The **Rough Gui**

Oman

written and researched by

Gavin Thomas

www.roughguides.com

Contents

◀◀ Illuminated dome of Sultan Qaboos Mosque, Muscat ◀ Schoolboys at Jabrin Fort

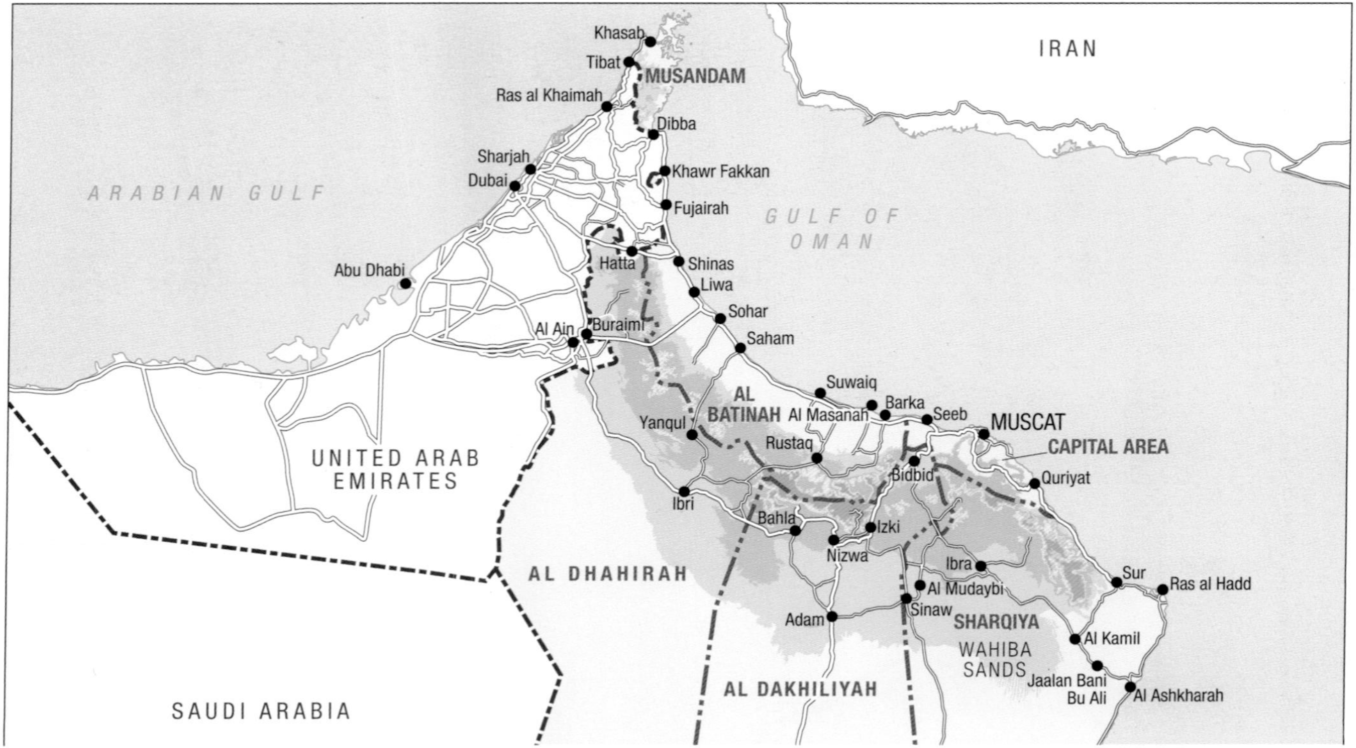

IRAN
Khasab
Tibat
MUSANDAM
Ras al Khaimah
Dibba
Sharjah
Dubai
Khawr Fakkan
Fujairah
ARABIAN GULF
GULF OF OMAN
Abu Dhabi
Hatta
Shinas
Liwa
Sohar
Al Ain
Buraimi
Saham
Suwaiq
Barka
Seeb
MUSCAT
CAPITAL AREA
AL BATINAH
Al Masanah
Yanqul
Rustaq
Bidbid
Quriyat
UNITED ARAB EMIRATES
Ibri
Bahla
Izki
Nizwa
Ibra
Sur
Ras al Hadd
AL DHAHIRAH
Al Mudaybi
Sinaw
Adam
SHARQIYA
Al Kamil
WAHIBA SANDS
Jaalan Bani Bu Ali
Al Ashkharah
AL DAKHILIYAH
SAUDI ARABIA

Meters
1500
1250
1000
500
250
0

0
100 km

N

Shana
Hilf
Masirah Island
AL-WUSTA
Madrakah
Duqm
ARABIAN ORYX SANCTUARY
ARABIAN SEA
Hayma
Marmul
Khuriya Muriya Islands
Hasik
Sadah
Mirbat
Taqah
Thumrait
Salalah
Mughsail
EMPTY QUARTER (RUB AL KHALI)
DHOFAR
YEMEN

Introduction to

Oman

Amid the ever-changing states of the Arabian Gulf, Oman offers a refreshing reminder of a seemingly bygone age. Overdevelopment has yet to blight its most spectacular landscapes and cultural traditions remain remarkably undiluted, making the sultanate one of the best places in the Gulf to experience traditional Arabia. Quiet stretches of coast are shaded with nodding palm trees and dotted with fishing boats. Mudbrick villages nestle amid sprawling date plantations or cling to the sides of remote valleys. Craggy chains of towering mountains are scored with precipitous canyons and rocky wadis, while the wind-blown dunes and gravel plains of the great inland deserts stretch away into the distance.

Of course, it's not all savagely beautiful, sparsely populated landscapes. Oman has embraced the modern world, and in parts of the country the contemporary is very much in evidence, particularly in the low-key glitter and bustle of the capital, Muscat, and in the burgeoning cities of Salalah and Sohar. Despite the trappings of modernity, however, much of the rest of the country retains a powerful sense of place and past. Busy souks continue to resound with the clamour of shoppers bargaining over frankincense, jewellery and food. Venerable forts and crumbling watchtowers still stand sentinel over towns they once protected, goats wander past huddles of ochre-coloured houses, and the white-robed Omanis themselves saunter quietly amid the palms.

Where to go

Most visitors begin in **Muscat**, the nation's sprawling modern capital. Much of the city now comprises a largely featureless suburban sprawl, though engaging reminders of times past persist in the lively commercial district of **Muttrah** and the historic quarter of Old Muscat, site of the sultan's palace and a pair of hoary old Portuguese forts. The city also boasts an alluring selection of upmarket hotels – including some of the Gulf's most memorably opulent Arabian-style establishments – with fabulously ornate decor, marvellous beaches, and a selection of the country's finest restaurants and bars.

Inland from Muscat rise the spectacular mountains of the **Western Hajar**, centred on the beguiling regional capital of **Nizwa**, Oman's most historic and personable town. Nizwa also provides a convenient base from which to explore the myriad attractions of the surrounding mountains, including the mighty Jebel Shams (the highest peak in Oman), the spectacular traditional villages of the Saiq Plateau and the exhilarating off-road drive down the vertiginous **Wadi Bani Auf**. Other highlights include the lovely traditional mudbrick town of Al Hamra and the even more picture-perfect village of **Misfat al Abryeen**. Slightly further afield lie two of the country's most absorbing forts: monumental Bahla, the largest in Oman, and the more intimate Jabrin, whose perfectly preserved interiors offer a fascinating insight into life in old Oman.

North of Muscat in the shadow of the Western Hajar lies the coastal region of **Al Batinah**, fringed with a long swathe of sleepy, palm-fringed beaches. A series of low-key towns dots the coast, including lively Seeb, sleepier Barka (home to a couple more interesting forts) and sprawling Sohar, one of the country's oldest cities, although few physical reminders of its long and illustrious past survive. The main attraction in Al Batinah is the day-long

Nakhal Fort

drive around the so-called **Rustaq Loop**, which winds inland in the shadow of the mountains via the majestic forts of Nakhal, Rustaq and Al Hazm, and provides access to some of Oman's most beautiful wadis – including Wadi Abyad, Wadi Bani Kharous and Wadi Bani Auf – en route.

At the far northern end of Oman (and separated from the rest of the country by a wide swathe of UAE territory) lies the **Musandam Peninsula**. This is where you'll find some of the sultanate's most dramatic landscapes, with the Hajar mountains tumbling down into the ultramarine waters of the Arabian Gulf, creating a spectacular sequence of steep-sided *khors* (fjords), best seen during a leisurely dhow cruise. Most visitors base themselves in the modest regional capital of **Khasab**, which also provides a good base for forays up into the magnificent interior, centred on the craggy heights of the Jebel Harim.

South of Muscat lies **Sharqiya** region, providing a beguiling microcosm of Oman, with historic forts, dramatic mountain canyons, rolling dunes and turtle-nesting beaches. The still largely unspoiled coastline is a major draw, thanks to its generous swathes of pristine sand, the historic

Fact file

- The oldest independent state in the Arabian peninsula, Oman has been a sovereign entity since the expulsion of the Persians in 1747.
- The population is a fraction over 3 million, including some 600,000 expats, mainly from India, Pakistan and Bangladesh.
- All native Omanis are Muslim. Three-quarters follow the Ibadhi creed (see p.219); the remainder are largely Sunni.
- Oman is an absolute monarchy, with the ruling Sultan Qaboos exercising ultimate power over all major decisions of state.
- Oil is the country's most important export, although dwindling reserves have forced the government into a wide-ranging programme of industrial diversification and tourist development.

Sultan Qaboos: father of the nation

You'll not go far in Oman without seeing a picture of the country's supreme ruler, **Sultan Qaboos**, whether framed in miniature above the counters of shops, cafés and hotels or emblazoned on supersized billboards towering above major highways. Coming to the throne in 1970 following the ousting of his father, the sultan has overseen the transformation of the backward and impoverished country he inherited into a prosperous modern state and is still held in almost religious reverence – even the tumultuous events of the Arab Spring in early 2011 (and their modest repercussions in Oman itself) failed to shake his universal popularity.

For more on the sultan's reign and achievements, see pp.230-232.

town of **Sur** and the turtle-watching beach at **Ras al Jinz**. Inland, Sharqiya is centred on the rugged Eastern Hajar mountains, cut through by some of the country's most scenic wadis. On the far side of the mountains, most visitors head for the magnificent dunes of the **Wahiba Sands**, while it's also worth visiting the old-fashioned towns of Ibra and Jalan Bani Bu Ali nearby, home to some of the country's finest traditional mudbrick architecture.

Tucked away in the far southwestern corner of the country lies **Dhofar**, separated from the rest of Oman by almost a thousand kilometres of stony desert. At the centre of the region is the engaging subtropical city of Salalah, famous for its annual inundation by the monsoon rains of the *khareef*, during which the surrounding hills turn a lush green and cascades of water flow down the mountains, creating impromptu rivers, rock pools and waterfalls – one of Arabia's most memorably improbable spectacles. The city also makes a convenient base for forays into the majestic Dhofar Mountains and the interminable sands of the Rub al Khali – Oman's final frontier, stretching across northern Dhofar and on into Saudi Arabia.

▲ Wadi Bani Khalid, Eastern Hajar

When to go

▲ Rub al Khali

Oman's climate is typical of the Arabian peninsula, with blisteringly hot summers and pleasantly mild, Mediterranean winters. During the **summer** months (March/April to September/ October) almost the entire country is scorchingly hot; from May to July the thermometer can often nudge up into the 40°C. Visiting during this period is best avoided, with the exception of Salalah, where temperatures remain bearable thanks to the annual *khareef* which descends from June to August or early September. It's a memorable time to visit the area, even if accommodation gets booked solid and prices go through the roof. The **winter** months (October/November to February/March) are pleasantly temperate by contrast, with an almost Mediterranean climate and daytime temperatures rarely climbing much above 30°C. Evenings and nights at this time of year can be pleasantly breezy and even occasionally slightly chilly especially up on the cool heights of the Saiq Plateau and other elevated spots in the mountains. Excepting Salalah during the *khareef*, the entire country is extremely arid, and **rainfall** is rare – although don't be surprised if you experience a modest shower or two, most likely from December through to March.

Average monthly temperatures and rainfall

	Jan	Feb	Mar	Apr	May	Jun	Jul	Aug	Sep	Oct	Nov	Dec
Muscat												
Max/min (ºC)	21/17	22/18	25/21	30/25	34/29	35/31	34/30	32/28	31/27	30/25	26/21	23/18
Max/min (ºF)	78/63	79/64	86/69	94/76	103/84	105/87	101/87	97/83	97/81	95/77	87/70	81/65
Rainfall (mm)	13	24	16	17	7	1	0	1	0	1	7	13
Salalah												
Max/min (ºC)	27/18	28/19	30/21	32/23	33/25	32/26	28/24	27/23	29/23	30/22	31/20	29/19
Max/min (ºF)	81/64	82/67	86/70	89/74	90/78	89/80	83/76	81/74	84/74	87/71	87/69	83/66
Rainfall (mm)	2	7	6	20	17	11	25	25	4	4	10	1
Khasab												
Max/min (ºC)	24/16	25/16	28/19	33/24	38/28	39/30	40/31	39/31	37/29	34/25	30/21	26/17
Max/min (ºF)	76/60	77/61	82/67	92/75	100/82	103/86	104/88	101/88	99/85	94/78	86/70	79/63
Rainfall (mm)	45	49	46	9	2	0	1	0	0	0	3	32
Sur												
Max/min (ºC)	26/17	27/18	31/21	36/25	40/28	40/29	39/28	37/26	37/26	35/24	31/20	28/18
Max/min (ºF)	79/62	81/64	88/69	96/77	104/83	104/85	103/83	99/80	99/78	95/75	87/68	82/64
Rainfall (mm)	18	40	11	11	0.5	6	4	5	0	1	10	8

19 things not to miss

It's not possible to see everything that Oman has to offer in a single trip – and we don't suggest you try. What follows, in no particular order, is a selective and subjective taste of the country, from traditional forts, souks and villages through to the spectacular landscapes of the country's mountains, deserts and coast. All are arranged in colour-coded categories to help you find the best things to see, do and experience, and all entries have a page reference to take you straight into the guide, where you can find out more.

01 **Turtle-watching at Ras al Jinz** Page **174** • The nation's most memorable wildlife spectacle: hundreds of Green turtles hauling themselves up out of the ocean to lay their eggs on this remote Sharqiya beach.

02 Sultan Qaboos Grand Mosque Page **67** • A splendid example of modern Islamic architecture – and also the only mosque in the country open to non-Muslims.

03 Muttrah Souk Page **56** • Oman's most colourful souk is a disorienting labyrinth of tiny alleyways piled high with a bewildering array of exotic merchandise.

04 Khor ash Sham Page **152** • Take a dhow cruise through Musandam's most spectacular *khor* (fjord), keeping an eye out for pods of frolicking dolphins.

05 Dhofar during the khareef Page **191** • Arabia with a difference, as the arid mountains encircling Salalah turn green during the annual *khareef* (monsoon).

06 Al Ayn Page **139** • Magical cluster of Bronze Age beehive tombs atop a ridge at the edge of the Western Hajar.

07 Sur Page **170** • Personable old port town, with a beautiful harbour and waterfront, and the last surviving dhow yard in the sultanate.

08 Hiking in the Western Hajar Page **93** • Tackle one of the exhilarating hiking routes which crisscross the airy heights and dramatic wadis of this stunning mountain range.

09 Frankincense Page 199 • Aromatic wafts of frankincense smoke pervade every corner of the country, from traditional souks to modern hotels.

10 Jebel Harim Page 156 • Follow the road up into the spectacular mountains of inland Musandam, looking out for cave dwellings, bizarre rock formations, fossils and petroglyphs en route.

11 Saiq Plateau Page 94 • Refreshingly breezy mountain plateau, dotted with a string of spectacular traditional villages teetering on the brink of the cavernous Wadi al Ayn.

12 Jabrin Fort Page 105 • Of the five-hundred-odd forts scattered around the country, this is the finest: an absorbing maze of a place showcasing some of the country's most memorable traditional architecture and interiors.

13 Misfat al Abryeen Page **101** • Traditional Oman at its most magical, with a time-warped cluster of antiquated mudbrick houses in a lofty mountain setting.

14 Diving Page **31** • Explore an unspoiled underwater paradise of colourful corals and magnificent marine life.

15 The Rustaq Loop Page **116** • Absorbing journey though the inland Batinah in the shadow of the Western Hajar, boasting some of the country's finest forts and most scenic wadis.

16 **Nizwa** Page **85** • Oman's most historic town, with a picture-perfect huddle of souks and sand-coloured buildings clustered around one of the country's mightiest forts.

17 **A night in the desert** Page **180** • Sleep out amid the vast dunes of the Wahiba Sands or Rub al Khali under a sky full of stars.

18 **Jebel Shams and Wadi Nakhr** Page **102** • The country's highest peak, tumbling dramatically into the depths of Wadi Nakhr, Oman's "Grand Canyon".

19 **Wadi Bani Auf** Page **99** • The classic Omani off-road drive, straight down the near-vertical escarpment of the Western Hajar via the idyllic village of Bilad Sayt and the spectacular Snake Canyon to the plains below.

Basics

Basics

Getting there

Oman is well plugged into international air networks, either through the national carrier Oman Air or through other Gulf airlines such as Emirates, Qatar Airways and Etihad, meaning that it's now possible to reach Muscat from most major air-hubs in Europe, North America and Australasia with only a single change of plane.

Overland routes into the country are more limited. Oman shares land borders with the UAE, Saudi Arabia and Yemen, though at the time of writing it was only possible to enter the country via the UAE border posts listed on p.20. There are no regular international **ferry** routes into Oman, although the country is an increasingly popular stop on many cruise itineraries.

Flights from the UK and Ireland

Oman Air is currently the only operator offering direct flights from **London Heathrow** to Muscat. There are numerous one-stop options with other Gulf carriers including Qatar Airways (via Doha), Etihad (via Abu Dhabi), Gulf Air (via Manama) and Emirates (via Dubai), while British Airways also fly via Abu Dhabi. Fares start at around £600; flying time is around 7hr 30min outbound, 8hr on the way back. Oman Air also operates codeshare flights with BMI to Muscat via Heathrow from Manchester, Edinburgh and Aberdeen. Travelling **from Ireland**, the easiest thing to do is to get yourself to Heathrow and pick up a flight from there. Oman Air and BMI operate codeshare flights from Belfast.

Flights from the US and Canada

The flight from North America to Oman is a long journey with myriad different route options. It's possible to get to Muscat with just one change of plane travelling from New York or Toronto (with Emirates or Etihad via Dubai or Abu Dhabi respectively), Washington (Qatar Airways via Doha), Chicago (Etihad), Houston (Emirates and Qatar Airways), and Los Angeles and San Francisco (both Emirates).

From Canada, you could fly from Toronto, Montreal, Vancouver and other destinations to London with either British Airways or Air Canada, and then pick up a direct flight to Muscat with Oman Air, or go via Abu Dhabi with BA. Flying times from the east coast to Muscat can be as little as sixteen to seventeen hours depending on connections, although other flights can take anything up to 24 hours. From the west coast you're looking at a minimum flight time of eighteen to twenty hours, possibly quite a bit longer. Fares from both coasts are around US$1300–1400.

Flights from Australia, New Zealand and South Africa

There are various one-stop routes from **Australia** to Oman. One option is to aim for a major Asian air-hub and pick up a direct flight with Oman Air (who currently operate nonstop flights to Muscat from Singapore, Kuala Lumpur, Bangkok, Hong Kong, Colombo, Mumbai and Delhi, among quite a few other places in Asia). Other one-stop routes include travelling via Dubai with Emirates from Sydney, Melbourne, Brisbane and Perth, or via Abu Dhabi with Etihad from Melbourne, Sydney and Brisbane. Fares are around A$2000, with flying times averaging around thirty hours.

From **New Zealand**, it's easiest to travel to either Bangkok (with Thai Airways), Singapore (Singapore Airlines) or Kuala Lumpur (Malaysia Airlines) and pick up an Oman Air flight to Muscat from there – or alternatively to follow one of the routes via Australia described above. Fares start at around $2700, with flying times from around 33 hours.

From **South Africa**, the simplest way of getting to Oman is to catch a direct South

African Airways flight from Johannesburg, Cape Town or Durban to Dubai, and pick up a connection there. Alternatively, you could fly to Dar es Salaam, from where Oman Air operates direct flights to Muscat. Fares start from around R8000. Another romantic, if slightly more time-consuming, option is to fly to Dar es Salaam and then make your way over to **Zanzibar**, from where direct Oman Air flights leave for Muscat, allowing you to combine a visit to Oman and its most important former colony in a single visit.

Air passes

Oman Air's "Visit Oman Air Pass" (VOAP) may prove useful if you're combining a visit to Oman with one to the UAE or other countries in the Gulf. The pass offers discounted airfares (at a fixed $100/flight, or "sector", as it's described) from Muscat to various regional cities including Dubai, Abu Dhabi, Al Ain, Ras al Khaimah, Bahrain, Doha, Kuwait City and Damman when bought in conjunction with a flight to Oman from London or other points outside the Gulf. The scheme is also valid for domestic flights to Khasab and Salalah, but at $100 per journey these actually work out more expensive than standard fares – although this may change in future.

By land

Oman shares land borders with the UAE, Yemen and Saudi Arabia, although at present it's only possible to enter the country overland **from the UAE**, either via Buraimi/Al Ain (see p.133), Khatmat Milahah (see p.131) or Hatta (see p.131). There's also a border between the UAE and the Musandam peninsula at Tibat (see p.145). Border formalities at all four posts are straightforward, and citzens of most European, North American and Australasian countries can buy a **visa** on the spot (see p.37 for full prices and details). The whole process shouldn't usually take more than fifteen to thirty minutes, although

Six steps to a better kind of travel

At Rough Guides we are passionately committed to travel. We feel strongly that only through travelling do we truly come to understand the world we live in and the people we share it with – plus tourism has brought a great deal of **benefit** to developing economies around the world over the last few decades. But the extraordinary growth in tourism has also damaged some places irreparably, and of course **climate change** is exacerbated by most forms of transport, especially flying. This means that now more than ever it's important to **travel thoughtfully** and **responsibly**, with respect for the cultures you're visiting – not only to derive the most benefit from your trip but also to preserve the best bits of the planet for everyone to enjoy. At Rough Guides we feel there are six main areas in which you can make a difference:

- Consider what you're contributing to the **local economy**, and how much the services you use do the same, whether it's through employing local workers and guides or sourcing locally grown produce and local services.
- Consider the **environment** on holiday as well as at home. Water is scarce in many developing destinations, and the biodiversity of local flora and fauna can be adversely affected by tourism. Try to patronize businesses that take account of this.
- Travel with a purpose, not just to tick off experiences. Consider **spending longer** in a place, and getting to know it and its people.
- Give thought to how often you **fly**. Try to avoid short hops by air and more harmful night flights.
- Consider **alternatives to flying**, travelling instead by bus, train, boat and even by bike or on foot where possible.
- Make your trips "**climate neutral**" via a reputable carbon offset scheme. All Rough Guide flights are offset, and every year we donate money to a variety of charities devoted to combating the effects of climate change.

you might have to wait considerably longer during weekends and local holidays.

Airlines, agents and operators

Airlines

Air Canada Ⓦwww.aircanada.com.
Air New Zealand Ⓦwww.airnewzealand.com.
American Airlines Ⓦwww.aa.com.
bmi Ⓦwww.flybmi.com.
British Airways Ⓦwww.ba.com.
Delta Ⓦwww.delta.com.
KLM Ⓦwww.klm.com.
Oman Air Ⓦwww.omanair.com.
Emirates Ⓦwww.emirates.com.
Etihad Airways Ⓦwww.etihadairways.com.
Gulf Air Ⓦwww.gulfair.com.
South African Airlines Ⓦwww.flysaa.com.
Qantas Ⓦwww.qantas.com.
Qatar Airways Ⓦwww.qatarairways.com.
South African Airways Ⓦwww.flysaa.com.

Agents and operators

Signing up for a **tour** of Oman – either tailor-made in your own car or 4WD, or as part of a larger group – takes the hassle out of organizing transport around the country, and can also get you some good deals on rates at better hotels. On the downside, travelling around in a group inevitably neuters your experience of the country, while the itineraries offered by most agents are boringly predictable – although booking a tailor-made package should at least enable you to customize your itinerary to suit your particular interests. Many foreign operators offer tours of the country while there's also a decent selection of operators in Oman itself.

If you just want some kind of discounted flight-plus-hotel package deal, Destination Oman (Ⓦwww.destoman.com), Dream Oman (Ⓦwww.dreamoman.com) and Travel Oman (Ⓦwww.traveloman.co.uk) all have a decent selection of offers.

Tour operators outside Oman

Abercrombie & Kent UK Ⓣ0845 618 2203, Ⓦwww.abercrombiekent.co.uk; US Ⓣ800 554 7016, Ⓦwww.abercrombiekent.com. Upmarket, tailor-made tours focusing on Muscat, Musandam, Nizwa, Salalah and the Wahiba Sands.

Destination Oman Ⓣ0844 482 1672, Ⓦwww.destinationoman.co.uk. Range of basic tours (5–7 days) plus flight-and-hotel packages to Muscat.

Kuoni Ⓣ01306 747002, Ⓦwww.kuoni.co.uk. Range of short tours including "Highlights of Oman" (6 days), combined tours of Oman (or just Muscat) and Dubai (8 days), plus various one- or two-day excursions focusing on themes such as forts, wildlife, the desert, and frankincense in Salalah.

North South Travel UK Ⓣ01245 608291, Ⓦwww.northsouthtravel.co.uk. Friendly, competitive travel agency, offering discounted fares worldwide. Profits are used to support projects in the developing world, especially the promotion of sustainable tourism.

Oman Bike Tours Ⓦwww.omanbiketours.com. German company offering exhilarating off-road motorbike trips from its camp in Wadi Bani Auf.

Responsible Travel Ⓣ01273 600030, Ⓦwww.responsibletravel.com/holidays/oman. Refreshingly different – and socially responsible – tour operator offering an excellent selection of unusual and ethical tours across Oman. These range from mainstream country tours through to camping, hiking, camel-trekking and Empty Quarter safaris, as well as the chance to work on local conservation projects.

Shaw Travel Ⓣ01635 47055, Ⓦwww.shawtravel.co.uk. Upmarket tailor-made tours, plus a range of one-day tours including off-road mountain and desert trips and dolphin- and birdwatching.

STA Travel UK Ⓣ0871 2300 040, US Ⓣ1800 781 4040, Australia Ⓣ134 782, New Zealand Ⓣ0800 474 400, South Africa Ⓣ0861 781 781; Ⓦwww.statravel.co.uk. Worldwide specialists in independent travel; also does student IDs, travel insurance, car rental, rail passes and more. Good discounts for students and under-26s.

Trailfinders UK Ⓣ0845 058 5858, Ireland Ⓣ01 677 7888, Australia Ⓣ1300 780 212; Ⓦwww.trailfinders.com. One of the best-informed and most efficient agents for independent travellers.

Travel CUTS Canada Ⓣ1866 246 9762, US Ⓣ1800 592 2887; Ⓦwww.travelcuts.com. Canadian youth and student travel firm.

The Ultimate Travel Company Ⓣ020 7386 4646, Ⓦwww.theultimatetravelcompany.co.uk. Two countrywide tours (11–12 days) of Oman, plus tailor-made tours, including trips into the Empty Quarter.

USIT Ireland Ⓣ01 602 1906, Northern Ireland Ⓣ028 9032 7111; Ⓦwww.usit.ie. Ireland's main student and youth travel specialists.

Voyages Jules Verne Ⓣ0845 166 7033, Ⓦwww.vjv.com. Reliable group tours: choose from "Muscat & Beyond" (6 days), with day-trips from the capital, and "Frankincense & Fortresses" (7 days), divided between Muscat and Salalah.

Tour operators in Oman

Arabesque Travel Ⓦ www.arabesque.travel. Long-established local company under mixed Omani–British ownership offering a range of day and overnight trips from Muscat and Salalah, including wadi, fort, wildlife and Empty Quarter tours.
Gulf Leisure Ⓦ www.gulfleisure.com. Good range of adventure tours. On land there are desert safaris, wadi- and dune-bashing, mountain-biking, climbing, trekking and canyoning, while water-based activities include game-fishing, diving and glass-bottom boat tours.
Mark Tours Ⓣ 2478 2727, Ⓦ www.marktours oman.com. One of the largest local travel agents offering an excellent selection of one-day and overnight tours (including trips to places like Wadi Abyad, Wadi Shatan, Bat and As Suleif which aren't covered by other operators), as well as customized camping trips. They can also arrange car hire, or 4WDs with guide-driver.
Muscat Diving & Adventure Centre Ⓣ 2454 3002, Ⓦ www.holiday-in-oman.com. Oman's leading adventure specialists, with a big range of energetic outdoor activities on land and sea, including canyoning, caving, mountain-biking, climbing, trekking and diving, along with more mainstream cultural tours and self-drive itineraries.
Zahara Tours Ⓣ 2440 0844, Ⓦ www.zaharatours .com. Reputable local travel agents offering a wide range of one-day tours from Muscat, plus a few longer trips (2–10 days). They can also arrange car hire.

Getting around

There's very little public transport in Oman. Buses will, at a pinch, get you between the main towns and cities, but to really see anything of the country you'll need your own transport, either by signing up for a tour, hiring a guide-driver, or getting behind the wheel yourself.

By car

Driving yourself is far and away the easiest way of getting around the country (for details of tour agencies providing cars with driver, see above & p.21). An extensive and ever-expanding network of modern roads now reaches most parts of the country and driving is largely straightforward, although not without a few challenges.

Standards of driving leave a certain amount to be desired, and the country's level of road-traffic accidents and fatalities is depressingly high (albeit not quite as bad as in the neighbouring UAE). Drive defensively at all times, expect the unexpected and be prepared for some lunatic in a landcruiser to come charging down on you at 150km/h.

Vehicles drive on the right in Oman. The usual **speed limits** are 120km/h on dual-carriageways, 100km/h on single carriageways, and either 60km/h or 80km/h in built-up areas. Cars are fitted with a speed alarm which will beep at you (irritatingly) when you reach 120km/h. A few of the main highways are monitored by speed-cameras.

Common **road hazards** include vehicles driving after dark with no lights on; vehicles cutting suddenly in front of you without indicating; and livestock wandering onto roads, particularly goats and (in Salalah especially) camels. Rain often leads to **flash floods** which can cut off roads within a matter of minutes. Driving around you'll see endless signs saying "Stop when water is at red!" whenever you pass through even a slight depression in the landscape, meaning stop if the water level reaches the red paint on the poles on either side of the road. Keep a lookout too for **speed bumps**. These are found in towns and villages all over the country, but in many places the paint has peeled off them and there are no warning signs – a nasty surprise if you hit one at 80km/h.

Penalties for **traffic infringements** are often stringent. Jumping a red light, for instance, leads to a mandatory two-day jail term. Wearing a seat belt is also obligatory, with an on-the-spot fine of 10 OR if you're caught without one on. Oman is also famous for its law requiring drivers to keep their vehicles clean; driving a dirty car can technically land you with a fine, although in practice the police will probably just direct you to the nearest car wash.

If you have an **accident** you'll need to inform the police (emergency number ⓣ9999). It's best, if possible, to leave your vehicle exactly where it is until the police

Off-road driving in Oman

Going off-road in Oman, either as a passenger or driver, is one of the country's essential experiences. Driving off-road **in the mountains** ("wadi-bashing") is mainly a matter of common sense, and knowing the limits of your vehicle – something that you only really acquire with experience. Going out with an experienced off-road driver is, of course, the best training. Whatever you do, always err strongly on the side of caution.

Driving on sand ("dune-bashing") is a more specialized skill. The key to avoid getting bogged down is to stick to low gears and keep your revs up – but without revving so hard that you end up spinning the wheels and digging yourself in. Anticipating the terrain ahead, selecting the best route, working out which gear you need to be in and finding the correct gear-plus-revs combination is something of an acquired skill – particularly so when driving over large dunes.

Wherever you're going, take plenty of water and, ideally, travel with another vehicle (this is particularly important in the desert, where you're most at risk of getting stuck in dunes and needing to be towed out). And finally, check, if hiring a 4WD, that the insurance provided by the rental company actually covers off-road driving (not always the case).

The useful *Oman Off-Road*, published by Explorer, covers 26 of the finest off-road routes around the country in microscopic detail. Useful general points to remember include:

In the mountains, be very aware of the hazards of **rain**: it can take just minutes for flash floods to inundate wadis – if there's any possibility of rain in rough or remote areas, turn back or get out of the wadi as quickly as you can. If you get stuck in a flash flood, head for the highest ground in the vicinity. If the waters look like enveloping your vehicle, get out of it while you still can – floodwaters can rise with frightening speed.

If you find yourself having to cross a **flooded wadi**, it's a good idea to wade in first to test the depth of the water and strength of the current. If you decide it's safe to cross, use a low gear and maintain a steady 5–10km/h and keep your revs up to avoid stalling (using the differential-lock or low-range settings available on 4WDs can be useful if you're going to be driving through water for some time).

If you get **stuck on rocks**, jack the vehicle up and fill in the gaps under the wheels with stones, creating a ramp to clear the obstruction.

Driving on sand, you should **reduce tyre pressure** to between two-thirds and half of normal pressure. This creates a larger contact area between tyre and sand, increasing traction.

When driving over large dunes, the key is to gain sufficient momentum before you reach the dune and then maintain it all the way to the top. Stick to a low gear and keep your revs up – changing gears halfway up the side of a dune will cost you precious momentum. Ascending and descending dunes, try to drive straight up and down rather than at an angle.

Always follow **existing tracks** (where they can be found) to avoid causing additional damage to the environment. These will also most likely follow the best route.

If you do get completely stuck and can't move your vehicle, it's usually better (especially in the desert) to stay with your car rather than wandering off on foot in search of help, unless you know exactly where you're going. A vehicle provides shade and is much easier to spot than a lone walker.

have arrived and had a look at it. Moving it before they reach the scene can be construed as an admission of guilt.

Car rental

Car rental is reasonably inexpensive. The international car-rental agencies can provide cars from around 13–15 OR per day, rising to around 35 OR for a 4WD. Local firms may be able to provide a vehicle for as low as 10 OR, although, obviously, such vehicles may not be in such good condition as those hired from a more reputable company. Collision-damage waiver costs around 2 OR per day – you may consider it money well spent for the extra peace of mind it gives you. Your national **driving licence** should be sufficient documentation, although if in doubt check in advance with the car rental firm you intend renting from. Note that most car-rental firms won't hire vehicles to those aged under 21. **Petrol** is extremely cheap by European standards, at roughly 20p per litre.

Car rental agencies

Avis Ⓦwww.avis.com.
Budget Ⓦwww.budget.com.
Dollar Ⓦwww.dollar.com.
Europcar Ⓦwww.europcar.com.
Hertz Ⓦwww.hertz.com.
SIXT Ⓦwww.sixt.com.
Thrifty Ⓦwww.thrifty.com.

By bus and micro

All the major towns in the country are connected by **bus**. These will do at a pinch to get you between the country's major towns and cities, but no more. Buses are mainly operated by the government-run Oman National Transport Company (ONTC; Ⓦwww.ontcoman.com, although the site wasn't operational at the time of writing), along with a few private operators on the Muscat–Salalah route (see p.193).

Buses are reasonably fast and comfortable, although there are only two or three departures daily, and getting information about exactly where they depart from and when can be difficult (although if you use buses much you'll learn to recognize the distinctive ONTC concrete bus-stops-cum-shelters). **Fares** are extremely modest – no more than 2–3 OR for most inter-city journeys, rising to 6–7.5 OR for the long journey to Salalah.

Within larger towns (Muscat especially – see p.51) local transport is provided by taxis (see below) and **micros** (also known as "baisa buses") – basically minivans painted white and orange and seating up to around fifteen passengers, at a squeeze. These are mainly used by low-wage expats from the Indian subcontinent and are easily the cheapest way of getting around, although it can often be difficult to work out where micros run. Vehicles aren't signed, so it's just a question of asking around (or waving at anything that passes) until you find one going where you want to go to. Outside Muscat, drivers are unlikely to speak more than a few words of English.

By taxi

Within larger towns, the easiest way of getting around is by taxi. These are easily recognizable thanks to their white and orange livery, and usually fairly easy to find – just flag down one at the roadside. All Omani taxis are **unmetered**, meaning that you'll have to agree the **fare** before you set out – bargain hard. Locals would expect to pay no more than 1–2 OR for trips within most cities (or up to around 5 OR for long trips within Muscat), although foreigners are likely to pay significantly over the odds – anything up to double these prices, depending on your bargaining powers. All taxi **drivers** are Omani (the profession is reserved for Omani nationals). In Muscat, virtually all speak at least basic English; outside Muscat, they may speak Arabic only.

Taxis can also operate on a **shared** basis, with three or four passengers splitting the fare. Shared taxis operate both within towns and also on longer-distance routes between towns, offering a convenient alternative to buses. The system works on an ad hoc basics, however, so you'll have to scout around locally to find out where the best places to pick up a shared taxi are, and you may feel that it's more bother than it's worth.

By plane

There are only two **domestic air services** within Oman at present, between Muscat and Khasab in Musandam (see p.143), and between Muscat and Salalah (see p.194) – both of which offer convenient alternatives to the long journey by road.

By ferry

There is currently only one long-distance boat service in Oman: the high-speed ferry service between Muscat and Khasab in Musandam (see p.144), operated by the National Ferries Company (NFC). A new NFC service around the southern coast between the Khuriyah Muria islands, Shumwaymiyah and Hasik is also in the pipeline, scheduled to come into operation by 2013 – although don't be surprised if it actually takes a year or three longer.

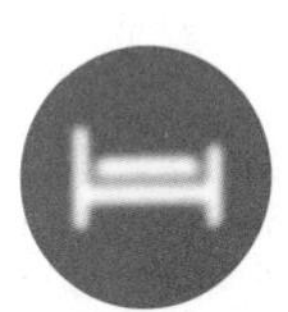

Accommodation

There are hotels in all major cities and towns in Oman, although outside Muscat standards are middling and you're not exactly spoilt for choice. Prices, too, tend to be rather expensive for what you get.

There are relatively few **tourist hotels** aimed specifically at foreign visitors. Far and away the best selection is in Muscat (see p.52), which boasts some of the most memorable hotels in the region. Outside the capital, however, there's very little to get excited about beyond a scattering of generally fairly humdrum resort hotels.

Most smaller towns boast a simple one- or two-star **local hotel** (usually in the range 12–20 OR/£20–33/US$30–50) aimed at Omani travellers. These are usually functional and somewhat basic places – most are passably comfortable and generally clean, though in the worst places you may have to put up with rock-hard mattresses, dodgy electrics and the occasional cockroach.

Camping is another possibility, and pitching a tent in a remote mountain wadi or on an unspoilt beach can be a memorable experience. There are no restrictions on wild camping in Oman, assuming the area you pitch your tent in is clearly uninhabited and uncultivated. If you want to camp anywhere close to a village or other signs of human habitation, you should ask permission first. A more upmarket alternative is to spend a night or two in one of the country's various **desert camps**, mainly found in the Wahiba Sands (see p.180).

Accommodation price codes

All the accommodation in the guide has been categorized according to the following price codes. These represent the cost of the cheapest double room including taxes.

❶ 16 OR and under
❷ 17–23 OR
❸ 24–30 OR
❹ 31–40 OR
❺ 41–50 OR
❻ 51–75 OR
❼ 76–100 OR
❽ 101–150 OR
❾ 151 OR and above

Prices

You won't find a room anywhere in the country for less than 12 OR (£20/$30), although in many places you'll pay 20 OR (£33/$50) for even the cheapest room. Rooms in the country's mid-range resorts generally go for around 40–60 OR (£65–100/$100–150), while rates at the top hotels in Muscat start from around 150 OR (£250/$400) or significantly more in some places. Always check whether local **taxes** (usually 17 percent) are included in the price or will be added on. Cheaper places tend to quote a "nett price" (as it's described locally, meaning inclusive of all taxes); more upmarket places often quote prices before tax.

Local hotels tend to maintain the same prices throughout the year. Rates at more upmarket tourist-oriented places are usually quite flexible and tend to change according to demand, usually most expensive during the winter months, and falling by as much as thirty percent during summer. Most mid- and top-range places have some sort of published **rack rate**, though in practice prices are usually significantly cheaper except during the very busiest times of year (around Christmas and New Year, for example). It's always worth checking out prices **online**, either on the hotel's own website or on booking websites such as Expedia – these can sometimes be significantly cheaper than simply arriving at the hotel without a booking.

Rooms and facilities

All hotel rooms in Oman boast the two essentials of modern Gulf living: air conditioning and a TV. Most places also give you a fridge, while hot water should also come as standard, although it doesn't always work reliably in the cheapest places (in budget places you'll usually have to turn the water heater on at least ten minutes before you hope to shower).

Some budget hotels also boast a simple in-house restaurant (and if there isn't one in house, there are likely to be other options close by). If you want a bar, licensed restaurant or swimming pool, however, you'll have to head somewhere a bit more upmarket.

Hotel nightlife

One peculiarity of accommodation in Oman is that many mid-range hotels double as local nightspots and drinking venues. Numerous hotels boast in-house **live-music bars** – essentially places where young, heavily made-up ladies dressed in (by Omani standards) relatively revealing clothing stand up on stage in front of a largely male audience and pout, simper and attempt to sing (and possibly dance as well). These venues usually host either Arabic or Indian performers; it's not uncommon for a single hotel to have two or three such venues, usually tucked away somewhere discreet, like the basement, and often reachable only from an entrance outside the hotel itself. Rooms in most hotels are reasonably well insulated from the massive amounts of noise generated in these places, although it's still worth trying to get a room as far away as possible to avoid being kept awake half the night.

Also popular with local Omanis (despite traditional Muslim strictures against the drinking of alcohol) are the so-called **sports bars** to be found in various hotels. These range from fairly civilized pub-style bars with TVs showing football through to raucous backrooms stuffed with pool tables and usually selling the cheapest beer in town – a good place to hang out with the locals, although they're unlikely to make much sense after a couple of pints.

Food and drink

Food in Oman is mainly a question of eating to live, rather than living to eat. The country's culinary traditions offer an interesting blend of Arabian and Indian influences, although the stuff served up in most local cafés and restaurants generally consists of a predictable selection of shwarmas and biryanis, with maybe a few other Middle Eastern meze and grills or Indian curries. Honourable exceptions exist, of course, but outside Muscat, good places to eat are few and far between.

Where to eat

There are plenty of places to eat in Oman, although few have any airs and graces. The basic eating venue is the **café**. At their simplest, these can be nothing more than a functional little room with plastic furniture and a strictly limited range of food and drink – perhaps one type of shwarma and one kind of biryani, washed down with cups of Lipton's tea. Better places will have bigger menus offering a range of Arabian- and/or Indian-style dishes, perhaps along with some fish, plus a few simple European dishes such as a burger and chips. You can usually get a filling meal at any of these places for around 1.5 OR, although culinary surprises are rare.

Restaurants are relatively thin on the ground – and the vast majority are located in hotels. These might have slightly fancier decor and a somewhat wider range of cuisines (including Indian, Chinese and European dishes) at inflated prices, although culinary standards are often no higher than those in local cafés – and often worse.

Cafés and restaurants do well enough for both lunch and dinner, although the only reliable source of Western-style **breakfasts** is hotel restaurants. More upmarket cafés may be able to rustle up some eggs or an omelette plus toast, although otherwise you'll probably be limited to traditional Indian-style breakfasts of dhal and bread.

Restaurants and cafés of all standards tend to **close** during the afternoons from around 3 to 6pm.

What to eat

Most of the food served up in Omani cafés and restaurants comprises a mix of Arabian standards (shwarma, kebabs and meze) alongside the ubiquitous biryani and other lacklustre Indian and Pakistani-style fare.

Arabian (aka "Lebanese") food is based mainly on grilled meats. If you want to eat cheaply and well in Oman, your best bet is the humble **shwarma**, spit-roasted chicken and/or beef carved off and served wrapped in bread with salads – the Gulf version of the doner kebab (also served laid out on a piece of bread on a plate with chips and salad – the so-called "shwarma plate"). A simple shwarma sandwich usually goes for under 0.4 OR, and two or three make a satisfying light meal. The fact that the meat is being spit-roasted in public also means that you can see what you're getting and how it's being cooked.

Other Lebanese- and Turkish-style grilled **kebabs** are also reasonably common and often as good as anything in the country – places styling themselves as "Turkish" cafés/restaurants are often the best for this sort of food. Common dishes include the Lebanese *shish taouk* (chicken kebabs served with garlic sauce) and Turkish-style *kofte* (minced spiced lamb) kebabs. Most kebabs are served with Arabian-style **flatbread** (*khubz*) and a bowl of hummus, while some places also offer other classic Lebanese **meze**.

Along with the shwarma, the other staple of Omani cooking is the **biryani**. This doesn't bear a great deal of relation to its fancier Indian and Persian cousins, usually being little more than a leg of chicken buried in rice flavoured with a few whole spices and bits of roasted onion. As a staple dish, it's usually good value and often quite tasty. Other similar biryani-style dishes you may encounter include the Afghan-style **kabuli** (or *qabooli*), the Saudi **kabsa** (*kebsa*, *kibsa* – also known as *maqboos* or *machbus*) and the Yemeni **mandi**. In theory, each of these regional variants has its own distinct character and manner of preparation (the meat used in *kabsa* and *mandi*, for instance, is traditionally slow-cooked in a tandoor oven dug in the ground, although obviously this is unlikely to be the case in your local Omani café). In practice, however, these dishes are prepared in so many different ways that it's impossible to generalize about exactly what to expect, beyond a basic combination of meat and rice, mildly spiced.

A lot of cafés also offer various other **pseudo Indian and Pakistani** dishes – anything from Pakistani-style meat curries through to Indian vegetarian classics like *mutter paneer* – although these (the vegetarian dishes especially) can often be astonishingly bad, and it's probably best avoiding ordering curries except in proper Indian restaurants.

Traditional **Omani dishes** provide an interesting, lightly spiced blend of Indian and Arabian culinary cultures, although they only rarely make it to restaurant menus. The nationwide *Bin Ateeq* chain (see p.71) is doing its best to revive local culinary traditions, while in Muscat places like *Kargeen* and *Ubhar* (see p.72) serve up old-fashioned creations like *harees laham* (lamb with wheat in cow ghee) and *shuwa* (slow-roasted meat cooked in a clay oven).

Chicken (*dijaj*) is the staple ingredient in most biryanis, kebabs and curries, although various other types of meat are also available going under the name **laham** (literally "meat"), which usually means beef or lamb, but might also conceivably mean goat or, in Salalah, camel.

There's lots of top-quality **fish** available along the coast, although to see it done justice you'll have to shell out for a meal at one of Muscat's upmarket seafood restaurants – or go to Dubai, which is where a lot of the catch ends up. The local kingfish (*kenadh*), shark (*samak al qersh*) and lobster (*sharkha*) are particularly good.

Outside Muscat and Salalah, **vegetarians** are likely to struggle. Your most reliable chance of getting fed is to find a café serving Indian vegetarian food, although a fair few Lebanese-style meze are also vegetarian. Alternatively, you can always put together some sort of a meal out of a bowl of hummus, a plate of bread and some salad.

Desserts and accompaniments

The classic Omani dessert is **halwa**, the local version of the much-travelled sweet which is made, in widely different forms, across Europe, the Middle East and Asia. Omani *halwa* is wheat-based, which gives it a quite different taste and texture to the nut-based *halwas* made in Eastern Europe, Greece and Turkey. It is traditionally made from semolina, ghee (butter), sugar and rose-water, flavoured with cardamom and almonds and slow-boiled over a wood fire. You'll see *halwa* for sale all over the country either in traditional ceramic bowls or in more functional plastic tubs stacked up in the fridges of cafés and grocery shops. It's worth a try, although something of an acquired taste: a rather sickly mush, somewhere in texture between porridge and blancmange.

Dates (also see p.129) are another Omani staple, traditionally served with coffee – the national symbol of hospitality. Dates come in a wide range of varieties both from Oman and neighbouring countries, with subtle variations in taste, size and colour.

Drinking

Perhaps the most distinctive local drink is traditional **coffee** (*gahwa*) – although this doesn't bear much resemblance to European coffee. Arabic coffee is traditionally served in tiny handle-less cups, without milk and sugar but flavoured with spices usually including cardomom and/or cloves – intense, aromatic and slightly bitter. The serving and drinking of coffee is an important element of traditional Omani hospitality, and it's not uncommon even now to enter a hotel lobby or other public place and see a coffee-pourer wandering about with a traditional metal coffeepot (*dallah*) and tray of dates. If offered coffee in a social situation, it is considered polite to accept one cup as a symbol of accepting the offered hospitality, even if you don't really want it. Your cup will be refilled whenever you empty it, although it's considered impolite to take more than three cups. When you've finished, shake the cup gently from side to side and say "*Bas, shukran*" ("Enough, thank you").

More conventional coffee, often described as **Nesafe** (or "Nescoffee"), is also available, as is tea (*shay*; usually a Lipton's tea-bag). **Fruit juices** are also often good, especially in local shwarma cafés and other Lebanese establishments. You may also come across **laban** (buttermilk).

Alcoholic drinks are relatively difficult to come by outside of Muscat, and often punitively expensive; the whole of Salalah, for instance, the country's second-biggest city, boasted just three functioning licensed venues at the time of writing. **Beer** is usually a stereotypical selection of European lagers (Heineken, Carlsberg, Amstel, Tuborg and so on), either canned or on tap. A 50cl can of beer usually costs around 2 OR, or 3 OR for a draught pint – significantly more in upmarket places. **Wine** is available at the country's upmarket hotel restaurants, although at a predictably hefty price.

The media

Like most other countries in the region, Oman isn't particularly noted for its freedom of speech, a fact reflected in its rather turgid media, which still serves more as a PR and propaganda vehicle than a forum for genuine debate and analysis.

Newspapers

The Omani press is unlikely to set pulses racing. All publications are kept heavily under the thumb of the state, and coverage of events in Oman consists of little more than dutiful PR puff about the meetings of assorted government bigwigs, industrial developments and the latest production statistics. Coverage of events abroad (which doesn't need to be censored) tends to be of a significantly higher quality, however. The *Oman Observer* (Ⓦmain.omanobserver.om) is perhaps the best of the country's four English-language dailies; the others are the *Times of Oman* (Ⓦwww.timesofoman.com), the *Oman Tribune* (Ⓦwww.omantribune.com) and the *Muscat Daily* (Ⓦwww.muscatdaily.com).

Television and radio

The state broadcaster, Oman TV, broadcasts in Arabic only, although the **televisions** provided in hotel rooms generally carry a range of satellite channels, usually including BBC World News and CNN. The country's only **English-language radio station**, Hi Fm (95.9 FM; Ⓦhi.yourhifm.com), serves up a bland diet of mainstream western pop and inane chat. You can't usually pick it up outside Muscat, however, which might be a good thing. Elsewhere in the country the radio airwaves can be disconcertingly empty.

Festivals

Oman's festival calendar is somewhat undernourished, barring the large-scale annual Muscat festival and its smaller cousin in Salalah. Alternatively, for a more traditional insight into the country's religious culture, visiting Oman during one of the annual Islamic festivals is especially rewarding – Ramadan is a particularly interesting time to visit, assuming you're prepared to put up with a certain level of practical inconvenience.

Muscat Festival Late Jan to late Feb Ⓦwww.muscat-festival.com. The highlight of the festival calendar, with a wide-ranging programme of events offering a mix of traditional arts, culture and heritage (including a special Oman Heritage and Culture Village in Qurum Park) along with fun events like the Muscat Fashion Show, Oman Food Festival and concerts at the Qurum Park Amphitheatre.

Salalah Tourism Festival (also known as the Khareef Festival) June 21 to Sept 21 Ⓦwww.salalahfestival.com. Held during the three months of the **khareef**, featuring assorted cultural attractions, sporting events, concerts and shopping promotions.

Ramadan Scheduled to run from approximately July 20 to Aug 18, 2012; July 9 to Aug 7, 2013; June 28 to July 27, 2014; precise dates vary according to local astronomical sightings of the moon. The Islamic holy month of Ramadan represents a period in which to purify mind and body and to reaffirm one's relationship with God. Muslims are required to fast from dawn to dusk, and as a tourist you will be expected to publicly observe these strictures, although you are free to eat and drink in the privacy of your own hotel room, or in any of the carefully screened-off dining areas which are set up in hotels throughout the city (while alcohol is also served discreetly in some places after dark, but not during the day). Eating, drinking, smoking or chewing gum in public, however, are definite no-no's, and will cause considerable offence to local Muslims; singing, dancing and swearing in public are similarly frowned upon. In addition, live music is also completely forbidden during the holy month (though recorded music is allowed), while many shops scale back their opening hours.

Fasting ends at dusk, at which point the previously comatose country springs to life in a celebratory round of eating, drinking and socializing known as **Iftar** ("The Breaking of the Fast"). The atmosphere is particularly exuberant during **Eid Al Fitr**, the day marking the end of Ramadan, when everyone lets loose in an explosion of celebratory festivity.

Renaissance Day July 23 Celebrating the 1970 coup which brought Sultan Qaboos to power and signalled the start of the Oman Renaissance (see p.230).

Eid al Adha Estimated dates: Oct 26, 2012; Oct 15, 2013; Oct 4, 2014. Falling approximately 70 days after the end of Ramadan, on the tenth day of the Islamic lunar month of Dhul Hijja, the "Festival of the Sacrifice" celebrates the willingness of Abraham (or Ibrahim, as he is known to Muslims) to sacrifice his son Ismail at the command of God (although having proved his obedience, he was permitted to sacrifice a ram instead). The festival also marks the end of the traditional pilgrimage season to Mecca. Large numbers of animals are slaughtered during the festival. No alcohol is served on the day of the festival or on the day before.

Outdoor activities and sport

Oman's wild mountain and desert landscapes offer enormous potential for outdoor activities and adventure sports – one which is slowly beginning to be realized, although the field remains in its infancy. The country is also a leading diving destination, with some of the region's most pristine underwater landscapes and marine life.

Hiking

The most obvious – and perhaps most rewarding – of the country's outdoor activities is **hiking**. An extensive network of hiking trails exists across the country, particularly in the Western Hajar (see box, p.93), with reasonably well-marked trails winding around and through some of Oman's most spectacular mountain ridges, wadis and canyons. Walks range from high-altitude treks along the mountain ridges through to exhilarating and challenging canyon walks, which usually involve scrambling over boulders and wading (and sometimes swimming) through rock pools and watercourses.

None of the treks should be attempted lightly. It's imperative to carry sufficient water and also to keep a watchful eye on the weather if trekking through wadis (especially narrower canyons). Rainfall in the mountains can be sudden and dramatic, leading to violent and potentially fatal flash flooding.

Twelve of the best routes are covered in *Oman Trekking*, published by Explorer.

Adventure sports

There is a range of **adventure sports and activities** around the country. Activities include canyoning (the rough scramble up Snake Canyon (see p.101) is especially popular), caving, abseiling, rock-climbing or tackling one of the country's three *via ferratas* (Wadi Nakhr, Snake Canyon and Bandar Khayran). Mountain-biking and kayaking are other possibilities. Leaders in the field are the Muscat Diving & Adventure Centre (Ⓦwww.holiday-in-oman.com), while Gulf Leisure (Ⓦwww.gulfleisure.com) also run a similar range of offerings.

Diving and snorkelling

Oman offers some of the region's finest **diving**, with good **snorkelling** too. Compared to other parts of the region, most of the coastal waters remain unspoilt, home to fine coral gardens and a few wrecks, and attracting some spectacularly large marine life.

It's possible to go diving straight from **Muscat**, which has a surprisingly extensive roster of dive centres (see p.49). Many operators here can also arrange trips to the spectacular **Daminiyat Islands** (see p.123) up the coast north of Barka. Further afield, **Musandam** (see p.149) is perhaps the finest diving destination in the country, while there are further excellent dive sites along the south coast, especially around Mirbat (see p.202).

Most of the country's dive centres are run by European and North American expats; all offer a fairly standard range of dives, along with PADI courses, while many places also run **snorkelling** trips and assorted **boat cruises**.

Sport

There's little in the way of organized sport in Oman, although if you're lucky you might catch a glimpse of one of the country's traditional competitive pastimes like **bull-butting** (see box, p.116) and **camel-racing** – the latter is held at many locations around the country, especially on public holidays and National Day, although it's difficult to pick up information about forthcoming events. Try asking locally to find out if anything's planned.

Currently, the only formal annual sporting event is the **Tour of Oman** (Ⓦwww.tourofoman.om) cycling race, first staged in 2010. Held over six days in February at locations around Muscat and the Western Hajar, it attracts a strong field of international riders.

Shopping

Oman offers a wonderful range of traditional Arabian products both natural and manufactured, ranging from inexpensive bags of aromatic frankincense and tubs of *bukhoor* through to elaborately wrought *khanjars* and chunky Bedu jewellery.

Where to shop

Many of the items described below can be found in souks all over the country, although for the finest array of Omani goods under one roof nothing beats a visit to the legendary Muttrah Souk (see p.56) in Muscat. The souks at Nizwa (see p.89) and Salalah (see p.198) also offer an excellent selection of merchandise – Nizwa is particularly celebrated for its handicrafts, while Salalah is perhaps the best place in the country to pick up samples of the greatly prized Dhofari frankincense. **Prices** are rarely fixed, however, and bargaining is very much the order of the day.

For a more contemporary, but in many ways equally rewarding, shopping experience, head to one of the many **Lulu Hypermarkets** which dot the country (the one between Muttrah and Ruwi in Muscat is convenient, and particularly good). A browse through the aisles here uncovers a fascinating array of local, Arabian and Asian produce, usually at bargain prices – anything from tubs of dates, jars of Yemeni honey, big packets of cut-price spices and great piles of outlandish vegetables through to traditional Indian tiffin-boxes and bars of sandalwood soap.

Aromatics

Oman is famous for all things fragrant – frankincense, *bukhoor*, myrrh and traditional perfumes – a cheap and portable memory of the sultanate.

Frankincense

Oman's most celebrated natural product is **frankincense** (see also box on p.199), widely available in souks all over the country, although you'll find the best selection in Muttrah Souk in Muscat and Al Husn Souk in Salalah. Frankincense is sold in various **grades**, referred to by a confusing variety of names. Cheapest is the rather blackish, low-grade stuff from Somalia. Local Omani frankincense is generally considered superior, though again there are many different qualities on offer, ranging from the generic, yellowish lumps of standard-grade frankincense through to the highly prized "silver" frankincense (also sometimes referred to as *hojari*, *hawjari* or *hugari*). As a general rule of thumb, the larger the chunks of frankincense resin and the clearer and lighter the colour, the better the quality. That from Dhofar (see Al Husn Souk account on p.198) is usually reckoned to be the best, although even here aficionados distinguish between different types of frankincense grown in different locations around the region.

Prices range from a rial or two for a bag of Somali frankincense through to 7–10 OR for higher-quality Salalah produce. Various types of **frankincense burner** (*mabkhara*) can also be found in shops around the country, ranging from functional little wooden and metal designs costing just a couple of rials through to brightly painted pottery frankincense burners from Salalah. Boxes of the tiny charcoal blocks used to burn the stuff are also widely available.

Bukhoor and myrrh

Almost as ubiquitous as frankincense is **bukhoor**, a distinctive local aromatic usually sold in cute little golden tins (a modern version of the traditional *mukkabbah* – see p.89) or in larger plastic jars – when it's easily mistaken for tea. *Bukhoor* is made from perfumed woodchips soaked in oil and blended with various perfumes in a range of styles. Traditional *bukhoor* will typically contain some combination of musk, frankincense, *oud* and sandalwood, although other ingredients are also sometimes added, creating a wide range of scents. Like frankincense, *bukhoor* is burnt using a charcoal burner (and works fine in a frankincense burner), although a tin of the stuff with its lid off will do very well as a kind of traditional Omani air-freshener. Prices range according to the quality of the ingredients used, although 2–3 OR is usual, despite what some optimistic shop owners might tell you.

Myrrh is another popular local aromatic, although less widely available than frankincense and *bukhoor*. It's produced by cutting the bark of a myrrh tree, collecting the resultant resinous sap and then burning it. Although Oman produces small quantities of myrrh, the stuff for sale in the country's souks will most likely have come from Somalia or Yemen. A small tub should cost a couple of rials.

Perfume

Traditional Arabian **perfumes** (*attar*) are another local speciality, although the flowery, oil-based scents are somewhat overpowering compared to more subtle European-style fragrances. Fine Arabian perfumes are usually founded on a base of essential oils derived from *oud* (aloes, or agarwood) leavened with other local fragrances, often including frankincense. As well as pre-packaged scents, most perfume shops (such as the nationwide Al Haramain chain) can mix up bespoke perfumes from the long lines of glass bottles kept behind the counter. For the ultimate in Omani *parfumerie*, check out the Amouage factory just outside Seeb (see p.113).

Handicrafts

Oman boasts a wealth of artisanal traditions, ranging from the country's famed metalworking (seen in elaborately detailed traditional *khanjars* and Bedu jewellery) through to traditional wooden walking sticks, pottery and clothes.

Khanjars

Perhaps the most appealling local souvenir is the **khanjar**, the traditional curved dagger which can be found around the Gulf, although those from Oman are often reckoned to be the finest. Modern replica *khanjars* are widely available, often sold ready-framed in small glass cases from as little as 10–15 OR; some are also given an artifically antique appearance through the use of black silver. These are often of poor quality, however, and don't begin to compare with the superb antique *khanjars* you'll find for sale in Muttrah and Nizwa Souks and a few other places around the country. No two antique *khanjars* are ever completely alike, and many display wonderfully intricate metalworking on their hilts and scabbards, along with deer-horn hilts (modern *khanjars* use plastic). Traditional Nizwa *khanjars* are characterized by their incredibly detailed silverwork, while those from Sur traditionally use gold thread to pick out designs. You'll also see plenty of antique Yemeni *khanjars* in Muttrah and Nizwa. These have leather rather than metal scabbards and generally show significantly lower standards of craftsmanship, although they are also very appealling in their own, slightly rustic, way, and significantly cheaper than their Omani equivalents. Prices for a genuine, high-grade Omani *khanjar* aren't cheap, and you won't get much for under 75 OR – it pays to shop around carefully.

Other handicrafts

Omani **pottery**, most of it manufactured in the workshops of Bahla (see p.104), is also widely available, particularly in Nizwa Souk, and includes a range of traditional pots and frankincense burners along with more touristy creations (miniature clay forts and watchtowers, for example).

Gold, **silver** and **jewellery** are also well represented. Oman is a particularly good place to pick up examples of distinctive antique **Bedu jewellery** – chunky necklaces, bracelets and anklets in elaborately worked silver. Traditional necklaces often sport the distinctive Maria Theresa Thaler coins which formerly served as the major currency in the Gulf, as well as cute boxes designed to hold fragments of Qur'anic text, meant to ward off the evil eye. Traditional Gulf-style gold bracelets are another eye-catching purchase – the Gold Souk section of Muttrah Souk is the place to go for these.

The traditional wooden **walking stick** is another popular souvenir, as are wooden **toy rifles**. Assorted **clothes and textiles** can also be found. An embroidered Omani cap makes a particularly cute souvenir, or you could go the whole hog and invest in a turban and dishdasha. Ladies will find a chintzy range of colourfully embroidered dresses, trousers and blouses, including local versions of the classic Indian *shalwar kameez*. Oman isn't a **carpet**-producing centre, although a few shops in Muttrah and Qurum in Muscat offer a decent range of Iranian, Afghan and other rugs and kilims at prices lower than you'd pay in the West. The country's large subcontinental population means that there's a good range of **Indian handicrafts** on offer (particularly in Muttrah), including Rajasthani-style patchwork and tie-dye fabrics and Kashmiri pashminas.

Consumables

Oman also offers an intriguing range of more perishable but equally memorable souvenirs. These include a packet of dates (those from Bateel – see p.75 – are particularly fine), a tub of *halwa* (see p.28) or a bottle of rose-water from Jebel Akhdar (see p.98). The nationwide chain of Lulu Hypermarkets is particularly good for stocking up on cheap local specialities.

Culture and etiquette

Foreigners are generally made to feel very welcome in Oman, although in return you'll be expected to abide scrupulously by Omani cultural norms. This remains a deeply traditional – and in many ways very conservative – country, and despite its sometimes superficially westernized appearance and growing openness to tourists, old attitudes run extremely deep.

Away from the main tourist centres, foreigners remain a source of considerable interest – often occasioning a certain amount of benign curiosity and clandestine staring. This is almost always friendly, and a smile, wave or (best of all) a cheery *salaam aleikum* (see p.244) will usually break the ice and lead to a conversation with whatever bits of a shared language you can muster.

Visiting traditional **Omani villages**, it's worth remembering that you are entering what is generally considered the private space of the locals who live there. Discretion is the order of the day, and the onus is on you, as the outsider, to behave in a friendly and open manner, and to exercise sensitivity when taking photographs (also see p.40). A few pre-prepared phrases of pidgin Arabic (see p.244) should help smooth the progress of any visit.

Dress

Dressing appropriately is perhaps the single most important thing to remember. Women should wear loose clothing, with arms and shoulders covered. Skirts, if worn, should reach at least beneath the knee, although wearing trousers is probably a better option. It's also useful to carry a shawl to cover your hair in more conservative areas. Dress codes are less crucial for men, although many Omanis will look rather askance at blokes dressed in tight or thigh-length shorts or singlets – below-the-knee shorts are probably OK, although it's best to err on the side of caution and wear trousers, even if it means foregoing a tan. For both men and women, it helps to dress conservatively, especially in rural areas. Ripped jeans, combat fatigues, dodgy T-shirts with inappropriate slogans or images and elaborate piercings are unlikely to play well in a rural village in deepest Sharqiya. Inside foreign-oriented tourist hotels more Western standards prevail, although it's still polite not to wander around in a bikini away from the pool or beach.

Behaviour

As throughout Arabia, it pays to keep your cool. Expressions of overt anger and any raising of the voice should be strictly avoided, whatever the situation. It's also worth knowing that even innocuous **hand gestures** are punishable under Omani law, if deemed offensive. Exact definitions are somewhat elastic, although it's a lesson well worth absorbing, particularly if driving, when the urge to flap your hands in exasperation (or give the idiot in the Toyota Landcruiser who has just cut you up at 150km/h the finger) may become overwhelming.

Meeting people

Traditional Arabic **greetings** serve as an important oil in the machinery of everyday Omani life (see p.244 for full details) – the elaborate, almost courtly, formality with which Omanis greet one another in even the most prosaic of circumstances (your driver stopping to ask for directions, for example) offers a fascinating insight into the forms of decorum which still regulate Omani life.

Physical modes of greeting are also important. Close male and female friends and relatives will kiss one another on either cheek, although between male strangers the standard form of physical greeting is a handshake. Members of the opposite sex do not generally touch – do not offer your hand to an Omani of the opposite sex unless they offer you theirs first.

Invitations to **visit an Omani home** are common – don't be surprised if your driver asks you back to his house at the end of a tour for coffee and dates. If invited for a formal meal, it's polite to take some form of small gift, ideally gift-wrapped – chocolates or dates are ideal. Remember to take your shoes off when entering any Omani house. Once inside, it's considered polite to take whatever form of food or drink is offered, since refusal may be construed as dissatisfaction or disapproval. For coffee-drinking etiquette, see p.28.

Taboo subjects

Conversations in Oman generally run along well-regulated lines – your country, age, marital status, number of children (if any), religion, profession, reasons for visiting Oman and impressions of the country being the usual topics.

Pride in their country is strong among Omanis, and criticisms of the nation of any type will not be well received (unless, perhaps, you are simply agreeing with an opinion expressed by your host). Negative statements about Islam should be even more strenuously avoided. In addition, if asked your own religion, it's easiest to profess Christianity, even if in fact you believe in nothing of the sort, given that concepts of atheism, agnosticism and alternative religions are not widely understood. Political discussion – except of the most general and harmless kind – also remains a sensitive subject to be approached with extreme care, while criticisms of Sultan Qaboos are a definite no-go.

Women travellers

Women travelling in Oman should experience few problems, although the sight of unaccompanied Western females, either solo or in pairs, is still something of a novelty in most parts of the country. Hassles are rare (assuming you dress conservatively – particularly crucial if travelling without a male companion), albeit not unknown, particularly in Muscat. On the downside, solo women travellers may feel particularly isolated, given that most Omani men will, out of respect, tend to studiously ignore you, while it's difficult to make friends with Omani women, at least without local contacts.

Travel essentials

Costs

Unfortunately, a visit to Oman doesn't come cheap. The major expenses are accommodation and transport/tours. The very cheapest **hotel** rooms start at around 12–15 OR per night (£20–25/US$30–40), at least double this for mid-range places, and anything from 75 OR (£120/$200) and upwards for top-end places.

The lack of reliable public **transport** options mean that to see the country properly you'll have to at least hire your own car (from around 15 OR/£25/$40/day), hire a car plus guide-driver, or go on a tour. The fact that so many of the country's highlights require 4WD adds further fiscal punishment, meaning either hiring your own 4WD (from around 30 OR/£55/$80/day) or, more realistically, taking a 4WD with guide-driver (from around 80 OR/£130/$210/day). At least petrol is cheap.

Once you've paid for lodgings and transport, other costs are relatively modest. **Eating** can be very cheap (if only because of the lack of proper restaurants), although the price of alcohol (if you can find it) is punitive. **Entrance fees** to the country's various forts and museums are extremely modest, however – seldom more than 1 OR.

Staying in the cheapest hotels, eating at local cafés, driving yourself and foregoing beer, you might scrape along on a bare minimum of 40 OR (£65/$100) per day per couple, without tours. Realistically, however, you're probably looking at around double this figure once you factor in the cost of taking a couple of off-road tours or a boat trip in Musandam. And of course it's very easy, in Muscat especially, to spend a lot more than this if staying in nice hotels and eating (and drinking) at good restaurants – in which case you could easily push this figure up to several hundred rials per day.

Many more upmarket hotels and restaurants levy a 17 percent **tax** (comprising an 8 percent service charge plus 9 percent government tax) on food and rooms. This is usually but not always mentioned in published room rates and menus – if in doubt, check. Cheaper places usually quote prices inclusive of taxes (the "nett" rate).

Crime and personal safety

Oman is an extremely safe country. Violent crime is very rare, and even petty crime such as burglary and pickpocketing is significantly less common than in most Western countries.

It pays to be sensible, even so. Make sure you have a good travel **insurance** policy (see p.38) before you arrive and protect all personal valuables as you would anywhere else, and take particular care of personal possessions in crowded areas such as Muttrah Souk.

If you are unfortunate enough to become the victim of theft, you'll need a police report for your insurance company, obtainable from the nearest police station. Don't count on finding any English-speaking officers, however; taking an Arabic-speaker with you will probably be a major help.

Far and away the major threat to personal safety in Oman is **traffic**, whether you're a driver, passenger or pedestrian (for more on driving in Oman, see p.22). As a **pedestrian**, bear in mind that traffic will not necessarily stop – or even slow down – if you start crossing the road, and may also be travelling a lot faster than you might expect.

Customs regulations

Visitors are allowed to import up to two litres (and not more than two bottles) of alcoholic beverages (non-Muslims only) and a "reasonable" quantity of tobacco. A yellow fever vaccination certificate is required for travellers arriving within six days from infected areas in Africa and South America.

Travellers carrying prescription drugs should take a letter from their doctor stating that they are obliged to take this medicine.

Electricity

UK-style **sockets** with three square pins are the norm. The country's current runs at 240 volts AC, meaning that UK appliances will work without problem directly off the mains supply, although US appliances will probably require a transformer.

Entry requirements

Citizens of most countries, including the UK, US, Ireland, Australia, New Zealand and South Africa, require a **visa** to enter Oman.

Tourist visas can be bought on the spot on arrival at Muscat airport, costing 20 OR (£37/US$55) for a one-month visa. Pay for your visa at the Travelex counter first; staff will give you a receipt which you then present at the immigration desk (signed "Tourist Visa"). Only single-entry visas are available at the airport (despite what signs say); multiple-entry visas have to be applied for in advance online (see below). If you're driving from the main part of Oman up to the Musandam peninusla through the UAE you'll need to buy a new visa every time you cross an Omani border – see p.145 for details. Note that embassy websites aren't well maintained, and the visa information and prices found on them may well be out of date; if in doubt, ring.

It's also possible to get your visa in advance by applying online at ⓦwww.rop.gov.om and then sending your passport into your nearest embassy or consulate. Visas acquired in advance currently cost £40 for a single-entry, or £100 for a multiple-entry visa valid for either one year (maximum stay 3 weeks at any one time) or the same price for a multiple-entry visa valid for two years (maximum stay six months). There's no point in going through the hassle of applying for a visa in advance unless you're going to be entering and leaving the country a lot and thus need a multiple-entry visa. Note, also, that when applying online for a multiple-entry visa you'll be required to fill in a section giving the details of a sponsor in Oman: enter your hotel name as your sponsor name and, for the sponsor ID, the figures "1111".

Having an **Israeli stamp** in your passport is not a problem when entering Oman.

Omani embassies and consulates abroad

Australia Level 4, Suite 2, 493 St Kilda Rd, Melbourne 3004 ⓣ03 9820 4096, ⓦwww.oman.org.au.
Canada c/o US embassy.
Ireland 4 Kenilworth Square, Dublin ⓣ01 491 2411.
New Zealand c/o Australian embassy.
South Africa 42 Nicholson St, Muckleneuk, Pretoria ⓣ012 346 4429.
UK 167 Queen's Gate, London SW7 5HE, ⓣ020 7225 0001, ⓦwww.omanembassy.org.uk.
US 2535 Belmont Rd, Washington DC, 20008 ⓣ202 387 1980, ⓦhttp://omanembassy.net & ⓦwww.omaninfo.us.

Gay and lesbian travellers

Oman shares the medieval attitudes prevalent around the Gulf with regard to same-sex relationships. Homosexuality remains illegal, and anyone caught in anything that might be classed as a homosexual act is technically looking at a spell in prison, although local police are unlikely to go after foreign gays and lesbians unless given good cause to.

As with other places around the Gulf, a scene does exist (particularly in Muscat), but it's extremely secretive. The only accessible online resource available at the time of writing is via Facebook (try "Gay in Oman" in the search box), although the few groups currently in existence appear to be largely made up of men looking for one-night stands.

In practical terms, the good news is that, given the sexually segregated nature of Omani society, male or female couples travelling together are unlikely to elicit any particular attention, assuming you behave in a manner consistent with local standards. Same-sex couples shouldn't attract too much attention when checking into a hotel room together, assuming you stick to twin, rather than double, beds. Discretion is naturally the order of the day, at all times,

Emergency number

In the event of an emergency, dial ⓣ9999 for an ambulance or to call the police.

and any public displays of affection or other unconventional behaviour should be strictly avoided, unless you know the people you are with very well.

Health

There are no serious **health risks** in Oman (unless you include the country's traffic). All the main cities in the country are equipped with modern hospitals and well-stocked pharmacies. **Tap water** is safe to drink, while even the country's cheapest cafés maintain good standards of **food hygiene**. One possible health concern is the **heat**. Summer temperatures regularly climb into the forty-degree Celsius range, making sunburn, heatstroke and acute dehydration a real possibility, especially if combined with excessive alcohol consumption. Stay in the shade, and drink lots of water.

Bilharzia is another possible risk if swimming in rock pools in the mountains.

Insurance

There aren't many safety or health risks involved in a visit to Oman, although it's still strongly recommended that you take out some form of valid **travel insurance** before your trip. At its simplest, this offers some measure of protection against everyday mishaps like cancelled flights and mislaid baggage. More importantly, a valid insurance policy will cover your costs in the event that you fall ill in Oman, since otherwise you'll have to pay for all medical treatment. Note, too, that most insurance policies routinely exclude various "adventure" activities. In Oman this will include adventure sports such as caving, abseiling and rock-climbing, and might conceivably also include trekking. If in doubt, check with your insurer before you leave home.

Internet

There's a decent number of **internet cafés** in some cities in Oman (Muscat, Salalah, Nizwa and Khasab, for example – all listed in the relevent guide chapters). Away from these places, however, it can be a real struggle to find anywhere to get online.

Internet access is also available in many mid-range and all top-end **hotels**, either via cable or wi-fi. Occasionally it's free in these establishments but most often chargeable, often at extortionate rates (2–3 OR/hr is common).

If you really need to be online you might consider subscribing to the **mobile internet service** provided by Nawras (ⓦwww.nawras.om), which uses a small modem that plugs into your computer's USB port, giving you your own portable wi-fi system – but with prices starting from around 25 OR it's a bit of an investment.

The **country URL** for Oman is ".om" – which looks confusingly like a typo for ".com". If you find a .om address not working, try replacing it with .com, or vice versa.

Mail

Oman has an efficient and reliable modern postal service. Postcards and letters cost between 200bz and 400bz to Europe and North America, rising to around 5 OR for parcels weighing over 1kg, although if sending anything valuable you may prefer to use an international courier such as DHL or FedEx, who have offices in Muscat and Salalah. There are no reliable **poste restante** facilities in Oman. If you need to receive a letter or package, it's best to have it delivered to your hotel (and to warn them in advance of its arrival).

Maps

The best **map** of the country is the *Reise Know How Oman* map (1:850,000). It's printed on (nearly) indestructible paper and covers the country in clear and commendably up-to-date detail. For off-road maps, *Off-Road Oman* (see p.23) includes excellent satellite maps of 26 routes around the country.

Money

The Omani currency is the **rial** (usually abbreviated "OR", or sometimes "OMR"), subdivided into 1000 **baiza** ("bz"). Banknotes are denominated in 100, 200 and 500 baiza and in 1, 5, 10, 20 and 50 rials (there are two types of one-rial note, coloured either red or brown). Coins are denominated in 5, 10, 25 and 50 baiza. Exchange rates at the time of writing were 1 OR = £1.60, $2.60 and €1.85.

ATMs and banks

There are plentiful **ATMs** all over the country, virtually all of which accept foreign Visa and MasterCards, as well as numerous **banks**, all of which will change travellers' cheques and foreign cash. Many more upmarket hotels will also change cash and travellers' cheques, usually at poor rates.

Opening hours and public holidays

Oman runs on a basically Islamic schedule. The traditional working week runs from **Saturday to Wednesday**, although some businesses also open on a Thursday morning, while Friday serves as the Islamic holy day (equivalent to the Christian Sunday). Usual **business hours** are 8am–5pm; government offices open 8am–2pm. **Banks** are usually open Saturday to Wednesday 8am–noon and Thursday 8–11.30am.

Shopping hours are slightly different. Shops in most souks generally open seven days a week, although most places remain closed on Friday mornings. Most places also shut down daily for an extended siesta from around noon or 1pm until 5 or 6pm, lending many smaller places a rather ghost-town ambience during the hot afternoon hours. Local **cafés** may stay open, although there's unlikely to be much food available past around 1pm (more upmarket restaurants tend to stay open until 2 or 3pm, but then usually close until around 7pm). Things fire back into life as

Public holidays

There are eight public holidays in Oman. Three of these fall on the same day every year; the other five follow the lunar Islamic calendar and therefore change date by around eleven days every year, moving gradually backwards through the year.

New Year's Day Jan 1

Mouloud (The Prophet's Birthday) Feb 4, 2012; Jan 24, 2013; Jan 14, 2014

Leilat al Meiraj (Ascension of the Prophet) June 16, 2012; June 5, 2013; May 25, 2014

Renaissance Day (see p.30) July 23

Eid al Fitr (End of Ramadan – see p.30) Aug 19, 2012; Aug 8, 2013; July 29, 2014

Eid al Adha (Feast of the Sacrifice – see p.30) Oct 25, 2012; Oct 15, 2013; Oct 4, 2014

National Day and birthday of Sultan Qaboos November 18

Islamic New Year Nov 26, 2011; Nov 15, 2012; Nov 4, 2013; Oct 25, 2014

dusk approaches, usually remaining busy until 9 or 10pm.

Museums tend to follow a similar pattern, opening Sunday to Wednesday from around 9 or 10am to 1pm and from 4 or 6pm to 7pm. Some remain closed for the whole of Thursday and Friday; others open, but only during the afternoon/evening. **Forts** broadly divide into two categories. Smaller forts tend to be open Saturday to Wednesday 8am–2pm; larger forts are generally open Saturday to Thursday 9am–4pm and Friday 8–11am.

Phones

The **country code** for Oman is ⓣ968. All Omani landline phone numbers are eight digits long, starting with ⓣ2. Area codes (eg ⓣ24 for Muscat) have now been integrated into the eight-digit format, and must be dialled irrespective of where you're calling from. Mobile numbers also follow an eight-digit format, but begin with ⓣ9. To call Oman from abroad you have to dial the country code plus full eight-digit number. **Emergency numbers** are listed on p.38.

Public phones are scarce in Oman and it's well worth bringing your **mobile** (cell phone) with you; check the relevant charges before you leave home. European GSM handsets should work fine in Oman, although North American cell phones may not (excepting tri-band phones).

If you're going to be using the phone a lot while you're in Oman, it might be worth acquiring a **local SIM card**, which will give you cheap local and international calls. The leading local phone operator is Nawras (ⓦwww.nawras.om), which has shops countrywide where you can pick up a SIM card (you'll need to show your passport when purchasing). The pre-paid Nawras Mousbak scheme (5 OR including SIM card and 2 OR credit) is the easiest to use. Funds can be added to your account using the widely available scratchcard-style recharge cards, available from many local shops – look out for the window stickers. Other operators include Oman Mobile (ⓦwww.omantel.om) and Samatel (ⓦwww.samatel.om), who run similar schemes at similar prices, although shops and recharge cards are less widely available.

Photography

Oman is a very photogenic country, although the often harsh light can play havoc with colour and contrast – for the best results head out between around 7am and 9am in the morning, or after 4pm. Don't take photographs of people without asking or you risk causing considerable offence, especially if taking photos of ladies without permission. In Arabic, "May I take you picture?" translates (roughly) as *Mumkin sura, min fadlak?* (to a man) or *Mumkin sura, min fadlik?* (to a woman). Men will probably be happy to oblige, women less so, while children of either sex will usually be delighted.

Smoking

Smoking is not permitted inside cafés, restaurants, bars, malls, offices and other public areas – although it's usually permitted on the outdoor terraces of bars and restaurants. Cigarettes are cheap; a pack of Marlboros, for example, costs under 1 OR.

Calling home from abroad

Note that the initial zero is omitted from the area code when dialling the UK, Ireland, Australia and New Zealand from abroad.

Australia ⓣ00 + 61 + area code + number
New Zealand ⓣ00 + 64 + area code + number
UK ⓣ00 + 44 + area code + number
US and Canada ⓣ00 + 1 + area code + number
Ireland ⓣ00 + 353 + area code + number
South Africa ⓣ00 + 27 + area code + number

Time

Oman runs on **Gulf Standard Time** (GST). This is 4hr ahead of GMT (or 3hr ahead of British Summer Time), 9hr ahead of US Eastern Standard Time, 12hr ahead of US Pacific Time; 4hr behind Australian Western Standard Time, and 6hr behind Australian Eastern Standard Time. There is no daylight-saving in Oman.

Toilets

There are no **public toilets** in Oman. If you get caught short, head to the nearest plausible-looking hotel, restaurant or café. Pretty much all tourist attractions, including museums and forts, also provide toilets. Most toilets in Oman are of Western-style sit-down design, although Asian-style squat toilets are also occasionally found.

Tourist information

There are no proper tourist information offices **in Oman** (apart from a small kiosk at the Muscat airport), and getting reliable local information can be a struggle. Your best bet is to talk to one of the local tour operators listed on p.22. Staff at better hotels may also be able to provide local information, though this is decidedly hit and miss.

There are no proper Oman tourist offices overseas. In the **UK**, tourist enquiries are handled by the PR company Representation Plus (Ⓣ020 8877 4524, Ⓔoman@representationplus.co.uk), whose response times can be extremely slow.

Websites

Useful websites for visitors include:

Ⓦ**www.omanet.om** Run by the Ministry of Information, packed with interesting background on the country's culture, history and tourist attractions.

Ⓦ**www.omanobserver.com** Latest news from the country's leading daily newspaper.

Ⓦ**www.omantourism.gov.om** Official website of the Ministry of Tourism, with extensive information and features on all parts of the country.

Ⓦ**www.muscatconfidential.blogspot.com** Insightful and entertaining musings on the latest political and other news from the sultanate.

Ⓦ**www.muscatdeli.blogspot.com** Perceptive reviews of restaurants in the capital and listings of forthcoming culinary events.

Ⓦ**www.muscatmutterings.com** Useful listings of forthcoming events in the capital plus links to other Oman-related blogs.

Travelling with children

Children form a central part of Omani life: treasured, fussed-over and generally integrated into most social situations. Families are usually large, and even quite young children are habitually included in social gatherings and night-time excursions at an hour when their Western counterparts are tucked firmly up in bed. For visitors with children, this means that your kids will generally be welcomed wherever you go (except perhaps in a few of Muscat's more exclusive restaurants and bars), and may well prove a bridge between you and the Omanis in whose company you happen to find yourself.

There are hardly any dedicated **children's attractions** in Oman, except the Children's Museum in Muscat (see p.65), although kids will enjoy many of the country's mainstream attractions. Exploring forts can be fun, while some of the less strenuous mountain walks (or parts of walks) may also appeal. Turtle-watching at Ras al Jinz is a guaranteed hit, as are dhow cruises amid the dolphins of Musandam. Various desert activities such as dune-bashing and camel-riding are also good for older kids.

The main child-related hazard in Oman is the **sun**. Children are particularly susceptible to the effects of sunburn and heatstroke and should be wrapped up carefully and made to drink plenty of fluids.

Outside Muscat, it can prove tricky to find supplies of nappies and other essential items for babies and toddlers. It's best to bring everything you might need with you from home.

Travellers with disabilities

Unfortunately, visiting Oman presents major challenges for travellers with disabilities. Many of the country's leading attractions – including its rugged mountains and rickety old forts – are, by their very nature, largely inaccessible to visitors with impaired mobility. Muscat is the country's most accessible destination. Some of the city's upmarket hotels have specially equipped rooms, while leading attractions including Muttrah Souk and Sultan Qaboos Mosque are fully accessible (although you'll have to check with your hotel as to whether they can provide you with suitable transport). Outside the capital things become more difficult, but you may be able to arrange transport through one of the tour operators listed on pp.21–22. Muscat Diving and Adventure Centre (Ⓦwww.holiday-in-oman.com) and Oman Travel (Ⓦwww.omantravel.uk.com) are two recommended operators for travellers with disabilities, while useful pointers about visiting the country can be found at Ⓦwww.able-travel.com.

Guide

Guide

1 Muscat

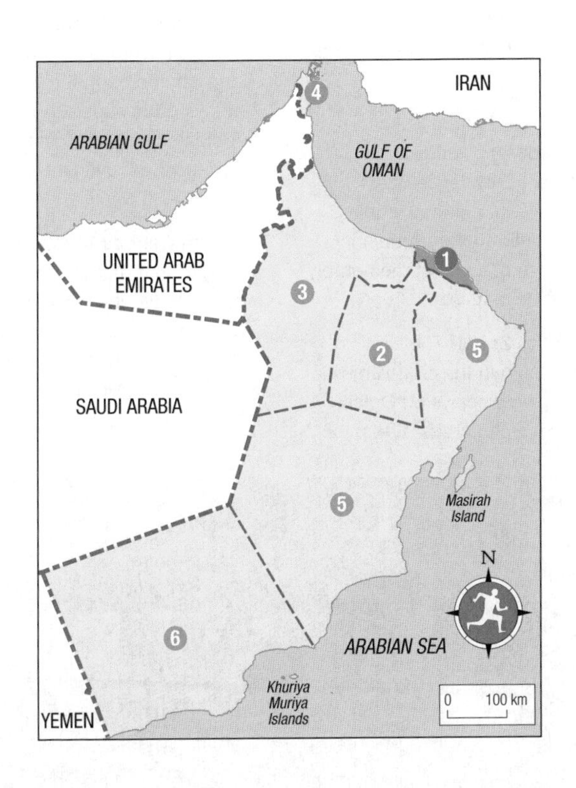
IRAN
ARABIAN GULF
GULF OF OMAN
UNITED ARAB EMIRATES
SAUDI ARABIA
Masirah Island
N
ARABIAN SEA
Khuriya Muriya Islands
0 100 km
YEMEN
1
2
3
4
5
5
6

CHAPTER 1

Highlights

* **Dolphin-watching** Take a boat trip out for a glimpse of frolicking dolphin pods, and for unrivalled views of the area's rugged coastline. See p.49
* **Muttrah Souk** Oman's most absorbing souk: a labyrinthine tangle of tiny shops piled high with Arabian curios and exotica. See p.56
* **Al Alam Palace** Sultan Qaboos's colourful Muscat residence offers an eye-catching example of contemporary Arabian design at its most memorably flamboyant. See p.60
* **Bait al Zubair** The best museum in the city, with wide-ranging displays on Omani culture and crafts. See p.62
* **Souq Ruwi Street** The vibrant commercial heart of Muscat's "Little India", crammed with colourful shops and curry houses. See p.64
* **Afternoon tea at Al Bustan Palace or the Grand Hyatt** Sit back over a traditional English afternoon tea while enjoying the super-fuelled Arabian kitsch of Muscat's two most extravagant hotels. See p.67 & p.68
* **Sultan Qaboos Mosque** Magnificent modern mosque rising above the western approaches to the city – and the only one in the country open to non-Muslim visitors. See p.67

▲ Muscat's waterfront and Muttrah Fort

1

Muscat مسقط

Oman's capital, and far and away its largest city, **MUSCAT** offers an absorbing snapshot of the country's past and present. Physically, much of the city is unequivocally modern: a formless straggle of low-rise, white-washed suburbs which sprawl along the coast for the best part of 25km, now home to a population nudging up towards the million mark – a quarter of the country's total. It's here that you'll find Oman at its most contemporary and consumerist, exemplified by the string of opulent hotels which line the city's sand-fringed coastline, backed up by swanky restaurants and modern malls, and honeycombed with a network of roaring, multi-lane highways. It's also unquestionably the commercial and administrative powerhouse of modern Oman, from the stately government buildings which line the main highway into town through to the high-rise office blocks of Ruwi's Central Business District.

Significant reminders of the city's past remain, however. These include, most notably, the engaging port district of **Muttrah** and the nearby quarter of **Old Muscat**, spread out along a salty seafront lined with old Portuguese forts, colourful mosques and assorted traditional Arabian buildings (many now converted to smale-scale museums). These are the places where you'll get the strongest sense of Muscat's sometimes elusive appeal, with its beguiling atmosphere of old-time, small-town Arabian somnolence, quite different from the somewhat faceless modern suburbs to the west. Muttrah and neighbouring **Ruwi** also offer the city's most interesting streetlife, and the best view of the patchwork of cultures which make up the city: Omani, Indian and Pakistani, with an occasional hint of Zanzibari, Baluchi and Iranian thrown in for good measure – a living memory of the city's surprisingly cosmopolitan past.

Some history

Evidence of human settlement in the Muscat area dates back to at least 6000 BC, although the city's rise to national pre-eminence is a much more recent affair. Muscat's port was sufficiently important to merit passing references in the works of Greek geographers, including Ptolemy and Pliny the Elder during the first century AD. For much of early Omani history though, it was overshadowed first by Sohar, to the north, and then Qalhat, to the south; one of the first European visitors to Muscat, Thomas Kerridge, writing in 1624 to the East India Company, described it as a "beggarly poor town".

Muscat suffered particularly at the hands of the **Portuguese**, who captured the town in 1508 and held onto it until 1650 – although ironically it was the Portuguese destruction of the nearby ports of Qalhat and Quriyat which cleared the way for Muscat's subsequent economic rise. The town began to flourish during the early Al Bu Said era (see p.223) in the second half of the eighteenth century when it established itself as the country's leading port and entrepot, while it also assumed increasing political significance during the reign of **Hamad bin Said** (1784–92), who moved the court to Muscat, where it has generally remained ever since. The city's economic position was confirmed during the nineteenth and twentieth centuries, thriving as a major centre for a range of economic activities including fishing, boat-building, slaving, arms-smuggling and general trade.

The sprawling metropolis you see today is a largely modern creation. Until the accession of **Sultan Qaboos** in 1970 the town comprised simply the old walled town of Muscat proper (or "Old Muscat", as it's now known), home to the residence of the sultan and other notables, and the separate port of Muttrah, the centre of the town's commercial activity.

Arrival

Muscat International Airport (Ⓦwww.omanairports.com), still sometimes referred to by its old name of Seeb International Airport, lies on the western edge of the city, around 30km from **Muttrah** and **Ruwi**, and around 15km from the modern city-centre suburbs including **Khuwair** and **Qurum**. It's usually around a thirty-minute drive to Muttrah and Ruwi, or fifteen to twenty minutes to Khuwair/Qurum, although the trip can take significantly longer depending on the city's unpredictable traffic. The airport is also about a twenty-minute drive from the nearby town of **Seeb** (see p.111) to the west. For **visa information** and requirements, see p.37.

Pre-paid airport **taxis** leave from directly outside the arrivals hall, costing 7–8 OR to most places in town (and also to Seeb) apart from *Al Bustan Palace* (10 OR) and the *Shangri-La Barr al Jissah Resort* (13 OR). There are also a few **ATMs**, plus Oman Mobile, Nawras and Samatel kiosks if you want to pick up a local SIM card (see p.40), and a string of **car-rental agents**.

Moving on from Muscat

The main ONTC **bus station** is in Ruwi (see map, p.63) from where buses run twice daily to Saham, Buraimi, Bahla, Birkat al Mauz, Ibra, Ibri, Nizwa, Sohar and Sur; these generally include one morning departure between 6.30am and 8am, and an early afternoon departure between 1pm and 2.30pm. There are also services to **Dubai** at 6am and 3pm, and to **Salalah** at 6am and 7pm, plus an additional departure at noon from mid-June to mid-September.

Various intercity **microbus** services run from Muscat. These mainly depart from **Rusayl roundabout**, close to the airport at the junction of the Nizwa and Sohar highways, and reachable by micro from Ruwi roundabout. A steady stream of micros depart from Rusayl inland to Nizwa, north to Sohar, and other destinations en route, usually costing just a few rials. You may also find **shared taxis** here running along the same routes at slightly higher prices. Note also that there's very little space inside a microbus – something of a challenge when you're travelling with even a modest amount of luggage.

Heading out to the **international airport**, micros to Seeb from Ruwi roundabout run directly past the airport, though once again the lack of space offers something of a challenge with luggage. Unless you're absolutely skint, it's best to catch a taxi (see p.51).

The only other way of leaving Muscat is by taking the **ferry** service to Musandam. For full details, see p.144.

Information

There's no official source of tourist information in Muscat beyond a small tourist information kiosk at the airport. Your best bet is to talk to one of the **local tour operators** listed on p.22. Useful local publications are equally thin on the ground. *Time Out Muscat* has fairly detailed listings of local restaurants, shops and tourist attractions, although it's not published regularly and so doesn't carry **listings** of what's on in the capital. For these, you're probably best off consulting local blogs like Ⓦwww.muscatmutterings.com (which also has useful links to other local blogs).

Diving, snorkelling and boat trips in Muscat

There are a surprising number of **diving operators** in Muscat offering a range of trips and PADI courses. The closest **dive sites** are just south of the city along the coast at **Bandar Jissah** and **Bandar Khayran** (which is also where you'll find the popular *Al Munassir* wreck) and, slightly further afield, at **Fahal Island** (40min–1hr by boat). Euro Divers, Omanta Scuba and the Oman Dive Centre also do trips out to the **Daminayat Islands** (see p.122), about a two- to three-hour trip by boat each way (or about half that in Omanta's high-speed catamaran). As throughout Oman, nutrient-rich waters attract a fine array of marine life, ranging from tiny nudibranchs to whale sharks. You stand a better chance of seeing larger sea life at the Daminiyats and Fahal, since they're further offshore. **Daminiyat Diving**, upstairs in the Jawaharat A'Shatti Complex in Shatti al Qurum (see p.67), stocks a reasonable range of diving gear; alternatively, try the shop at Bluzone Diving.

All diving operators also run **snorkelling** trips to explore the coral gardens at Bandar Jissah, Bandar Khayran and Fahal Island, and most (plus a couple of other operators) also run **boat trips** around the coast. These include **dolphin-spotting boat trips** – you should have a better than ninety percent chance of seeing dolphins (mainly spinner, sometimes bottlenose); whale sharks and humpback whales are also very occasionally sighted. Some operators also offer **sunset cruises**, leaving at around 4.30pm and lasting a couple of hours.

Dive operators

Bluzone Diving Marina Bander al Rowdha Ⓣ2473 7293, Ⓦwww.bluzonediving.com. Offers diving, snorkelling and sunset cruises, and also sells a good range of diving gear.

Euro Divers Capital Area Yacht Centre, Haramil (just north of Marina Bander al Rowdhah) Ⓣ2477 6042, Ⓦwww.euro-divers.com. Branch of a Swiss company, offering diving, snorkelling and dolphin-watching.

Oman Dive Centre Bandar al Jissah Ⓣ2482 4040, Ⓦwww.extradivers.info. Part of the worldwide Extra Divers network, this is one of the city's leading dive centres, and also runs snorkelling and dolphin-watching trips.

Omanta Scuba *InterContinental*, Shatti al Qurum Ⓣ2469 3223, Ⓦwww.omantascuba.com. Newly opened dive centre boasting a fast catamaran that can whisk visitors to the Daminiyats in just one hour, or to Fahal in a mere fifteen minutes. They also run leisurely boat trips, including dolphin-watching tours with snorkelling and lunch.

Boat tour operators

Arabian Sea Safaris *InterContinental*, Shatti al Qurum Ⓣ2469 3223, Ⓦwww.arabianseasafaris.com. Dolphin-spotting trips, plus kayaking and snorkelling.

Sidab Sea Tours Ⓣ9965 5783, Ⓦwww.sidabseatours.com. Glass-bottomed boat tours. Trips offer the chance to go snorkelling en route, plus a good chance of spotting dolphins.

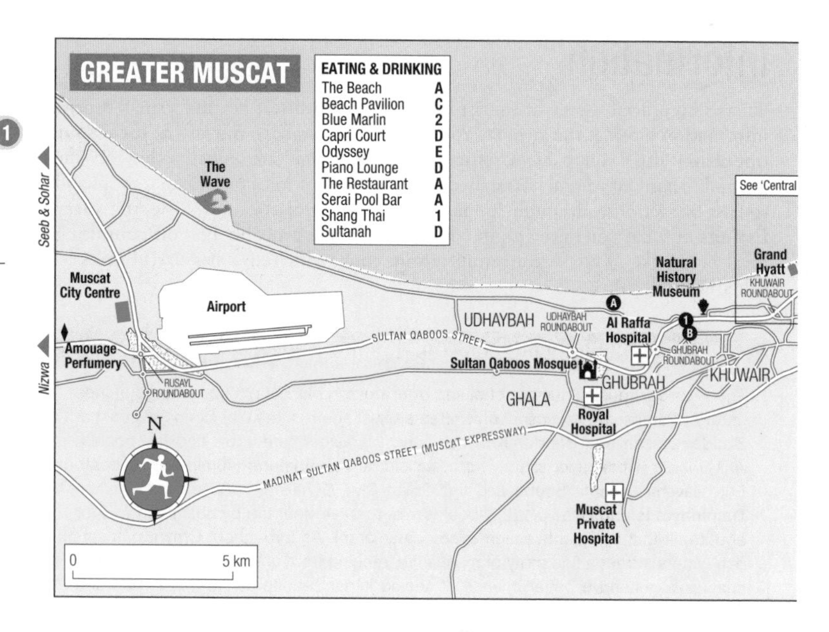

The best **maps** of the city are published by Explorer, either the handy, pocket-sized *Muscat Mini Map* (1.8 OR) or the excellent full-size *Explorer Muscat Map* (4 OR), which shows every street in the city with admirable clarity.

Orientation

Greater Muscat boasts an unusual geography and layout which can be somewhat perplexing at first impression. The entire city is extremely linear: a narrow ribbon of urban development spread out along 30km of coastline. As such, it's useful to think of Muscat not so much as a conventional city but rather as a collection of disparate towns and modern suburban developments without a single defining centre.

Broadly speaking, the city divides into two parts: **modern Muscat**, which stretches in a largely formless expanse of monotonous suburbs from just east of the airport through the suburbs of Ghubrah and Khuwair and on to Qurum; and the **older parts** of the city, comprising the three disparate districts of Muttrah, Old Muscat and Ruwi, divided from the rest of the city (and each other) by ridges of untamed, red-rock hills which give the eastern end of the metropolis a strangely lunar appearance in places.

The entire city is bisected from west to east by the main Highway 1, known as **Sultan Qaboos Street**, which runs from the airport to Shatti al Qurum and then splits (just beneath the rocky bluff topped by the *Mumtaz Mahal* restaurant – a useful landmark, since signage is poor) into two branches, with one arm, Qurum Heights Road, heading off to Muttrah and Old Muscat, and the other, Al Nahdah Street, to the centre of Qurum and then Ruwi. The newly constructed **Muscat Expressway** runs parallel to Sultan Qaboos Street a couple of kilometres inland, joining up with Al Nahdah Street at Qurum.

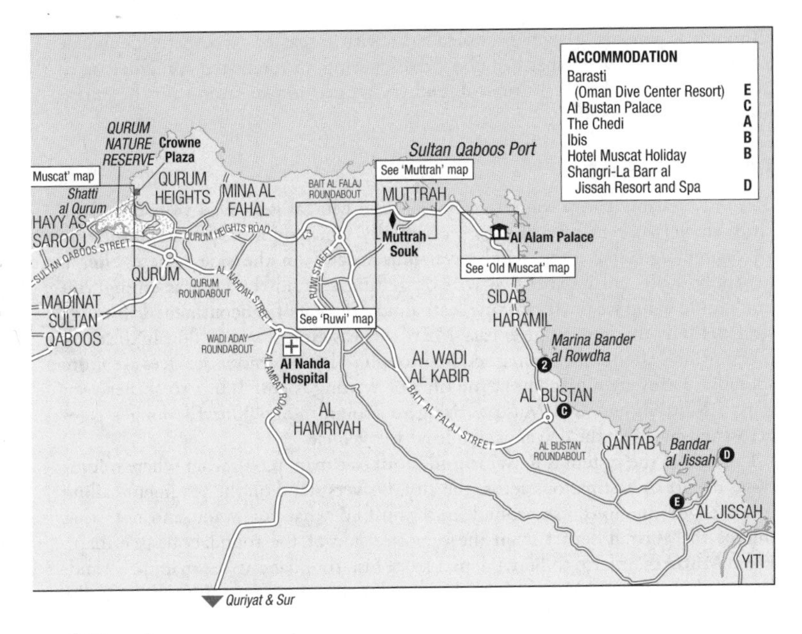

City transport

Greater Muscat is extremely spread out, and although parts of the city lend themselves to casual wandering, to explore the city in its entirety you'll need transport. Unfortunately, like virtually everywhere else in the Gulf, Muscat is determinedly car-centred, and public transport options are somewhat limited.

Taxis

The most convenient way of getting around is to hop in one of the city's plentiful **taxis**, painted a distinctive orange and white. These can be found virtually everywhere, at any time of the day and night – indeed, it's difficult to walk anywhere in the city without being persistently honked at by passing drivers for custom. Unfortunately, all the city's taxis are **unmetered**, meaning that you'll have to haggle over the fare before you set off – usually a frustrating business. Muscat's taxi drivers are an engagingly rogue-ish bunch: virtually all of them speak some kind of English, and they're often entertaining company to boot, although few are averse to making an extra rial or two out of visiting tourists.

As a rough rule of thumb, it's worth bearing in mind the following **sample taxi fares** from Muttrah: to Ruwi or old Muscat 1 OR; to Qurum 3 OR; and to the airport 6 OR (although note that all these prices double after midnight). In practice, as a foreigner, you'll probably end up paying anything from a third to twice as much, depending on the length of your journey and your bargaining powers. Trying to agree a reasonable fare outside the city's more upmarket hotels is a particularly frustrating experience.

An alternative to hiring your own cab is to grab a seat in a **shared taxi** – roughly double the price of a seat in a microbus (see below) but significantly cheaper than hiring the whole vehicle yourself. Unfortunately, finding a shared taxi is something of a challenge. The system operates on an entirely ad hoc basis, although if you see a semi-occupied taxi with a seat or two spare it's worth asking – just be aware that the taxi driver, seeing an interested foreigner, may evict the people already in the cab and try to get you to stump up the entire (inflated) fare yourself.

Microbuses

The only reliably cheap way of getting around Muscat is to avail yourself of the citywide network of **microbuses** – essentially white minivans, distinguished by an orange sign above the windscreen plus rosette on the side. These offer a generally swift and inexpensive way of getting around the city, assuming you don't mind being sardined into tiny seats amid a throng of subcontinental workers, students and other low-wage expats. Micros are easiest to come by during the early morning and after dark. From midday through to late afternoon services are more sporadic. **Fares** are a bargain: at the time of writing it cost 100bz to go between Ruwi, Muttrah and Old Muscat, rising to around 300–400bz for longer rides across the city. Pay the driver as you leave the vehicle.

The hub of the system is **Ruwi roundabout** (see map, p.63), from where microbuses depart to destinations across the city. Drivers stand on the pavement calling out their destinations; ask around until you find what you want, and note that micros to Muttrah depart from the opposite side of the roundabout (see map). From **Muttrah**, micros to Ruwi depart from Fish roundabout (see map, p.57) and, less regularly, for Old Muscat from the opposite side of the road. **Elsewhere** in the city, the easiest way to pick up a micro is to head for one of the major roundabouts along Sultan Qaboos Street; micros generally stop on the slip roads underneath roundabout flyovers. Make sure you're on the right side of the highway for the direction you want to travel in and, if in doubt, follow any likely-looking crowd of Indian or Pakistani workers, who can usually be found looking for transport until late at night.

Self-driving

Given the vagaries of public transport in Muscat, **hiring a car** (see p.22) is an appealling option, assuming you're going to be moving around the city a fair bit – if not, it may well be easier and no more expensive to catch taxis as required.

A couple of caveats apply, however. The first is the general standard of driving in the city, which is (by Omani standards) unusually aggressive, and occasionally downright homicidal, especially after dark, when Muscat's resident kamikaze petrolheads take to the streets. The second is the baffling complexity of the city's road systems and the lack of useful signage, meaning you're likely to spend considerable amounts of time going round and round like a laboratory hamster in some infernal road-traffic experiment. Equip yourself with a good map (such as Explorer's Muscat Map) and expect to get lost on a fairly regular basis.

Accommodation

Muscat is the only place in Oman where you're even slightly spoilt for choice when it comes to **accommodation**, while the level of competition here helps keep **prices** a bit more honest than in other parts of the country, although still no bargain. **Muttrah** is the place to head to for budget accommodation – with the added attraction of placing you right at the heart of Muscat's most absorbing area, although if you're looking for more upmarket lodgings you'll have to go

Guesthouses in Muscat

As an alternative to a conventional hotel, Muscat boats a number of low-key but appealing guesthouses. The following are the best.

Lanavilla 47th St, PC 106, Ghubrah North ⓣ9335 6310, ⓦwww.lanavilla-oman.com. Simple but very pleasant accommodation in an attractive modern house close to the beach. ❺

L'Espace 77 Al Ezdehar St, Ghubrah North ⓣ9628 2472, ⓦwww.lespaceoman.com. Overlooking the beach, with six colourful rooms decorated with Rajasthani fabrics and artefacts. ❺

Nomad Guest House Way 4468, Athaiba, Ghubrah North ⓣ9549 5240, ⓦwww.nomadtours.com. Homely guesthouse with helpful staff, cosy rooms and a pleasantly sociable atmosphere. ❺

Villa Shams PC 116 Mina al Fahal ⓣ2456 1197, ⓦwww.villashams-oman.de. German-owned guesthouse, in a central location close to Qurum Park. The small pool is a bonus. ❻

elsewhere. Accommodation in **Ruwi** is mainly aimed at business travellers, with a couple of budget options thrown in, and although none of the hotels here is of any particular distinction it's one of the liveliest and most fun areas of the city in which to base yourself.

Further accommodation options can be found scattered across modern Muscat. These include a trio of mid-range places in the attractive suburb of **Qurum Heights**, along with a mix of mid- and top-end places further west around **Shatti al Qurum** and the contiguous suburbs of **Hayy as Saruj** and **Ghubrah**, plus a few mid-range, business-oriented options in nearby **Khuwair**. The peaceful area **south of the city** is home to a few further hotels, including the opulent *Al Bustan Palace* and the vast *Shangri-La Barr al Jissah Resort*.

Muttrah

The following places are shown on the map on p.57.

Corniche Hotel Muttrah corniche ⓣ2471 4636, ⓔcorniche_hotel@mjsoman.com. After the *Naseem*, this is the best of Muttrah's budget options, with relatively spacious, comfortable and well-maintained rooms (some with a sea view) at a competitive price. ❷

Al Fanar Hotel Muttrah corniche ⓣ2471 2385, ⓕ2471 4994. At the far end of the Corniche, this is Muttrah's most down-at-heel option, with shabby corridors and dog-eared furniture, although only a couple of rials cheaper than the competition. Rooms on the lower floors are beginning to look a bit battered, but are reasonably well-maintained and generally clean, albeit the promised hot water may not be available. There are also some even cheaper rooms on the top floor, but these are filthy and falling to bits. ❷

Marina Hotel Muttrah corniche ⓣ2471 3100. The nicest of the old Muttrah hotels, albeit a bit more expensive than other places nearby, with friendly service and neat rooms – a bit dated, but well maintained and very comfortable; doubles also boast superb harbour views (though the twins and singles don't). The hotel is also home to the popular *Al Boom* restaurant (see p.70) and a pair of Arabian and Indian live-music bars. ❸

Al Mina Hotel Muttrah corniche ⓣ2471 1829, ⓔminahotl@omantel.net.om. Rooms here (a few with slight sea view through small windows and from private tiny balconies) are rather past their best and relatively expensive compared to the competition, though rates may be susceptible to bargaining. ❸

Naseem Hotel Muttrah corniche ⓣ2471 2418, ⓕ2471 1728. The best of the Muttrah cheapies, right in the thick of things and virtually within spitting distance of Muttrah Souk. Rooms (some with wonderful harbour views through big windows) are showing their age, but are well looked after, and excellent value, while the consistently friendly and professional service is another major bonus. Breakfast is available in the small in-house restaurant, but no other meals. ❷

Ruwi

The following places are shown on the map on p.63. The *Sheraton* hotel on Bayt al Falaj Street, one of the district's landmark buildings, was closed until further notice at the time of writing, with no planned reopening date.

Al Falaj Hotel Al Mujamma St ⓣ2470 2311, ⓦwww.omanhotels.com. Dated four-star on the quiet northern edge of Ruwi. Rooms are a bit drab, although there's a decent range of in-house facilities including a pair of spacious pools and sun terrace, an eighth-floor pub (with crooning Filipino singers nightly) and the good *Tokyo Tara* Japanese restaurant next door, both with fine views over the Ruwi sprawl. Published rates are overpriced, but significant discounts are available on the website. ❻

Haffa House Ruwi St ⓣ2470 7207, ⓦwww.shanfarihotels.com. Cosy four-star in a good, central location. Rooms are pleasantly furnished, while facilities include a swimming pool, massage centre (Thai and Swedish), in-house restaurant (unlicensed) and coffee shop, but no bar – meaning that it's at least quieter than certain other places around town. ❻

Mutrah Hotel Muttrah St ⓣ2479 8401, ⓦwww.mutrahotel.com. Oman's oldest hotel, founded in the historic (for Oman) year of 1970, generally manages not to look its age, at least apart from the lifts, which groan like an octogenarian climbing Mount Everest. It now serves as one of Ruwi's leading downmarket drinking holes, with a pair of live-music bars, sports bar and a 24hr licensed restaurant, although the large and well-maintained rooms are good value, and quieter than you might imagine. ❸

Ruwi Hotel Next to Ruwi roundabout ⓣ2470 4244, ⓦwww.omanhotels.com. Functional three-star in an excellent location right in the thick of the Ruwi action. Rooms are pleasantly spacious and kitted out with crisp modern furniture, while facilities include a small pool, restaurant, pub, plus a couple of live-music bars in the basement. Published rates are overpriced, but significant discounts are available on the website. ❺

Sun City Hotel Al Jaame St, next to ONTC Bus Stand ⓣ2478 9801, ⓔhotel.suncity@hotmail.com. One of the cheapest places to stay in Ruwi, with bright, reasonably modern rooms, but no in-house facilities. It overlooks the ONTC bus stand (convenient if you've got an early-morning departure) and is just seconds from the rest of the Ruwi action, although it's a bit overpriced for what you get. ❸

Qurum Heights

The following places are shown on the map on p.66.

Crowne Plaza Al Qurum St ⓣ2466 0660, ⓦwww.crowneplaza.com. This pleasantly low-key four-star boasts one of the best locations of any hotel in the city, hugging the top of the rocky ridge at the southern end of Qurum beach, and with sweeping views down the coast. Facilities include the good *Come Prima* Italian and *Shiraz* Iranian restaurants (see p.71), the attractive *Duke's Bar* (see p.74), a health club, gym and a decent pool (plus a second, shaded, pool for kids) enclosed in attractive gardens; there's also a nice little secluded cove on the beach directly below. Rooms (with sea or land view) are on the small side, but given the location, price and facilities, this adds up to one of Muscat's most appealing packages. ❼

Qurum Beach Hotel Al Qurum St ⓣ2456 4070, ⓔqbhotel@omantel.net.om. Rather eccentric-looking two-star within walking distance of Qurum Beach, with passable rooms, a tiny in-house restaurant and two live-music bars (Indian and Arabian). It's pleasant enough, although overpriced for what you get, while the big central atrium – an eccentric combination of hanging greenery, arabesque walls and what looks like a fire escape – is something of an acquired taste. ❻

Ramee Guestline Al Qurum St ⓣ2456 4443, ⓦwww.rameehotels.com. Disinterested service, ugly rooms and public convenience-style architecture don't exactly inspire, although overall it's better value than the *Qurum Beach* next door. Other plus points include a pair of good North and South Indian restaurants and the swinging *Rock Bottom Cafe* (see p.74), plus Indian and Arabian live-music bars. There's also a pool in a rather ugly interior courtyard hemmed in by high red walls. Book online for big discounts. ❺

Shatti al Qurum and Hayy as Saruj

The following places are shown on the map on p.66.

Coral Hotel Off As Sarooj St ⓣ2469 2121, ⓦwww.coral-international.com. Deserves an extra star for the sheer madness of its design, from the wacky facade fashioned out of stylised coral fans through to the weird interior with ship's-wheel motifs on virtually every surface and lashings of gold paint. The large and slightly bare rooms are disappointingly ordinary after the design extravaganza outside, while a simple restaurant (unlicensed) is all that's on offer in the way of in-house facilities – although you're just a couple of minutes' walk from the various bars and restaurants of the adjacent *Grand Hyatt.* ❻

Grand Hyatt Off As Sarooj St ⓣ2464 1234, ⓦwww.muscat.grand.hyatt.com. This enjoyably overblown hotel (see p.67) is one of Muscat's top addresses – although often significantly less expensive than its major rivals. Rooms (from around 160 OR) are beautifully furnished and unusually spacious, arranged around the hotel's lovely (albeit rather small) gardens, bisected by an attractive serpentine pool-cum-river; there's also a public beach immediately to the rear of the hotel with plenty of sand to stretch out on (and where you'll also find the popular *Al Candle Café* – see p.72). The hotel is home to some of the city's top eating and drinking venues including *Tuscany* restaurant (see p.72), the *Copacabana* nightclub (see p.74) and the lovely *John Barry Bar* (see p.74). Facilities include a steam room, sauna and gym (but no spa) in the hotel's Club Olympus. ❾

InterContinental Al Kharjiyah St ⓣ2468 0000, ⓦwww.muscat.oman.intercontinental.com. This big dour concrete box of a hotel is easily mistaken for a multistorey car park from the outside, but is much nicer once you're through the doors. Rooms have land or sea views and are arranged around a stylish atrium up and down which glass-walled elevators silently shuttle, while the back of the hotel is enclosed by immaculate, expansive gardens, with two fine pools (one under a shady trellis) and a health club, a dive centre and an attractive swathe of public beach beyond. ❽

Al Qurum Resort (formerly the *Sheraton Qurum Resort*) Back of Jawaharat A'Shatti Complex ⓣ2460 5945, ⓔreservations.qbr@gmail.com. An intimate little place, with just seven rooms, tucked away behind the *InterContinental*, and right next to the beach. There's a decent-sized pool in the neat little gardens out back, plus two gyms and the good attached *Jade Garden* restaurant (see p.72). It's reasonable value if you can score one of the three very spacious sea-facing doubles with king-size beds; the four twin-bedded rooms (including two sea-facing) are only slightly cheaper but much smaller and less appealing. ❽

Khuwair and Ghubrah

The following places are shown on the map on p.50.

The Chedi Off 18 November St, Ghubrah ⓣ2452 4400, ⓦwww.ghmhotels.com. One of Muscat's finest hotels, although compared to the size and extravagance of the city's other top-end options, this is a model of understated cool. The pseudo-tented Arabian-style lobby offers a stylish nod towards its Gulf-side location, although the rest of the hotel is pure Asian designer Zen, with a minimalist decor of white pillars, feng-shui-style water features and maze-like hedges. The huge canopied pool is a work of abstract art in its own right, and the whole place looks particularly magical after dark, when hundreds of candles flicker in the gardens. Rooms (from around 225 OR) come with all designer mod-cons ranging from rain showers to iPod docks, while in-house facilities include a pair of gorgeous restaurants (see p.72) and one of Oman's finest spas. The only caveat is that the grounds, though beautiful, are rather small, and the public beach at the end of the hotel grounds is disappointing. ❾

Ibis Dawhat al Adab St, next to *Hotel Muscat Holiday*, Khuwair ⓣ2448 9890, ⓦwww.ibishotel.com. Aimed squarely at business travellers, with functional but modern and attractively designed rooms, plus restaurant (unlicensed), business centre and gym, but no bar (although there's one in the *Hotel Muscat Holiday* next door). ❺

Hotel Muscat Holiday (formerly the *Holiday Inn*) Dawhat al Adab St, next to *Ibis*, Khuwair ⓣ2448 7123, ⓦwww.holidayhotelsoman.com. Pleasant four-star, aimed mainly at business travellers although it manages to feel appealingly homely, from the plush, rather old-fashioned foyer through to the spacious and comfortably furnished rooms. Facilities include an in-house restaurant, the pleasant *Churchill's Bar* and a good-sized, if rather functional, pool. ❻

South of the centre

The following places are shown on the map on p.50.

Barasti (Oman Dive Center Resort) Oman Dive Center ⓣ2482 4240, ⓦwww.omandivecenter.com. The most chilled-out place to stay in Muscat, spread out along the Oman Dive Center's little private beach with accommodation in a string of pretty barasti (palm-thatch) huts. Huts are all a/c, although otherwise desert-island simplicity prevails, with not much furniture and no TVs, although all come with verandas out front and attractively rustic stone-walled outdoor bathrooms to the rear. Slightly too many huts have been crammed into the available space, and it's a bit pricey for what you get, but even so this is still one of Muscat's nicer, and more unusual, places to stay. ❻–❼

Al Bustan Palace ⓣ2479 9666, ⓦwww.albustanpalace.com. Oman's most famous hotel (see p.68), this remains one of the most attractive places to stay in the city, thanks to its alluring, Arabian-nights interior and superb location on an unspoiled stretch of rocky coastline amid vast, palm-studded gardens, fringed with a fine swathe of private beach. Rooms (from around 200 OR; with a sea or garden view) have been attractively updated, while facilities include a good selection of upmarket eating and drinking venues (see pp.73–74). 9

Shangri-La Barr al Jissah Resort and Spa ⓣ2477 6666, ⓦwww.shangri-la.com/muscat. The largest of Muscat's top-end options, the vast Shangri-La resort sprawls for around a kilometre along one of the city's most beautiful stretches of coastline, squeezed in between rugged mountains and a generous swathe of beach. There are actually three hotels here: the relatively downmarket, family-oriented *Al Waha*, the fancier *Al Bandar*, aimed at business travellers, and the very exclusive *Al Husn* "private resort". Facilities include some of Muscat's finest restaurants and bars, (see p.73 & p.74), acres of sand, huge pools, the opulent Chi – The Spa and excellent children's play areas. There's also a decent selection of shops in the mock mudbrick "Omani Heritage Village" and adjacent Souk al Mazaar. The complex as a whole has plenty of alluring style, with a sumptuous blend of Arabian chintz and Asian Zen-cool, although the sheer scale of the development has rather overwhelmed the pristine natural setting and the security guards on every corner can make the whole place feel like some kind of five-star prison camp. Average rates run from around 150 OR at *Al Waha* up to 225 OR at *Al Husn*. 9

The City

The logical place to begin any tour of Muscat is in the old city's commercial heart, **Muttrah**, home to the famous Muttrah Souk and a cluster of other attractions, as well as the city's most engagingly authentic streetlife. From here, it's a pleasantly breezy 2km walk (or short taxi ride) along the attractively landscaped corniche to **Old Muscat**, home to Sultan Qaboos's florid Al Alam Palace, a pair of crusty old Portuguese forts and the absorbing Bait al Zubair museum. Some 2km inland from Muttrah, the bustling district of **Ruwi** is the cultural heart of the city's sizeable Indian and Pakistani communities, best appreciated during an after-dark stroll along the vibrant Souq Ruwi Street.

West of Ruwi stretches the endless sprawl of modern Muscat's Legoland suburbs. Attractions here include the fine beach of **Shatti al Qurum**, close to many of the city's most appealing hotels and restaurants, while nearby **Qurum** is home to a string of interesting shops. A smattering of further low-key museums lies scattered here and there, while most visitors also head out to Ghubrah, on the western edge of the city, to visit the magnificent **Sultan Qaboos Mosque**.

Muttrah مطرح

Sweeping around a beautiful seafront corniche, **MUTTRAH** (also spelled Mutrah or Matrah) is the city's old commercial centre, and still far and away the most interesting part of the city. The area retains much of its mercantile importance thanks to the presence here of the large **Sultan Qaboos Docks**, the city's **Fish Market** and the enduringly popular **Muttrah Souk**, as well as reminders of its past in the form of the old Portuguese **Muttrah Fort**.

Muttrah Souk

The main draw in Muttrah is the famous **Muttrah Souk**, probably the single most popular tourist attraction in the country. This is Muscat at its most magical: an absorbing labyrinth of narrow, perfume-laden alleyways packed with colourful little shops stacked high with tubs of frankincense and *bukhoor*, old silver *khanjars*, Bedu jewellery and other exotic paraphernalia – one of the few markets in the world where it's possible to buy gold, frankincense and myrrh all under a single roof. You could spend many enjoyable hours here, haggling over handicrafts and attempting to make sense of the maze, especially if you venture away from the heavily touristed main drag into the tangled backstreets beyond.

The souk can be somewhat deceptive at first acquaintance: it's a lot larger, and a lot more confusing, than you might initially suspect. Heading in from the **main entrance** on the corniche it's possible to walk across the souk in under five minutes, following the main thoroughfare which bisects the area from north to south. This stretch – at its liveliest after dark – is where you'll find the souk's most touristy (and expensive) shops, lined with neatly restored old buildings under a fine wooden roof and thronged with an eclectic mix of robed Omanis and camera-toting coach parties.

In fact, this is just a small part of the overall complex, which continues for a considerable distance to either side, especially to the west. Turn right off the main drag and, if you know where you're going (or see the directions below) it's possible to work your way back to the **Muttrah Gold Souk** building which fronts the corniche a couple of hundred metres west of the main souk entrance, passing through a fascinating series of alleyways stuffed with gold and silver jewellery en route. Further alleyways head off in every direction, lined with increasingly run-of-the-mill shops and eventually shooting you out of the souk either back onto the corniche or into the tangle of narrow backstreets and tiny alleyways which honeycomb the area behind Sur al Lewatia (see p.59) and the *Naseem Hotel* – a fascinating, if disorienting, walk.

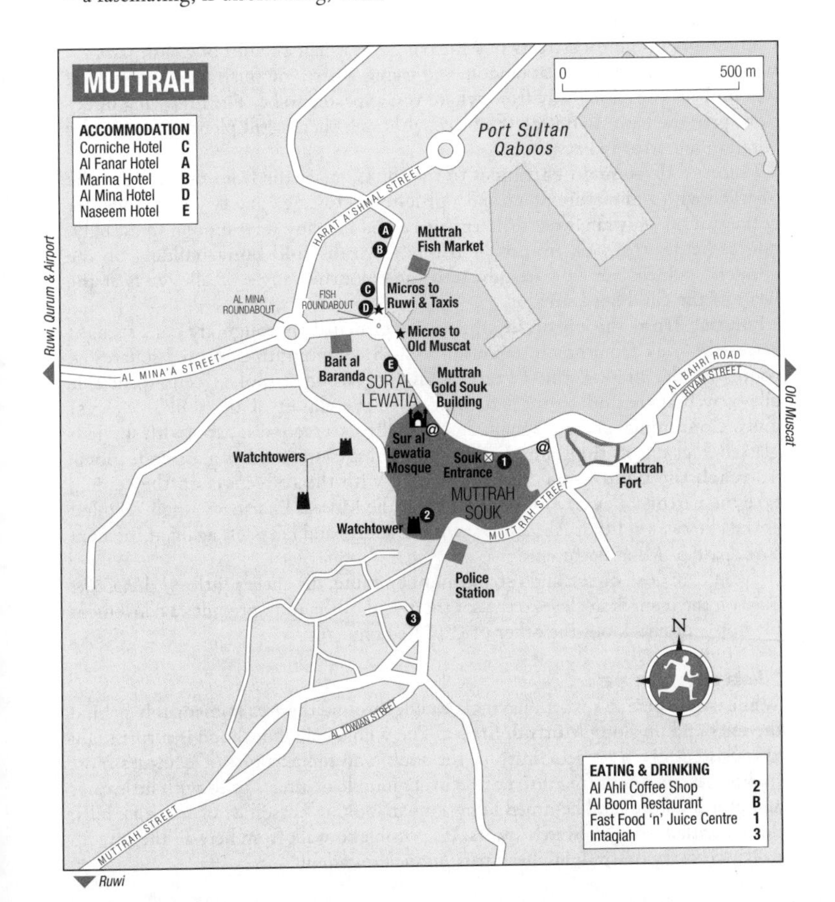

Shopping in Muttrah Souk

Pretty much anything and everything of Omani provenance can be found for sale in Muttrah Souk, including vast quantities of frankincense and *bukhoor*, herbs, *halwa*, spices and crushed rose petals and rose water from Jebel Akdhar (see box, p.98), alongside traditional perfumes, pashminas and Omani caps, robes and turbans. Many shops also sell old Bedu silver jewellery and *khanjars*, including museum-quality pieces which retail for hundreds of dollars alongside pieces of "Omani silver" (which might mean anything from antique jewellery and Maria Theresa dollars through to worthless modern junk) heaped up in tubs and sold by weight. The **Gold Souk** area is packed with shops selling gold and silver jewellery in a range of Arabian and European designs.

It's difficult to generalize about **prices**, although for more workaday items you're likely to pay significantly more here than in less touristed parts of the city. A tub of *bukhoor*, for example, which might be found in local supermarkets for less than a rial, usually goes for around 2.5–3.5 OR, while some rogue traders might try to sell you an equivalent for as much as 10 OR. It goes without saying that it's best to shop around, while virtually all shop-owners are amenable to **bargaining**.

Souk orientation

Getting lost in the backstreets of Muttrah Souk is half the fun of a visit, and it's well worth wandering off at random and seeing where you finally end up – which will probably be a long way from where you expected to be. The following directions give the basic layout of the place, although there's still plenty of room for entertaining error in between.

There are **three main entrances** to the souk, one at the front on the corniche (marked with a miniature dome and a pedestrian crossing), and two close together at the rear on Muttrah Street. Alternatively, and in many ways more interestingly, you can enter the souk from behind the **Muttrah Gold Souk** building on the corniche, which puts you straight into the colourful tangle of alleyways at the heart of the Gold Souk area.

Entering **from the corniche**, the souk's principal thoroughfare runs straight across the souk from north to south, with three diminutive covered squares en route. At the first of these (with a kind of wooden-spoked ceiling), a side alleyway branches off to the left, leading to the closest of the souk's two rear exits. Continuing along the main drag you'll pass a second square (with stained-glassed *khanjars* on the ceiling) and then a third (with stained-glass coffeepots). To **reach the Gold Souk** from the square with the coffeepots on the ceiling, take the narrow alleyway on your right by the Muscat Pharmacy, then keep left as the alleyway splits at Ahmed Darwish Trading, and keep left again at the next fork, past Al Mina Perfumes.

If you're in need of rest and **refreshment** en route, the cheery little *Al Ahli Coffee Shop* on the main drag close to the southern end of the souk provides a convenient pit stop – or check out the other places listed on p.70.

Muttrah Street

While you're here, it's worth having a wander around the area immediately behind the souk and up along **Muttrah Street**. The whole neighbourhood is surprisingly untouristed, given its proximity to the souk, and remains one of Muscat's most traditional and interesting districts – a lively jumble of streets lined with little cafés and grocery stores and hemmed in by a lunar-looking horseshoe of red-rock hills, dotted with a string of watchtowers. It's possible to walk from here all the way up to Ruwi: carry on straight ahead past *Intaqiah* restaurant.

Bait al Baranda

A five-minute walk west of Muttrah Souk lies **Bait al Baranda** (Sat–Thurs 9am–1pm & 4–6pm; 1 OR), literally "The Veranda House" (the veranda actually being on the first floor). This fine old traditional Omani mansion was built in the late nineteenth century and was formerly home to the American Mission clinic, followed by the British Council. It now houses a museum devoted to the history of Muscat, although the main draw is the building itself, centred on an airy central courtyard-cum-atrium, supported on wooden columns.

The ground floor hosts temporary art exhibitions. Upstairs, well-presented displays cover the history of Muscat from the Stone Age settlements (c.10,000 BC) discovered at nearby Bowshar, Ras al Hamra and Al Wataya, through to modern times, with particularly good coverage of the colonial era and various maritime skirmishes between British and French forces, backed up with a smattering of old maps, navigational charts, prints and other documents.

East to Muttrah Fort

Bait al Baranda is a good place to begin exploring Muttrah's fine seafront **corniche**, which stretches from **Fish (As Samak) roundabout**, just below the Bait al Baranda and continues for around 3km east along the Muttrah seafront and beyond towards Old Muscat.

Right next to Fish roundabout stands Muttrah's lively **fish market**, busy every morning until around 9–9.30am with local fishermen and traders haggling over piles of freshly caught seafood (at the time of writing, a new market building was under construction nearby, slated to open in 2012). Next door to the fish market stand the **Sultan Qaboos Docks**, one of Oman's largest ports, opened in the 1970s, whose gantries, silos and great piles of stacked-up containers dominate views from all around the harbour, and which also provide moorings for the vast cruise ships that dock here during their tours of the Gulf.

East of Fish roundabout stretches Muttrah's attractive **seafront**, an elegant curve of snow-white buildings hemmed in between the sea in front and the chain of craggy red-rock mountains which flank Muttrah to the rear. There's a particularly fine parade of traditional seafront **mansions** between Fish roundabout and the entrance to Muttrah Souk: venerable old whitewashed two- or three-storey structures with intricately carved windows and ornate wooden balconies. Immediately past these lies the large, blue-tiled Shia **Sur al Lewatia mosque**, next to which a small gateway leads into the walled Shia area of **Sur al Lewatia**; casual visitors are not welcomed here, and a local resident can usually be seen sitting at the gate turning back inquisitive tourists. A few further steps along the corniche brings you to **Muttrah Souk**, covered on p.56.

High above the waters at the far eastern end of Muttrah harbour sits the modest **Muttrah Fort**. It's not really a proper fort so much as a single high wall with a round tower at either end, balanced precariously atop a craggy ridge – particularly dramatic when illuminated after dark. You can climb the rough concrete steps up to the top for sweeping harbour views and a closer look at the crumbling fortifications.

Al Riyam and Kalbuh Parks

Beyond Muttrah Fort it's a fine, breezy walk along the attractively landscaped seafront, with assorted gardens, fountains and gold-domed pergolas en route, dotted with an extraordinary number of statues of fish. Another ten minutes' walk brings you to a rocky headland poking out into the sea and topped with a pair of **watchtowers**; steps lead up to the watchtower nearest the sea (closed for building work at the time of writing). On the opposite, land-side of the road lies **Al Riyam Park** (Sat–Wed 4–11pm, Thurs & Fri 9am–midnight; free), a shady park with extensive children's play areas and a small funfair. The bizarre structure on the rock outcrop overlooking the park is a supersized model of an **incense burner**, although it looks more like some kind of rococo spaceship.

Continuing along the road, you'll see the tower of Muscat Gate Museum (see p.62) poking up ahead. On your left is **Kalbuh Park** (Sat–Wed 4–11pm, Thurs & Fri 9am–midnight; free), a pleasant strip of palm-fringed grass in the lee of the cliffs, with a watchtower perched high above on a ridge at the far end and plenty of drinks kiosks. From here's it's just another five minutes' walk on to Old Muscat.

Old Muscat

Clustered around a small bay at the far eastern end of the capital lies **MUSCAT** proper – often referred to as **Old Muscat** to distinguish it from the surrounding city to which it has now given its name. Despite serving as the home of the ruling sultan, Old Muscat retains the feel of a small and decidedly sleepy little town, quite distinct from the rest of the city, from which it's separated by a swathe of craggy mountains. Additional protection is afforded by the unattractively restored **city walls** which guard the landward approaches. Right up until the mid-twentieth century the gates were closed three hours after dusk, and anyone venturing out onto the streets afterwards was obliged to carry a lantern with them – just one of the unusual local laws which also included a ban on smoking in the main streets and playing music in public.

Al Alam Palace

At the heart of Old Muscat is **Al Alam Palace** ("Flag Palace"), the most important of the six royal residences of the ruling monarch, Sultan Qaboos, which are dotted around Muscat, Salalah and Sohar. Built in 1972, the palace is Oman's most flamboyant example of contemporary Islamic design, with two long wings centred on a colourful, cube-like central building, its flat, overhanging roof supported by extravagantly flared blue and gold columns. The palace isn't open to

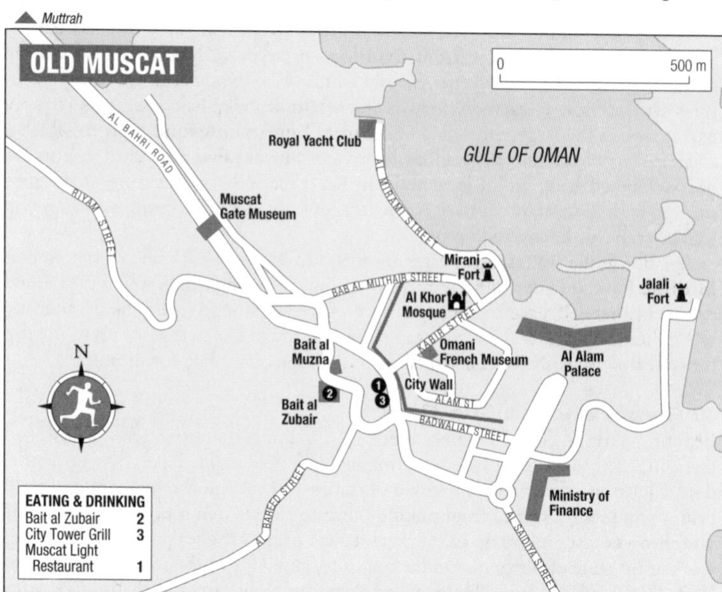

the public, although you can get a good view of the facade from the iron gates at the front.

The palace complex is impressively stage-managed, approached via a long pedestrianized boulevard framed by two arcaded colonnades, with copious amounts of highly polished marble covering every available surface. On either side stretches a cluster of impressive **government buildings**: huge, snow-white edifices sporting crenellated rooftops, traditional wooden balconies and window shutters. Look right as you approach the palace and you'll also see a fine section of the original city **walls** snaking up the hillside, punctuated with three large watchtowers en route.

The harbour and Portuguese forts

Immediately behind the palace lies Old Muscat's neat little harbour, flanked by a pair of rocky headlands on which sit the Portuguese forts of **Jalali** and **Mirani**. Like Muttrah Fort (see p.59), just down the road, these are quite unlike the traditional Omani forts you'll see elsewhere in the country: essentially just a sliver of wall plus flanking watchtowers squeezed into the tiniest of spaces on top of the rocks – seriously cramped, but virtually impregnable.

Mirani Fort stands directly behind Al Alam Palace above the pretty blue-tiled Al Khor mosque. Walk around the back of the fort for a good view of the rear of the palace and of the fort's major structure, a soaring five-storey tower, each storey slightly narrower than the one below, like an enormous telescope. From here there are good views over to the similar **Jalali Fort**, which crowns the rocky ridge on the opposite side of the harbour, although it lies out of bounds to the general public thanks to its location beyond the assorted government buildings next to the Al Alam Palace.

Past Mirani Fort you can walk a short distance along the water as far as the Royal Yacht Club, with pleasant views of the **harbour** itself, its two forts, and of further considerable fortification erected at the end of the headlands to either side of the entrance to the harbour. You'll also notice the names of assorted **ships** (HMS *Falmouth* and HMS *Perseus* prominent among them) on the cliffs opposite, painted onto the rockface by the crews of visiting vessels – like a kind of maritime visitors' book. According to legend, the young Horatio Nelson himself scrambled up the rocks here during a visit to Muscat in the 1770s, despite his fear of vertigo.

A Mirani marriage

The virtual impregnability of Mirani and Jalali Forts has meant that those wishing to capture them have had to resort to some unconventional stratagems over the centuries. The most famous incident in the forts' colourful history – and the final *coup de grâce* to the Portuguese occupation in Oman (see p.221) – occurred in 1650. The Portuguese had already been driven from virtually every other part of the country and were now holed up in their Muscat strongholds. The commander of Muscat's Portuguese garrison, a certain Pereira, was besotted with a local Hindu girl, whom he wished to marry. Her father, Narutem, feigned obedience to Pereira's wishes and ordered preparations for a great wedding celebration at Mirani Fort, during which he proposed cleaning the water tanks, replacing the fort's contaminated gunpowder and restocking its provisions. At the moment when the fort had been stripped of all food and ammunition, Narutem gave the signal and Omani fighters attacked, eventually retaking the old city.

Ironically, less than a hundred years later the Omanis themselves would lose both Mirani and Jalali Forts to the Persian forces of Taqi Khan under perhaps even more embarrassing circumstances (see p.223).

Bait al Zubair

Of the various small museums scattered about Old Muscat, easily the most interesting is the **Bait al Zubair** (pronounced "Zubeer"; open Sat–Thurs 9.30am–1pm & 4–7pm; 2 OR; no photography; Ⓦwww.baitalzubairmuseum.com), with wide-ranging exhibits relating to Omani culture, customs and craftsmanship, all collected over the years by the Zubair family, who still own and run the museum.

The museum is spread across three separate buildings. The bulk of the collection is concentrated in the **Bait al Bagh** ("Garden House"), a large, white but not particularly exciting building dating from 1914, when it served as a former Zubair family residence. Displays include antique *khanjars* and firearms, as well as assorted household articles ranging from coffeepots to kohl holders and a good selection of traditional clothing and jewellery (look out for the ingenious *salwa*, a style of necklace worn by unmarried girls – the main "jewel" is actually a recycled bicycle reflector). Exiting the rear door of the building brings you into the surrounding **gardens**, where you'll find a traditional barasti *majlis* and a *falaj*, along with an entertaining Omani-style model village.

Diagonally opposite the Bait al Bagh stands the **Bait Dalaleel**, where you'll find the museum's coffee shop (see p.71) along with a little cluster of rooms quaintly refurbished in traditional Omani style. Opposite the Bait Dalaleel stands the third of the museum's trio of buildings, the **Bait al Oud** ("Grand House"). The ground floor is used for temporary exhibitions of contemporary art. Upstairs, the **first floor** has interesting displays of old maps and wooden models of traditional dhows. Next door, a large room is stuffed full of an eye-catching array of household items from the original home of Sheikh al Zubair bin Ali. The **second floor** houses a random assortment of displays, including black and white photos from the late nineteenth century (unlabelled, unfortunately), and rooms full of old Islamic coins and historic prints.

Opposite the Bait al Zubair, the **Bait al Muzna** art gallery (Sat–Thurs 9.30am–7pm; Ⓦwww.baitmuznagallery.com) displays original or limited-edition artworks in a wide range of styles, usually either by local artists or with an Omani theme. Prices start from around 50 OR up into the thousands.

Omani French Museum and Muscat Gate Museum

A couple of other museums and galleries lie scattered around the western end of Old Muscat. A five-minute walk around the block and through Al Kebir Gate brings you to the **Omani French Museum** (Sat–Wed 10am–1pm & 5–8pm, Thurs 10am–1pm; free), located in the former house of the French consul, Bait Faransa, a gift from Sultan Faisal bin Turki in 1896, during a period of rising French influence in the Sultanate (see p.227). The museum houses various mildly interesting historical exhibits covering the history of the French in Oman, although the whole place was closed for renovation at the time of writing.

At the western edge of the district, the **Muscat Gate Museum** (Sat–Wed 8am–2pm; free) occupies a single large room inside the restored gateway which spans the main road at the entrance to Old Muscat (staff tend to keep the heavy wooden doors shut at all times, making the place look closed even when it's open; push hard). The museum doesn't have much in the way of exhibits, bar a couple of small models, although the detailed boards covering the history of Oman and Muscat feature some interesting old pictures and black-and-white photographs, along with detailed explanations of the various historical periods involved.

Ruwi روي

Some 3km inland from Muttrah lies **RUWI**, the de facto commercial heart of the city. It's relatively small beer compared to other urban areas around the Gulf, though if you've spent long in the quieter backwaters of Oman the district's blaze

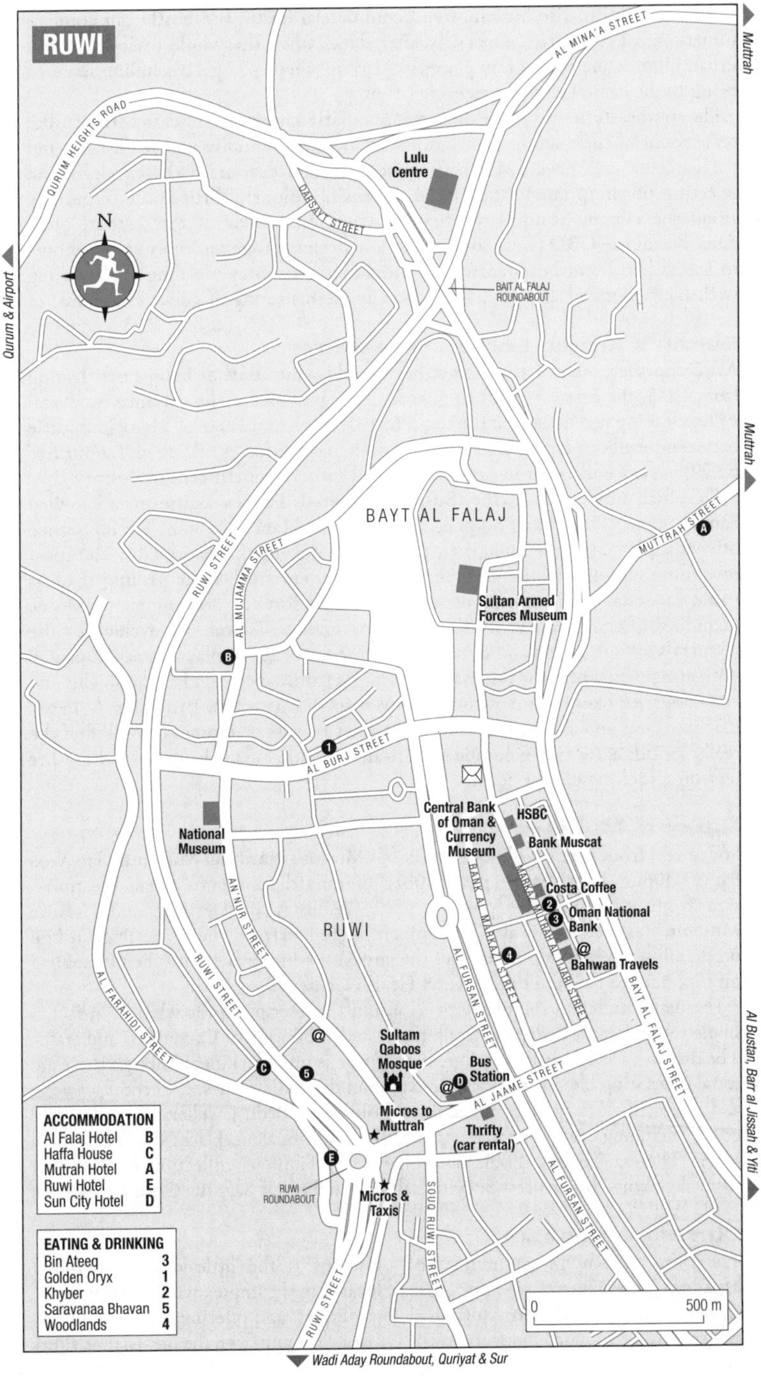

RUWI

Al Mina'a Street
Muttrah
Qurum Heights Road
Darsayt Street
Lulu Centre
N
Bait Al Falaj Roundabout
Qurum & Airport
Muttrah
BAYT AL FALAJ
Muttrah Street
Ruwi Street
Al Mujamma Street
Sultan Armed Forces Museum
Al Burj Street
National Museum
Central Bank of Oman & Currency Museum
HSBC
Bank Muscat
Costa Coffee
Oman National Bank
Bahwan Travels
Bank Al Markazi Street
Markaz Mutrah Al Tijari Street
An'Nur Street
RUWI
Ruwi Street
Al Farahidi Street
Al Fursan Street
Bayt Al Falaj Street
Al Bustan, Barr al Jissah & Yiti
Sultam Qaboos Mosque
Bus Station
Al Jaame Street
Micros to Muttrah
Thrifty (car rental)
Ruwi Roundabout
Micros & Taxis
Souq Ruwi Street
Al Fursan Street
Ruwi Street
0 500 m
Wadi Aday Roundabout, Quriyat & Sur

ACCOMMODATION

Al Falaj Hotel	B
Haffa House	C
Mutrah Hotel	A
Ruwi Hotel	E
Sun City Hotel	D

EATING & DRINKING

Bin Ateeq	3
Golden Oryx	1
Khyber	2
Saravanaa Bhavan	5
Woodlands	4

of neon, high(ish)-rise buildings and commercial hustle and bustle can come as something of a surprise, especially after dark, when the whole place has a real urban buzz – one of the few places in Muscat where you get a genuine sense of being in the capital city of a sizeable country.

The southeastern side of the district is popularly known as Muscat's **Little India**, on account of the many Indian and Pakistani expats who live and work here, and parts of the area have a distinctly subcontinental flavour, with the city's best selection of cheap curry houses and dozens of colourful little shops, especially along the vibrant **Souq Ruwi Street**. The western side of the district, often described as the **CBD** (Central Business District), is altogether more sedate, home to the rather grand headquarters of most of the country's leading banks, along with assorted travel agents, airline offices and a smattering of good restaurants.

Sultan's Armed Forces Museum

At the northern end of the district lies the old white **Bait al Falaj Fort**. Dating from 1845, the fort was built to guard a strategic point at the entrance to several valleys leading to Muscat and the coast. In 1915 the fort was site of a ferocious battle between rebellious tribesmen from the south and the forces of Sultan Taimur (see p.227) – a key encounter in Oman's troubled early twentieth-century history.

The fort now houses the **Sultan's Armed Forces Museum** (Sat–Wed 8am–1.30pm, Thurs 9am–noon & 3–6pm, Fri 9–11am & 3–6pm; 1 OR), signed off Mujamma Street. Along with the Bait al Zubair, this is arguably the most rewarding museum in the city, and actually covers much more ground than its name suggests, with informative exhibits on all sorts of non-military subjects, including Omani history, Ibadhism and navigation, as well as coverage of the country's various rulers and dynasties. All the historical displays are accompanied with armaments from the relevant era, ranging from superb old Persian shields and enormous Arabian swords through to Martini-Henry rifles, Browning & Lewis machine guns and assorted mortars and rocket launchers. Upstairs, you'll find the really serious hardware including an anti-aircraft gun, missile launcher and a rather fearsome-looking cluster bomb.

National Museum

Southwest from here on A'Noor Street lies Muscat's **National Museum** (Sat–Wed 8am–1.30pm, Thurs 9am–1pm; 500bz). Finding the museum is half the fun: a sign from A'Noor Street points to the "Ministry of Heritage and Culture Museum" (as the place is also known), although bizarrely, there's no English sign on the museum building itself – it's the large-ish white block with the Omani flag on top, next to the sign to the Ruwi Health Center.

The name itself is a singularly over-optimistic description for what is, in fact, a single room, largely dedicated to a rather dated exhibition of Omani arts and crafts. The displays are decidedly random and signage is often lacking, although there are some interesting old artefacts scattered among the endless rifles, coffeepots, *mandoos* and scraps of pottery. The collection of old silver Bedu jewellery is particularly good, including some fine old *mazrad*, the traditional necklaces decorated with Maria Theresa Thalers. Look out too for the fabulous collection of jewellery formerly owned by Princess Seyyida Salma, daughter of Said the Great (see p.225).

Currency Museum

The third of Ruwi's triumvirate of museums is the little-visited **Currency Museum** (Sun–Thurs 9am–1pm; 250bz), located in the impressive Central Bank of Oman building on Markaz Muttrah al Tijari Street, and offering a well-presented and surprisingly absorbing overview of Omani currency from the pre-Islamic times to the present. Access to the museum is by guided tour only; you'll have to present yourself to reception and wait for a member of staff to show you around.

Dry as it might sound, the story of Omani currency provides some interesting insights into the history of the region. The bulk of the collection focuses on nineteenth- and twentieth-century coins and banknotes. These include the Indian rupee notes which were formerly used as legal tender in Oman, Maria Theresa Thalers (which served as a kind of international currency throughout the Gulf) and locally produced *baiza* coins used for small sums – meaning that three different currencies were in simultaneous circulation right up until 1970, when Oman issued its first banknotes. Other exhibits include a fine selection of pre-Islamic coins, stamped with some engaging portraits of the various rulers under whose jurisdiction they were issued. Pride of place goes to the first ever Islamic coin, one of only two in the world, minted in 700 AD during the caliphate of Ummayad ruler Bin Marwan.

Mina al Fahal

East of Qurum Heights, the industrial district of **MINA AL FAHAL** is home to one of the country's major oil refineries, and the centre of operations for the government-owned PDO (Petroleum Development Oman). If you want to find out more about the black gold, the **Oil & Gas Exhibition Centre** (Sat–Wed 7am–3pm, Thurs 8am–noon; free), run by PDO, has a good array of educational exhibits on oil exploration and production (although, disappointingly, nothing on history or details of production in Oman today). Many of the exhibits are interactive, giving you the chance to try your hand at prospecting for oil, loading a tanker or launching an "intelligent pig".

Qurum (القرم) and around

The suburb of **QURUM** (also spelled Qurm) is, from a tourist point of view at least, the heart of modern Muscat, and the place where you'll find the densest concentration of shops, upmarket hotels and good places to eat, as well as the city's best public beach, Shatti al Qurum. The centre of the suburb is marked by Qurum's lively **commercial district**, close to the junction of Sultan Qaboos Street and the Muscat Expressway, which is home to a cluster of low-brow restaurants and small-scale malls dotted with some interesting shops (see p.75). North of here lies the very upmarket suburb of **QURUM HEIGHTS**, with tree-lined streets and discreet, low-rise white villas surrounded by bougainvillea-filled gardens.

Shatti al Qurum شاطي القرم

West of Qurum Heights stretches the attractive **Shatti al Qurum** (Qurum Beach), a fine swathe of golden sand which extends west to the neighbouring suburb of Hayy as Saruj and beyond, with views of the rocky **Fahal Island** (one of the city's leading dive sites – see p.49) offshore. If you want to sunbathe, you're better off sticking to the areas of beach around the back of the *InterContinental* or *Grand Hyatt* hotels, where the number of other sun-worshipping Westerners on the sands guarantees relative anonymity and hassle-free relaxation; elsewhere on the beach, female visitors may attract unwanted attention.

The northern end of the beach is bounded by a small rocky outcrop, topped by the distinctive, cruiseliner-shaped *Crowne Plaza* hotel, while south of the beach stretches the low, green expanse of the **Qurum Nature Reserve**, protecting a rare surviving stretch of coastal mangrove forest (not open to the public). Next door is **Qurum Park** and the adjacent **Children's Museum** (Sat–Wed 8am–1.30pm, Thurs 9am–1pm; 500bz), located in the larger of two distinctive dome-shaped

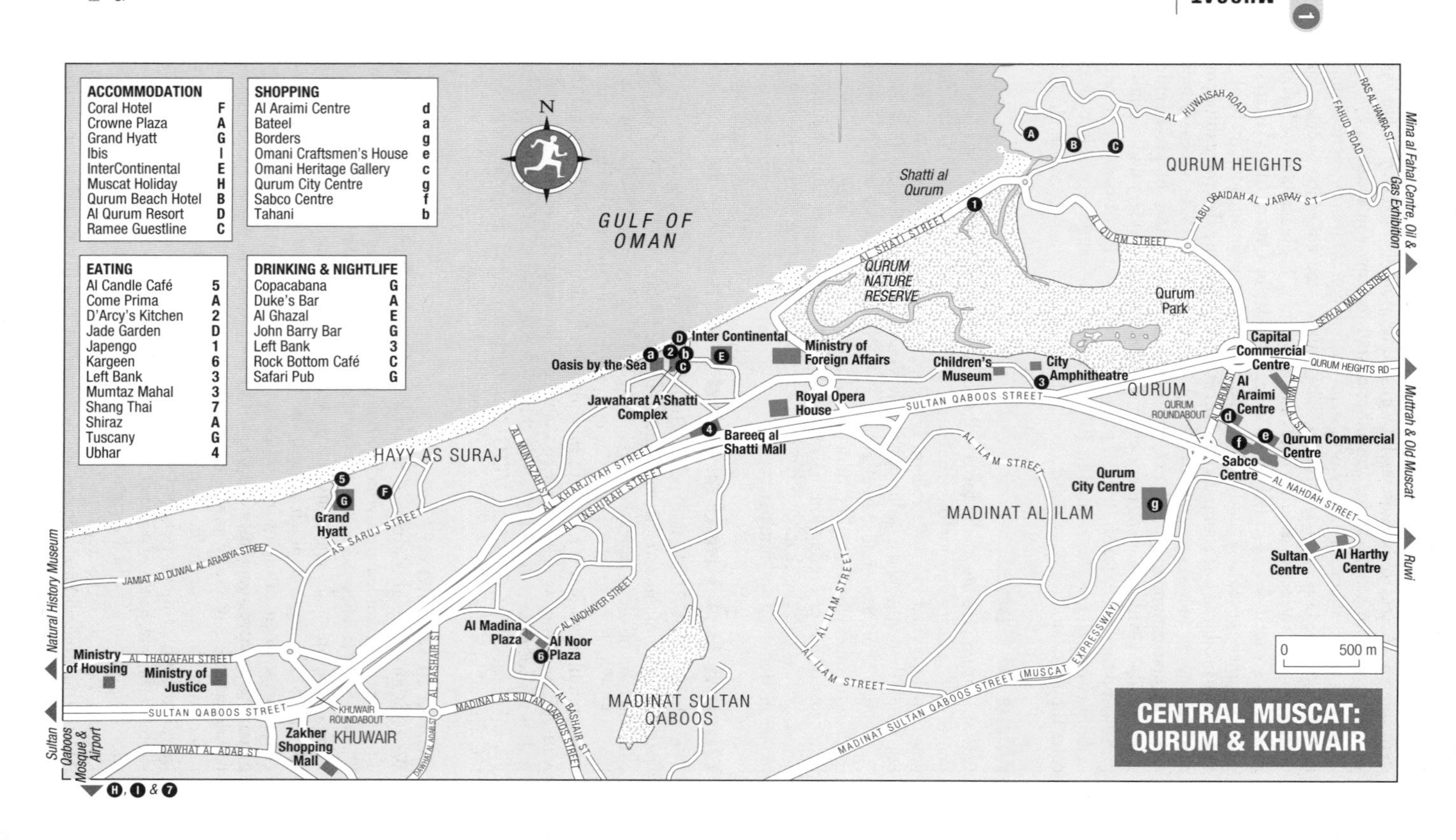

ACCOMMODATION	
Coral Hotel	F
Crowne Plaza	A
Grand Hyatt	G
Ibis	I
InterContinental	E
Muscat Holiday	H
Qurum Beach Hotel	B
Al Qurum Resort	D
Ramee Guestline	C

SHOPPING	
Al Araimi Centre	d
Bateel	a
Borders	g
Omani Craftsmen's House	e
Omani Heritage Gallery	c
Qurum City Centre	g
Sabco Centre	f
Tahani	b

EATING	
Al Candle Café	5
Come Prima	A
D'Arcy's Kitchen	2
Jade Garden	D
Japengo	1
Kargeen	6
Left Bank	3
Mumtaz Mahal	3
Shang Thai	7
Shiraz	A
Tuscany	G
Ubhar	4

DRINKING & NIGHTLIFE	
Copacabana	G
Duke's Bar	A
Al Ghazal	E
John Barry Bar	G
Left Bank	3
Rock Bottom Café	C
Safari Pub	G

buildings sitting next to Sultan Qaboos Road. Inside you'll find a big array of enjoyable interactive exhibits on sight, sound, the body and science – a guaranteed hit with kids, and fun for grown-ups too.

From below the Crowne Plaza, a pleasantly breezy road heads along the open seafront for around 1km to reach the cluster of hotels and restaurants centred around the *InterContinental* hotel. The main attraction here is the attractive **Jawaharat A'Shatti Complex**, a poky and old-fashioned little mall on the inside, although its exterior terrace, and that of the **Oasis by the Sea** restaurant complex opposite, has been colonized by a sociable string of restaurants, including the popular *D'Arcy's Kitchen* (see p.72).

Grand Hyatt

Continuing past the Jawaharat A'Shatti complex, an attractive ten-minute stroll along the pedestrianized seafront walkway brings you to the rear of the **Grand Hyatt**, one of Muscat's most flamboyant hotels. Owned by a Yemeni sheikh, the rather peculiar exterior looks like the bastard lovechild of a Yemeni fort and a French chateau. It's worth going inside, though, for a look at the hotel's fabulous interior. This is pure Orientalist chintz at its most extravagant, with soaring gold and cream pillars, a great tumbling staircase, 25m-high stained-glass windows, plus assorted palm trees and Bedu tents. The whole place is best appreciated over a superior afternoon tea at the *Sirj Tea Lounge* in the shadow of the impressive bronze statue of an Arabian falconer on horseback, who glares out across the foyer – the whole statue actually rotates, imperceptibly, every hour, which explains why it never seems to be quite where you remembered it.

Khuwair الخوير

Heading west, the next suburb you reach is **KHUWAIR**, home to an impressive string of **government ministries** – large, white buildings with traditional architectural decorative touches – which line the northern side of Sultan Qaboos Road. At the western end of the ministry area, right next to the main highway, lies the modest **Natural History Museum** (Sat–Wed 8am–1.30pm, Sun also 4–6pm, Thurs 9am–1pm; 500bz). This is worth a visit if you're interested in Omani wildlife, geography and geology, offering a good introduction to the different regions of the country, and their associated flora and fauna, although some of the displays are rather out of date. Exhibits range from curios such as enormous fossilized marine gastropods (prehistoric snails) and a neat set of mastodon teeth, through to more predictable offerings including glass cases full of petrified insects and pickled snakes, plus various stuffed animals and birds. Perhaps most impressive is the adjacent **Whale Hall**, containing the complete skeleton of a sperm whale.

Sultan Qaboos Grand Mosque

Towards the western end of Muscat's long urban sprawl, the suburb of Ghubrah (pronounced something like "*Hob*-rah", with throaty *h*) is where you'll find the stunning **Sultan Qaboos Grand Mosque** (Sat–Thurs 8–11am; free). Opened in 2001, this is the only mosque in Oman open to non-Muslims and one of the largest in the Gulf, with room for an estimated 20,000 worshippers in the two prayer halls and surrounding courtyard. The mosque itself sits within a walled compound with a minaret at each corner, plus a fifth, larger minaret halfway along the northern wall. The overall style is a kind of stripped-down contemporary Islamic, clad in vast quantities of white and red-brown marble. The minarets offer a nod towards traditional Egyptian architecture, while other decorative touches (such as the wooden ceilings and elaborate tilework) were inspired by Omani and

Persian traditions. Other architectural details, such as the impressive latticed golden dome over the central prayer hall, are entirely original.

Entrance to the mosque is from its eastern end, through spacious gardens bisected by water channels. The first building you reach is the **Ladies' Prayer Hall** (although men are allowed in), relatively plain compared to the rest of the building. Beyond this a pair of distinctively tall and narrow arches, embellished with Qur'anic script, connect the ladies' prayer hall to the opulent **main prayer hall** (*musalla*), supported on four enormous pillars and decorated in whites, greys and sea-greens. The **carpet** covering the prayer hall floor is the world's second largest and took 400 female weavers from the Iranian province of Khorasan four years to make – the whole thing measures 60 x 70m, contains 1.7 million knots and weighs 21 tonnes. The huge Swarovski crystal **chandelier** in the centre of the hall is a staggering 14m tall and was often claimed to be the largest in the world until the construction of an even bigger crystalline monster in Qatar in 2010.

Visiting the mosque, note that its popularity and limited opening hours mean that it often gets absolutely overrun with coach parties by around 10am. The earlier you can visit the better. Visitors are required to dress appropriately (no shorts or uncovered arms, while women are required to cover their heads) and to remove their shoes before entering either prayer hall. Under-10s are not allowed into the main prayer hall.

South of the centre

The city **south of old Muscat** (see p.50 for a map of this area) is much less developed than that to the north, with attractively landscaped roads winding through largely unspoilt mountains and a string of self-contained fishing villages shoehorned into the rocky little bays which dot the coast. There are no must-see sights here, although you might be tempted to drop into the landmark **Bustan Palace Hotel** for afternoon tea, or to spend an evening over drinks and a meal at the vast **Shangri-La Barr al Jissah Resort**, which boasts some of the city's finest restaurants and bars.

Marina Bander al Rowdha

A kilometre or so south of Old Muscat lies the village of Sidab, arranged around a neat little horseshoe harbour, and the contiguous village of Haramil. A further kilometre south of Haramil is the little harbour, usually packed with lines of posh yachts moored up in the **Marina Bander al Rowdha**, home to the Bluzone Diving centre (see p.49) and *Blue Marlin* restaurant (see p.73).

Follow the road down into the marina, where there is ample parking. On your right at the bottom of the hill you'll see the Marine Science & Fisheries Centre, home to the **Aquatic Exhibition of Marine Living Species** (Sun–Thurs 8am–2.30pm, Fri 4–6pm; free), an underwhelming aquarium boasting a few tanks of local marine life such as parrotfish, wrasse, surgeonfish, butterfly fish, trigger-fish and pop-eyed mudcrabs, plus a few turtles in depressingly small tanks.

Al Bustan Palace

It's a further kilometre south from here to the flamboyant *Al Bustan Palace* hotel. Now somewhat ignominiously beached in the middle of the roundabout at the entrance to the hotel lies the famous wooden dhow, the **Sohar**. The *Sohar* was constructed during 1979–80 using traditional Arabian boat-building techniques (including the unusual method of "stitched" construction: literally sewing planks together using coconut twine) and then sailed to China by a team led by redoubtable British adventurer Tim Severin – a fascinating adventure described in his *The Sindbad Voyage* (see p.240).

Follow the driveway from here down to **Al Bustan Palace** itself. Opened in 1985, this is the oldest of Muscat's super-deluxe hotels and was for many years the jewel in the crown of the fledgling Omani tourism industry, regularly cited as the most opulent and visually spectacular hotel in the Gulf. More recent hotel openings in neighbouring Dubai and Abu Dhabi, not to mention increasing competition within Muscat itself, have rather eroded the hotel's unique appeal, while the quirky exterior – like a kind of hexagonal Arabian spaceship – is beginning to look decidedly passé. The interior, however, remains undeniably impressive, centred on a huge soaring central atrium covered in gilded geometrical designs and supported by eight enormous gold arches – well worth lingering over while indulging in one of the hotel's sumptuous afternoon teas.

Bandar Jissah بندر جصة

A further 5km or so down the coast from *Al Bustan Palace* lies the beautiful bay of **Bandar Jissah**, dotted with a couple of rocky islands and ringed with gently shelving cliffs and headlands, one of them hollowed through with a modest **sea arch** which tour boats usually take the opportunity to duck under. The beach here was formerly an unspoilt **turtle-nesting site** before the construction right on top of it of the massive *Shangri-La Barr al Jissah Resort* complex. Green and hawksbill turtles can still be seen nesting on the beach from November to March, and the resort employs a dedicated "turtle ranger" to look after them. Sadly, the beach is only accessible to hotel guests and diners, and the way in which one of Muscat's most compelling natural spectacles has effectively been appropriated by the resort and turned into an in-house attraction leaves a slightly sour taste in the mouth.

There's also rewarding diving and snorkelling here (see p.49), plus accommodation and good food either at the *Shangri-La* (see p.73) or at the nearby **Oman Dive Centre** (1.5 OR entrance, or 3 OR at weekends for use of pool and beach, waived if you buy food or drink).

Yiti (يتي) and beyond

Some 20km from Muscat, at the end of the road past the Oman Dive Centre and *Shangri-La* resort, the tranquil little fishing village of **YITI** (or Yitti) makes a good target for a picnic, with a spacious beach dotted with fishing boats and wading birds, and attractive views along the rocky coast. The whole place feels remarkably rural and traditional given its proximity to Muscat, although this may soon change if the proposed **Yenkit** project (Ⓦwww.yenkit.com) goes ahead – a US$2 billion "luxury integrated tourist resort facility" featuring five-star hotels and a golf resort. Mercifully, recent economic difficulties mean that the scheme has been shelved, temporarily at least.

Some 3.5km inland from Yiti, a road heads off left, winding through the mountains for 9km to reach the village of **BANDAR AL KHAYRAN** at the end of a beautiful rocky sea inlet fringed with sandflats and mangroves. Beyond here, it's a further 14km to **AS SIFAH**, set around a bay hemmed in by low, rocky headlands and lined with another generous stretch of sand. The northern end of the beach is particularly popular. If you have 4WD you can continue 5km south along the graded coastal track to reach a further cluster of much quieter coves – a perfect spot for some wild camping.

Wadi Mayh

A twenty-minute drive south of Ruwi off the main road to Quriyat (see p.165) lies the idyllic **Wadi Mayh** – a wonderful stretch of untamed countryside in the shadow of the Eastern Hajar, offering a beguiling taste of rural Oman within an easy afternoon's drive of the capital. The wadi offers a perfect snapshot of traditional Arabia in miniature, its broad, gravel-strewn river bed interspersed with rock pools and flanked by craggy limestone cliffs, while an extended *falaj* connects the sand-coloured villages and date plantations which dot the valley – all remarkably unspoilt given its proximity to Muscat.

To **reach the wadi**, head south along the road to Quriyat from Wadi Aday roundabout in Ruwi. Around 23km south of Ruwi, a surfaced road heads off left into the wadi. The first half of the road (around 10km) is tarmacked, after which a graded track continues, eventually joining up with the road to Yiti.

Eating

Muscat has far and away the best selection of **places to eat** in the country, albeit relatively modest compared to other capital cities in the region. There's a good spread of upmarket restaurants, mostly based within the various hotels in the city's more modern districts around **Qurum**. More down-at-heel options can be found in the older parts of the city: **Ruwi** has the best range of cheap curry houses alongside slightly fancier restaurants, while **Muttrah** has the most enjoyable traditional Arabian shwarma cafés.

Muscat offers a rare chance to sample traditional **Omani** food at places like *Kargeen*, *Ubhar* or *Bin Ateeq*; you'll also do well for **seafood**, most of which comes fresh out of the local market at Muttrah. There's also a glut of good **Indian** restaurants thanks to the city's sizeable subcontinental population, along with a passable assortment of **Italian**, **Chinese** and **Thai** establishments, plus a couple of **Iranian** and **Moroccan** joints. Most restaurants close from 3–7pm. All the venues listed below are open daily for lunch and dinner unless otherwise stated; phone numbers are listed for establishments where it's a good idea to book ahead.

For restaurant reviews Ⓦwww.muscatdeli.blogspot.com has some excellent in-depth critiques of various places around the city, plus details of forthcoming culinary events.

Muttrah

The following places are shown on the map on p.57.

Al Ahli Coffee Shop Squirrelled away inside the northern end of Muttrah Souk, this popular little café attracts a mix of bargain-hunting Muscatis and souvenir-laden tourists alike. Good either for a quick drink or something more substantial, with a wide range of milkshakes and juices plus cheap sandwiches, burgers and shwarma. Virtually everything under 1 OR.

Al Boom *Marina Hotel* (see p.53). The main draw at this little hotel-top restaurant is the gorgeous views of the Muttrah corniche from one of the tightly packed tables lining the tiny outdoor terrace – arrive early to be sure of bagging a seat, or settle for a place in the more spacious but less spectacular interior. The short menu features an unexceptional mix of Indian, Arabian, Chinese and Continental dishes, plus a reasonable selection of seafood fresh from the adjacent fish market – try the shark vindaloo. It also boasts the additional attraction of being Muttrah's only licensed restaurant. Most mains 3–4 OR.

Fast Food 'n' Juice Centre Muttrah corniche. Busy, touristy café in a plum location right next to the entrance to Muttrah Souk – prices are slightly above average, although it's worth the premium for the breezy outdoor seating overlooking the corniche. Food includes all the usual snacks, burgers, sandwiches and shwarmas along with more substantial grills, fish and pizza, plus juices, shakes and proper coffee. Mains 2–3 OR. *Gulf Fast Food* next door is very similar.

Intaqiah Muttrah St. This pleasant garden restaurant offers a tourist-free taste of local life virtually within spitting distance of Muttrah Souk – best after dark, when it's prettily illuminated. There's no menu: either snack on a shwarma sandwich or fill up on one of the café's big and tasty set dinners (3 OR) of grilled chicken or beef accompanied by soup, falafel, salad, hummus and bread. The restaurant is directly behind the souk. Leave the souk through either of the rear exits and walk straight ahead up the road; the restaurant is on your right after about 100m.

Old Muscat

The following places are shown on the map on p.60.

Bait al Zubair Bait al Zubair Museum (see p.62). Old Muscat's best museum is home to a pleasant modern café (with reasonable coffee to boot); entry to the café is free, and there's seating either in the rather chic modern interior or outside in the museum gardens, although not much in the way of food, for which you'll have to head to one of the nearby restaurants listed below.

City Tower Grill The best of Old Muscat's virtually non-existent eating options, with a tourist-friendly menu of burgers, sandwiches, shwarmas, salads and juices, plus more substantial grills and biryanis. *Muscat Light Restaurant* next door has more of a mainstream Omani-Indian menu with assorted biryanis and curries. Mains at both places around 1–1.5 OR.

Ruwi

The following places are shown on the map on p.63.

Bin Ateeq Markaz Muttrah al Tijari St. Part of a nationwide chain (with branches in Nizwa and Salalah), *Bin Ateeq* makes a commendable, if not entirely successful, stab at re-creating an authentic local dining experience. Food is traditional Omani, with a range of meat and seafood curries and biryani-style dishes served up in one of the dozen or so little, traditionally furnished rooms into which the place is divided – you eat sitting on the floor. It's a nice idea, although the dining rooms are a bit drab (while the TVs in each room don't do much for the atmosphere either) and the food is average. Mains 1.2–2.5 OR.

Golden Oryx Al Burj St. An attractive upmarket Chinese restaurant, with a pleasantly soothing atmosphere and eye-catching decor – a bit like being inside an old wooden junk. The menu runs through a fairly mainstream selection of meat, fish and veg dishes, mainly Cantonese, with a few Szechuan options plus Thai curries – competent rather than exceptional, although portions are huge. Mains 3.5–6.5 OR. Licensed.

Khyber Markaz Muttrah al Tijari St. Sociable little restaurant, serving up big portions of North Indian classics, both veg and non veg (most mains 2–3 OR). Food is competent rather than memorable, and service is friendly, albeit decidedly erratic. The bottled Kingfisher is a bonus, although the wine selection is unlikely to set pulses racing.

Saravanaa Bhavan Ruwi St. Omani offshoot of the global chain of South Indian vegetarian restaurants offering above-average food at below-average prices, and usually rammed with local Indians (expect to queue during busy periods). Choose from the extensive menu of South Indian *dosas*, *vadas* and *uttapam*, plus a solidly prepared range of North Indian staples and a few Chinese dishes, with everything under 1.5 OR (and many items under 1 OR).

Woodlands Bank al Markazi St. Ruwi's top dining choice, owned by the same people who run the excellent *Mumtaz Mahal* (see below), serving up excellent South Indian cuisine in a pleasantly rustic dining room with cane furniture and lots of potted plants. The restaurant specializes in feisty Chettinad cuisine from Tamil Nadu: spicy meat, fish and veg *poriyals*, *varuvals* and *kuzambu*. There's also a good selection of North Indian standards and South Indian snacks – *dosas*, *uttapam*, *vadas* and *appam*. Mains 3–4 OR. Also boasts a reasonable wine list, plus beer and other drinks.

Qurum and Qurum Heights

The following places are shown on the map on p.66.

Come Prima *Crowne Plaza*, Al Qurum St. Small but suave Italian restaurant, in an airy modern dining room with white chairs, red glasses and big green pots. The menu offers a range of pasta and pizza (around 8 OR) plus more elaborate, modern-Italian-style mains (around 15 OR), with fresh, authentic ingredients and a keen nose for flavour.

Left Bank Off Sultan Qaboos St, below *Mumtaz Mahal* (see below). Very suave modern bar-restaurant, with seating either inside or (better) on the gorgeous outdoor terrace overlooking the city lights below. Food (mains 6–9 OR) comprises a big and eclectic selection of international dishes – everything from fish and chips to curries – although prices feel a bit steep for what is essentially glorified pub food. There's also an excellent drinks list, including one of Oman's best cocktail selections. Alternatively, you might prefer to eat at the superior *Mumtaz Mahal* upstairs, then come here for a drink afterwards.

Mumtaz Mahal Off Sultan Qaboos St, next to the Children's Museum ⑦2460 5907. One of the city's best-loved restaurants, occupying a large and pleasantly airy dining room with picture windows offering fine views over the city below. The inventive menu features a mix of classic Mughlai and Punjabi dishes such as the signature *raan-e-mumtaz* (marinaded whole leg of lamb slow-cooked in a tandoor), alongside some original house specials and other dishes offering a nod towards South Indian culinary traditions, including assorted fish curries and the chef's special mutton pepper fry. The wine list is decent, and there's also superior live music Sun–Thurs. Mains 5–7 OR, veg mains 3–4 OR.

Shiraz *Crowne Plaza*, Al Qurum St. This small and rather plain-looking restaurant serves up some of the best and most unusual Iranian food in the city, including inventive *polos* (Iranian-style biryanis featuring ingredients such as orange-flavoured chicken, chicken and blackberry, and salmon & saffron), traditional "stews" (duck and pomegranate, shrimp and tamarind, green hammour) and meaty kebabs. Mains around 10–15 OR.

Shatti al Qurum and Hayy as Saruj

The following places are shown on the map on p.66.

D'Arcy's Kitchen Jawaharat A'Shatti Complex. This popular expat hangout does a fair impression of an English-style country teashop, with chintzy decor and waitresses in frilly white pinafores – even if they are from the Philippines. The menu features all-day breakfasts, salads, sandwiches and soups plus more substantial burgers, pasta dishes and other mains (around 3–4 OR) ranging from fish and chips to stir-fries.

Al Candle Café Hayy as Saruj. Breezy and very chilled-out little seafront café, tucked away on the beach at the back of the *Grand Hyatt*. It's best after dark, when a mellow crowd of local Omanis and other expat Arabs settles in over the café's cheap shisha (1.2 OR). Food comprises a short but well-prepared menu of burgers, falafel sandwiches and a few grills plus assorted beverages including Turkish coffee and Moroccan tea.

Jade Garden *Al Qurum Resort*, behind the Jawaharat A'Shatti Complex. Homely little restaurant, offering a range of well-prepared Thai and Chinese dishes (mains 4–6 OR), plus sushi, sashimi and teppanyaki. Licensed.

Japengo Al Shatti St. The most appealling of the string of cafés dotted along the beachfront road, with sea views through the wall-to-ceiling windows or outdoor seating on the breezy rooftop terrace. The shamelessly eclectic menu rolls out a veritable culinary encyclopedia ranging from salads and sandwiches through to sushi, pasta, pizza, stir-fries, Lebanese grills and fish & chips – all reasonably, if unexceptionally, prepared. Unlicensed. Mains 4–7 OR.

Tuscany *Grand Hyatt* ☎2464 1234. One of the top restaurants in the city, the *Grand Hyatt*'s signature eating venue serves up a fine selection of authentic Italian cuisine under the leadership of its Piedmontese chef, with seating in a rather solemn-looking dining area reminiscent of a domed Roman temple. The menu features a small but carefully crafted selection of meat and fish mains, using a range of authentic Italian ingredients alongside local seafood, plus a good selection of superior pasta dishes and wood-fired pizzas. Pizza and pasta around 7–9 OR; mains 9–14 OR.

Ubhar Bareeq al Shatti Mall (due south of Jawaharat A'Shatti Mall). One of Muscat's more original places to eat. The inventive menu features traditional Omani cuisine given a contemporary makeover, with dishes like camel biryani, fish *machbus*, *harees* (chicken with wheat), plus novel desserts including date ice cream and the signature "Ubhar's Dream" (*halwa* in puff pastry). There's also a choice of mainstream pastas, burgers and sandwiches if none of the above appeals. Mains 5–7 OR.

Madinat Sultan Qaboos

The following place is shown on the map on p.66.

Kargeen Madinat Sultan Qaboos shopping complex, between Al Noor Plaza and Al Madine Plaza. One of the most enjoyable places to eat in Muscat, occupying a rambling series of small buildings set amid large, shady gardens, with seating either inside or out, on wooden benches scattered with colourful cushions under the trees. The vast menu seems to have a little bit of everything, from crepes, pasta, pizzas, steaks, seafood, sandwiches, grills and no less than six types of shwarma through to traditional Omani-style mains (most 3–4 OR) including *shuwa* (slow-roasted meat) and other local specialities. Service can be decidedly random, however, so don't expect to get served in a hurry. There are now several other branches around town, but none is a patch on the original.

Khuwair and Ghubrah

The following places are shown on the map on p.50.

The Beach *The Chedi*, Off 18 November St, Ghubrah ☎2452 4343. The second, and perhaps the best, of *The Chedi*'s two main dining venues. Follow the candles through the Japanese-style hedges to this magical outdoor pavilion-style restaurant, right on the seafront, which manages to combine high contemporary Asian style with beachside informality. The menu features all things marine, with a fine selection of international seafood, plus oyster and caviar selection. Mains from around 15 OR. Open for dinner only, apart from Friday brunch (which costs around 50 OR/ person including as much Moët as you can drink – which will probably be quite a lot, given the price).

Bin Ateeq Sultan Qaboos St, Khuwair. Khuwair branch of the Oman-wide chain. See p.71.

The Restaurant *The Chedi*, Off 18 November St, Ghubrah ☎2452 4343. The main restaurant in the idyllic *The Chedi* hotel – slightly cheaper than, although perhaps not quite as memorable as *The*

Beach (see above). There are four separate kitchens here, turning out accomplished Arabian, Asian, Indian and "Contemporary" (meaning modern European/international) food, backed up by a selection of more than 300 wines. There's indoor seating, although you might prefer the lovely palm-studded courtyard outside. Most mains around 12–16 OR.

Shang Thai Sultan Qaboos St, Khuwair (above *Pizza Express* in the building behind *McDonald's*). Soothing Thai restaurant, despite the unpromising location next to Sultan Qaboos St (whose crazy traffic you can admire through big picture windows). The menu features a good range of well-prepared meat, seafood and vegetarian Thai classics (plus a few Szechuan and Hokkien dishes), served in big portions and with plenty of flavour. It's especially handy if you're staying at the nearby *Ibis* or *Hotel Muscat Holiday* hotels. Most mains 3–4.2 OR.

South of the centre

The following places are shown on the map on p.50.

Beach Pavilion *Al Bustan Palace* ⓣ2479 9666. On the beach at the *Al Bustan Palace* hotel, and one of the most beautiful locations in town. Not surprisingly, seafood is the speciality here, with a range of local and international offerings either fresh from Muttrah fish market or flown in, although there are also some meat alternatives. Non-guests will need to reserve in advance. Most mains are around 15 OR.

Blue Marlin Marina Bander al Rowdha. Attractive modern restaurant, with alfresco seating overlooking the marina. There's a good range of international breakfasts, snacks and mains ranging from sandwiches, burgers and pasta dishes through to more substantial seafood dishes using ingredients straight from the Muttrah fish market, all backed up by a decent drinks menu featuring cocktails, wine and beer. Mains 4–7 OR.

Capri Court *Al Bandar, Shangri-La Barr al Jissah Resort* ⓣ2477 6565. Vying with the *Grand Hyatt*'s *Tuscany* for the title of the best Italian in Oman, with an intimate and very chic dining room or tables on the terrace. The menu showcases both classic and contemporary Italian – anything from a traditional porcini risotto or squid-ink linguine through to fine-dining creations like beef tenderloin with goose liver and black truffle. There's also an excellent (if expensive) wine list. Open for dinner only. Mains are around 12 OR.

Odyssey Oman Dive Center. One of Muscat's most relaxing places to eat, set on a lovely outdoor terrace overlooking beach and bay, and offering an international menu of well-prepared pastas, salads and sandwiches (around 5 OR) plus more substantial meat and fish mains (6–7 OR), including lots of daily specials. Licensed.

Sultanah *Al Husn, Shangri-La Barr al Jissah Resort* ⓣ2477 6565. One of the finest restaurants in the city, situated in the exclusive *Al Husn* section of the vast *Shangri-La* resort and named in honour of the original *Sultanah*, which in 1840 became the first Omani ship to cross the Atlantic. The decor features sea views and subtle, marine-inspired designs, while the menu offers a range of top-notch international à la carte meat and seafood, plus a regularly changing section based on the day's "port of call" – a surprisingly cheesy touch for a restaurant which takes itself this seriously. Open for dinner only. There's a good but very pricey wine list and the food is predictably expensive, with mains at around 20 OR.

Drinking, nightlife and entertainment

Muscat has far more **licensed** pubs, bars and restaurants than anywhere else in Oman, mainly (but not exclusively) found in hotels. There are three main options: the swanky **bars** found in the city's upmarket hotels; the somewhat more downmarket English-style **pubs**, also found in most mid- and upper-range hotels; and the raucous **live-music bars** with live Arabian or Indian stage shows. Nowhere is drinking cheap, however, and the city's fancier bars, although undoubtedly alluring, can empty your wallet very quickly.

Hanging out over a freshly pressed juice or a cup of coffee in one of the city's local **cafés** offers a far cheaper and more typically Omani experience – the coffee shops in and around Muttrah Souk and along the nearby corniche (see p.70) are particularly attractive places to shoot the breeze and watch the world go by. It's also worth heading to somewhere like *Al Candle Café* or *Kargeen* (see opposite) after dark and chilling out over a **shisha** and a cup of Turkish coffee. For a more upmarket variation on the same theme, **afternoon tea** in either the *Grand Hyatt* or *Al Bustan* are both enjoyable.

All the following are marked on the map on p.66, unless otherwise noted.

Al Boom Restaurant *Marina Hotel*, Muttrah. Muttrah's only licensed restaurant (see p.70; see map, p.57) is also a good place for a drink, if you can bag one of the terrace tables overlooking the corniche. See map, p.57.

Duke's Bar *Crowne Plaza*, Qurum Heights. Spacious English-style pub-bar with views of palms through big picture windows.

Al Ghazal *InterContinental*, Shatti al Qurum. Strangely Arabian name for thoroughly British pub, with wood-panelled interior, a couple of pool tables and live sport on TV. There's live music nightly except Monday, plus quiz nights, pool and darts competitions, and karaoke.

John Barry Bar *Grand Hyatt*, Al Khuwair. One of the most stylish bars in the city (with prices to match), featuring nautically themed decor complete with foaming portholes, a ceiling covered in ships' rigging and bar staff in sailors' uniforms. There are lots of big comfy seats to crash out on inside, plus an outdoor terrace overlooking the hotel gardens. A jazz duo performs most evenings from around 9pm.

Left Bank Qurum. Swanky establishment overlooking the modern city from a bluff above Sultan Qaboos St. Functions mainly as a restaurant (see p.71) but does equally well for a moody drink, with lovely views, chilled-out ambient music and a good selection of beverages including one of the city's best cocktail lists.

Piano Lounge *Al Bandar* Hotel, *Shangri-La Barr al Jissah Resort*. Gorgeously svelte little bar, with very cool decor, shelves full of temptingly back-lit bottles and an accomplished pianist tinkling the ivories from her perch on top of what looks like a miniature aquarium. Alternatively, head outside to the long outdoor terrace, with beautiful sea views.

Safari Pub *Grand Hyatt*. Small African-themed bar with poky, uninspiring decor and rather lacking in seats, although the live music, provided by a regularly changing roster of international bands, is usually among the best in the city.

Serai Pool Bar *The Chedi*, Ghubrah. Beautiful outdoor bar next to *The Chedi*'s lovely canopied pool. Drinks include a rather modest list of wines, cocktails, beers and mocktails, and you can also order a selection of food from *The Restaurant* (see p.72) next door.

Nightlife

Nightlife in Muscat is a pretty low-key affair – it can often seem like the city's two most popular after-dark activities are driving at maniac speeds up and down Sultan Qaboos Street or piling into the nearest Lulu hypermarket for late-night shopping. Western expat and tourist nightlife tends to focus around drinking in one of the city's bars or pubs. **Listings** of forthcoming events are also hard to come by – have a look at the "Oman Nightlife" group on Facebook or check out Ⓦwww.muscatmutterings.com.

Quite a few of the city's pubs have **live music** most nights, ranging from the accomplished international cover bands (or occasional jazz acts) which play the city's five-star drinking joints through to the gyrating Filipina chanteuses who can be heard murdering classic tunes in the city's more downmarket pubs. For a quintessential slice of Omani nightlife, head to one of the **live-music bars** (see p.26) found in some of the city's mid-range hotels (such as the *Marina* in Muttrah, or the *Mutrah* and *Ruwi* hotels in Ruwi). The nearest you'll get to a genuine **club** is either the *Copacabana* at the *Grand Hyatt* or the *Rock Bottom Café* – the only two places in the city which currently have a "dancing permit", without which the Omani authorities forbid any form of disco activity.

Copacabana *Grand Hyatt*. Muscat's leading nightspot hosts resident and visiting international DJs playing anything from r'n'b and hip-hop through to Arabian and Bollywood tunes; at busy times you may struggle to get in if you're not in a couple. For latest events, check their Facebook page. Closed Fri.

Rock Bottom Café *Ramee Guestline Hotel*, Qurum. Downmarket alternative to the *Copacabana*, with a raucous crowd of under-age, under-dressed drinkers and far too much testosterone floating around; in 2009 the US Embassy in Muscat banned their staff from visiting the place after a series of particularly spectacular punch-ups. Still, the band's usually quite good – just don't antagonize the bouncers.

Entertainment

Big-name international **music acts** (although think Tom Jones and Bryan Adams rather than Shakira and Dizzee Rascal) occasionally pass through the city, during which the gardens at the *InterContinental* hotel are pressed into service as an impromptu concert arena.

More upmarket forms of **cultural entertainment** are virtually nonexistent at present, although this may change following the opening of the city's new Royal Opera House (Ⓦwww.rohmuscat.org), next to Sultan Qaboos Street in Qurum (currently scheduled to open in mid-2011). This will provide the city with a much-needed large-scale performance space – expect a mix of classical music, jazz, dance and Arabian cultural events, plus visiting opera productions.

Shopping

The majority of visitors to the city do all their shopping in **Muttrah Souk** (see p.56), although there are a few other places worth checking out. The most interesting area is the commercial district in central **Qurum**, around Qurum roundabout, where a cluster of old-fashioned malls harbour an interesting range of shops selling traditional arts and crafts, gold, jewellery and perfumes. Standard **opening times** for most shops and malls are roughly Saturday to Thursday, from 10am–1pm & 5–10pm, and Friday from 5–10pm (some places open and close half an hour earlier than this). All the following places are shown on the **map** on p.66.

Al Araimi Centre Qurum. This poky little mall is a good spot to pick up local perfumes, with branches of the Gulf-wide Arabian Oud and Ajmal chains (although the English sign on the latter is bafflingly tiny); if you don't like any of the ready-made perfumes on offer, both these shops will help you create your own bespoke scent, mixed at your pleasure from the big glass jars behind the counter.

Bateel Oasis by the Sea Complex (opposite the Jawaharat A'Shatti Complex), Shatti al Qurum. If you're a lover of the date, this place has the best in the city, with a top-quality range of Saudi varieties either sold plain or stuffed with lemon, orange or almond, from 7.5 OR/kg. They also do a good range of chocolates, as well as beautiful gift boxes and date-derived drinks.

Borders Qurum City Centre, Qurum. In a city of very few bookshops, this modest branch of Borders is one of the best, stocking a decent range of English-language titles, plus magazines and local-interest books.

Omani Craftsmen's House Opposite Sabco Centre, Qurum. Similar to the well-known Omani Heritage Gallery (see below), selling good-quality traditional craftsmanship including pottery, rugs, incense burners and the like.

Omani Heritage Gallery Jawaharat A'Shatti Complex, Shatti al Qurum. Traditional Omani handicrafts including Bahla pottery, frankincense burners from Dhofar, rugs, caps, coffeepots and some attractive jewellery with traditional Bedu designs given a contemporary makeover. Relatively expensive, although at least the quality is assured.

Qurum City Centre Qurum roundabout, Qurum. This shiny modern mall is one of the smartest in the city, hosting a mainstream range of high-street shops including a good branch of Borders (see opposite) and a large Carrefour supermarket. It also stays open throughout the day, unlike most other places in town (Sat–Thurs 10am–10pm, Fri 2–10pm).

Sabco Centre Qurum. Home to one of the city's better selections of carpet and handicrafts shops, including Village Arts & Crafts, Art of Loom and one of the nationwide branches of Al Haramain Perfumes, all of which stand lined up to the right of the entrance, facing the street. Further jewellery, carpet and perfume shops line the road past the entrance, while inside the centre is a pleasant *Barista* coffee shop set in a fake tropical garden, a branch of Amouage (see p.113) and, for those who should know better, an Arsenal shop.

Tahani Jawaharat A'Shatti Complex, Shatti al Qurum. Next door to the Omani Heritage Gallery, with a very upmarket selection of museum-quality antique Bedu jewellery, *khanjars*, coffeepots and *mandoos* plus quirky Western curios such as old box cameras, wind-up telephones and retro clocks.

Listings

Airlines British Airways, at the airport ⓣ2456 8777; Emirates, Villa 714, Way 2114, Al Inshira St, Madinat Sultan Qaboos ⓣ2440 4444; Etihad, Way 3506, Building460, New MBD Area, Hayy al Mina ⓣ2482 3500; Gulf Air, 428 Mussandam Building, Ruwi St, just north of Ruwi roundabout ⓣ2448 2777; Oman Air, Building 1713, Way 2720, Block No.157, CBD, Ruwi (just off Markaz Muttrah al Tijari Street south of the Central Bank of Oman) ⓣ2451 8977; Qatar Airways, Haffa House Hotel, Ruwi St, Ruwi ⓣ2416 2700; Thai Airways, c/o Bahwan Travel Agencies, Markaz Muttrah al Tijari Street, CBD, Ruwi ⓣ2470 4455.
ATMs There are plentiful ATMs all over the city. Almost all accept foreign-issued Visa and/or MasterCards.
Car rental The usual international car rental chains are at the airport; reserve in advance, especially for larger vehicles. Some hotels in the city have car rental desks, including the *Radisson Blu* (Thrifty), the *Crowne Plaza* (Dollar) and the Grand Hyatt (Mark). Thrifty also has a branch opposite the Ruwi bus station. Local operators have offices in Ruwi along Al Nahdah St; prices are usually cheaper, although vehicles may not be as modern or as reliable.
Embassies and consulates Virtually all the city's embassies are located in the diplomatic quarter of Hayy as Saruj, south and west of the *Grand Hyatt* hotel. Australia, New Zealand and Ireland are represented by their embassies in Saudi Arabia (although Ireland maintains an honorary consul in the city). Canadian consulate, Trade Links Building, Building 1738, Way 2728, CBD, Ruwi ⓣ2478 8890; Ireland, Honorary Consul, Dr Mohammed H. Darwish, Haggan Haider Darwish, O.C. Centre, 8th Floor, Suite #807, Ruwi ⓣ2470 1282; UK embassy, Jamiat ad Duwal al Arabiya St, Hayy as Saruj ⓣ2460 9000, ⓦukinoman.fco.gov.uk; US embassy, Jamiat ad Duwal al Arabiya St, Hayy as Saruj ⓣ2469 9771, ⓦoman.usembassy.gov.
Hospitals For an ambulance, call ⓣ9999. There's a well-developed network of public and private hospitals in the capital. Two of the main government hospitals are The Royal Hospital (ⓣ2459 9000, ⓦwww.royalhospital.med.om) in Ghubrah south of the Sultan Qaboos Mosque, and Al Nahdha Hospital (ⓣ2483 7800) in Ruwi near Wadi Aday roundabout. The main private hospital is Muscat Private Hospital (ⓣ2458 3600, ⓦmuscatprivatehospital.com) in Bowshar; Al Raffah Hospital (ⓣ2461 8900, ⓦwww.asterhospital.com), next to Ghubrah roundabout, is another possibility, more conveniently located, although with not such a good reputation.
Internet There are a number of useful internet cafés dotted around Muttrah and Ruwi, all marked on the maps on p.57 and p.63. In Muttrah, the New Millenium Generation Internet Café on the corniche south of the souk entrance also provides wi-fi access if you have your own computer. There's also the Khamis bin Daud Khamis Internet Cafe around the east side of the Muttrah Gold Souk building. In Ruwi, the two most convenient places are Online Always, on A'Noor St, and Highest Summit Internet Cafe, right next to the *Sun City Hotel*. In Ruwi's CBD, try City Cyber Cafe around the back of the building next to Bahwan Travel Agencies (see Thai Airways listing, above). Most places charge 500bz/hr.
Police Emergency number ⓣ9999. The most conveniently located police stations are in Muttrah, next to the southern entrance to Muttrah Souk, and in Ruwi at the northern end of Souq Ruwi St.
Post and couriers The main post office (Sat–Wed 8am–8pm, Thurs 8am–noon) is at the northern end of Markaz Muttrah al Tijari St in Ruwi's CBD (see map, p.63). There's a DHL office around the back of the National Bank of Oman nearby on the west side of the same street. FedEx have an office in the Al Araimi Centre in Qurum, and there's another DHL office on the lower floor of Qurum City Centre (see p.75) close by.
Spas There are two superb, international-standard spas in town. The Spa at *The Chedi* (see p.55) specializes in elaborate oriental-style treatments including body polishes, bathing ceremonies, beauty rituals and massages drawing on a range of Indian, Balinese, Thai and Arabian techniques. Chi – The Spa at the *Shangri-La Barr al Jissah Resort* (see p.56) has a similar Asian slant, along with locally inspired rituals including rasul, hammam, frankincense and rose body-wrap treatments. Neither comes cheap, however, with treatments at both places starting at around 45–50 OR/hr. The Palm Beach Club in the *InterContinental* offers massages (Asian, Thai, Sports) and reflexology (16 OR/25min).
Travel agents See p.22 for a list of leading local travel agents. Useful offices include Zahara, on the lower floor of Qurum City Centre, and Mark Tours on Al Iskan St in Ruwi and at the *Grand Hyatt* hotel.

The Western Hajar

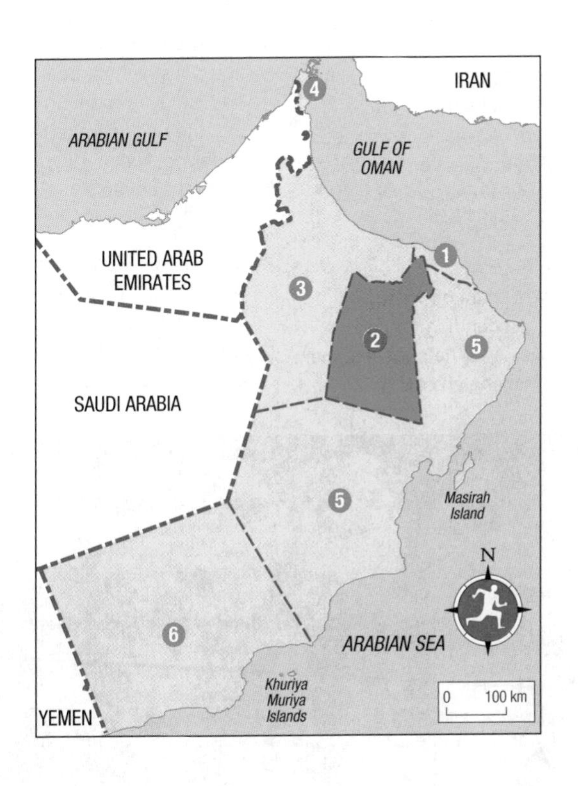

CHAPTER 2

Highlights

* **Nizwa** Historic capital of the interior and Oman's most personable town, with a grand fort and an absorbing string of souks. See p.85

* **Goat Market, Nizwa** One of Oman's most entertaining traditional markets, where hundreds of locals congregate to haggle over goats, cows and other livestock. See p.89

* **Saiq Plateau** The scenic heart of the Jebel Akhdar, with a string of old-fashioned villages clinging to the edge of the spectacular chasm of Wadi al Ayn. See p.94

* **Wadi Bani Awf** The classic Omani off-road drive, descending from the mountains to the coast via the dramatic chasm of Wadi Bani Awf, with the picture-perfect traditional village of Bilad Sayt en route. See p.99

* **Misfat al Abryeen** Picture-perfect traditional mountain village, with a labyrinthine tangle of beautiful mudbrick buildings and an idyllic *falaj* set amid beautiful upland scenery. See p.101

* **Jebel Shams** Drive up the country's highest peak, for spectacular mountain scenery and stomach-turning views into Wadi Nakhr – Oman's "Grand Canyon". See p.102

* **Jabrin Fort** Fairy-tale fort, whose beautifully restored interiors offer a fascinating glimpse into Omani life in centuries past. See p.105

▲ Earthenware pots and souvenirs, Nizwa Souk

2

The Western Hajar

Inland from Muscat, Highway 15 winds up into the craggy Hajar mountains, Oman's geological backbone, which extend all the way along the east coast of the country, from Sur to the Musandam Peninsula. The region southwest of Muscat is home to the Hajar's highest and most dramatic section, often described as the **Western Hajar**, or Al Hajar al Gharbi (as opposed to the somewhat lower and less extensive Eastern Hajar, covered in chapter five). The area is also sometimes referred to as **Al Dakhiliya** (literally, "The Interior"), one of the seven administrative regions into which Oman is divided and which encompasses the towns and mountains of the Western Hajar, as well as a large swathe of desert to the south.

The main focus for most visits to the region is the famous old town of **Nizwa**, the pre-eminent settlement of the Omani interior and formerly home to the country's revered imams. Nizwa also provides a convenient base from which to explore other attractions around the hills, with its mix of rugged mountainscapes and dramatic wadis along with historic old mudbrick towns and idyllic date plantations bisected with traditional *aflaj*. Leading attractions include the spectacular massifs of the **Jebel Akhdar**, east of Nizwa, and **Jebel Shams**, to the west, the highest summit in Oman. There are also memorable traditional villages at **Al Hamra** and **Misfat al Abryeen** plus a number of the country's finest forts, including those at **Bahla**, the largest in the country, and **Jabrin**, perhaps the most interesting.

Inland from Muscat to Nizwa

It's around 140km from Muscat to Nizwa, an easy drive (roughly 1hr 30min–2hr) along the fast, modern **Highway 15** which is now dual carriageway virtually the whole way – a fine drive up into the mountains, or an even more exhilarating downward swoop when descending from Nizwa towards the coast.

The route covered by the modern highway is one of the most significant in Omani history, winding through a gap between the towering uplands of the Jebel Akdhar on one side and the more modest peaks of the eastern Hajar on the other. This was once perhaps the most important commercial conduit in the country, and the principal trade artery between the highland capital of Nizwa and Muscat on the coast, its former importance signalled by the extraordinary surfeit of forts, watchtowers and fortified settlements which still flank the modern highway. These include the massed watchtowers and hilltop village of **Fanja**, the fort at **Bidbid**, the walled town at **Izki**, and the oasis-smothered valley and massed fortifications of **Sumail**, all of which offer rewarding diversions from the main road up into the hills.

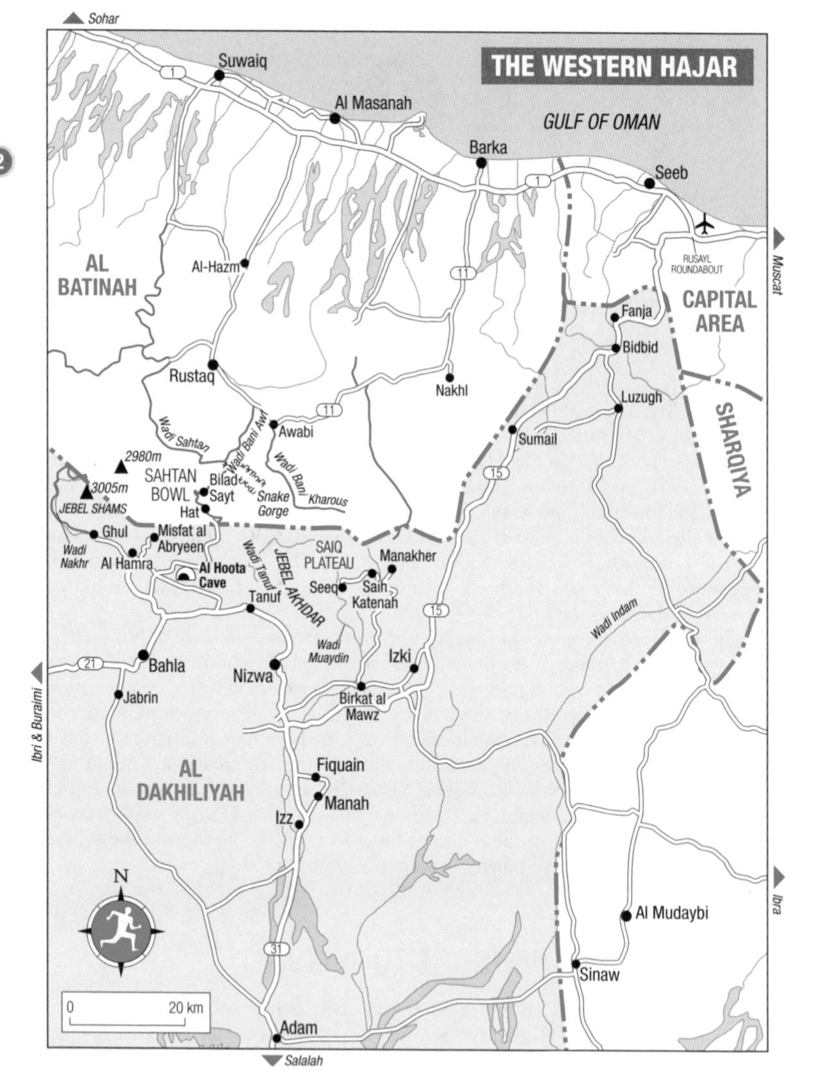

Fanja فنجاء

Some 30km from Rusayl roundabout along Highway 15, the town of **FANJA** is home to a dramatically situated old **walled village and watchtower**, perched high on a hilltop overlooking the modern town and providing commanding views over the valley below. The area's former strategic significance is signalled (as at Sumail, further up the road) by the extraordinary quantity of towers which stand watch from the surrounding hills. Entrance to the village is via a well-preserved gateway flanked by a very solid-looking stretch of stone wall. Inside, the old walled village comprises a decaying muddle of ruined mudbrick buildings plus, incongruously, a couple of modern concrete houses, still apparently inhabited. It's a five-minute scramble from the entrance up to the tower itself. This is built in an unusual lozenge shape, rather than the usual circle or square, commanding 360-degree views over the surrounding hills, dotted with a dozen or so further watchtowers.

Getting to Fanja

Getting to the old village is slightly convoluted. The following directions assume that you're approaching from the direction of Muscat, but work in reverse if approaching from Nizwa. Follow the signs off Route 15 into Fanja. This road runs through the centre of the modern town, descending to a big modern bridge across the wadi. On the far side of the bridge you'll see a large round watchtower on your right. Take the small side road on your right after about 150m which loops back to the watchtower; it's easiest to park here and walk the rest of the way (around 15–20min), given the narrowness of the roads. Walk along this road (keeping left at the first fork) – there's another watchtower directly ahead at this point – this isn't the one you're aiming for. Continue ahead through a high-walled date plantation, then turn left in front of two small shops signed "Sale of Food Stuffs" and "Manufacturing of Cuttain" (sic). A few metres later you reach a T-junction, with the mudbrick houses of the old village visible on the rocky bluff above. Turn left, climbing uphill until the tarmac ends, then head right up a rough track – you'll see a section of wall and the main gateway ahead.

Bidbid بدبد

A few kilometres beyond Fanja, just off the main highway, the small town of **BIDBID** is worth a quick detour for its quaint **fort** (not open to the public). This is one of the prettiest small castles in the country: a rustic little structure, built with mudbrick walls on a stone base, with windows and rifle-slits cut lopsidedly out of the adobe, half-hearted little rounded battlements above and a large watchtower perched on a small rock outcrop beside. Unusually, the walls have been left unplastered following restoration, so you can see the pebbles and bits of straw mixed in to strengthen the mudbrick, adding to its rather homespun charm. A swiftly flowing *falaj*, in which villagers are wont to do their washing, runs around one side of the fort.

The fort is about 1km off Highway 15. To get here **from Nizwa**, take the signed turn-off and follow the road into town until you reach a modest line of shops. Take the unsigned road on the left here just past a medium-sized white mosque, bear left over two oversized speed bumps and the fort is in front of you. There's no exit to Bidbid from the highway approaching **from Muscat**; you'll need to continue along the highway for about 1km then turn around at the Ibra/Sur roundabout, head back down the highway and follow the directions from Nizwa.

Sumail سمائل

Just over 20km beyond Bidbid, the town of **SUMAIL** (also spelled Samail) was historically one of the most important in the area thanks to its position at the head of a narrow pass through the mountains, the so-called **Sumail Gap**. The Gap stretches for about 10km north of town, lined with kilometre after kilometre of lush date plantations squeezed in below rocky ridges to either side, their summits crowned by dozens of watchtowers, walls and other fortifications – a picture-perfect slice of traditional Oman.

From either Muscat or Nizwa, follow the signs from Highway 15 into Sumail and through the ugly modern sprawl of Al Madrah. After about 3km you'll see Al Karama Hypermarket on your right. Just past here there's a dramatic change of scenery as the road swings round to the left and emerges into the Gap itself: a broad, lush wadi, with endless date plantations stretching ahead below the low rocky outcrops which enclose the wadi on either side. The rock outcrops themselves are topped by literally dozens of watchtowers – about 1km past the hypermarket you'll notice a particularly eye-catching pair of towers atop a prominent outcrop on the far side of the wadi, worth a closer look. Standing in front of these two towers you can see a further five watchtowers dotted along hilltops opposite.

Continuing along the road, the wadi and palm plantations continue for the best part of 10km, overseen by further watchtowers. The largest of the various fortifications dotting the valley, **Sumail Fort** (not open to the public) lies right next to the road, about 3km past the hypermarket, although only its tower is visible from the road itself, the main part of the structure being obscured by the large rock outcrop on which it sits. The fort is one of Oman's more unusual constructions, its high, zigzagging walls moulded around the contours of the rock outcrop on which it's built, with a large tower at the summit of the outcrop, and some modest living quarters clustered around the gateway at the bottom. To find the fort, look out for the blue sign (itself quite easy to miss) announcing Al Ujm, immediately past which you'll cross a bridge. Take the first turning on the right after the bridge for around 200m and you'll arrive at the fort.

About 3km further north along the road beyond the fort, a sign on the left points to the **Bait al Sarooj** ("Sarooj House" – *sarooj* being the traditional Omani-style plaster which was formerly used to protect the exterior of mudbrick constructions), a couple of hundred metres off the road. This traditional Omani fortified house isn't open to the public, but you're free to admire the nicely restored exterior, large but rather plain, although enlivened with a finely carved wooden door. A pair of watchtowers stand on the ridge above, offering further fine valley views.

If you've made the detour to Sumail and are heading down to Muscat there's no need to retrace your steps back to Highway 15. It's just as quick, and considerably more pleasant, to continue on along the road down the Gap and on to **Luzugh**, from where another back road heads north, eventually rejoining Highway 15 just south of Bidbid.

Izki إزكي

South of Sumail, the mountain scenery flanking Highway 15 becomes increasingly dramatic. To the west rise the towering uplands of the Jebel Akdhar, with their huge slabs of tilted limestone. To the east stretch the much smaller and more irregular ophiolite hills which mark the edges of the Eastern Hajar.

Just under 50km beyond Sumail, a few kilometres off the main highway, lies the town of **IZKI**, overlooking the broad **Wadi Halfayn**. Izki is popularly claimed to be the oldest town in Oman, and was also formerly notorious for its tribal intrigues, being divided into Yamani and Nazari villages; until quite recent times, relations between the two communities remained strained and suspicious – a long-standing example of one of Oman's most ancient ethnic divides (see p.218).

The old town

Modern Izki is a large and formless place which straggles alongside the main highway for more than 5km. The main attractions are the ruins of the old walled town and adjacent fort, situated on a bluff overlooking Wadi Halfayn, with the mountains to either side. The **old town** is particularly beautiful, an extensive complex of disintegrating mudbrick buildings enclosed within a rectangle of impressively solid walls, built on raised stone foundations; the walls have survived the years relatively intact, unlike many of the buildings within.

Entrance to the old town is via the large **gateway** on the wadi-facing side of the town nearest the date plantations. Next to the gateway stands a well-preserved

The falaj

One of the most distinctive sights in the Omani mountains is the **falaj**: the traditional system of narrow, mud-walled water channels used to irrigate fields and date plantations, and to provide villages and towns with reliable water supplies. The **origins** of the system go back into the mists of prehistory (the name itself perhaps derives from an old Semitic word meaning "distribution"; the true Arabic plural is *aflaj*, although "*falajes*" is often used instead). One theory holds that it was introduced by the Persians – who had developed a similar irrigation system, know as the *qanat* – in around the sixth century BC, although there is evidence that *falaj*-like irrigation systems were present in Arabia even before then.

Estimates of the **total number** of *aflaj* in Oman vary from five thousand to well over ten thousand, of which perhaps as many as four thousand are still in use. Traditionally, the reliability and size of the local *falaj* was the key factor underlying the size and prosperity of settlements in Oman. Nizwa, for instance, flourished thanks to its abundant water sources, including the mighty Falaj Daris. By contrast, if a *falaj* ceased flowing, it usually spelled the end of the village that relied on its water. Mosques can also often be seen near important sections of a *falaj*, offering a reliable source of water for ritual ablutions before prayers, while most of the country's larger forts also boasted their own dedicated *falaj*, often flowing from an underground source directly into the building and guaranteeing a steady supply of water in the event of a siege. *Aflaj* remain an integral part of the traditional Omani date plantation or village – even today, many locals still use them to wash clothes in or even, in larger ones, to take a bath.

Construction and operation

The communal effort and expense involved in constructing and maintaining a *falaj* was a heavy burden on traditional Omani society, although it also helped foster social cohesion and a sense of shared responsibility. Locating a suitable water source using the services of a specialist water diviner was the first challenge. There are two basic types of *falaj*: a **ghaily falaj**, drawn from a water source above ground such as a river bed or mountain spring, or, more commonly, an **iddi** or **daudi falaj**, drawn from an underground well, anything up to 50m beneath the surface – many *aflaj* start with extensive tunnels before they emerge into the light of day. Creating such subterranean conduits was obviously a major engineering feat, as was constructing the **channels** themselves. In order to make sure the water keeps running, these are built on a constant, if often imperceptible, downward gradient from source to destination (although in places – such as the mountain villages of the Saiq Plateau – you'll see channels tumbling steeply down the hillside between layers of agricultural terracing).

The **operation** of the typical *falaj* is another highly developed part of the Omani social fabric. *Aflaj* are collectively owned, with villagers holding shares which give them the right to a certain amount of water. Water is diverted into adjoining fields by unblocking holes in the sides of the channel for a certain amount of time (traditionally calculated by the movement of stars at night and by sundials during the day, although nowadays most people just use clocks). Large villages usually employ a full-time manager (*aref*) to oversee the running of the *falaj*, assisted by an agent, who looks after repairs and maintenance.

mosque on a raised platform, with a pair of fine arches, an unusually large *mihrab* and a red-painted wooden roof decorated with fragments of Qur'anic text within. From here, you can spend a peaceful twenty minutes nosing around the remains of the old streets, laid out on an approximate grid plan, with a wide main thoroughfare running dead-straight through the middle. Many fine buildings still survive in various states of dereliction; a number preserve their original carved wooden doors and beamed roofs. At the far end of the village stands a second, unusually large, mosque. The roof has long since vanished, but the interior survives partially intact, with two long lines of stone arches on chunky circular columns and a rustic *mihrab* and *minbar*.

On the far side of the old town lie the similarly crumbling remains of Izki's large **fort**, with the remains of the impressive central keep (including one round tower built, unusually, entirely of stone) set within a square of collapsing walls. Following the road past the fort as it dips back down from the ridgetop brings you to a further fine collection of old mudbrick houses, now surrounded by modern buildings.

Izki is also home to the **Falaj al Malki** (or Mulki), thought to be the oldest in the country, whose tributaries water the date plantations beneath the old town – the entire *falaj* consists of a network of around 360 channels (although only two are now in use), drawing water from a source 20m below ground. In 2006 this became one of five Omani *aflaj* protected as a UNESCO World Heritage Site.

Getting to Izki

Approaching **from Muscat**, take the exit off Highway 15 signed Izki and Qaroot al Janubiah then follow the main road into town for about 2km until you see a sign saying "Izki 4km" on your left. **From Nizwa**, take the road through Birkat al Mawz towards Nizwa, passing through about 5km of built-up straggle to reach the "Izki 4km" sign (on your right). Turn right/left (depending on which direction you're approaching from) at the sign and follow the road for about 3km through mostly open countryside until you reach a roundabout. Take the (unsigned) right-hand turning here. This road runs alongside the oasis then veers right, narrowing as it passes through the oasis, and then climbs the ridge beyond, which is where you'll find the old town and fort.

Birkat al Mawz بركة الموز

Some 11km beyond Izki is the small town of **BIRKAT AL MAWZ**, slightly over an hour from Muscat, and just 25km east of Nizwa. Birkat al Mawz (literally "Pool of Bananas", which are still grown in the oasis here) is of interest mainly as the starting point for the stunning road up to the Saiq Plateau (see p.94), although there are a couple of sights in the town itself. The main attraction is the town's fort, the **Bait al Ridaydha**. This is a relatively modern structure, the original having been destroyed by the British during the Jebel War (see p.228); the fort has recently been renovated, and although there are rumours that it will eventually reopen to the public, no one seems to know when this might happen. The impressive **Falaj al Khatmeen** (one of five *aflaj* across the country that were collectively listed as a UNESCO World Heritage Site in 2006) flows through the middle of the fort, emerging at the front in a raised, walled channel which continues on past a small stone-built mosque and watchtower.

Largely obscured by the modern town is **Old Birkat**, just east of the centre – one of the region's most atmospheric abandoned villages, with a higgledy-piggledy pile of ruined mudbrick houses stacked up virtually on top of one another on a steep hillside, with a *falaj* (still flowing) running through the middle and a watchtower perched at the top. It's possible to climb (with care) most of the way up, following the main pathway between the houses, and then a series of steps between and within the ruined structures, emerging on a terrace offering views of further mudbrick structures and five or so watchtowers dotted on the surrounding hills.

Old Birkat is surprisingly well hidden among the backstreets of the modern town. To find it, continue along the main road through town, about 500m past the turn-off to the castle. Look out for the small shop signed "Bicycles & Motorcycles Sale" on your right, and a small mudbrick watchtower just beyond (if you reach a patch of open date plantation on your right you've gone too far). Past the shop but before the watchtower, take the narrow road on your left and follow it for about 100m to reach the old village.

Birkat al Mawz is a convenient place to **rent a 4WD** to go up Jebel Akhdar – see p.94 for further details. If you want **to stay** hereabouts, the *Golden Tulip* hotel (see p.87) is just 5km down the road in the direction of Nizwa.

Nizwa نزوى

The principal city of the interior, **NIZWA** played a key role in the history of Oman for well over a thousand years, from the earliest days of Islam through to the 1950s, when the country was finally unified under the rule of Sultan Said bin Taimur. For much of this time, the city served as the capital of the interior and seat of the country's ruling imams, the religious leaders who presided over an independent state quite separate from the sultans of Muscat down on the coast. As such, Nizwa had until quite recently a reputation for tribal belligerence and religious conservatism verging on fanaticism. Ibn Battuta, visiting Nizwa in 1329, described the Omanis as "a bold and brave race … the tribes are perpetually at war with each other", while Wilfred Thesiger, travelling through the area some six centuries afterwards in the late 1940s, was advised by his Bedu companions to avoid the town on pain of arrest, imprisonment or worse.

Ironically, in the sixty years since Thesiger's aborted visit, Nizwa has reinvented itself as one of Oman's most welcoming destinations for foreign travellers. It's a thoroughly enjoyable place to while away a few days, with a string of attractions including a magnificent fort, fine souks and a famous goat market, while the town's conveniently central location puts you within easy striking distance of pretty much anywhere in the Western Hajar, making it the perfect base to explore one of Oman's most rewarding regions.

Some history

One of the oldest cities in Oman, Nizwa owes its importance to its strategic location at the crossroads of trade routes between the Buraimi, Muscat and Dhofar, as well as its proximity to unusually abundant water sources (the town's Falaj Daris, see p.91, is the largest in the country). Known as "The Pearl of Islam", Nizwa served as capital of Oman under the Julanda dynasty in the sixth and seventh centuries AD – according to legend it was in Nizwa that the Julanda leaders became the first Omani converts to Islam in 630 AD. The town was chosen as capital in 793 AD at the beginning of the second imamate (see p.220), as its inland position made it a safer base for the imams than coastal Sohar, the previous capital, which was prone to attacks by the seafaring Persians. Nizwa subsequently remained the pre-eminent town of the interior for almost a millennium until challenged by Rustaq, to which the Ya'aruba imams (see p.221) decamped in 1624. Religion aside, Nizwa also developed into a major craft centre, home to skilled artisans working in silver, copper and leather.

Nizwa was caught up in the **Jebel War** (see p.228) – in the early 1950s the city's historic fort even suffered the indignity of being bombed by the British RAF. Since 1970, the city has begun to modernize and open up to the world. The city was connected to Muscat by a modern highway, while a major renovation of fort and souk was carried out during the 1990s and the new University of Nizwa opened in 2002.

Arrival, orientation and information

Nizwa sprawls along the main highway for the best part of 15km, although the historic centre itself is extremely small – scarcely a ten-minute walk from top to

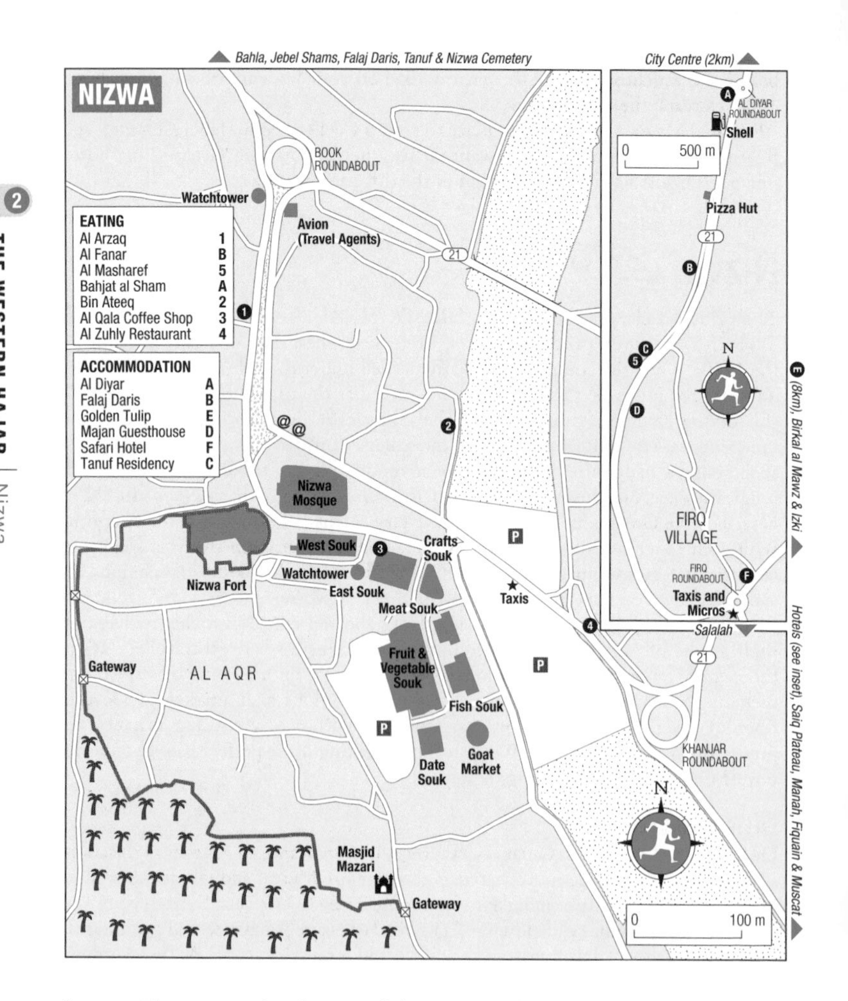

bottom. The main road makes a small detour around the centre, bounded by a pair of distinctive roundabouts. At the south end of town lies the **Khanjar Roundabout** (boasting a large sculpture of a *khanjar*), right next to the main parking area. The **Book Roundabout** (adorned with a pile of supersized books) is at the northern end. All the town's accommodation (see opposite) is strung out along the main road south of town.

There are a couple of good **internet** places on the north side of the Friday Mosque: the well-equipped Al Mutalik Internet Café and, a few doors down, Yanabiah Dharis Trading Internet Café above Al Esala City for Fashion shop; both charge 100bz per fifteen minutes.

Unlike virtually every other town in Oman, Nizwa is small enough to walk around. For trips further afield plentiful **taxis** can be found in the vast car park by the Khanjar roundabout, which is also the best place to pick up local micros. For bus and micro services to Muscat, it's usually quickest to head out to the Firq roundabout some 5km south of town, which sees a steady stream of passing traffic, much of which bypasses the town itself. The better hotels can probably set you up with a **car and/or guide**. Alternatively, try Ali al Rashidi at Avion travel agents (Ⓣ2541 0600) in the middle of town.

Accommodation

Disappointingly, there are no places to stay in the centre of Nizwa itself. All the following hotels are ranged along the main highway to Muscat, south of the centre, and are shown on the Nizwa map inset, opposite.

Al Diyar 2.5km from the centre, next to the Al Diyar roundabout Ⓣ2541 2402, Ⓦwww.aldiyarhotel.com. This plain modern hotel is one of the nicer places to stay in Nizwa, and the closest to the centre. Rooms (some with balconies) are spacious and nicely furnished, though come with shower only. There's also a small pool, and passable food at the attached *Bahjat al Sham* restaurant (see p.91). ❺

Falaj Daris 4km from the centre Ⓣ2541 0500, Ⓦwww.falajdarishotel.com. Designed like a miniature fort with discreet Omani touches, this well-run three-star is easily the most appealing place to stay in Nizwa. Rooms are nicely furnished (though with rather poky bathrooms) and arranged around a pair of attractive courtyards. Facilities include a gym and two pools (one "cool", the other at normal outdoor temperature), plus a kids' pool and pool bar. The in-house *Al Fanar* restaurant (see p.91) is easily the best in town, and the hotel is also home to Nizwa's only licensed venues, including a couple of noisy live-music bars and the much more soothing *Castle Lounge* (see p.90). They can also arrange a vehicle with driver-cum-tour guide for mountain excursions. ❻

Golden Tulip 18km from the centre (and just 5km from Birkat al Mawz – see p.84) Ⓣ2543 1616, Ⓦwww.goldentulipnizwa.com. This rather charmless four-star is the most upmarket place to stay in the Nizwa area, although the setting in a windy and exposed spot next to the Muscat highway more or less in the middle of nowhere has zero appeal. The whole place is strangely overblown but also a little drab – and the public areas have the personality of a conference centre. Rooms are arranged around a pair of enclosed courtyard gardens; all come with balconies and are comfortable enough, if a bit chintzy. Facilities include a good-sized pool, plus a nice English-style pub, sports bar and pool bar and gym. Staff can arrange 4WDs with driver-cum-guide, although at rather pricey rates. Large discounts are available during the summer. ❼

Majan Guest House 5km from the centre Ⓣ2543 1910. This neat and cosy "guesthouse" (although it's really just a homely sort of hotel) is the nicest semi-budget option in town, with clean and cheerily furnished rooms. There are no in-house amenities, although the sociable *Al Masharef* café is just a five-minute stroll away, and the restaurant and bar at the *Falaj Daris* hotel are also within walking distance (around 15–20min) or a short drive. ❸

Safari Hotel 8km from the centre, just east of the Firq roundabout on the side road to Birkat al Mawz Ⓣ2543 2150, Ⓔsafari@motifoman.com. Some way from the town centre, this rather moribund place has clean but unappealing rooms and a small pool, but not much else. Rates are expensive for what you get – which isn't a lot. ❹

Tanuf Residency 4.5km from the centre Ⓣ2541 1601, Ⓕ2541 1059. The cheapest option in town, although still no bargain. Rooms are large but decidedly grimy, with dodgy electrics, erratic plumbing and a cockroach problem – fortunately, they're quite small. ❸

The Town

Nizwa is perhaps the only town in Oman which truly lives up to the sort of mental pictures which most foreigners have of Arabia, with a picture-perfect huddle of old-fashioned sandstone buildings clustered around the huge fort and mosque, surrounded by a quaint tangle of traditional souks. It's not entirely authentic, of course: the entire town was massively restored, rebuilt and generally scrubbed up in the 1990s, and now looks a lot neater than it ever did in its traditional heyday (at least excepting the wonderful old quarter of Al Aqr – see p.90), and you'll see more tourists here than anywhere else in the country outside Muttrah Souk in Muscat.

Even so, Nizwa preserves a decidedly traditional appeal. The whole place retains a fetchingly village-like atmosphere, particularly after dark, when the tourists who throng the town by day have largely disappeared and locals come out to sit on the streets and share news and gossip. Things are particularly colourful during the Friday Goat Market (see p.89), when Bedu women in traditional face masks descend on town, accompanied by old-timers in lopsided white turbans, with perhaps a traditional *khanjar* shoved into their belts and a rifle slung jauntily over their shoulders.

Nizwa Fort

At the very heart of the town, squeezed in tightly between souks and mosque, squats Nizwa's mighty **fort** (Sat–Thurs 9am–4pm, Fri 8–11am; 500bz). The fort is said to date back to the days of the ninth-century imam Al Salt bin Malik, although the present structure dates from the later seventeenth and early eighteenth centuries – part of the large-scale Ya'aruba building programme which also saw the construction of nearby Jabrin and Al Hazm forts.

The main tower

The complex actually consists of two separate elements: the "fort" proper (*q'ala*), essentially a single huge round tower; and the attached "castle" (*hisn*), containing the imam's residential quarters, the entire complex enclosed within a large, walled compound. The **fort-cum-tower** was constructed between 1649 and 1661 by the second Ya'aruba imam, Sultan bin Saif al Ya'aruba. This is the largest such structure in the country, 30m high and 36m in diameter – a fearsome symbol of military power which compensates for Nizwa's defensively vulnerable location in the middle of a wadi. The inside of the tower is filled to a depth of 15m with rocks and rubble, while the rounded walls are designed to withstand cannon fire, a combination which lends the entire structure unusual strength – anti-tank rockets, fired against the tower during the 1950s Jebel War (see p.228), are said to have simply bounced off the walls.

The **interior** of the tower is an excellent example of the defensive ingenuity of Oman's military architects. Access to the roof is provided by a single narrow, zigzagging staircase protected by five spiked metal doors with a "murder hole" overhead (look up to see the narrow slits above), down which boiling date syrup could be poured or heavy objects dropped, as well as water, in the event that hostile forces attempted to set fire to the fort. In the unlikely event that attackers did manage to force the doors, they were likely to fall into the deep holes, or "pitfalls", located immediately beyond. Fortunately for modern tourists, these are now glassed over, and light up helpfully as you approach.

At the **top** is a huge rooftop terrace, designed to provide a high, stable platform for the fort's twenty-odd cannon, which sit ranged around the perimeter, capable of providing 360-degree fire over considerable distances. Here you'll also see the openings of the various murder holes, along with a couple of wells and a vertiginous flagpole – pity (or admire) the fool who is tasked with changing the three light bulbs at the very top. A further 10m-high battlemented wall encloses the terrace, ringed with a walkway from which the garrison could fire on the enemy with rifles in the event that they got close enough to the fort without being blown to smithereens by the cannon. It also commands a bird's-eye view over the town and sprawling oases – a convenient vantage point from which to keep an eye on passing trade.

The residential quarters

Next to the tower stand the fort's extensive **residential quarters**, which acquired their present shape during the rule of imam Nasir bin Murshid al Ya'aruba in the early seventeenth century – a confusing little labyrinth of rooms, passages and stairwells. Rooms on the **ground floor** house an absorbing sequence of displays on just about every aspect of traditional Nizwa life: the *falaj*, silver and copper-working, forts, the Omani imams, keys, padlocks, the souk, mosques, all copiously illustrated and excellently explained, along with a couple of interesting old films.

A series of four rooms kitted out with traditional furnishings occupies most of the **first floor**, unusually spacious and high-ceilinged. Steps lead up to the roof from here for further views over the complex.

Nizwa mosque and the souks

Virtually in the shadow of the fort walls lies Nizwa's second major landmark, the **Nizwa Mosque** or **Friday Mosque** (officially the Sultan Qaboos Mosque; non-Muslims not permitted inside), with its distinctive – and much photographed – brown-tiled dome and minaret, best seen from the fort walls.

Stretching around the southern side of the mosque lies Nizwa's absorbing sequence of **souks**, one of the most interesting in the country. The souks were extensively renovated during the 1990s and now look picture perfect (apart from the East Souk, see below) – far from authentic, of course, but undeniably pretty. Most shops open for business around 8am but close between 10am and 11am and don't reopen until around 5pm in the afternoon, so don't expect to get much shopping done in the middle of the day.

The craft souks

The souks nearest the fort are the most touristy, showcasing Nizwa's celebrated artisanal traditions. The town is one of Oman's major **craft centres**, particularly famous for its silver jewellery and *khanjars*, as well as copperware, leatherwork and *mukkabbah*, the traditional round airtight containers with fluted lids, made from copper, which were used to store volatile items like frankincense and *bukhoor*. The number of tourists passing through tends to inflate prices – you might find cheaper Nizwa silverware in the Muttrah Souk in Muscat – although things are quieter later on in the day and after dark.

Opposite the castle, the attractive **West Souk** houses a mix of quaint shops with big wooden doors; some are devoted to touristy items like *khanjars* and walking sticks, others to more workaday items. East of here, the small **East Souk** is the most atmospheric in Nizwa, and the only one to have escaped restoration, with tiny shops clustered beneath crumbling mudbrick arches and columns, with weathered old wooden beams overhead propping up a makeshift corrugated-iron roof and Nizwa's most venerable collection of shopkeepers, most of whom appear to be almost as old as the buildings they sit in. Offerings here are fairly humdrum, featuring assorted foodstuffs, miscellaneous hardware and household items, although there are also a couple of photogenic spice stalls at the far end.

At the eastern end of the East Souk a miniature square is lined with shops displaying shelves full of quaint **Bahla pottery**; you can also see a short section of the old city **walls** here, running south from the pottery stalls along the back of the fruit and vegetable souk. Past here, the tiny **Crafts Souk** houses a further handful of shops stocking all the usual staples of the Omani souvenir hunter including *khanjars*, old Bedu silver jewellery, coffeepots, walking sticks, *mandoos* (traditional wooden chests) and old-fashioned rifles.

The food and livestock souks

The southern end of the souk area is more functional, with specific areas devoted to fish, meat and dates, plus a colourful **Fruit and Vegetable Souk**, with piles of produce and a string of stalls at the back selling tubs of *halwa*. Immediately south of here is the **Goat Market**, home to Nizwa's famous **Friday Market** where locals come to trade livestock – cows and goats in particular – which is sold by auction.

The market starts at around 8am and finishes at around 11am in time for *sala al Jumu'ah*, the congregational Friday prayers. Animals are walked around the circular stand at the centre of the market and auctioned off to the highest bidder, a lively scene featuring hundreds of locals, a fair few tourists, and an overwhelming smell of animal poo. Things can get particularly lively during the cattle auctions, as some of the more restive animals (including some rather large bulls) attempt to break free of their handlers and charge to freedom through the surrounding throng.

Al Aqr and the city walls

To get a sense of how Nizwa looked in the days before it was buffed up for the tourists, head to the old walled quarter of **Al Aqr**, within spitting distance of the fort and souks, though it sees surprisingly few tourists. To reach the heart of the quarter, head through the car park at the back of the Fruit and Vegetable Souk and exit via the steps at the back. You'll find yourself facing a marvellous traditional Omani townscape of imposing two- and three-storey houses in various stages of decay – although a surprising number are still in use, many of them inhabited by the town's sizeable Pakistani community.

It's a wonderful place for idle wandering along the narrow, shaded streets which honeycomb the area, looking out for the colourful doorways and finely carved wooden windows which still adorn many of the houses. There are also a couple of very old mudbrick mosques hereabouts: boxlike structures, lacking the usual minaret, with only a small pepper-pot dome of the roof betraying the buildings' function. The finest is the **Masjid Mazari** on the southern side of the district (no English sign; it's opposite Basateen Hai Alain Laundry), raised up on a high terrace, with access via a narrow flight of steps from street level.

Bounding the edge of Al Aqr is a section of Nizwa's surprisingly extensive and well-preserved **city walls**. These begin around the back of the fort (with whose own walls they link up) and continue for the best part of 1km, dotted with a fine sequence of crumbling gateways and watchtowers – Nizwa at its most memorably time-warped.

Nizwa cemetery

An even more ancient relic of Nizwa's past can be found at the old **Nizwa cemetery**, on the edge of town about 1km north of the centre (head north along the Bahla road then take the turning on the left signed Hay al Ain immediately in front of a large watchtower). The cemetery is huge, stretching for around 1km along either side of the road, and dotted with thousands of graves dating back to the arrival of Islam; many of the religious scholars and *qadis* (judges) for whom the town was once famous are said to be buried here. The actual gravestones themselves are extremely modest, typical of the Islamic tradition in general (and the Ibadhi tradition in particular), which discourages the construction of elaborate funerary monuments. Most are little more than simple, uncarved fragments of stone set upright in the ground, and at first sight the whole place can look more like some strange kind of rock plain than a man-made cemetery – an unusual and strangely haunting glimpse into Nizwa's distant past.

Eating and drinking

There are few culinary delights in Nizwa. Apart from the pleasant *Al Fanar* restaurant at the *Falaj Daris* hotel, you're limited to a string of no-frills cafés in the centre and along the main road south of town. For **drinking**, the only licensed venues in town are at the *Falaj Daris*, where you can choose between the pleasantly sedate *Castle Lounge* or hang out with the pool-playing locals at the *Sahara* bar, or at the deafening belly-dancing show next door.

Al Arzaq No-frills little café right in the centre of town serving up a short menu of the usual chicken, mutton, beef, fish and prawn curries and biryanis, plus a few local biryani-style dishes including *maqboos* and *kabooli*. Mains 1–2 OR.

Bahjat al Sham Set in the pleasant *Al Diyar* hotel (see p.87), this functional restaurant resembles the changing room at a municipal swimming pool. There's a wider-than-average selection of food, however, including a small selection of Lebanese meze, assorted "Gulf dishes" (chicken, mutton, fish biryanis and *maqboos*), lots of grills such as *shish taouk*, plus a few Indian and Chinese dishes (including a tiny vegetarian selection) and allegedly even pizzas, not to mention "hummus with foal" (they mean *foul* – beans) and, appropriately enough for a hotel restaurant, "checkin soup". Mains 1.5–2 OR.

Bin Ateeq Next to the wadi just east of the mosque. Identikit Nizwa branch of the countrywide chain. See p.71.

Al Fanar Restaurant *Falaj Daris* hotel (see p.87). Easily the best place to eat in town (and the only one that's licensed), with seating inside the bright dining room or in the pretty courtyard outside, set on a terrace around the hotel pool and with fairy lights twinkling in the trees after dark. The menu runs through all the usual staples, including meze to start with followed by a choice of Indian, Chinese and Continental standards, plus a few Omani options – try the tasty *kabsa dijaj*, chicken pieces buried in a mound of cardamom-scented orange rice with coriander on top. Note, however, that there may only be a buffet available some nights if the hotel is full. Most mains 3–6 OR.

Al Masharef Next to the *Tanuf Residency* (see p.87). Cheery Turkish restaurant – particularly good for grills and shwarma, while there's also a good selection of Lebanese-style pastries and fruit juices. There's plenty of outdoor seating, and usually a big screen rigged up showing live football – a popular evening hangout among locals.

Al Qala Coffee Shop Built into the side of the archway linking the East and West Souks, this hole-in-the-wall café offers a good pit stop for hot and cold drinks while exploring the town, with shady outdoor seating under the trees, and plenty of people-watching opportunities.

Al Zuhly Restaurant Unpretentious streetside joint, with fine views of the town (beautifully floodlit after dark) from its outdoor seating and plumes of smoke from the kebab grills outside. The inexpensive menu features the usual meat and fish curries, masalas and biryanis, although you're probably better off sticking to the tasty shwarma sandwiches and plates (the chicken is a lot better than the beef). Expect to eat your meal to a soundtrack of locals driving up and honking their horns for in-car takeaways. Mains 0.8–1.3 OR.

Around Nizwa

There are several rewarding sights in the immediate environs of Nizwa. North of the city lie the crumbling remains of the atmospheric old mudbrick town of **Tanuf**, while nearby you can have a look at a section of the **Falaj Daris**, the largest in Oman. South of the city lies another extensive ruined mudbrick town at **Manah**, and the quaint little **Al Fiyquin Fort**.

North of Nizwa: Falaj Daris and Tanuf

One of the keys to Nizwa's former prosperity was its plentiful water supplies – there were formerly 134 *aflaj* in the Nizwa *wilayat*, of which over a hundred are still in use. The biggest of the lot is the mighty **Falaj Daris**, the largest *falaj* in Oman, and one of the five collectively listed as UNESCO World Heritage Sites in 2006. A short section of the *falaj* to the north of Nizwa has now been restored and turned into a popular little park and picnic area. To get here, head out on the road to Bahla. A blue sign on your right around 7km from Nizwa points downhill to the *falaj*, just 100m off the main road. The *falaj* here is impressively large, big enough to take a bath in places, which you'll probably see locals doing, and has been preserved in more or less its original condition, built up with stones (although some sections have been patched up with ugly concrete blocks). Unfortunately, only around 200m of *falaj* is actually visible here before it disappears underground at either end, while the suburban park, complete with kids' playground and a junior quadbiking centre, doesn't add to the atmosphere.

Altogether more memorable are the remains of the old town of **TANUF**, 12km north of Nizwa. The main draw here is the atmospherically ruined **old town**, a large swathe of fragmentary mudbrick buildings which sprawls over the best part of a kilometre next to the modern village. This is all that's left of the original town, which was bombed by the RAF during the 1950s Jebel War (see p.228) at the request of Sultan Said bin Taimur, who wished to crush the power of local warlord Suleyman bin Himyar al Nabhani, the self-styled "King of the Jebel Akhdar". Not much remains beyond the occasional wall or eroded tower, apart from a small mosque, which survives with internal arches and *mihrab* intact, although the whole site is eerily beautiful, in a rather melancholy way.

Immediately beyond the old town the road heads into the fine narrow gorge of **Wadi Tanuf**, best known nowadays as the source of the popular Tanuf mineral water, which is bottled from a spring here and sold countrywide. Look to your left and you'll see a remarkable elevated *falaj*, built into the base of the mountain several metres above the floor of the wadi – in wet weather the *falaj* sometimes overflows and cascades down the rock, creating a spectacular little impromptu fountain. A rough track (4WD only) continues down the gorge for a further 5km or so, hemmed in by increasingly sheer cliffs, leading into **Wadi Qashah** and the village of Al Far. The track ends here, although it's possible to continue even further into the mountains on foot, aiming for the abandoned village of Al Rahbah (around 90min one-way).

To **reach Tanuf**, follow the brown sign off the Nizwa–Bahla highway signed Wadi Tanuf (if approaching from Bahla, ignore the blue sign to Tanuf about 5km further down the road by the Al Maha petrol station and continue until you reach the brown sign).

South of Nizwa: Fiquain (الفيقين) and Manah (منح)

South of Nizwa you leave the mountains behind, entering the great swathe of largely flat and featureless gravel desert which blankets the south of the country, bisected by **Highway 31** as it begins its long and lonely journey to Salalah, almost 1000km distant.

There are two attractions here, both within easy striking distance of Nizwa. The first is the sleepy village of **FIQUAIN**, home to the attractively restored **Al Fiyquin Fort**. Despite its name, this is a fortified house (*sur*) rather than a traditional fort, an unusually tall and narrow structure which towers over the crumbling remains of the old mudbrick village. Inside, 66 steps climb up past a sequence of small, bare rooms to the rooftop terrace; look out for the series of circular openings in the middle of each floor, running the entire height of the building, which were formerly used for drawing up buckets of water and other supplies. You can't actually see much from the rooftop terrace thanks to the high walls which enclose it – unless, that is, you fancy climbing up the watchtower which crowns the building via a series of perilous handholds projecting from the outer wall. The house opens according to no discernible pattern, depending on when the guardian or anyone else is around; mornings are probably your best bet.

To **reach Fiquain**, head to the Firq roundabout and drive 5km south along Highway 31 until you reach the left turn with a blue sign to Manah and Karsha and a brown sign to the fort itself. Head some 8km along this road and then take the turning on the right marked with a blue sign to Al Feequain and a brown sign to Al Fiyquin Fort and drive through the village to reach the fort, clearly visible above the surrounding houses.

A short drive beyond Fiquain lies **MANAH**, home to one of the country's most impressive ruined towns, which sprawls for 1km or so around the edge of modern Manah. Unfortunately, the extensive site is currently closed for restoration, although you can still get a decent sense of the ruins of the mudbrick houses, dotted with a number of impressive stone watchtowers including one particularly tall and slender square tower whose top has crumbled dramatically away like a rotten tooth.

Walks in the Western Hajar

The Western Hajar boasts virtually limitless **trekking** possibilities, with spectacular mountain scenery and a well-established network of trails – many of them along old donkey tracks through the mountains. Many of these paths have now been officially recognized as public trekking routes by the Oman government; some have been waymarked with yellow, white and red flags painted onto rocks en route to assist with route-finding, although you may still prefer to enlist the services of a specialist guide to make sure you don't get lost in what is often inhospitable terrain. The high altitude of many of the treks means that temperatures are pleasantly temperate, although it's wise not to underestimate the possible challenges of even relatively short hikes. Carry ample supplies of water and warm waterproof clothing at all times – weather conditions can change with spectacular suddenness up in the *jebel*.

For an excellent overview of some of the most rewarding routes, pick up a copy of **Oman Trekking**, published by Explorer, which details some of the country's finest hikes, including ten in the Western Hajar, and one through Wadi Tiwi in Sharqiya. Unfortunately, virtually all the treks are linear rather than circular, meaning that you'll either have to retrace your steps or arrange for transport to collect you at the end of the walk. The following are the best of the Western Hajar routes.

Around Jebel Shams and Wadi Nakhr

Route W4: Al Qannah Plateau to Jebel Shams (9.5km; 5–6hr one-way). This extended and challenging hike follows the sheer cliffs ringing the top of Wadi Nakhr (Oman's "Grand Canyon") to the summit of the country's highest mountain, with views into Wadi Sahtan and Wadi Bani Awf en route.

Route W6: Al Qannah Plateau to As Sab (3.5km; 1.5hr one-way). Probably the most famous walk in Oman, popularly known as the "Balcony Walk", this spectacular trek follows an old donkey trail inside the rim of Wadi Nakhr to the abandoned village of As Sab (aka Sab Bani Khamis). Links up with route W6a.

Route W6a: Al Qannah Plateau, Wadi Ghul to Al Khatayam (6km; 3–4hr one-way). Moderate trek following an old donkey path above the southern end of Wadi Nakhr. Links up with route W6.

Around Wadi Bani Awf

Route W8: Balad Sayt (5km; 3–4hr one-way). Challenging high-level walk which climbs from the beautiful village of Bilad Sayt up the northern flank of the Western Hajar above Wadi Bani Awf. Links up with routes W9 and W10h.

Route W9: Misfat al Abryeen (9km; 5–6hr one-way). Long trek along old donkey trail starting at the beautiful village of Misfat al Abryeen, with views into Wadi Bani Awf en route. Links up with routes W8 and W10h.

Route W10h: Sharaf al Alamayn (3.5km; 1.5–2hr one-way). Relatively easy high-altitude walk from the village of Sharaf al Alamayn along the top of the mountains. Links up with routes W8 and W9.

Around Jebel Akhdar

Route W18b: Seeq to Al Aqr (4km; 2hr one-way). An easy but spectacular walk through the traditional villages lining the edge of the Saiq Plateau, following the rim of the cavernous Wadi al Ayn.

Route W24a & W25: Wukan to Hadash via Jebel Akdhar (14km; 7–10hr one-way, 10–13hr circular walk if combined with Route W24b). Challenging and extremely exposed high-altitude trek around the northern edge of the Jebel Akdhar above the Ghubrah Bowl. Links up with trek W24b to form a circular route, just about doable by very fit walkers in a single day.

Route W24b: Hadash to Wukan via Al Qawrah (4km; 2.5–3hr one-way). Short but challenging walk through a trio of mountain villages.

To **reach Manah**, continue for about 2km along the main road beyond Fiquain, passing a large mosque on your left to reach a roundabout at the entrance to the town. Turn right here (signed to Al Sooq) and continue for 1.5km until you see the ruins rising on the left-hand side of the road behind the modern shops.

Jebel Akhdar (الجبل الأخضر) and the Saiq Plateau

Northeast of Nizwa rises the great limestone massif of the **Jebel Akhdar**, centred on the **Saiq Plateau** (pronounced "Sirq", and often spelt Sirq or Seeq). This is one of Oman's more unusual natural curiosities: an extensive upland plateau, lying at an altitude of around 2000m and ringed by craggy summits to the north and the vertiginous gorge of Wadi al Ayn to the south. The plateau has been extensively farmed for at least a thousand years thanks to its temperate Mediterranean climate, which allows for the cultivation of many types of fruit which cannot survive the heat of the lowlands: peaches, pears, grapes, apples and pomegranates all flourish here, along with a wide range of vegetables and the area's famed roses (see p.98). The plateau is particularly beguiling during the hot summer months, and deliciously cool after the heat of the plains below.

The plateau was formerly one of the highest and most inaccessible inhabited regions in Oman, although it's been largely tamed by a carpet-smooth modern tarmac road which allows access to the plateau from Birkat al Mawz (see p.84) in around forty minutes (compared to the gruelling six-hour hike which was formerly required) – though you'll still need a 4WD to get up it, thanks to the local police regulations described below. The top of the plateau is surprisingly developed in places. The sprawling modern town of Saih Katenah is the main local eyesore, while the presence of a large military camp and firing range at the top doesn't help, accompanied by endless barbed-wire fences and assorted military hardware. Away from these areas, however, the plateau remains one of the most beautiful places in the Western Hajar, dropping into the huge natural chasm of **Wadi al Ayn** and ringed by the idyllic traditional villages of **Al Aqr** and **Al Ayn**.

How green was my mountain

The name Jebel Akhdar means "The Green Mountain", a somewhat unlikely moniker, given the massif's largely inhospitable terrain, with vast expanses of bare rock on which only the hardiest shrubs and ground plants are able to survive. The most convincing explanation for the unlikely name is that it refers to the days when the Saiq Plateau and other parts of the surrounding mountains were covered in a dense carpet of agricultural terracing, pieces of which can still be seen today below the villages of Al Ayn and Al Aqr. An alternative if slightly less convincing theory holds that the name derives from the colour of the limestone from which the mountains are formed, and which can take on a decidedly greenish coloration in certain lights – in complete contrast to the reddish ophiolite hills which surround the plateau to the east and south.

Further ambiguity surrounds the present use of the name. On maps, the name **Jebel Akhdar** is generally used to refer to the entire section of the Hajar mountains running west from the Sumail Gap as far as Jebel Shams. In practice, however, most locals (and local road signs) use the name to describe the area of mountains immediately north of Nizwa, around the Saiq Plateau (which is the sense used in this guide). The area further west, beyond Al Hamra, is usually described as **Jebel Shams** (see p.102).

Wadi Muaydin

Leaving Birkat al Mawz along the road to Jebel Akdhar, you'll pass the entrance to the dramatic **Wadi Muaydin** (on your left about 5km from Birkat, and 1km before you reach the police checkpoint at the bottom of the road up to Jebel Akdhar). This is the starting point for a steep six-hour hike up to the top of the plateau, formerly one of the principal routes up into the mountains, and far more direct than the modern road, which loops its way circuitously up the back of the hills. It's probably best to find a guide if you fancy tackling the hike up to the plateau – most reliably done via a travel agent in Muscat, although you could try asking around among the drivers who hang out at Birkat al Mawz (see p.84). The initial section of the wadi is also driveable (even in a 2WD) for the first 5km or so along a good graded track between towering limestone walls – a good place to get your rental car dirty.

The Saiq Plateau

It's 32km along the twisting road from Birkat al Mawz up to the plateau – a journey of around forty minutes. Some 6km beyond Birkat al Mawz, the road up to the Saiq plateau begins to climb in earnest. There's a police **checkpoint** here, and if you're not in a 4WD you'll be forced to turn back – a shame, given that the wide and beautifully engineered road up into the hills would be perfectly feasible in a 2WD.

From here the road begins to hairpin dramatically upwards into the hills, with huge sweeps of rocky mountainside dotted with the small, hardy shrubs and trees – *butt*, wild olive and the occasional stately juniper – which manage to suck a living out of the bare rock. The mountains are a study in naked geology, formed out of huge slabs of limestone which have been tilted sideways over millions of years to produce the evenly sloping mountainsides and neat right-angle summits you see today, and whose colour changes according to the light from a sere, green-grey with occasional splashes of brownish-orange – a striking contrast to the much smaller and more irregularly shaped reddish ophiolite hills below. A series of viewpoints on the road up allows you to stop and admire increasingly expansive views.

Manakher and Saih Katenah

After about thirty minutes' drive you'll get your first sight of the plateau away on your left: a spacious expanse of flat upland ringed by mountains, although the views from this direction are rather spoilt by the sprawling development of Saih Katenah – something of a surprise after the pristine mountain scenery on the way up. Shortly afterwards, a narrow side road heads off on the right to **MANAKHER** (pronounced "M'Nakhr"), a pretty little village clustered around a narrow lush wadi, although less memorable than the villages further into the plateau.

Back on the main road, a further ten minutes' drive brings you to the top of the plateau and its major settlement, the unattractive town of **SAIH KATENAH** – a surprisingly extensive place this high up in the hills, complete with a large modern mosque, petrol station and the nearby *Al Jebel Al Akhdhar* hotel (see p.97).

Wadi al Ayn and around

On the far side of Saih Katenah lies the spectacular **Wadi al Ayn** (although throaty local pronunciation can make it sound something like "al Rin"), a wonderful, Grand Canyon-like chasm which ploughs through the heart of the plateau. The initial stop on most tours is just south of Saih Katenah at **Diana Point**, the first of many memorable viewpoints over the gorge – named in honour of the lonely Princess of Wales, who stared into the abyss here during a state visit in the 1980s.

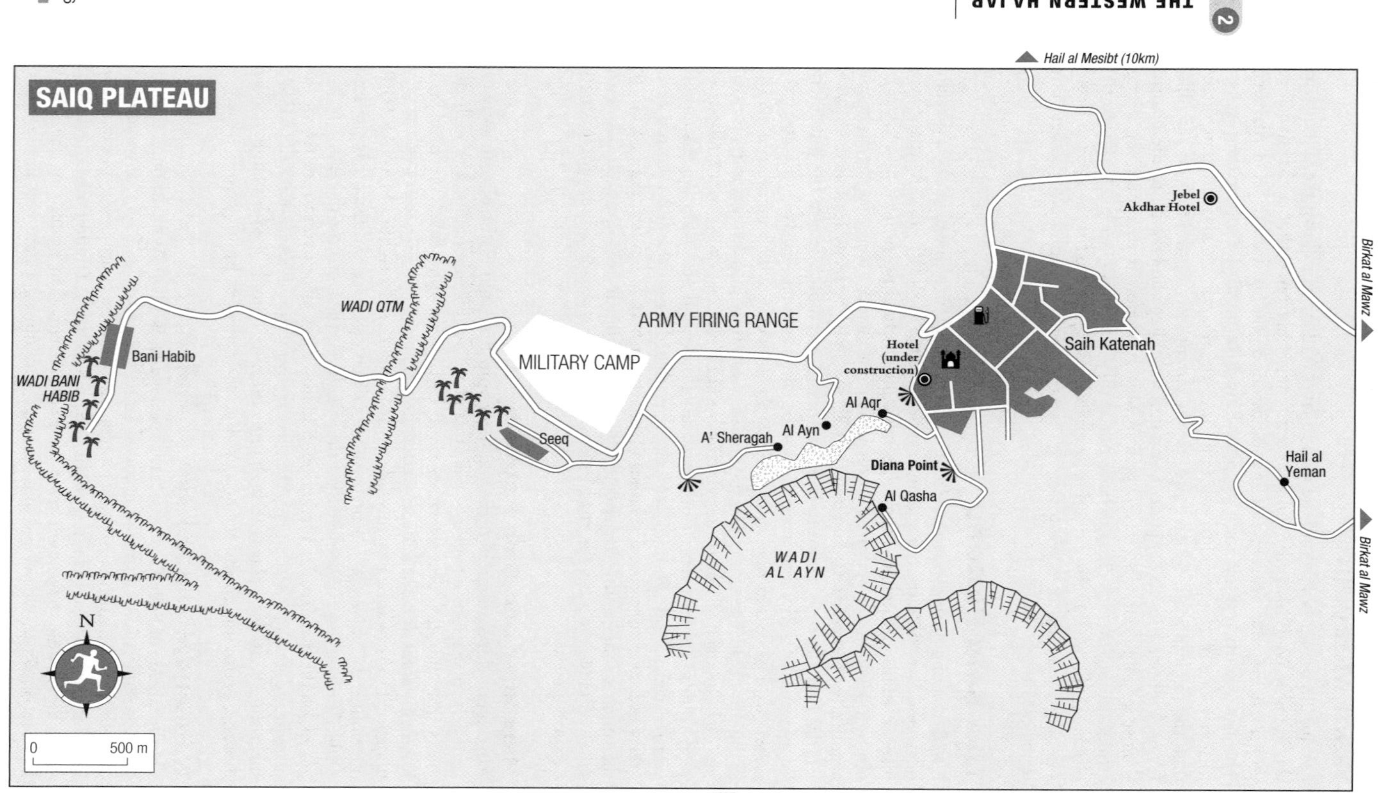
SAIQ PLATEAU
Hail al Mesibt (10km)
Birkat al Mawz
Birkat al Mawz
Wadi Muaydin
Jebel Akdhar Hotel
Saih Katenah
Hotel (under construction)
Hail al Yeman
ARMY FIRING RANGE
MILITARY CAMP
WADI QTM
Bani Habib
WADI BANI HABIB
Seeq
A' Sheragah
Al Ayn
Al Aqr
Diana Point
Al Qasha
WADI AL AYN
N
0
500 m

Beyond Fayadiah, a trio of remarkable hanging villages clings perilously to the edges of the chasm, with an intricate layer-cake of terraced fields edging their way down into the gorge (there's a spectacular view over all three from the edge of Saih Katenah near Diana Point). The first is the village of **AL AQR**, famous for its rose gardens (see p.98) and one of the prettiest villages in the country, with a cluster of little houses, walled gardens bisected with *aflaj* and an amazing viewpoint over Wadi al Ayn below. A short distance beyond lies the similarly picturesque village of **AL AYN**, perched on an unusual rock-spur projecting out from the escarpment (known to geologists as a "travertine cone", formed over hundreds of thousands of years by the evaporation of mineral-rich springs). It's possible to walk between Al Aqr and Al Ayn in around twenty minutes along a pretty little trail, following the yellow, white and red flags painted onto the rocks. This is part of the longer **hiking route** W18b (see p.93) which continues on to the village of Seeq – around two hours' walk one-way.

Beyond here, the main road continues past an army firing range and then a side turn to the village of **A'SHERAGEH**, more modern and less interesting than Al Ayn and Al Aqr, though with further spectacular views into the gorge below. Note that the final section of road down into the village is perilously steep and it's best not to attempt it if you're driving yourself. Park at the top, just before the houses begin.

West to Bani Habib

Past A'Sherageh, the main road continues west across the plateau, flanked by an ugly military camp which stretches alongside the road from the A'Sherageh turning as far as **SEEQ**, after which the plateau is named – another surprisingly large (but largely modern) village tucked away in a hollow.

Past here the road twists down through the narrow, palm-filled **Wadi Qtm** and on to the uninspiring modern village of **BANI HABIB**, where the main road across the plateau terminates. Park your vehicle at the end of the road and follow the stone steps leading down into a lush narrow wadi filled with fruit trees and flowering shrubs – a solid mass of greenery amid the bare surrounding rock. Turn left here and scramble along the wadi floor for about 50m and you'll see some rough steps on the far side. It's possible to climb up these to reach part of the old village, its abandoned houses made of stone rather than mudbrick. From here there are memorable views over the rest of the old village, clinging to the edges of the narrow, steep-sided wadi, running between sandstone cliffs.

Plateau practicalities

There's no public transport to the plateau, and 2WDs aren't allowed up, meaning that you'll have to **hire a 4WD** to visit. The cheapest option is to get yourself to Birkat al Mawz (see p.84) and pick up a car with driver-cum-guide there. A few drivers with cars can usually be found hanging around the square in front of the fort; stand around looking lost for a couple of minutes, and someone will probably come and talk to you (or, failing this, try one of the car rental places at the entrance to the village). The current going rate is 30 OR for a tour of the plateau. These last around three to four hours, although drivers are pretty relaxed timewise and won't rush you. You could easily drive yourself if you have a 4WD, although the drivers double as guides and will show you places and viewpoints you might otherwise well miss. Alternatively, you may be able to arrange a tour through your hotel in Nizwa.

Currently, the only **accommodation** option on the plateau is the friendly and well-run *Jebel Akdhar Hotel* (Ⓣ2542 9009, Ⓦwww.jabalakhdharhotel.com.om; ⑤ Sun–Tues, ⑥ Wed–Sat), about 1km east of Saih Katenah. This makes a pleasant place to hole up for a night or two, with bright and cheery rooms, clean and very comfortably furnished. Meals are available in the attractive restaurant (licensed) under a

The rose harvest

The Saiq Plateau – the small village of Al Aqr (see p.97) in particular – is famous for its **rose gardens**, probably brought to Oman from Persia, where rose cultivation has a long history. The damask rose (*Rosa Damascena*) flourishes here thanks to the plateau's temperate climate; the gardens are at their most colourful for a few weeks in April, when the flowers come into bloom.

Aesthetics aside, the Saiq Plateau's rose gardens are also of considerable economic value thanks to their use in the production of the highly prized Omani **rose-water**. The petals of the fully grown roses are carefully plucked (usually early in the morning, when the weather is coolest, to help preseve their intense aroma) and then taken off for processing. This remains a largely traditional affair. The petals are stuffed into an earthenware pot with water, sealed up in an oven (traditionally heated using *sidr* wood, although nowadays it's more likely to be gas) and boiled for about two hours. The resultant rose-flavoured steam condenses into a metal container inside the pot, which is then repeatedly filtered to produce a clear liquid. Demand for the area's rose-water usually outstrips supply. Genuine Omani rose-water is itself an important ingredient in Omani *halwa* (see p.28), while it can also be added to drinks and food. Locals believe that it's also good for the heart, and can ease headaches if rubbed into the scalp.

stained-glass dome, and staff can provide details and sketch-maps of local walks and attractions, and summon local guides on request. Two **new hotels** are apparently under construction on the other side of Saih Katenah (see map, p.96), the first due to open in October 2011, though no details were available at the time of writing.

Al Hamra and around

Tucked in at the foot of the mountains some 40km northwest of Nizwa (and 20km north of Bahla) lie several of the region's most memorable attractions, including **Al Hamra**, one of Oman's most atmospheric traditional towns, and **Misfat al Abryeen**, one of its prettiest villages, while it's also worth making a short detour to the impressive **Al Hoota cave** nearby.

Al Hamra الحمراء

Magical **AL HAMRA** is one of the best-preserved old towns in Oman, with a warren of stony, rubble-strewn alleyways lined with endless traditional mudbrick houses tumbling down the hillside to the idyllic oasis below; it's hauntingly time-warped, although as throughout the rest of Oman these old dwellings are now being systematically abandoned.

Much of the pleasure of a visit here simply consists of getting lost amid the winding streets, although there are a couple of low-key attractions to head for, close to one another on the main street which runs through the bottom of the old town. Best of the two is the **Bait al Safah** (daily 9am–5.30pm; closed June–Aug; 2 OR), a kind of living museum of old Oman occupying an exquisitely restored traditional house done up with old artefacts and traditional furnishings. It gives a nice (although perhaps rather sanitized) impression of what these houses might originally have looked like, while a few jolly old ladies from the town sit around baking bread, grinding coffee and flour, and so on.

Close by lies the **Beit al Jabal** (daily 9am–5pm; 2 OR), also on the main street through the bottom of the old town. Occupying another of Al Hamra's traditional houses, this is a much less manicured offering than Bait al Safah, with rough-hewn mudbrick walls and rickety steps – very atmospheric, and probably a lot more authentic as well. Unfortunately, the entrance price is a rip-off and there's not much to actually see apart from a dusty collection of not particularly interesting antiques and curios, including the usual old swords, coins, pots and suchlike.

Getting to Al Hamra

The **turning to Al Hamra**, and also Al Hoota Cave, is off the main Nizwa–Bahla highway by the shops with the big Toyota sign on top. Head along this road for 12km to reach the roundabout on the outskirts of Al Hamra by the Shell garage. Go straight across this roundabout (signed towards Al Hoota Cave), and then straight across a second roundabout (signed Center City). Follow this road as it curves left through the new town, passing a brown sign on your left to **Misfat al Abryeen** (see p.101). Ignore this turning, continuing straight ahead until you reach a fork in the road by a mosque at the edge of the old town. Take the right-hand fork, which climbs up to a ridge above the old town (you'll see lots of mudbrick houses on your left). Park somewhere along here and walk down into the old town.

Al Hoota Cave كهف الهوتة

Around 9km past Al Hamra (see directions above) lies **Al Hoota Cave** (also spelled Al Hota; Sat–Thurs 9am–1pm & 2–6pm, Fri 9am–noon & 2–6pm; last tours at 5.15pm daily. 5.5 OR; no photography; Ⓦwww.alhootacave.com), a spectacular cave complex which offers a rare opportunity to look underneath Oman's remarkable geological surface. Access to the cave is via guided tour only; these depart between every fifteen minutes and every hour depending on the time of day. There's also an interesting exhibition on the cave and Omani geology upstairs, as well as a pleasant café.

A quaint little **train** shuttles visitors between the entrance and the cave itself, about 300m distant. The caves are some two to three million years old and stretch for 5km in total, of which slightly less than 1km is open to visitors, accessible via a metal walkway with handrails all the way around (plus a few flights of stairs). The section open to visitors is impressively large: a huge, sepulchral cavern, though the stalagmites and stalactites are unimpressively gloopy, like the melted stumps of enormous candles. At the far end steps lead down to the edge of a lake, the largest of three in the caves – a rather spooky expanse of water stretching away under a low rock ceiling. The lake is 900m long and up to 10m deep in places, and is home to a unique species of blind fish, although you probably won't see any.

Wadi Bani Awf وادي بني عوف

Beyond Al Hoota Cave lies the start of the spectacular descent of the Western Hajar down a sheer escarpment through **Wadi Bani Awf** (or Auf), widely considered the most memorable off-road drive in the country. This is Oman at its most nerve-janglingly dramatic, with stupendous scenery and a rough, vertiginous track which challenges the skills of even experienced off-road drivers – not to be attempted lightly, and best avoided during or after rain.

The entire off-road section between Sharafat al Alamayn and the main road at Awabi (see p.120) takes around 2–3hr. The track is regularly graded but gets very churned up after spells of bad weather. It's also possible to tackle the route in reverse, driving up from the Batinah, although the driving is easier and the views generally better heading downhill.

Geology of the Hajar

Geology is all around you in Oman in a way that's matched by few other places on earth. For professional geologists, the country is one of the most interesting on the planet, and even casual visitors cannot fail to be intrigued by the spectacular rock formations which fill every corner of the Hajar mountains, where the lack of vegetation and soil cover leaves milllions of years of complex geological processes exposed, often with textbook clarity.

Much of Oman's geological interest (and, by extension, its spectacular mountain scenery) is the result of its location at the southeast corner of the **Arabian continental plate** where it meets the Eurasian (aka Asian) oceanic plate. As the Red Sea grows wider, Oman is being pushed slowly north and forced underneath the Eurasian plate (a rare example of a continental plate being "subducted" by an oceanic plate), a geological pile-up which has created the long mountainous chain of the Hajar.

Most of the rocks now making up the Hajar mountains were actually formed **underwater**. As the Arabian plate was driven underneath the Eurasian, large masses of what was originally submarine rock have been pushed on top of the mainland ("obducted"), sometimes travelling hundreds of kilometres inland – which explains the incongruous abundance of marine fossils found buried near the peaks of some of Arabia's highest mountains. Most of the main part of the range is made of up various types of limestone, ranging from older grey and yellow formations through to outcrops of so-called geological "exotics" – pale, whitish "islands" of younger limestone, such as Jebel Misht and Jebel Khawr, north and south of Al Ayn (see p.139) respectively.

Surrounding the limestone are Oman's celebrated **ophiolites** – rocks from the oceanic crust which have been lifted out of the water onto a continental plate. These are of particular interest to geologists in that they reveal processes which are normally buried kilometres underwater. They also provide Oman with one of its most distinctive landscapes, forming the fields of low, irregular, crumbling red-rock mountains which you can see along the Sumail Gap, around the Rustaq Loop and in many parts of the Eastern Hajar.

If you're interested in exploring further, pick up a copy of Samir Hanna's *Field Guide to the Geology of Oman* (see p.240).

Sharafat al Alamayn

The route starts between Al Hamra and Al Hoota Cave – follow the signs to Hat and Bilad Sayt. The first section is along good tarmac road which twists up to the top of the escarpment and the wonderful viewpoint of **Sharafat al Alamayn**, one of the finest panoramas in Oman, with views across the entire Western Hajar and down towards the coast below – it's worth the trip up in a 2WD even if you don't plan to continue. The fine **hiking route** W10h (see p.93) heads west from here along the top of the ridge, connecting with route W9, which heads up to the top of the *jebel* and Mifat al Abryeen, and route W8, which descends to the village of Bilad Sayt.

If you want to **stay** hereabouts, *Al Hoota Rest House* (Ⓣ9282 8873; ❺ half-board only), about 1km down the road before you reach Sharafat al Alamayn, provides simple lodgings in a mix of spacious modern chalets or rooms; it's a pleasant spot above the mountains though the rest house itself is a bit cheerless and rather expensive for what you get.

Bilad Sayt and Wadi Bimah

Past Sharafat al Alamayn the tarmac ends and a rough track begins worming its way down the almost vertical escarpment, offering spectacular views all the way. It's around thirty minutes of bumping and grinding from here to the village of

HAT, which you'll see off the track on your right, watered by a spectacular *falaj* which comes tumbling down from the mountains. Past here the track continues across a very rough wadi bed – difficult going even in a 4WD, and not to be attempted after rain.

Another ten to fifteen minutes down the track brings you to the village of **BILAD SAYT**, 2km down a (signed) side-turning off the main track. Tucked away in the folds of the mountains, this Shangri-La-like settlement is one of the most famous traditional villages in Oman, although its size and relative modernity (complete with a big red-and-white pylon, telephone wires and a large modern school) come as something of a surprise given the remote and inhospitable location. The core of the village remains magical, however, with a picturesque pile of small houses, crowned with a tiny fort, sitting above a lush swathe of immaculate terraced fields.

Another fifteen minutes beyond Bilad Sayt you'll see a deep gorge in the mountains below you on the right. This is **Wadi Bimah**, or "Snake Gorge", as it's popularly known, an impossibly narrow crack running through the surrounding mountains. The entrance to the gorge lies a couple of kilometres further down the track, about twenty minutes beyond Bilad Sayt. It's possible to scramble into the gorge over the jumble of boulders lining the wadi floor, although the gorge should be avoided if there's any hint of rain – people have drowned here in flash floods, during which the wadi can fill up with frightening speed.

Past here the track finally levels off, running through a narrow pass between red cliffs before reaching the junction with the side-track leading into **Wadi Sahtan** and the extensive **Sahtan Bowl**, a large natural hollow in the hills, rather like the Ghubrah Bowl (see p.119), dotted with old-fashioned villages. The area is particularly famous for its honey, and many of the locals still keep bees. From here, it's a short drive back to the main road near Awabi.

Misfat al Abryeen مصفاة العبريين

Sleepy **MISFAT AL ABRYEEN** (often abbreviated to Misfat, or Misfah) is one of the prettiest traditional villages in Oman, a picturesque huddle of old ochre-coloured stone buildings looking, from certain angles, a bit like a medieval Italian hill village. Arriving at the small parking area at the edge of the village you'll see only a single street climbing steeply up the hillside. Dive down one of the side alleys, however, and you'll find yourself amid a marvellous warren of twisting lanes, covered passages, gateways and meandering flights of steps – all of which bring you down, sooner or later, to the *falaj* which runs below the village, surrounded by lush bougainvillea, banana palms and other greenery.

Once you've explored the village, head back to the main road, walk up the hill and then down the steps on the far side to rejoin the **falaj** as it exits the village running through a rocky, steep-sided gorge crowded with date palms and tiny terraced fields. You can walk along the *falaj* walls or the footpath which runs just above it for about 1km up into the gorge until the *falaj* disappears into a large rock. En route, notice the regular gaps in the side of the *falaj* from where subsidiary channels run off into fields below; these are kept blocked up with stones, which are removed when the adjacent fields need irrigating.

Back in the centre, it's also possible to scramble up the rocky hillside to the picturesquely ruined **watchtower** which stands above the village, and which is said to be over a thousand years old.

To **reach Misfat**, take the turning from Al Hamra described on p.99, then follow the road for around 8km. The road is narrow and twisty, but fine for a 2WD. If you want to see more of the surrounding area, **hiking route W9** (see p.93) heads west of here across the top of the hills.

Jebel Shams جبل شمس

The mountains on this side of Nizwa are much less developed than those on the Saiq Plateau, which makes for more continuously spectacular scenery, although there's no equivalent here to the Saiq Plateau's dramatic hanging villages. The highpoint (in every sense) of a visit out here is the drive up the flanks of **Jebel Shams** (3005m), the highest mountain in Oman.

Hotels in Nizwa may be able to arrange a **4WD with guide** for the trip up Jebel Shams from Nizwa; alternatively, try Avion (see p.87) in the town centre. Expect to pay around 45–50 OR, possibly more if booked through one of the town's more upmarket hotels.

Wadi Ghul وادي غول

The road up Jebel Shams starts by running past the entrance of the narrow, steep-sided **Wadi Ghul**, which connects with the spectacular Wadi Nakhr (see below) directly below the summit of Jebel Shams. It's possible **to walk** up to Wadi Nakhr along hiking route W6/W6a (see p.93), which climbs from here up along the cliffs above the wadi to the village of Khateem.

At the entrance to the wadi you'll see the remains old **Ghul village**, a collection of ruined mudbrick houses clinging to the hill on the far side of the river bed, above lush date plantations, and disintegrating back into (and becoming increasingly indistinguishable from) the orangey-coloured rocks of the hillside whence it came. The modern village faces it on the other side of the wadi. You can explore the oasis at the bottom of the hill, with a *falaj* running between tiny banked-up plots, although there's no longer any safe way of scrambling up to the old buildings and fortifications on the hilltop above. The name *ghul* means, literally, "ghoul" – a devilish kind of jinn (the English word is derived from the Arabic, which also gave us the name of the star Algol). Quite why the village is named thus is unclear, although it may conceivably have something to do with the supernatural behaviour of the nearby jinns of Bahla (see opposite).

Wadi Nakhr and the Balcony Walk

Beyond Ghul, the road begins to climb steadily upwards towards the summit of Jebel Shams, surfaced for about the first half of the journey, though nearer the top the tarmac gives out and the track becomes quite steep and rocky in places, meaning that 4WD is essential. The landscape hereabouts is very similar to that on the road up to the Saiq Plateau, with huge sedimentary limestone formations, their colours ranging from chalky greys and greens through to sandstone oranges and reds. En route you'll notice the distinctive outline of Jebel Misht (see p.139) standing in proud isolation away to the west. The final few kilometres (past the *Jabal Shams Base Camp*; see opposite) are particularly spectacular, with grand views down into the great chasm of **Wadi Nakhr** (also sometimes referred to as Wadi Ghul, to which it's joined), and popularly known as the "Grand Canyon" of Oman.

The main road up the mountain finishes at the *Jabal Shams Resort* (see opposite), from where a side track runs a couple of kilometres to the windswept hamlet of **KHATEEM** (also spelt Khatayam, but pronounced something like "Hootm", with throaty *h*), just a handful of tiny houses clinging to the edge of the canyon. Getting out of your vehicle you'll probably be greeted by local children trying to sell you some of the area's traditional black-and-red rugs, or smaller woven trinkets made from the fleece of the long-haired goats which browse the mountains hereabouts.

Khateem is also the starting point for the spectacular **Balcony Walk** (part of hiking route W6 and clearly waymarked with the usual red, white and yellow painted flags; see p.93). This is probably the most famous hike in the country, winding around the cliffs halfway up the rim of Wadi Nakhr to the abandoned village of As Sab. The scenery here is some of the most dramatic anywhere in Oman: a kind of huge natural amphitheatre, with kilometre-high cliffs, the tiny village of Nakhr way below in the shadowy depths of the canyon and birds of prey – such as the Egyptian vulture, with its distinctive black-and-white-striped wings – hovering silently on the thermals overhead. Count on around three hours for the return journey from Khateem to As Sab, although even a ten-minute walk from Khateem offers memorable views and a good taste of the scenery hereabouts.

The road to the **summit** itself (topped by a golfball-style radar installation) is off limits due to military use, although you can still walk up to the southern summit (2997m), known as Qarn al Ghamaydah, along hiking route W4 (see p.93), with marvellous views into Wadi Nakhr, Wadi Sahtan and Wadi Bani Awf en route.

Accommodation

Rather surprisingly, there are a couple of **places to stay** right on top of the mountain, either of which offers an excellent base for walks around the mountain.

Jabal Shams Base Camp About 5km before the end of the road ⓣ9668 6303. Cheaper but much more basic than the nearby *Jebel Shams Resort*, although upgrades are planned. Accommodation is in a mix of rather glum-looking rooms in a string of cheerless little concrete blocks or in some passable tents with attached bathrooms and proper beds. The camp is located in a natural hollow in the hills, which provides a measure of shelter but also means that there are no views. There's a small (unlicensed) restaurant and a neat little tented sitting room. ❹–❺

Jabal Shams Resort At the end of the road (signed as Camping & Travelling Center) ⓣ9938 2639, ⓦwww.jabalshams.com. The best of Jebel Shams' two accommodation options, with a stunning location and extremely helpful staff. The attractively furnished "Sunset Chalets" boast superb mountain views through big French windows; the cheaper "Private Chalets" are similar, but lack the views. There's also a massively overpriced Arabian tent with mattresses on the floor for 50 OR (including dinner), although you can also bring your own tent and camp here for a very modest 6 OR. There's also a trim little on-site unlicensed restaurant. ❻

Bahla بهلا

Some 40km west of Nizwa, the small town of **BAHLA** is famous for its gigantic fort and its distinctive earthenware pottery – and it also has a certain reputation as the favoured haunt of mischievous jinns and other supernatural phenomena – a kind of Omani Glastonbury. Unfortunately the town's fort, one of the most splendid in Oman, is closed indefinitely for repairs, although you can still enjoy fine views of the exterior, while the atmospheric old town and city walls are also worth a look, as is the engaging little souk.

The Town

There's nothing subtle about Bahla's **fort**. One of the biggest in Oman, its immense walls and irregular skyline of assorted towers, bastions and crenellations loom massively above the modest modern town, looking like some kind of gigantic medieval factory. As with many of Oman's forts, Bahla is believed to have been established in pre-Islamic times, though the present structure dates back to the days of the Banu Nebhan, the dominant tribe in the area between the twelfth and fifteenth centuries, although the fort was largely rebuilt during the seventeenth century. During the twentieth century the fort fell into an advanced state of disrepair and was in danger of collapsing entirely until, in 1987, it was listed as a UNESCO World Heritage Site and closed for the huge renovation works which continue to this day, and with no scheduled end yet in sight. If you want to have a (virtual) glimpse inside the fort, check out the 360-degree panophotographs at Ⓦwww.world-heritage-tour.org/middle-east/oman/bahla.

While you're here, it's also worth exploring the area running down to the wadi below the fort on the western side of town. Start at the **mosque** sitting directly in front of the fort on top of a large raised terrace – a plain, mudbrick box. The mosque's terrace offers probably the best view of the fort in town, as well as a bird's-eye view over the extensive remains of **old Bahla**, a dense cluster of mudbrick houses in various states of disrepair, bounded by a couple of old gateways and the remains of old defensive walls and towers. Some of the buildings are surprisingly grand, including a number of very fine, but very decayed, three-storey houses, many of which retain their solid original wooden doors (or colourful modern metal replacements). The houses are largely uninhabited now and, as with so many similar places throughout Oman, it's difficult to imagine the ruins surviving for much longer.

Continuing away from the fort brings you to even more considerable remains of Bahla's **city walls**, which stretch for some 12km around the fort, town and surrounding date plantations. The best-preserved section is down along the wadi. Walk down along the main road towards Jabrin until you reach the bridge over the wadi, look left, and you'll see an impressive line of fortifications stretching away in the distance, well over 5m high in places. There's also another stretch of walls on your right as you drive into town from Nizwa, shortly before you reach the fort.

The souk and around

Back near the fort on the other side of the main road lies the town's **souk**, one of the more attractive in the north, with dozens of little shops lined up within a cluster of arcaded buildings. The souk was once home to a famous old **tree**, said to be the home of a jinn, which locals tied down with chains for fear that the resident supernatural spirit might fly off with it. The original tree is now gone, although a young replacement has been planted in its place, surrounded by a circular concrete wall decorated with symbolic chains (quite handy for keeping things secured where jinns are concerned – a mosque on the edge of town is said to have flown here one night all the way from Rustaq). To reach the tree head into the souk. Near the entrance, just past the Omani Sweets shop, you'll notice an open area to your left which serves as the souk's fruit and vegetable market. Diagonally opposite here, a doorway leads into a quaint covered alleyway lined by shops; the tree is in the diminutive square at the far end.

Bahla is also well known for its **pottery**, said to owe its superior quality to the unusual excellence of the local clay (collected from the local wadi) and the skill of the town's artisans, although you won't see much in town – most of it is sent off to the souk in Nizwa. Follow the road through the souk and out the far side into an attractive area of date plantations for about 1km to reach the **Aladawi Clay Pots Factory**, where you can see pots being made, and also buy them at prices significantly below what you'll pay elsewhere. Even if you're not interested in pots it's an attractive walk, along narrow shady streets dotted with the occasional old mudbrick house or fortification.

Jabrin جبرين

The small town of **JABRIN** (also spelled Jabreen, Jibreen, Gabrin, Gibrin and so on) is best known for its superb **fort** (Sat–Thurs 9am–4pm, Fri 8–11am; 500bz) – if you only visit one fort while you're in Oman, this is probably the one to choose. The fort dates mainly from around 1670, one of several built during the Ya'aruba building boom of the later seventeenth century, constructed at the behest of the future imam Bil'arab bin Sultan (reigned 1680–92), who lies buried here in a crypt beneath the fort. Further alterations were made to the castle during the eighteenth century by imam Muhammad bin Nasr al Ghafiri (reigned 1725–27), and the whole thing was restored between 1979 and 1983.

The fort is located around 5km south of Jabrin town, a picture-perfect structure nestled amid palm trees. The fort's main building is surrounded by high walls and a gravel courtyard, home to a small mosque; you can also see the deep *falaj*, which formerly provided the castle with water (and which flows right through the building), to the rear. The interior is absorbingly labyrinthine, with dozens of little rooms packed in around a pair of courtyards. Essentially, the building divides into two halves, which, for the sake of clarity, are described below as the **northern** and **southern wings**, although you won't find this terminology used in the fort itself.

Accommodation

Jabrin is home to the modest **Jibreen Hotel** (Ⓣ2536 3340; ❸), an uninviting place in a cheerless location in the middle of town right next to the main road (about 200m west of the roundabout where the road heads south to the fort). Rooms are large and reasonably comfortable, although you'll have to put up with some of the ugliest furniture in Oman. Unless you're really stuck, you'd be better off pushing on to Ibri or Nizwa.

The fort's northern wing

Walk through the entrance and you'll find yourself in the fort's extraordinarily deep and shady central courtyard. A right turn here brings you immediately into a second courtyard at the centre of the northern wing, centred around a similarly narrow and deep courtyard, with beautifully carved windows and wooden balconies above. Rooms on the **ground floor** are devoted to practical matters. These include a huge date store (with distinctive corrugated stone floor; sacks of dates were stacked up here, and the resultant juice collected in the channels running across the floor), a kitchen area (with the adjacent *falaj* providing constant running water), and a guard room with a microscopic jail sunk into the floor, like a cupboard in the ground.

From next to the date store, steep steps lead directly up to the rooftop, passing an entrance into the low-ceilinged guard tower en route. Emerging onto the rooftop, note a second flight of steps immediately to your right which descend back into the fort, and to which you'll return in a moment. The **rooftop** itself is covered in a further jumble of buildings and towers. The largest structure is a fine pillared mosque, with traces of old painting on its arches and a finely painted ceiling. Steps lead up onto the roof of the mosque, the highest point of the whole fort, with superlative 360-degree views. A Qur'anic school (*madrasah*) stands next door.

Take the steps mentioned above back down to reach the fine set of rooms on the **first floor**, signed as "Conference Room, Dining Rooms & Courtroom"; all unusually spacious and high-ceilinged compared to most apartments within Omani forts (as are similar rooms in the southern wing). These include the large **courtroom**, with scales of justice hanging from the wall and a small opening at the far end of the room through which those convicted were forced to crawl out before being taken away for punishment. Next door is a **dining room** and the so-called "conference room", a curious translation for what is simply a traditional **majlis**, or meeting room, with carpeted floor, cushions around walls, shelves lined with old swords, pots, kettles and a fine pair of wooden doors and painted ceiling hung with three big brass lamps. The high ceiling and line of floor-level windows keep things pleasantly cool, even without air conditioning. Close by on the same floor you'll find a horse stall in which the imam was wont to stable his favourite steed. Continuing down the stairs from here you'll pass a women's jail (a standard feature of Omani forts) – not especially inviting, although it's at least a bit less claustrophobic than the men's jail a few steps below.

The fort's southern wing

Continue to the bottom of the steps and you'll find yourself back next to the central courtyard. Turn right at the bottom of the stairs to enter the fort's southern wing, home to the finest sequence of interiors of any fort in Oman.

Once again, rooms on the **ground floor** have a practical emphasis, including soldiers' quarters, an armoury and yet another jail (entered via a tiny hole in the wall). Climb the stairs around the back of the soldiers' quarters to reach the **first floor**, home to a further superb pair of *majlis* (signed "public reception rooms") embellished with richly painted ceilings – the red, black and gold ceiling in the second room is particularly fine. A library stands on the opposite side of the stairs with two-tiered windows with rustic little wooden shutters.

A further flight of stairs, framed with delicately moulded arches, leads up to the **second floor**, formerly the inner sanctum of the ruling imam and home to a suite of even more lavish rooms. These include the so-called "Sun and Moon" room, with yet another richly painted ceiling, the imam's beautiful private *majlis* and, finest of all, the imam's personal "suite" (as it's described), a pair of rooms with intricately carved, rather Indian-looking filigree stone arches and wooden shuttered windows, although only one small section of the original painted ceiling survives. Steps continue from here up to the top of the fort, emerging opposite the rooftop mosque.

Return to the entrance into the central keep and head through the door on your right to reach the crypt-like grotto beneath the northern wing. Here you'll find the wonderfully atmospheric **tomb of imam Bil'arab bin Sultan bin Saif** (see p.222), who is said to have died by his own hand at Jabrin in 1692 at the end of his unhappy thirteen-year reign. The tomb is surrounded by arches carved with Qur'anic script and with the *falaj* flowing beneath. Yet another flight of stairs heads up next to the tomb, leading to the public reception rooms on the first floor.

Al Batinah and Al Dhahirah

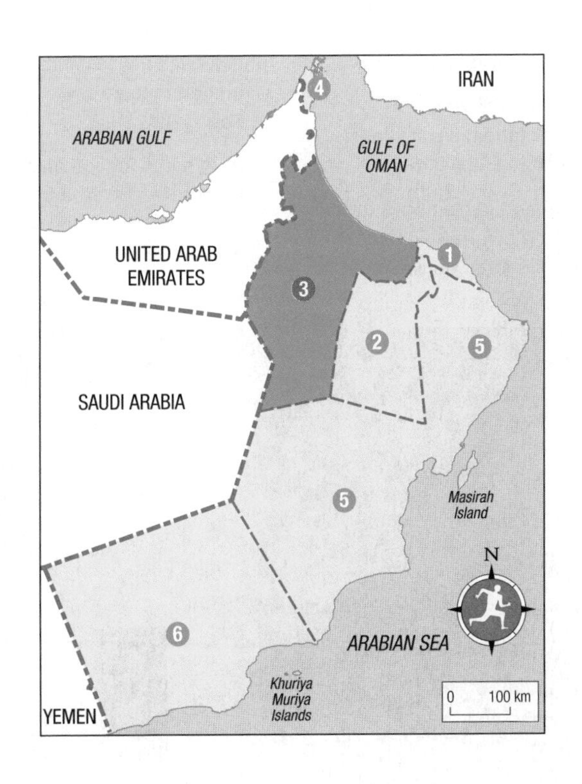

CHAPTER 3

Highlights

* **Seeb** One of the region's most interesting towns, with colourful shops and souks, and a breezy seafront. See p.111

* **Bait Na'aman, Barka** Atmospheric old fortified house whose beautifully restored interiors offer a fascinating glimpse into the life of Oman's former rulers. See p.115

* **Nakhal** Fairy-tale fort at the foot of the towering Jebel Akdhar. See p.118

* **Wekan** Spectacular mountain village perched high above the Ghubrah Bowl. See p.119

* **Daymaniyat Islands** These rocky little islands offer a wealth of wildlife along with some of the country's finest diving and snorkelling. See p.123

* **As Suleif** Absorbing ruins of one of Oman's finest old walled villages, with a labyrinthine tangle of mudbrick houses, mosques and watchtowers. See p.138

* **Al Ayn** Intriguing collection of Bronze Age beehive tombs in a dramatic mountain location. See p.139

▲ View from Nakhal Fort

3

Al Batinah and Al Dhahirah

North of Muscat lies **Al Batinah** region, which stretches along the coast beyond the capital all the way up to the UAE border. This was once the most vibrant and cosmopolitan region in Oman, thanks to its wealth of natural resources and proximity to the great civilizations of Mesopotamia and, subsequently, Persia, although the gradual emergence of Muscat as the country's principal city and port led to a steady decline in the Batinah's economic fortunes, and things are a lot quieter now. Away from the main coastal highway, most of the region is pleasantly comatose, with a sand-fringed coastline, dotted with fishing boats and old forts and backed by endless date plantations.

At the southern end of the region lies the personable town of **Seeb**, within hailing distance of the capital and international airport, and sleepier **Barka**, home to a fine fort, the absorbing old Bait Na'aman and occasional bull-butting contests. Both Seeb and Barka make good bases from which to explore the Batinah's main attraction, the so-called **Rustaq Loop**, a fine drive between the coast and the foot of the Hajar mountains, taking in the superb forts at **Nakhal**, **Rustaq** and **Al Hazm**, with numerous dramatic wadis shooting off into the hills en route, offering myriad off-road opportunities. Back on the coast, the **Sawadi and Daymaniyat islands** offer some superb diving, although otherwise there's not much to detain you before you reach **Sohar**, Oman's former commercial capital and still the largest town in the north, although there are disappointingly few physical reminders of its long and illustrious history.

Inland from Al Batinah, **Al Dhahirah** region covers a wide and largely featureless expanse of desert. Few tourists make it here, unless transiting between Oman and Al Ain in the UAE via Al Dhahirah's main town, **Buraimi**, home to a pair of fine forts and with a lively mercantile atmosphere. Further down the road lies **Ibri**, home to yet another fort and the remarkable old mudbrick village of As Suleif, while clusters of Bronze Age tombs lie scattered around the nearby hills at **Bat** and **Al Ayn**.

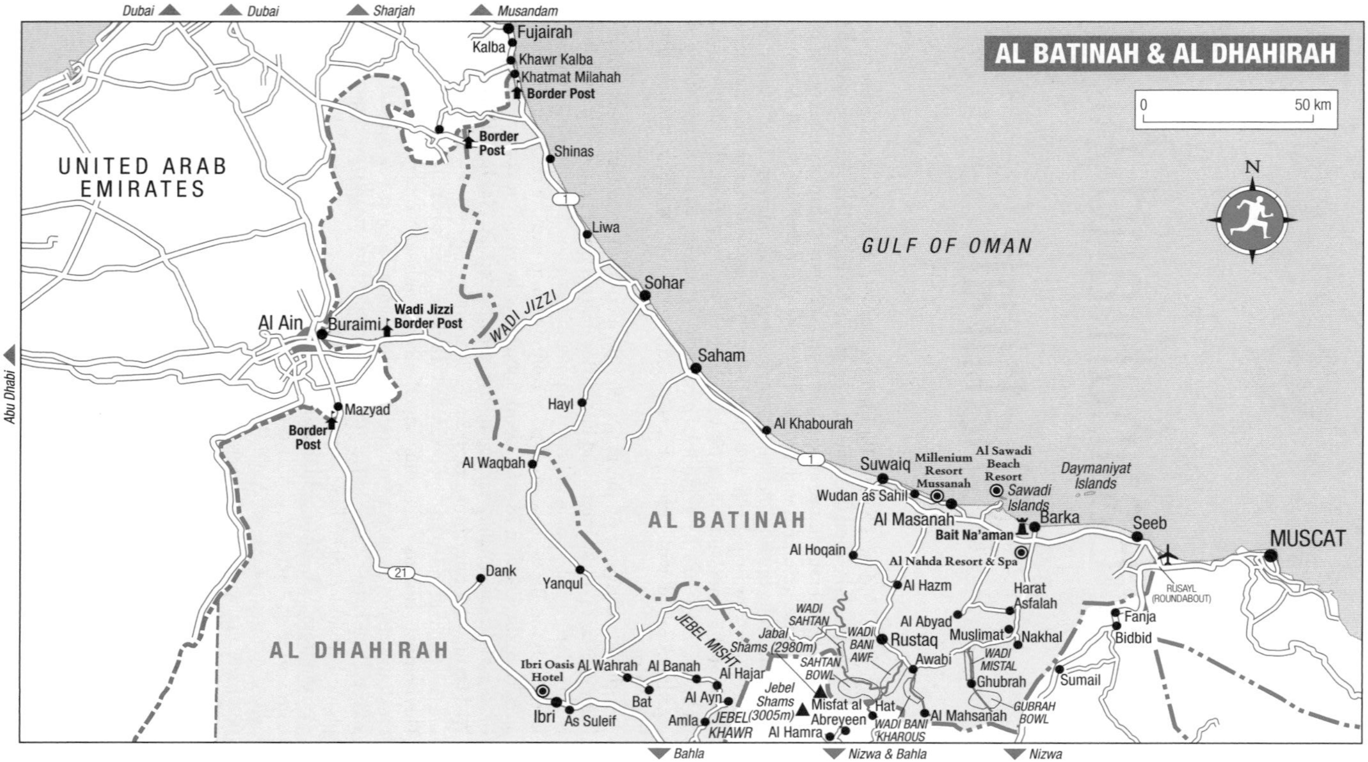

AL BATINAH & AL DHAHIRAH

0 50 km
N

GULF OF OMAN
UNITED ARAB EMIRATES
AL BATINAH
AL DHAHIRAH

Dubai
Dubai
Sharjah
Musandam
Abu Dhabi
Bahla
Nizwa & Bahla
Nizwa

Fujairah
Kalba
Khawr Kalba
Khatmat Milahah
Border Post
Border Post
Shinas
Liwa
Sohar
Saham
Al Khabourah
Suwaiq
Millenium Resort Mussanah
Al Sawadi Beach Resort
Sawadi Islands
Daymaniyat Islands
Wudan as Sahil
Al Masanah
Barka
Bait Na'aman
Seeb
MUSCAT
RUSAYL (ROUNDABOUT)
Al Nahda Resort & Spa
Al Hoqain
Al Hazm
Harat Asfalah
Al Abyad
Muslimat
Nakhal
Rustaq
Awabi
WADI MISTAL
Ghubrah
GUBRAH BOWL
Al Mahsanah
Fanja
Bidbid
Sumail
WADI SAHTAN
WADI BANI AWF
Jabal Shams (2980m)
SAHTAN BOWL
Jebel Shams (3005m)
Misfat al Abreyeen
Hat
WADI BANI KHAROUS
Al Hamra
JEBEL KHAWR
Amla
Al Ayn
Al Hajar
JEBEL MISHT
Al Banah
Bat
Al Wahrah
Ibri Oasis Hotel
Ibri
As Suleif
Dank
Yanqul
Al Waqbah
Hayl
WADI JIZZI
Wadi Jizzi Border Post
Buraimi
Al Ain
Mazyad
Border Post
1
1
21

Seeb السيب

A fifteen-minute drive west of the international airport, the engaging town of **SEEB** (or As Seeb, as it's usually signposted, also spelled As Sib, or just plain Sib) sees few tourists, but is well worth a couple of hours of your time or, even better, an overnight stay in order to experience a slice of quintessential contemporary Omani life. Despite now being in danger of being swallowed up by the suburban sprawl of Muscat, Seeb is easily the liveliest and most interesting of all the towns along the coast north of the capital, with a vibrant commercial atmosphere and a colourful main street.

Seeb's proximity to the airport makes it a convenient first or last stop on a tour of the country, while it's also a good base from which to tackle the Rustaq Loop. A pre-paid taxi **from the airport** to Seeb costs 7 OR, and there are plenty of taxis cruising the streets around the town itself.

Accommodation

Given its size, Seeb musters a reasonable choice of accommodation options, with the added bonus of a couple of decent hotel restaurants and other licensed venues thrown in for good measure.

Al Bahjah Wadi al Bahais St ⓣ2442 4400, ⓦwww.rameehotels.com/seeb-hotels.html. Pleasantly old-fashioned and slightly chintzy hotel with spacious and very comfortably furnished rooms (although some are a bit grubby in places, and the distant thumping of the various in-house entertainment venues occasionally intrudes). Facilities include (erratic) internet access, free use of the pool at the *Dream Resort* (see below) and the decent *Keranadu* restaurant (see p.113), while the hotel is also home to a cluster of nightspots including the usual sports bar and Indian and Arabian live-music bars. ❹

Dream Resort 1.5km west of the centre, just behind the Corniche ⓣ9238 4588, ⓦwww.rameehotels.com/seeb-hotels.html. This scruffy hotel isn't much to look at from the outside (and isn't actually on the coast) but offers spacious and well-furnished rooms, plus the bonus of Seeb's only pool (non-guests 3 OR/hr; *Al Bahjah* hotel guests can use it for free). Facilities include the good *Kapaka* Indian restaurant (with a similar menu to that at the *Keranadu* restaurant at *Al Bahjah* – see p.113), plus a nicer than average sports pub, Indian and Arabic live-music bars, and the *Blackout* disco, with an African band. ❺

Seeb Guest House Main road, diagonally opposite *Al Bahjah* hotel ⓣ2442 3212, ⓔseebguesthouse@hotmail.com. Simple but comfortable no-frills guesthouse with bargain room rates. No facilities, but the restaurant and bars of the *Al Bahjah* hotel are just over the road. Tends to get booked solid, so advance reservations are pretty much essential. 14 OR single/double.

The Town

A walk along Seeb's principal thoroughfare, **Wadi al Bahais Street**, is surprisingly absorbing; the architecture may be modern and functional, but the various merchandise on display offers a fascinating snapshot of Omani trade in miniature – pretty somnolent during the day, although lively (and brilliantly illuminated with neon shop signs) after dark.

The main road describes an extended loop (all one-way traffic) through the town centre, splitting just past the Oman Oil petrol station. Where the main road divides into two you'll see a number of furniture shops selling **mandoos**, modern versions of the traditional wooden chests with elaborate metalwork decoration which can be seen in forts all over the country, their design largely unchanged for hundreds of years.

Past here, the first section of the road is dedicated to a colourful array of **textile shops**, their windows filled with pouting mannequins dressed in eye-poppingly

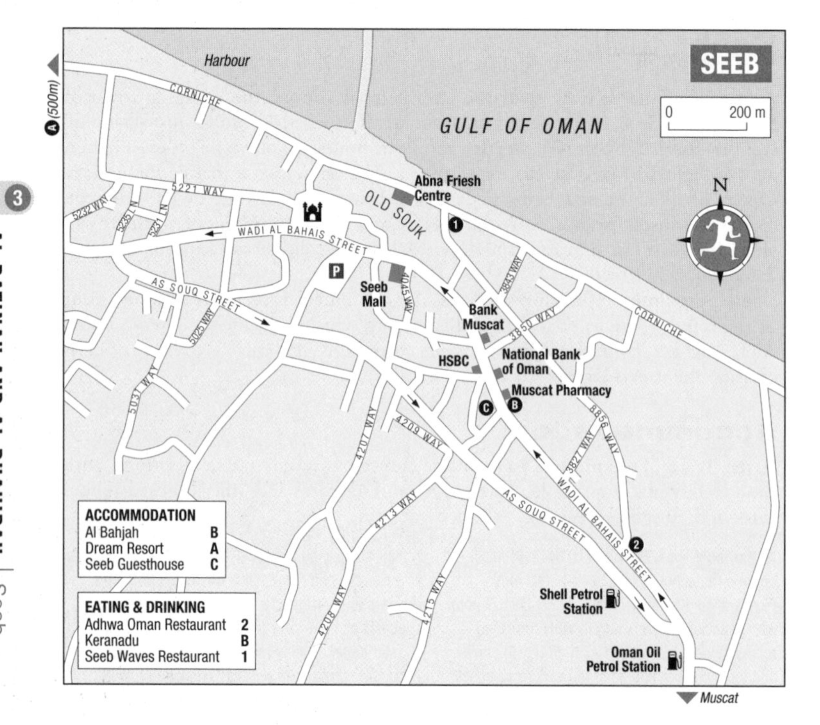

spangly dresses, alongside other places retailing more sober (but still richly embroidered) abbayat, the black robes which most Omani women wear in public over their house clothes. Many of the fabric shops offer **tailoring** services – a good place to get cheap clothes made up, or to pick up a cut-price copy of your favourite shirt or frock. There are also a large number of shops selling **gold jewellery** in traditional Omani designs. Past here (around *Al Bahjah* hotel) the mercantile angle changes, with shops specializing in Omani **caps** and **musar** (turbans) alongside others selling traditional **perfumes**, some with pretty window displays of chintzy glass perfume bottles.

The old souk and corniche

Further along, the street becomes more workaday. Continue past the large but uninteresting Seeb Mall on your left. Ahead you'll see the town's main mosque. Before reaching this, head into the tangle of alleyways on the right (seafront) side of the road. This is Seeb's **old souk**, one of the most interesting in the north, small but surprisingly labyrinthine, with narrow alleyways lined with little shops selling *halwa*, nuts and honey, along with further places selling clothes and fabrics, and a line of vegetable stalls under tattered awnings.

It's also worth hunting out the **Abna Friesh Centre**, in the Friesh Sons Centre on the east side of the souk. Specializing in traditional herbal treatments, this popular shop boasts one of Oman's most absorbing window displays, with shelves packed with all manner of exotic purgatives and restoratives ranging from soap nut, toothbrush tree and humble plant through to purging garlic, arsenic and bright yellow chunks of sulphur. The Abna Friesh Ayurvedic Medical Centre next door offers a selection of similarly traditional nostrums including the treatment of

Mountain Oman

Oman's mountains encapsulate Arabia at its most magnificently untamed: a forbidding wilderness of naked red rock, with towering limestone massifs rising to craggy summits and scored through with narrow, sheer-sided canyons. Fascinating vestiges of traditional life survive amid the wilderness too, with spectacular mountain villages buried deep amid remote wadis or clinging to the vertiginous

The north face of Jebel Shams, Oman's highest peak ▲

Waterfall in the Dhofar Mountains ▼

Al Hoota Cave ▼

The ranges

Oman's geological backbone, the mighty Hajar mountains run the length of the eastern coast in a bewildering tangle of peaks, plateaus and wadis. At the heart of the range lie the towering **Western Hajar**, home to the country's highest peak, Jebel Shams, and many of its most dramatic mountainscapes. Abutting the Western Hajar, the **Eastern Hajar** are less lofty but scenically no less enthralling, especially the canyon-like wadis which score the coastal side of the range. At the northernmost tip of Oman, the Hajar reach a suitably dramatic conclusion amid the rugged heights and magnificent fjords of **Musandam**. At the opposite end of the country, a second major chain of peaks, the **Dhofar Mountains**, encircle the city of Salalah, and are particularly memorable during the annual *khareef* (monsoon), when the hills turn a lush, misty green.

Wadis, canyons & khors

Oman is a geological treasurebox (see p.100), home to a series of dramatic and often outlandish landscapes in which the forces of nature lie spectacularly revealed, exposing millions of years of tectonic history with textbook clarity.

An essential feature of Omani geography are **wadis**: seasonal watercourses which cut through the mountains, creating a wide variety of landscapes ranging from broad, gravel-strewn mountain bowls to the narrowest of **canyons**.

All the mountains are riddled with caves, many of which are still little explored, although the sepulchral **Al Hoota Cave** in the Western Hajar gives a good sense of the country's subterranean landscapes. Elsewhere, similar cave formations have collapsed, creating vast **sinkholes**, such as those at Tawi Attair and Taiq in Dhofar. Oman's coastal ranges are particularly impressive, nowhere more so than in the huge **khors** (fjords) of Musandam, where the red rock of the Hajar mountains plunges into the waters of the Arabian Gulf, and along the dramatic sea-cliffs of Dhofar's Jebel al Qamar.

Villages in the clouds

The uplands of Oman are home to a string of old-fashioned **mountain villages**, often maintaining a perilous toehold amid some of the country's most inhospitable landscapes. Many of these villages are miniature marvels of traditional landscape design, with picturesque layers of agricultural terracing and date gardens carved out of near-vertical mountainsides, with water piped in by ingeniously engineered *aflaj*.

In the Western Hajar, the villages of the **Saiq Plateau**, teetering at the end of the kilometre-deep precipice above Wadi al Ayn, are perhaps the most spectacular examples, while the idyllic **Misfat al Abryeen**, a fascinating tangle of mudbrick houses poised above a burbling *falaj*, is perhaps the prettiest. Other celebrated mountain settlements include the picture-perfect **Bilad Sayt**, buried amid precipitous slopes halfway down Wadi Bani Auf, and the magical mountain top eyrie of **Wekan**, high above the Ghubrah Bowl.

Further north, the mountain villages of Musandam offer an even more impressive example of the Omanis' ability to scratch a living out of the hills. Rudimentary dwellings (now uninhabited) lie scattered across the mountains, constructed out of caves, rock-slabs and tumbled boulders – offering a compelling picture of a now-vanished way of life.

▲ Mountain village, Wadi al Ayn

▼ A *falaj* at Misfat al Abryeen

Rock climbing in the Western Hajar ▲

Wadi Shab ▼

Exploring the mountains

The mountains contain seemingly limitless **off-road driving** possibilities – popularly referred to as "wadi bashing" – but you'll require nerves of steel and a head for heights either as driver or passenger. A more peaceful alternative, particularly in the Western Hajar, is to make use of the well-developed network of **hiking** routes (see p.93). These offer a range of excellent and often challenging treks along old donkey trails, reaching places even the stoutest 4WD cannot. Adrenaline junkies will also find **adventure sports** opportunities, including caving, abseiling and rock climbing.

Top ten mountain landscapes

▸▸ **Saiq Plateau** Set amid the heights of the Jebel Akdhar and dotted with spectacular traditional villages. See p.94.

▸▸ **Wadi Nakhr** Oman's own "Grand Canyon": a vast natural amphitheatre ringed with sheer cliffs. See p.102.

▸▸ **Wadi Bani Auf** Off-road driving - and scenery – at its most thrilling. See p.99.

▸▸ **Snake Gorge** Hike over boulders and wade through rock pools. See p.101.

▸▸ **Wadi Mistal** Sensational drive through the Ghubrah Bowl, up to the dramatically situated village of Wekan. See p.119.

▸▸ **Khor ash Sham** Cruise the waters of Musandam's finest *khor*. See p.152.

▸▸ **Wadi Shab** Stunning wadi with palm gardens and rock pools nestled below sheer sandstone cliffs. See p.167.

▸▸ **Road to Jaylah** A dizzying off-road drive over mountain crests, passing Bronze Age tombs en route. See p.168.

▸▸ **Jebel Samhan** Cloud-capped limestone cliffs rising high above the Dhofar coast. See p.204.

▸▸ **Jebel al Qamar** A magnificent road twists and turns through the depths of these wild Dhofari mountains. See p.210.

cancer using hot irons and herbs, Qur'anic exorcism and "therapy of the haunted by demons and magic".

On the far side of the souk you come out on Seeb's long seafront **Corniche**, where you'll find the town's fish market along with a long swathe of rather muddy sand – usually busy with half-a-dozen football matches later in the day. Continuing west along the Corniche you'll pass a few shops selling small pet birds and others specializing in fishing equipment before reaching the harbour, enclosed by a large breakwater and lined with boats and piles of large, hemispherical wire-mesh fish traps, a bit like skeletal igloos with funnel-shaped openings.

Amouage perfumery

Given Oman's obsession with all things olfactory, it's no surprise that the country is home to one of the world's most expensive and unusual perfumes. The upmarket **Amouage** (Ⓦ www.amouage.com) brand was founded in 1983 by a member of the royal family and now produces around ten different scents for men and women, with sales outlets in around forty countries worldwide. Amouage perfumes all feature traditional Omani ingredients such as silver frankincense, myrrh from Salalah and rock roses from Jebel Akhdar; scents are packaged in quaint bottles inspired by the shape of a *khanjar* (for men) and the dome of a miniature mosque (for ladies).

Visitors are welcome at Amouage's **factory** (daily 8am–5pm; free) just outside Seeb, a surprisingly small and homely place where you can watch bottles being individually hand-filled and packaged, and learn more about the various scents from the resident staff. If you fancy buying some, a bottle of the premier scent, "Gold", will set you back around 100 OR for a 100ml bottle, although there are also less expensive products on offer including soaps, body lotion, travel sprays and candles. The factory is on the main highway to Nizwa about 1km west of Rusayl roundabout (look out for the blue signs on your right), down the small road just before Al Dar Interiors.

Eating and drinking

The only **licensed** venues in the town centre are all in *Al Bahjah* hotel: choose between the relatively sedate *Keranadu* restaurant (see below) or one of the hotel's live-music bars. Alternatively, head out to the nice sports pub at the *Dream Resort* (see p.111).

Adhwa Oman Restaurant Wadi al Bahais St. This run-of-the-mill local café stands out for its attractive streetside terrace. Food comprises the usual assortment of chicken, mutton and fish masalas, biryanis and *qabooli*, along with a few other Indian dishes which may or may not be available depending on what mood the chef is in. It's also a good spot for a traditional Indian breakfast of tea and stuffed *paratha*. Most mains around 1 OR.

Keranadu *Al Bahjah* hotel. One of the few half-decent Indian restaurants in northern Oman, specializing in spicy Keralan cuisine, and with a good spread of North Indian favourites too – anything from *malai kofta* and butter chicken through to masala dosa and malabar fish curry (and with a good vegetarian selection too), plus a few Chinese and continental options. Dishes are flavoursome and reasonably authentic, although the chef tends to deluge most offerings with vast amounts of cream and/or oil. Most mains around 1.5–2.5 OR.

Seeb Waves Restaurant Corniche, just east of the souk. This breezy seafront café is a good place to sit out and people-watch after dark. Food is average, with the usual Omani café fare including shwarmas plus chicken/mutton/prawn/fish/cuttlefish biryanis, *qabooli* and *kebsa*, along with some Chinese options. Mains around 1 OR.

Barka بركاء

A forty-minute drive west of the airport lies the low-key **BARKA**. As with many other places along the Batinah coast, the rather sleepy town you see today gives little sense of its former importance, when it was a major centre of local Gulf trade. The original town sits on the coast, just north of the coastal highway – to **get here**, take the turning off the roundabout by the big Lulu hypermarket and drive for 4km to reach the T-junction in the middle of the town.

Accommodation

The only place to **stay** around Barka at present is the five-star **Al Nahda Resort & Spa** (Ⓣ2688 3710, Ⓦwww.alnahdaresort.com; 25–30 percent discounts in summer, otherwise ❽–❾). The resort occupies a huge swathe of lush grounds, with accommodation in spacious and attractively furnished chalets. Facilities include a big pool complete with eye-catching rock waterfall, plus Arabian à la carte and international buffet restaurants. The resort is also home to one of the best **spas** north of Muscat offering a range of classic Balinese, Thai, Indian and Abhyanga treatments along with various more overtly medical treatments and health checks, including regeneration, detox and colonic irrigation.

To **reach** the resort, take the road inland to Rustaq off the Lulu roundabout heading inland (on the left if approaching from Muscat) and drive for around 3km; the resort is signposted on the right.

The fort

Turn right at the T-junction in the centre of town and head along the road past the shops for about 200m to reach the Barka's imposing **fort** (Sun–Thurs 8am–2pm; free), built during Ya'aruba times and subsequently expanded by the Al Bu Saids. Climb the steps through the large gateway-cum-entrance hall to reach the fort's raised central courtyard. Ahead, at the top of the steps, stands a simple little mosque. On your right, a second gateway leads into the residential section of the fort, housing the former apartments of the town's *wali* (local governor), spread over two floors. The two rooms on the upper floor are positioned so as to make the most of refreshing sea breezes (as well as enjoying a strong aroma of fish from the adjacent souk); both are furnished with the usual motley assortment of old rugs, crockery and wooden chests, while the room on the far side also sports delicate moulded pictures of trees, vases and abstract geometrical designs on its walls. As in many rooms in Omani forts, the windows here are set at floor level, making it possible to loll on a rug while enjoying the sea winds. Steep wooden steps lead up from here to the rooftop terrace at the highest point of the fort – on a clear day you can see the Daymaniyat Islands, way out to sea, as well as the humped, rocky outline of the main Sawadi Island closer to hand on your left.

The remainder of the structure has a more military emphasis, with high curtain walls punctuated with three towers, two round and one hexagonal. The latter, entered via a particularly impressive pair of spiked doors, is the biggest, and the strongpoint of the fort, with a spacious interior supported by a single enormous column and six large cannon pointing out over town.

On the far side of the fort, next to the ocean, lie Barka's **fish and vegetable souks**, busiest in the morning.

The banquet massacre at Barka

Barka fort's main claim to fame is as the site, in 1747, of one of the most important events in Omani history: the final expulsion of the Persians from the country and the foundation of the Al Bu Said dynasty (see p.223), whose descendants continue to rule Oman to this day.

The architect of the affair was **Ahmad bin Said**, the popular governor of Sohar and Barka, who had a few years previously signed a treaty with the Persians. Ahmad decided to affirm his friendship by inviting the entire Persian garrison at Muscat to a banquet at Barka fort. The banquet was well under way when, it is said, there was a sudden beating of drums and the public crier announced: "Anyone who has a grudge against the Persians may now take his revenge!" According to one version of the story, all the Omanis present immediately fell upon their unarmed guests and did away with the lot of them, apart from two hundred soldiers who cried for mercy. These were put on a ship for Persia, although according to legend a mysterious fire swept through the ship, and all aboard, with the exception of Ahmad's sailors, were burned alive or drowned. An alternative version of the event states that Ahmad bin Said simply executed a few of the Persians, but allowed the rest to go free, or sent them back to Persia.

Bait Na'aman

Rather more interesting than Barka's fort is the beautiful old fortified house of **Bait Na'aman** (Sat–Thurs 7.30am–2.30pm, closed Fri; free, although a tip is welcomed – 1 OR/person should suffice). The unusually tall and narrow house, with alternating square and round towers, is thought to have been constructed around 1691–92 by imam Bil'arab bin Sultan (or possibly his brother, and successor as imam, Saif bin Sultan), and was used by both imams during their visits to the area. According to one tradition, this is also where Sultan Said bin Sultan murdered his unpopular predecessor Badr bin Saif in 1806 (see p.225) with a single blow from his *khanjar*. The entire building was beautifully restored in 1991.

Unlike most of Oman's forts, the house has been fitted out with a lavish selection of traditional furnishings and fittings, giving the place an engagingly domestic atmosphere and making it much easier to imagine what life was like for its former inhabitants than in most other Omani heritage buildings. **Downstairs** you'll find the original bathroom and stone toilet, both connected to an underground *falaj* which formerly brought water all the way from Nakhal. There's also a storage room, in which dates were pressed (the holes in the floor were used to siphon off the juice), as well as a pitch-black ladies' jail.

The main living areas are situated **upstairs**, with a sequence of rooms attractively furnished with traditional rugs, cushions, crockery and jewellery. These include the men's and ladies' *majlis*, plus a quaint bedroom with four-poster bed and a wooden hatch in the floor through which water could be drawn up from below. Nearby is the private *majlis* of the imam, equipped with a secret escape passage, and a watchtower with pit-like jails for miscreants. Further stairs lead up to the **roof**. The main tower is supported by beautiful teak beams, with old pictures of ships scratched onto the walls. The tower originally housed six cannon, backed up by three more cannon in the house's second tower – an impressive array of firepower for what was essentially a private residence rather than a proper fort.

To **reach the house**, drive around 5km north of the roundabout by the Lulu hypermarket along the main coastal highway then turn right off the highway, following the signs to A'Naaman and (just afterwards) the Barka Health Center, following the road as it twists back towards the coast. The house is about 3km down the road on your left – it's not signposted, but is instantly recognizable.

Bullfighting à la Batinah

Barka is one of the various locations along the Batinah coast where you can catch the traditional Omani sport of **bull-butting** (which can also be seen in neighbouring Fujairah in the UAE). Unlike Spanish bullfighting, bull-butting is a bloodless contest between animals, rather than bull and matador. The sport is thought to have been introduced by the Portuguese, although its origins probably go back to antiquity, and appears to have roots in both ancient Persia and classical Greece.

Contests are between large Brahma bulls, traditionally fed up on a diet of milk and honey. Animals are matched according to weight and led into the area to do battle, at which point (all being well) they will lock horns – although some bulls just turn around and run away, frantically pursued by their owners. The winning bull is the one which either pushes the other to the ground or forces it to give up its ground. Most fights last less than five minutes, and ropes attached to the bull mean that they can be pulled apart (with difficulty – some of the bulls weigh around a ton) if things start turning ugly.

Meetings are held on Fridays during the winter months from around 4pm, lasting a couple of hours and attracting a good-natured, but exclusively male, audience. Contests alternate on a weekly basis between Sohar, Shinas, Barka and Seeb.

Barka's **bull-butting arena** is on the northern edge of town. To reach the arena, turn left at the T-junction in the town centre and follow this road for around 3km; the low-walled enclosure is down the side road signed to the Barka Health Center.

Inland from Barka: The Rustaq Loop

Easily the most rewarding attraction in Al Batinah is the so-called **Rustaq Loop**, a fine day's drive combining magnificent mountain scenery with three of Oman's finest castles – at **Nakhal**, **Rustaq** and **Al Hazm**. There are also a few other minor sights en route, while the surrounding mountains offer endless possibilities for off-road driving through spectacular wadis. Unfortunately, the loop has (temporarily, at least) lost some of its lustre thanks to the closure for renovation of the castles at Rustaq and Al Hazm. Hopefully these will have been restored to working order by sometime in 2012, although as with all Omani restoration projects, it's best not to hold one's breath.

The loop is strung out along single-carriageway **Highway 13**, a fast, and usually fairly traffic-free (except between Barka and Nakhal) stretch of road. The only **accommodation** on the loop itself is a single, rather unappealing option at Rustaq, although the trip can easily be done in a day from either Barka, Seeb or even Muscat. The following account describes the loop travelling in a **clockwise direction**, although there's absolutely no reason why you shouldn't tackle it in the opposite direction.

Harat Asfalah

Highway 13 heads off from the main coastal road at Barka. The opening section of the loop is fairly humdrum, with featureless scenery either side of the road until you approach Nakhal and the mountains begin to come increasingly into view.

Some 7km before Nakhal (and 22km from the coastal highway), brown signs point west off Highway 13 to the little-visited remains of the fort at **HARAT ASFALAH**. Compared to the other, much more grandiose forts around the Rustaq Loop, this is a decidedly homely affair, with a nicely restored section of crenellated wall bounded by a pair of towers (with a couple of old cannon) and a neat little gateway. Walk through the gateway to reach a small, windowless mosque (with an unusual little *mihrab* on the external wall) and a small kitchen, with a hole for fires in the floor and a neat little round chimney directly above. Steps lead from here up to the rooftop, offering fine views over the adjacent date plantations. The rest of the fort has now disappeared, the space it formerly occupied now covered by the modern village, dotted here and there with a few collapsing old mudbrick buildings. The fort is about 2km off the main road – follow the brown signs, turning right off Highway 13, then right and then left along increasingly narrow and twisting roads until you descend into a date plantation, at which point you'll see the castle on your right.

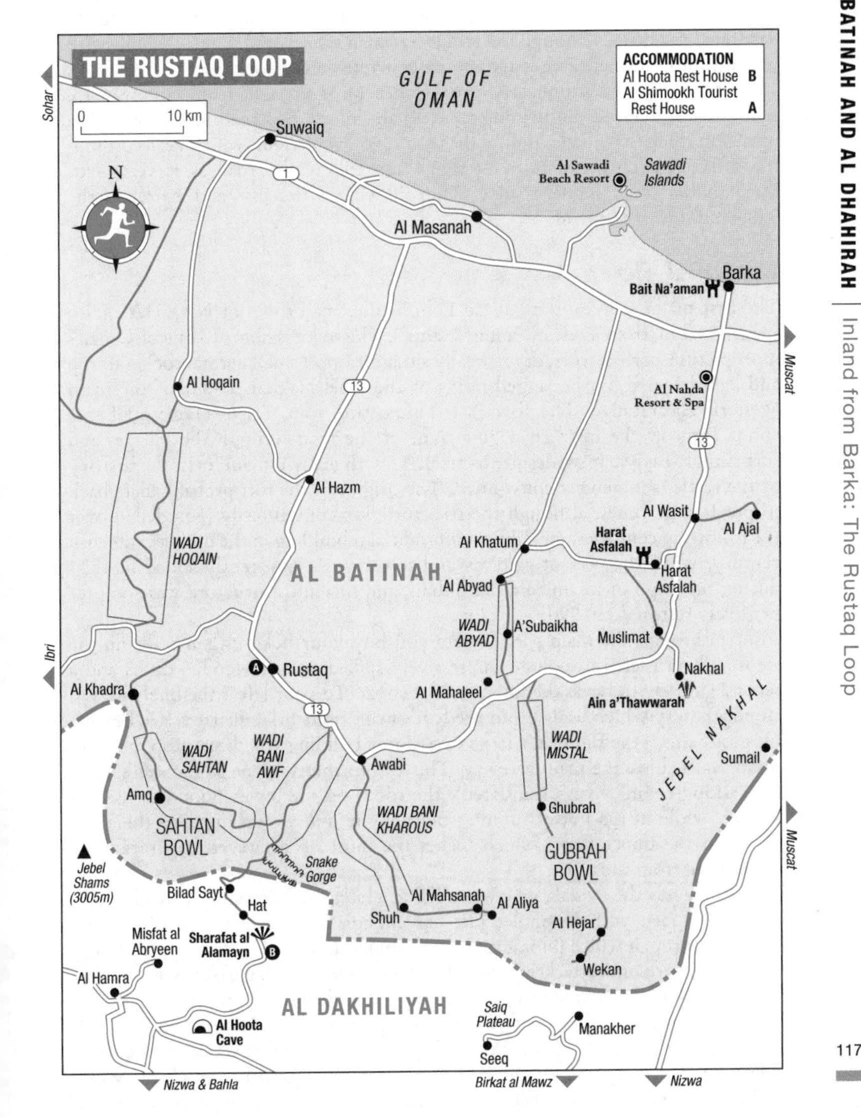

Muslimat

Around 6km further down Highway 13 lies another of the loop's buried curiosities at **MUSLIMAT**. Drive through the modern village (see directions below) and park by the trio of old cannon which still stand guard by the roadside under a tree. Behind here, a neatly restored gateway leads into the remains of Muslimat's old mudbrick village. Steps to the right lead up to the usual mudbrick mosque on a high raised terrace. On the other side of the gateway lies a rubble of collapsed buildings plus a single intact round watchtower with a distinctive tapering upper section (designed to reduce the impact of cannonball fire). Next to this stands an unusually imposing two-storey battlemented mudbrick mansion with finely decorated windows, although the facade has been rather unpleasantly rebuilt with incongruous Italianate arches and lumpy concrete breezeblocks.

The **turn-off** to Muslimat is clearly signed on your right from Highway 13, around 750m before the turning to Nakhal. Follow this road for around 1km until you reach the village. Ignore the turning on your right (which heads off into the village's extensive date plantations) and follow the road as it veers left, through the small modern souk. The old village lies just past here, on the left-hand side of the road.

Nakhal Fort نخل

The first major stop on the Rustaq Loop is the small town of **NAKHAL** (also spelled Nakhl, from *nakhl*, meaning "palm"). The town is home to one of Oman's most picture-perfect forts, dramatically situated atop a small natural rock outcrop and backdropped by the jagged peaks of the Jebel Nakhal, a spur of the main Western Hajar range. The **fort** (Sat–Thurs 9am–4pm, Fri 8–11am; 500bz) is about 1km off the main road, just right of the road through the village (and surprisingly easy to miss, despite its size). As with many Omani forts, the **history** of the castle is somewhat convoluted. The origins of the fort probably date back to pre-Islamic times, although the structure was continuously remodelled over the following centuries, including a substantial rebuilding in the mid-seventeenth century, while the present gateway and towers were apparently added in 1834 during the reign of imam Said bin Sultan, and the entire structure was comprehensively restored in 1990.

Enter through the main gate (where you buy your ticket), then walk up the steps and turn left through an impressively spiked pair of wooden doors and a second gateway to reach the interior of the fort. To your left is the finely carved stone archway which leads up to the fort's main residential quarters (see below). Opposite this is the **Barzah**, a large two-storey building which sits atop the fort's outer walls above the main gateway. This was formerly home to the *wali*'s *majlis* (or "sitting room", as it's translated); the room on the lower floor was used in winter, while in the hotter summer months the *wali* would move to the airier room on the upper floor, which makes the most of whatever sea breezes are blowing in from the coast.

Continue past the Barzah, where you'll find a kitchen, followed by a small watchtower equipped with loopholes just big enough for a rifle barrel, plus wider openings through which (in traditional Omani fashion) boiling date juice or honey could be poured onto attackers below. Past here is the imposing **east tower**, reached by a narrow flight of stone steps and equipped with further rifle-sized apertures, plus wider embrasures for the fort's cannon, one of which survives *in situ*.

Retrace your steps to the Barzah and head through the archway opposite, from where further steps lead up past a date store and a large jail to reach the **wali's living quarters**. This was the castle's main residential section, with a series of rooms arranged around a small terrace at the highest point of the fort, including the *wali*'s own bedroom, along with a living room, guest room and rooms for boys, girls and women, all modestly furnished with old rugs, crockery and fine old wooden chests, plus a couple of antique (and very rickety) four-poster beds. The women's room, despite being the highest in the fort, is notably less breezy than the *wali*'s bedroom opposite, as it faces inland.

Exiting the women's room, turn left and follow the steps and walls around the rest of the complex and thence back to the entrance. En route you'll pass the fort's **middle** and **western towers**. The latter is equipped with a neat little wooden ladder built into the internal wall, while there are particularly fine views from the small watchtower immediately outside across the fort's impressive quantity of spade-shaped battlements and out over the sprawling date plantations and rugged mountains beyond.

Ain a'Thawwarah hot springs

A short drive from Nakhal Fort lie the **Ain a'Thawwarah** hot springs, a popular picnic spot with locals – the whole place tends to get crammed at weekends. The springs are at the end of the main road through Nakhal. Carry on past the fort and follow the pretty but narrow little road for around 2.5km as it twists between high-walled date plantations to reach the springs (there's parking space at the end of the road). The water here is invitingly clean and clear, and full of tiny fish. Walk up past the small picnic area, at the end of which you'll find the spring itself, with surprisngly warm water gushing out of the rock.

Wadi Mistal and Wekan

About halfway between Nakhal and Awabi, a sign points south off Highway 13 towards **Wadi Mistal** (tarmac road for the first 6km, then good graded track for another 25km before the final ascent to Wekan village). The wadi begins by passing through a narrow gorge, its floor covered in a tumble of huge grey boulders, before opening out into the **Ghubrah Bowl**, a huge, flat gravel plain, ringed on the left by the cliffs bounding the southern edge of the Jebel Nakhl and, at the far end, by the peaks of the Jebel Akhdar.

It's a swift if rather bumpy ride across the bowl to reach the village of **Al Hejar** on the far side, from where a very steep, rough and slightly stomach-churning road (4WD essential) climbs up to **WEKAN** (also spelled Wakan, Wukan), one of the most spectacular mountain villages anywhere in Oman. There's parking in the village, while a restored watchtower provides an optimal viewing platform from which to admire the bowl and encircling mountains below.

Wekan is also the starting point for the **hiking routes** W24b and W25 (see p.93). Even if you don't fancy tackling either walk in its entirety, it's well worth exploring the opening section of walk W25, which winds up through the picture-perfect terraced gardens to the rear of the village, running alongside a bucolic little *falaj* which tumbles down from the mountainside above – arguably the prettiest short walk in Oman. The walk is waymarked (albeit not very clearly) from the village centre and it takes around twenty minutes to reach the top of the village.

Wadi Abyad

About 3km beyond the turn-off to Wadi Mistal, a signed turn-off on the right points to the village of **A'Subaikha**, the starting point for trips into the pretty **Wadi Abyad** ("White Wadi"). This is quite different in character from the wadis on the southern side of Highway 13, set between low ophiolite hills and dotted with palm trees and rock pools. The water in some of the pools often turns a distinctive milky white due to the high concentrations of dissolved calcium it contains, and which sometimes crystallizes into a fine covering, like warm ice. The whole place is particularly lovely towards dusk, when the low light brings out the rich russet colouring of the surrounding hills and the whole valley seems almost to glow.

Driving the wadi is something of a challenge. There's no actual track here, it's simply a question of picking your way across the gravel-covered wadi bed, treacherously loose and deep in many places – speed is of the essence in order to avoid getting bogged-down. There's also usually a fair bit of water hereabouts, so expect to ford a few streams en route. You can get about 5km down the wadi before your way is blocked by rocks. Wadi Abyad is also a popular camping spot, particularly at weekends, meaning that if you do get stuck, you should be able to find someone to help pull you out.

Awabi العوابي

The section of Highway 13 between Nakhal and Rustaq is easily the most scenic of the entire loop (and usually fairly traffic-free), with the high mountains of the Western Hajar towering above the road on your left, while to your right lies an unusual landscape of small, crumbling red-rock hills with jagged ridgetops and summits – a good example of Oman's characteristic ophiolite landscapes (see p.100).

A further 35km on from Nakhal, the town of **AWABI** is home to yet another **fort** (Sun–Thurs 8am–2pm; free), around 2km off Route 13 on the far side of the modern town – follow the brown signs. The quaint, toy-like structure is built in a mixture of stone and mudbrick with a small mosque, looking like an oversized shoebox, standing in front of the gates. Inside, the roughly moulded walls, covered with coarsely finished *sarooj*, give the place a pleasantly rustic look – a lot more authentic than the polished surfaces of most other restored Omani forts. The main tower is an interesting study in traditional Omani living arrangements, boasting no less than three hole-in-the-floor toilets, all carefully designed so that waste products would fall outside the castle walls and into the village below.

Wadi Bani Kharous

Immediately behind Awabi fort, a narrow cleft in the mountains announces the start of **Wadi Bani Kharous**, one of the most spectacular along the Rustaq Loop, and now easily accessible thanks to the construction of a new black-top road stretching all the way to the end of the wadi at Al Aliya, some 25km from Awabi (although the last couple of kilometres are extremely narrow and twisty as they run through the wadi's final two villages). The wadi is surprisingly developed, with a string of seven villages forming a ribbon of almost continuous settlement, although the scenery is beautiful throughout, hemmed in between high limestone cliffs, their summits sculpted into delicate rock pinnacles. The last few kilometres are especially pretty, as the wadi narrows and fills up with date palms and mango trees, with houses stacked up on rock ledges on the hillside above. The wadi is also one of the most important geological sites in Oman, exhibiting a range of rock formations spanning over 500 million years, from the Cretaceous period to the Late Proterozoic era, the latter being some of the oldest in the country.

A few kilometres west of Awabi you pass the end of the spectacular track which descends from the mountains via **Wadi Bani Auf**, covered on p.99.

Rustaq الرستاق

Tucked up beneath the northern escarpment of the Hajar mountains, **RUSTAQ** is one of the most venerable settlements of the interior. The town owes its place in Omani history to the redoubtable imam **Nasir bin Murshid al Ya'aruba** (see p.221), founder of the Ya'aruba dynasty, who was elected imam at Rustaq in 1624 and made the town his principal centre of operations during his subsequent 25-year reign. The town was also a favoured base for Ahmed bin Said (see p.223), founder of the later Al Bu Said dynasty.

Rustaq's importance was the result of its strategic position between the coast and the mountains, guarding the exit points of several nearby wadis through which goods would have been transported from the *jebel* above. The town developed into a major centre for local commerce, craftsmanship and other trades, home to some of the country's finest metalworkers and silversmiths, and also renowned as the source of some of Oman's best *halwa* and finest honey – bee-keeping remains a popular local occupation to this day.

Sadly few remains of the town's illustrious history survive, however. Modern Rustaq is a sprawling and rather characterless place, and far less interesting than its old rival, Nizwa, while the closure for extensive renovations of the town's majestic fort has robbed it of its one stellar attraction, for the time being at least.

Accommodation

There's only one **place to stay** in Rustaq (indeed around the whole of the Rustaq loop). This is the one-star *Al Shimookh Tourist Rest House* (Ⓣ2687 7071, Ⓕ2687 7072; 30 OR, including breakfast), in the new town about 500m down the Ibri road opposite the Makkah hypermarket (just past the Oman Oil petrol station on the right-hand side of road), about 4km from Rustaq fort. The welcome is friendly, although it's rather expensive for what you get, with simple and slightly dog-eared rooms with TV and fridge, plus squat toilets in the small attached bathrooms.

The Town

Rustaq is effectively divided into two distinct sections: the "old" town and fort, which lies just south off Highway 13, and a "new" town, about 3km further north along Highway 13 on the way to Al Hazm, clustered around the turn-off to Ibri and the modern Rustaq Mosque, a vast white structure with a pair of soaring minarets.

Tucked away at the back of the old town (and clearly signposted from Highway 13) is Rustaq's mighty **fort**, one of the biggest in the country, with a huge, soaring central keep surrounded by extensive walls. The fort was closed at the time of writing as part of a major two-year restoration project, due (in theory, at least) to finish sometime around early 2012.

The fort is one of the most ancient in Oman. The original fort is thought to have been built by the Julanda dynasty fifty years before the arrival of Islam, and was subsequently expanded in 670 ADand again in 1698, while further towers were added by Sultan Faisal bin Turki in 1906. The extensive compound is provided with its own *falaj* and surrounded by low exterior walls topped by a quartet of towers, the tallest rising to almost 20m. Inside sits the tall central keep, built over three levels, with the usual living quarters (including the finely decorated chambers of the imam himself) plus an armoury and a fine mosque. The old **souk** in front of the fort – which formerly hosted a good range of stalls selling traditional handicrafts and souvenirs – is also being rebuilt.

Most of the rest of Rustaq is modern and largely forgettable, although it's worth strolling around the back of the fort, where a cluster of decaying mudbrick houses stands around a small blue-domed mosque. Close by a diminutive, rather Indian-looking mudbrick mausoleum sits atop a small rise, offering a superb view of the fort and the vast swathe of date palms which envelop the old town.

Eating

Assuming you're exploring the loop in a single day, you'll probably find yourself in Rustaq around lunchtime, although unfortunately there's not much on offer when it comes to **eating**. For no-frills drinks and snacks, the most convenient option is the simple *Rawabi al Kasfa* coffee shop around the eastern side of the fort (the side opposite the entrance) – or walk five minutes to the stretch of main road nearest the fort where you'll find a few basic coffee shops and cafés serving up the usual Indian curries and biryanis. Alternatively, it might be worth checking the new souk in front of the fort (see p.121) once it's open.

Al Hazm

The last point of interest on the Rustaq Loop is the modest little town of **Al Hazm**, home to another oversized **fort** (Sat–Thurs 9am–4pm, Fri 8–11am; 500bz). At the time of writing, the fort was closed for extensive renovations, probably until sometime in 2012 at the earliest – although you can at least sneak a peek at the entrance gateway's magnificently carved wooden doors. The fort was built by the Ya'aruba imam **Sultan bin Saif II** (see p.222), who briefly established Al Hazm as capital of Oman in preference to Rustaq, and who is buried inside. This is one of the biggest of all Oman's fortified structures: a huge stone box containing a disorienting labyrinth of corridors and rooms, complete with the usual living quarters, prisons, mosque and its own dedicated *falaj*, clustered around a diminutive central courtyard – although there's not much to see from the outside, which is disappointingly plain.

To **reach** the fort approaching from Rustaq, turn left at the roundabout in the centre of Al Hazm town. The fort is 1km along this road, clearly visible on your left.

North from Barka to Sohar

The long swathe of fertile coastline **between Barka and Sohar** shows the Batinah at its most untouched, with interminable date plantations meandering along the coast, interspersed with sleepy villages, the occasional fort and endless swathes of beach littered with boats – if you're lucky you may spot examples of the traditional *shasha*, an antique style of reed-boat made from bundles of dried palm fronds, which was once common throughout the Gulf. It's around 150km from Barka to Sohar, a ninety-minute drive along the busy coastal highway (which doesn't actually run within sight of the sea), although it's much more enjoyable to get off onto the small roads which run alongside the coast here and there.

The Sawadi and Daymaniyat Islands

The main tourist draw between Barka and Sohar is the Sawadi and Daymaniyat islands (and the adjacent *Al Sawadi Beach Resort*), one of the country's leading dive spots, but equally rewarding to visit for a snorkel or swim. The rocky and windswept **Sawadi Islands** lie just offshore. The largest of the seven islands lies almost within spitting distance of the beach, a large rocky hump topped by a string

Diving the Daymaniyats

Diving and snorkelling trips to the Daymaniyat Islands can be most conveniently arranged through **Extra Divers Al Sawadi** (Ⓣ2679 5545, Ⓦwww.extradivers.info), based at the *Al Sawadi Beach Resort* (see below); count on around 30 OR for a trip including two dives. Most dive operators in Muscat (see p.49) also arrange trips here, though obviously it's a much longer (and somewhat more expensive) trip. It's a 30min–1hr boat trip from *Al Sawadi Beach Resort* to the Daymaniyats, depending on exactly which of the twenty-odd dive sites scattered around the islands you're going to. Contrary to what is sometimes said, **diving** at the Daymaniyats is technically easy and suitable even for non-PADI-qualified divers. The waters around the islands boast excellent visibility, abundant soft and hard corals, descending in places to depths of 20m, and swarms of colourful little tropical fish and nudibranchs. The main attraction, though, is the islands' oversized **marine life**, including leopard sharks, barracuda, shoals of moray eels, rays, turtles and huge sea horses, while you're almost guaranteed the chance to spot a whale shark between July and September.

Extra Divers also run night dives around the Sawadi Islands, and **snorkelling** trips to both the Sawadi and Daymaniyat islands; it's also possible to just go along for the boat trip, without getting in the water. Extra Divers can also arrange various **water-sports**, including kayaking, water-skiing, jet-skiing and wakeboarding.

of watchtowers, while the other smaller islands lie further out to sea. It's possible to walk across the sand to the main island at low tide, though take care you don't get stranded when the tide comes back in; at other times **boat trips** can be arranged by bargaining with the local fishermen on the beach for around 5 OR, while **snorkelling trips** can be set up through Extra Divers at the *Al Sawadi Beach Resort* (10 OR including snorkelling equipment, or 5 OR without). The **beach** here is littered with exotic-looking seashells, perfect for a stroll and a spot of beachcombing.

Much further out to sea (30min–1hr by boat), off the coast midway between Barka and Seeb, the **Daymaniyat Islands** (also spelled Dimaniyat or Dimaaniyat) are one of Oman's premier dive spots. Virtually everyone who comes here does so to dive, or at least snorkel (see box above). There are nine low, rocky little islets here, strung out in a line from east to west and clustered in three quite widely separated groups, surrounded by coral reefs (you'll probably fly directly above them when landing at Seeb international airport). The islands have been protected as a **nature reserve** since 1996 and provide an important nesting site for hawksbill and green turtles, as well as a wide range of migratory birds including the increasingly rare sooty falcon (which can also be found in the Sawadi Islands), one of the few migratory raptors which actually nests and breeds in the region. Given their protected status, access to the Daymaniyats is restricted, and you're not allowed to land on the islands from the beginning of May until the end of October; the rest of the year you'll require a permit (4 OR/day), which can be arranged by your tour operator.

Accommodation

Enjoying a prime location on the long swathe of beach more or less opposite the Sawadi Islands (and around 9km off the coastal highway) is the rather dated **Al Sawadi Beach Resort** (Ⓣ2679 5391, Ⓦwww.alsawadibeach.com; ❼). Rooms (with either a sea or garden view) are plain and old-fashioned, although there's a decent stretch of beach and attractive, spacious grounds with pool and children's playground. Other facilities include Arabian, Indian and international restaurants, a health and fitness centre and the small Whisper spa. It's a pleasant enough spot, although unless you're here for the diving (see box, p.123), the *Sohar Beach Hotel* (see p.128) further north is a better option.

Al Masanah (المصنعة) and around

Back on the main coastal highway, it's another 10km north to reach the turning for **AL MASANAH**, then a further 5km to reach the town itself, where you'll find the town's **fort**, a square high-walled structure next to the road by the seafront. The fort is unusual in being built almost entirely of stone, rather than mudbrick, with bands of roughly hewn rocks (including the occasional piece of coral) held together with layers of pebble-encrusted mud. Some kind of restoration work appears to be under way, although it looks like it will be a long time before anything's finished.

From Al Masanah you can follow signs along the coast (but out of sight of the sea) through the village of **Wudan as Sahil**, passing assorted construction sites connected with the Blue City project (see below) en route. It's not a particularly scenic drive, although the road is fast and largely deserted, and at least gets you away from the mad traffic on the main coastal highway for a bit.

Wudan as Sahil also provides the slightly unlikely setting for the sprawling **Millennium Resort Mussanah** (Ⓣ2687 1555, Ⓦwww.millenniumhotels.com; ❼), a brand-new resort complex sitting on a fine stretch of coast overlooking a small marina, with stylish modern rooms and a good spread of restaurants – although rather a long way from anywhere else.

Suwaiq (السويق) to Saham

Follow the road north for just over 20km and you'll find yourself in **SUWAIQ**, a neat little town arranged around a large seafront **fort**, typical of the numerous similar structures which dot the Batinah coast, encircled by long crenellated walls

Blue City blues

For many visitors, much of the appeal of Oman lies in the striking dissimilarities it presents with the neighbouring UAE, Dubai in particular. However, proof that Oman is not entirely lacking Dubai's taste for vast new mega-developments and infrastructure projects – and all the attendant financial woe that they can create – is provided by the troubled **Blue City** project (Ⓦwww.almadinaazarqa.com), now officially known as Al Madina A'Zarqa, although still usually referred to by its original name.

Launched in late 2007, Blue City was intended to serve as a major peg in Oman's ongoing strategy to diversify its oil-based economy, featuring four hotels, two golf courses, 200 villas and 5000 apartments spread along 16km of coastline near Al Sawadi, at a total cost of around US$20 billion. As with many projects in the neighbouring UAE, however, the credit crunch crippled development, and by early 2010 the scheme was close to liquidation, until the Abu Dhabi-backed Essdar Investments stepped in to rescue it. After a year of attempting to revive the project, Essdar gave up and sold it back to the Oman government, who are now left holding the baby.

The future of Blue City remains uncertain, although it seems that the project will still go ahead, in some form at least. Driving along the coast at present there's not much to see apart from the distant outlines of some half-hearted construction work, although the possibility that a fine stretch of unspoiled Omani coastline will be buried under an expanse of ersatz Arabian villas, chintzy hotels and water-hungry golf courses remains at least distantly on the cards.

with a tower (three round and one square) at each corner and a tall, narrow keep poking up inside. It's not open to the public, unfortunately, so you won't get any further than the impresssively large wooden doors.

North of here it's another 36km along the coastal highway until you reach the turn-off to **AL KHABOURAH**, 2km away on the coast and home to yet another of sturdy little square forts which guard the Batinah coast. The fort here stands right on the seafront – a rather plain little structure, its entrance guarded by a pair of very rusty cannon. It's not open to the public, though it compensates with its magnificent coastal views.

North of Al Khabourah, it's possible to follow a winding little back road which hugs the coast all the way up to Saham, twisting through an endless straggle of sand-coloured villages, occasionally running alongside the sea and little scraps of boat-covered beaches – a lovely glimpse of the backwaters of the Batinah which few tourists ever see. It's decidedly slow going, however – don't expect to get from Al Khabourah to Saham in anything under an hour – and there are no signs so you'll have to follow your nose, keeping to the right whenever there's a choice of roads.

At the end of the road, **SAHAM** is a lively, slightly scruffy little place. The obligatory **fort** (with four chunky square towers) sits on the seafront. A long road runs north and south from here, lined with a few unusually grand (though now decidedly dilapidated) ocean-facing villas, an impressive number of mosques and a long strip of muddy beach with hundreds of boats pulled up on the sand and, towards dusk, dozens of football matches in progress.

Sohar صحار

The major city in northern Oman, **SOHAR** boasts a long and eventful history, and a leading place among the nation's seafaring exploits – according to local tradition, no less a personage than Sindbad hailed from Sohar (see p.130), while for a number of centuries the town served as the capital of Oman, and was the centre of an extensive trading network stretching up and down the Gulf.

Sadly, despite its lustrous Arabian Nights heritage, modern Sohar is a somewhat anodyne place. Nothing remains of the old town, while its major attraction, the imposing Sohar Fort, was closed for extended renovations at the time of writing. The best reason to come here is to crash out for a few days on the beach at the attractive *Sohar Beach Hotel*. Otherwise there's little cause to visit unless passing through en route to the UAE border crossings at Buraimi and Khatmat Malahah, or as a jumping-off point for the scenic road up to Yanqul and Ibri in the Dhahirah.

Some history

Sohar is one of the oldest towns in Oman, and was for many centuries the most important port and commercial centre in the country, until the rise of Muscat from around the sixteenth century onwards. The Sohar region has enjoyed continued prosperity for at least six millennia, probably forming part of the legendary country of Magan (see p.217), which once supplied Sumer with many of its raw materials. Copper was mined in the nearby Wadi Jizzi (see p.132) as far back as the fifth century BC, and Sohar developed as a properous centre for smelting and mining, as well as a major agricultural centre.

By the time **Islam** arrived in Oman, Sohar had established itself as the capital of the region, and remained so until the beginning of the second imamate in 793 AD,

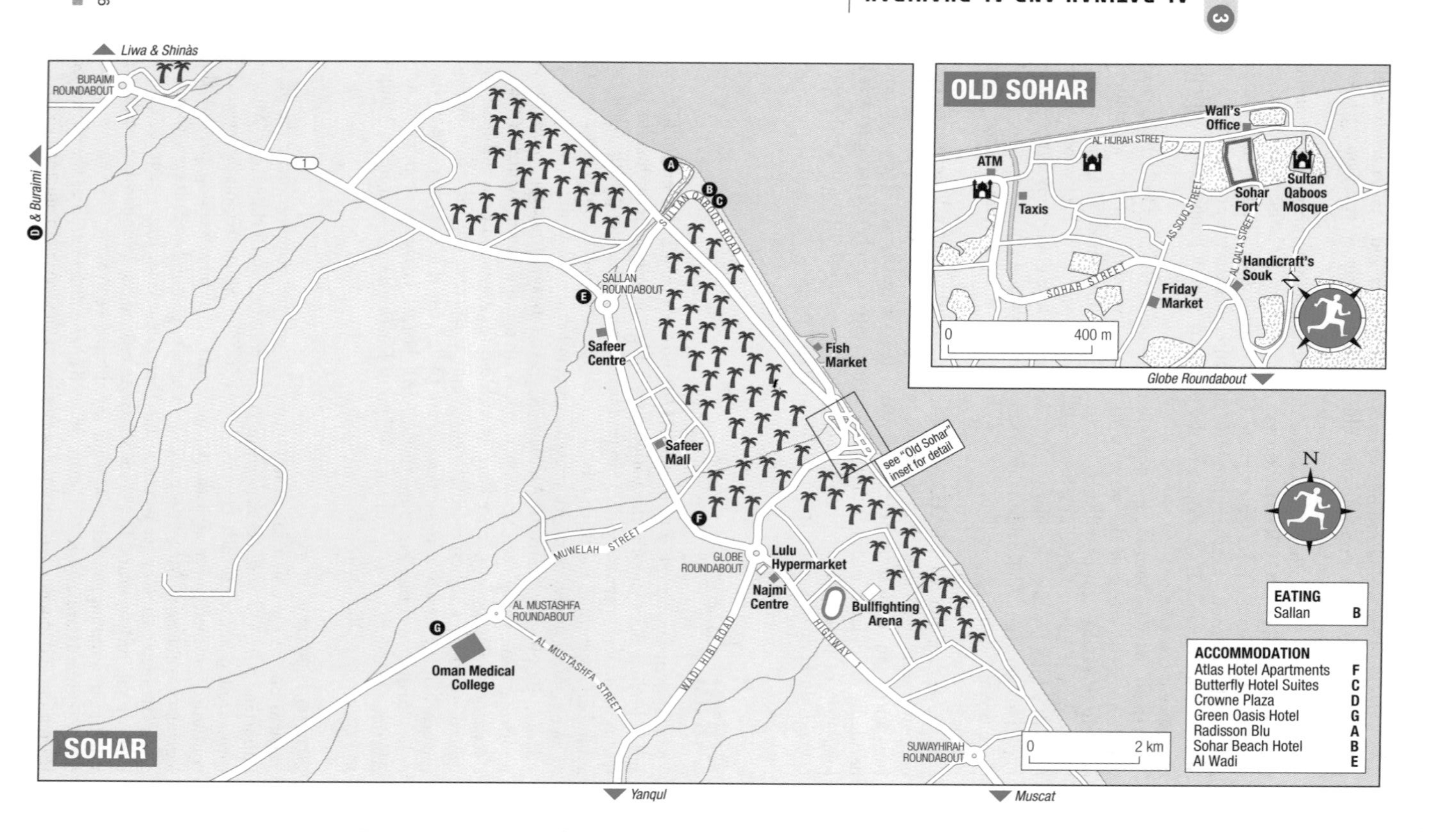
SOHAR
OLD SOHAR
Liwa & Shinàs
D & Buraimi
Yanqul
Muscat
Globe Roundabout
BURAIMI ROUNDABOUT
1
SULTAN QABOOS ROAD
SALLAN ROUNDABOUT
Safeer Centre
Safeer Mall
Fish Market
see "Old Sohar" inset for detail
MUWELAH STREET
GLOBE ROUNDABOUT
Lulu Hypermarket
Najmi Centre
Bullfighting Arena
HIGHWAY 1
WADI HIBI ROAD
AL MUSTASHFA ROUNDABOUT
AL MUSTASHFA STREET
Oman Medical College
SUWAYHIRAH ROUNDABOUT
N
0
2 km
Wali's Office
AL HIJRAH STREET
ATM
Taxis
AS SOUQ STREET
AL QAL'A STREET
Sohar Fort
Sultan Qaboos Mosque
Handicraft's Souk
SOHAR STREET
Friday Market
0
400 m
EATING
Sallan B
ACCOMMODATION
Atlas Hotel Apartments F
Butterfly Hotel Suites C
Crowne Plaza D
Green Oasis Hotel G
Radisson Blu A
Sohar Beach Hotel B
Al Wadi E

when the seat of the imams was moved for security reasons to Nizwa, which was judged, correctly, to be less vulnerable to attack.

Sohar retained its pre-eminent commercial position, nonetheless – "The hallway to China, the storehouse of the East", as the eminent tenth-century historian Al Muqaddasi described it. Unfortunately, the city's wealth also attracted less welcome visitors, usually hailing from neighbouring Persia. In 971 and again in 1041 a Persian fleet overran and sacked the city, while around 1276 the city suffered at the hands of almost five thousand Mongol raiders from Shiraz, although it had at least partly revived by the time Marco Polo visited around 1293.

Worse still was to follow the arrival of the **Portuguese**, who occupied Sohar in 1507 and controlled the city until 1643, when they were finally evicted by the Omani forces of Nasir bin Murshid (see p.221). The Persians returned to Sohar yet again in 1738 under the command of Nadir Shah, but were beaten off by **Ahmad bin Said**, the city's brilliant governor and future ruler of Oman (see p.223), who endured another nine-month-long Persian siege in 1742 before finally capitulating to the far larger forces of his attackers.

Sohar remained an important city following the establishment of the Al Bu Saidi dynasty, but was gradually eclipsed by Muscat as the country's major seaport and slipped increasingly into the sidelines of Omani history – apart from a brief moment of notoriety in 1866 when Sultan Thuwaini was murdered by his son Salim in the city's fort.

Sohar has enjoyed something of an **economic resurgence** over the last few decades – during the 1980s, the old copper mines of Wadi Jizzi were reopened by the Oman Mining Company for the first time in over a thousand years, with further large new deposits being discovered inland around Yanqul and Ibri. More recently, the vast new **Sohar Port**, opened in 2004, may yet restore the city to its maritime pre-eminence.

The city also leapt briefly into the international headlines in early 2011 when it became the focal point of nationwide protests (see p.232) against the government.

Arrival and orientation

Even by Omani standards, Sohar is exceptionally spread out, sprawling along the coast for over 20km. Most activity is now focused around the main coastal highway and the big malls which flank it rather than the small and decidedly comatose "old" town.

ONTC **buses** will drop you at the centre of the old town; there are usually some **taxis** hanging around in the parking lot on the other side of the wadi. A new **airport** is planned for Sohar out near the *Crowne Plaza* hotel, although recent delays mean that it is now not due to open until 2015.

Accommodation

In addition to the accommodation options below, Sohar will shortly be home to a new *Radisson Blu* (Ⓦwww.radissonblu.com/hotel-sohar), due to open in early 2012 and occupying a plum location on the beach just north of the *Sohar Beach Hotel*; check the website for the latest information.

Atlas Hotel Apartments Around 1km north of the Globe roundabout behind the Diwan Silk building Ⓣ2685 3009, Ⓕ2685 3011. Functional modern block with comfortable apartments sleeping one to four; the larger ones come with kitchen and sitting rooms. Uninspiring, but as cheap as anywhere in town. ❹

Butterfly Hotel Suites On the seafront next to the *Sohar Beach Hotel* Ⓣ2684 4531, Ⓦwww.butterflyoman.com. Upmarket hotel block, with apartments sleeping two to six people, spacious and stylishly furnished; all come with kitchen and washing machine and most have a sitting room as well. There's also a small indoor pool, a gym and an attractive in-house restaurant (unlicensed) and coffee shop, while the facilities of the *Sohar Beach Hotel* are only a stone's throw away. Non-smoking throughout. Two-person apartment around ❺

Crowne Plaza Buraimi Highway ⓣ2685 0850, ⓦwww.crowneplaza.com. Vast new five-star standing in monumental isolation next to the Buraimi highway some 3km from the coastal road (and the best part of 20km from the town centre) – a slightly surreal slice of upmarket opulence more or less in the middle of nowhere. The whole place has plenty of smooth contemporary style, with suave (if smallish) modern rooms with dark wood finishes and all mod-cons, a pair of stylish restaurants plus bar. There's also a large and attractive pool and poolside terrace lined with sunloungers, though unfortunately the view is of pylons, distant factories and rubble-strewn desert. ❻

Green Oasis Hotel 5km inland off the coastal highway along Muwelah St ⓣ2684 6077, ⓕ2684 6441. The cheapest option in Sohar, though no bargain, in an uninspiring setting next to a main road about 5km from the coastal highway, or 8km from the fort. Standard rooms are simple and functional; deluxe rooms are big but still fairly plain. There's also a small pool and a restaurant, but no bar. The hotel is directly opposite the big Oman Medical College – a useful landmark, given the lack of signage. Standard rooms ❹, deluxe rooms ❺

Sohar Beach Hotel On the coast 4km from Sallan roundabout ⓣ2684 1111, ⓦoman .swiss-belhotel.com. The nicest resort in northern Oman, this relaxing four-star sits on the beach a few kilometres north of the town centre. The main building is built to resemble a miniature white fort, with low-key Arabian touches and rooms spread in wings around the garden. Rooms are attractively plush, and there are also some family-sized chalets. There's a nice big pool in the attractive gardens, plus a strip of rather brown and pebbly beach. Facilities include a simple in-house spa offering massages and reflexology treatments, the pleasant *Al Jizzi* lounge bar, a beach bar and the attractive *Sallan* restaurant. The hotel also hosts various nightspots including a disco, and Filipino and Arabian live-music bars. ❻–❼

Al Wadi Just off Sohar Roundabout ⓣ2684 0058, ⓦwww.omanhotels.com. Old-fashioned three-star just off the main coastal highway. Rooms are comfortable enough, if somewhat plain and worn, although some, next to the hotel's small pool, have been attractively restored and are available at the same rate. There's also a passable international restaurant plus Arabian, Indian and Filipino live-music bars and a sports bar; all are usually fairly raucous, although far enough from the main building not to be a nuisance. Unfortunately, it's seriously overpriced at current rates. ❺

The fort

Sohar's snow-white **fort** sits proudly atop a small natural mound, next to the sea just south of the old town centre, an imposing structure with a tall keep rising within the enclosing walls. The fort is thought to date back to pre-Islamic times; Amr bin Al Aas, envoy of the Prophet Mohammed, is said to have been received here by the ruler of Sohar in the year 630 AD. Archeological surveys suggest that the present-day fort was rebuilt on the rubble of the original structure in around 750 AD, and probably modified at various times by later Omani rulers, as well as by the Portuguese. At the time of writing, the fort had been closed for three years while undergoing intensive renovation by a French team. The most optimistic estimate is that it will reopen in late 2011, although it could take much longer.

Around the fort

Almost next door to the fort stands the large **Sultan Qaboos Mosque**, with its eye-catching gold dome, while a five-minute walk inland is the town's new **handicrafts souk** (signed 'Omani Craftsman's House' on one side of the gate and 'Al Qala'a Souq for Handcrafts [sic] Industries' on the other), occupying a neat little walled enclosure decorated with miniature watchtowers. There are sixteen shops here, although only six were open at the time of writing, including a silversmiths, a shop selling traditional medicines and a few other places flogging the usual *khanjars*, *mandoos*, guns (real and toy) and other souvenirs. The nearby **Friday Market** (open daily, despite its name) occupies an open-air pavilion filled with

The date palm: tree of life

There are an estimated eight million date palms (*Phoenix dactylifera*; in Arabic, *nakhl*) in Oman, and travelling around the Batinah you'll rarely be out of sight of the endless plantations which blanket the coast. Dates have been a staple food in the Middle East for thousands of years; the wood of the date palm also provides an important source of building material, while leaves and fronds are used to make baskets, ropes and medicines – a remarkable variety of uses which has led to the date palm's popular description as the "tree of life".

The date palm is one of the oldest cultivated fruit trees in the world. They are believed to have been grown since ancient times from Mesopotamia to prehistoric Egypt, possibly as early as 6000 BC – one of the first human efforts at systematic agricultural cultivation. The date palm is mentioned in both the Bible and the Qur'an. Mohammed urged his followers to "cherish your father's sister, the palm tree", and Muslims still traditionally break their Ramadan fast each night by eating a date.

Dates also underpinned the traditional nomadic lifestyle of the Omani interior, providing a small, light, concentrated and long-lasting source of nutrition which was perfectly adapted for the Bedu's itinerant lifestyle. Dates are something of a self-contained nutritional super-fruit, and an excellent source of protein, vitamins and minerals. Their high sugar content (40–80 percent) also protects them against bacterial contamination and makes them extremely durable – dried dates can last for years. They can also be pressed for their juice, used to make wine, syrup and vinegar; in earlier times, boiling date syrup was used as an offensive weapon poured onto attackers below fort walls.

Cultivation

According to a traditional saying, the date palm "needs its feet in water and its head in fire", a combination provided in Oman by intensive *falaj* irrigation and the country's burning summer temperatures. Date palms grow rapidly, up to 40cm per year, reaching heights of up to around 30m. Trees can live for around 150 years, producing over 100kg of dates annually. Over forty varieties of date are grown in Oman, with over 150,000 tonnes of fruit produced annually – easily the largest crop in the country, and, until the discovery of oil, far and away the most economically important.

Dates take around seven months to mature. Unripe dates range in colour from green through to red or yellow, becoming darker and sweeter as they ripen. There are hundreds of different varieties, ranging widely in size and colour — the best are highly prized by local connoisseurs, much as fine wines are in France. There are three basic types: soft (such as the popular Medjool variety), semi-dry (such as Deglet Noor) and dry. Only the female date palm produces fruit, however. In the wild, trees are entirely wind-pollinated, and yield little fruit. Cultivated date palms are pollinated by hand, with flowers from male date palms being sold in local souks and then strategically placed in the branches of female trees (although wind machines to blow pollen onto the female flowers are also sometimes used). Most fruits are harvested between August and December. In many places, dates are still handpicked, although mechanical shakers may be used in larger plantations.

stallholders selling fruit, vegetables and animal feed – worth a look if you're around in the morning, although things are usually pretty dead after around 11am.

North of the fort

North of the fort lies **old Sohar**, the site of the original town, bounded by dried-up wadis to the north and south, though it's now old in name only: the eminently forgettable shops and villas here date back only to the 1990s, when the old souk was demolished. More appealing is the parallel seafront **Corniche**, with

Sindbad and Sohar

Sohar is often claimed to be the birthplace of the legendary **Sindbad** (or Sinbad), hero of the "Seven Voyages of Sindbad the Sailor", one of the most famous tales in the *One Thousand and One Nights*, subsequently recycled into countless films, cartoons and books. It's a nice story, given Oman's historic seafaring prowess, and one you'll probably see recycled a few times in local tourist literature, although sadly it has little basis in fact – attempts to claim the legendary sailor as a local Sohari appear to be simply an attempt to acquire prestige by association, rather as the English have adopted St George (who was actually a Roman soldier from Palestine).

Sindbad himself is clearly a mythical figure, a composite hero whose legendary adventures derive from centuries of seafaring folklore and assorted travellers' tales derived from a wide variety of sources. According to the *One Thousand and One Nights*, Sindbad was a merchant from Baghdad, who set sail from Basra, although the stories of his seven voyages most likely derive from Persian sources, or perhaps from the famous collection of Sanskrit fables known as the *Panchatantra*. The name Sindbad itself is Persian rather than Arab, and may even be derived from Sindh (now a province in Pakistan), from which the names of both the Indus River and, ultimately, India, derive.

a breezy waterside walkway under interminable blue lampposts. Continuing along the Corniche some 750m north of the old town centre brings you to the town's striking modern **fish market**, its elegantly curved roofline designed to echo that of a traditional Arabian dhow.

The best bits of **beach** are at the top end of town, just north of the *Sohar Beach Hotel*, with a wide, mud-coloured swathe of sand, scattered with seashells and with fine coastal views. Next to the beach lies an attractively shady **park** arranged around a large lake.

South of the fort

South of the fort, you can follow the road for about 5km through an attractive string of oases before turning inland to reach the coastal highway at As Suwayhirah roundabout. This part of town is also where you'll find the local **bullfighting arena** (see p.116) in a large circular enclosure with sloping stone sides. The arena is two blocks east of the large stadium.

Eating

Even by Omani standards there's a distinct lack of decent places to **eat** in Sohar, and you'll most likely end up eating where you're staying. If you fancy heading out, the best place to aim for is the *Sallan* restaurant at the *Sohar Beach Hotel*, which dishes up a well-prepared selection of continental, Chinese, Indian and Arabian mains (around 6–8 OR) on its attractive outdoor candlelit terrace, or inside, if it's too hot.

Onward from Sohar

Sohar is the nexus for several of the north's major routes, either continuing north along the coast to **Shinas** and the two UAE border crossings beyond or heading inland to either **Buraimi** (and another entry point into the UAE) or south along the newly surfaced road to **Yanqul and Ibri**.

North of Sohar

The area **north of Sohar** doesn't boast any stand-out attractions, although if you're driving up to the UAE or Musandam, there are a couple of low-key sights to break the journey.

Some 25km north of Sohar, the coastal settlement of **LIWA** is home to the inevitable **fort** (not open to the public), its extensive curtain wall and five round towers topped with unusually spiky sawtooth battlements, with a tall and narrow keep inside – a design somewhat reminiscent of that of Suwaiq Fort (see p.124) further down the coast. Unusually, the fort doesn't lie on the coast, but 1km or so inland. Continue along the road past the fort to reach the seafront. South of here stretches the enormous new **Sohar Port** complex with its impressive tangle of cranes, cargo ships and containers; to the north, in complete contrast, a meandering sea inlet threads its way behind the beach, lined with mangrove thickets and with abundant birdlife – a fine place for a quiet picnic.

A further 36km north of Liwa, the town of **SHINAS** is notable mainly for being the most northerly town in Oman (excepting Musandam, of course). As throughout the Batinah, fishing is the main industry here, with a busy harbour enclosed by two curling breakwaters; much of the local catch ends up on the restaurant tables of Dubai. There's also yet another identikit **fort** (more or less behind the harbour), while the neat little covered souk next door is also worth a quick look.

If you're in Shinas, you're probably continuing on into the UAE through one of two border crossings in the area (for details of border formalities, see p.20). The first continues due north to reach the border at **Khatmat Milahah**. The second heads inland to reach the border at **Hatta**.

South to Ibri via Yanqul

The recently opened highway between **Sohar and Yanqul** offers perhaps the easiest way of getting between the coast and the mountains. It's 110km from Sohar to Yanqul, a drive of around 75 minutes along a fast and scenic highway, with hardly any traffic. The road to Yanqul runs off the Globe roundabout in Sohar (although it's not signed to Yanqul, only to Wadi Habib). Note that there are **no petrol stations** between Sohar and Yanqul, while there are also a couple of wadis about 30km out of Sohar which are prone to flooding. The road is fairly tedious for the first 40km or so (excepting a sign to the jovial-sounding village of Beer Jam about 25km out of Sohar) but becomes increasingly dramatic as the mountains approach and the road begins to hairpin upwards, eventually breasting the crest of the ridge slightly over halfway to Yanqul, before descending into the village of Al Waqbah.

YANQUL itself is a remote and rather sleepy little place lying in the shadow of the huge triangular Jebel al Hawra and surrounded by eye-catching mountain formations – slender rock pinnacles, craggy ridgetops, table mountains – which make for enjoyable viewing during the drive from Sohar to Ibri. It's worth stopping here to have a look at the town's attractive mudbrick fort, the **Bait al Marah** (not open to the public), built at the beginning of seventeenth century by the Nabhani dynasty (see p.221). The **old village** behind is also interesting, with dozens of crumbling mudbrick houses in an advanced state of decay, plus more modern concrete homes with colourful (though faded) metal doors. Most of the houses are now abandoned, although the *falaj* still flows in places. To reach the fort, turn right at the T-junction at the beginning of Yanqul (if approaching from Sohar) and turn right along the road to Dank. The fort is about 1km along this road, on the right.

West to Buraimi

The 100km trip from Sohar to Buraimi takes around ninety minutes along **Highway 7**. The highway follows the course of **Wadi Jizzi**, formerly one of the most important trading routes in Oman, linking the coast and hills, and also important since antiquity for its copper deposits, which were exported as far afield as Mesopotamia and Persia. The stretch up to the **Wadi Jizzi border post** en route to Buraimi (see below) is dual carriageway, fast and normally pleasantly traffic free, with the added bonus of superb mountain scenery en route. The first section of the road is dominated by the outline of Jebel Sohar, the high and isolated peak away to your left. Later on the highway winds up into the hills, past a long succession of magnificently craggy peaks – the Omani landscape at its barest and most dramatic.

Past the Wadi Jizzi border post, the road climbs up on a broad plateau ringed by distant peaks. The road is single carriageway from here into Buraimi, and normally significantly busier with traffic, although major roadworks are afoot in an attempt to ease traffic flow.

Al Dhahirah

Inland from the Batinah, **Al Dhahirah** region is one of the least visited parts of the country, a largely uninspiring and dusty stretch of featureless gravel desert stretching from the UAE border down to the mountains around Bahla. The region's main town, **Buraimi**, serves as a convenient entry or exit point if you're heading to or from Abu Dhabi or Dubai, although it's also well worth a visit in its own right. From Buraimi, a spectacular road runs over the mountains and down Wadi Jizzi to the coast at Sohar.

Alternatively, the fast and relatively traffic-free Highway 21 arrows south from Buraimi to the little-visited but surprisingly interesting town of **Ibri**, worth a stop-off for a look at its old fort and souk, and for the extraordinary old kasbah at **As Suleif** nearby. Beyond Ibri lie the villages of **Bat** and **Al Ayn**, home to a fascinating scatter of Bronze Age beehive tombs and other structures, some of Oman's most important archeological remains.

Buraimi البريمي

Highway 7 from Sohar ends at the town of **BURAIMI**, pushed up right against the border next to the more or less contiguous UAE city of Al Ain. Evidence of human settlement here dates back for some five thousand years, and the Buraimi oasis was historically one of the most important inland settlements in this part of Arabia thanks to its position astride the major trade route between Sohar, Wadi Jizzi and the interior, with a string of villages growing up around the various oases which dot the area. These have now been divided by the modern Oman–UAE border, while Buraimi itself has been comprehensively overtaken by the neighbouring – and now much wealthier and busier – Al Ain. Because of the town's distance from pretty much everywhere else in Oman and the border hassles associated with visiting it (see box, p.133), Buraimi doesn't feature on many Omani

Visiting Buraimi: border practicalities

Visiting Buraimi is significantly complicated by the bizarre fact that you have to technically "leave" Oman in order to reach the town. **Approaching from Sohar**, there is a border post on the main Highway 7 at **Wadi Jizzi** about 40km before Buraimi. You will be stamped out of Oman here (and, if you are on a single-entry visa, have it cancelled), even though the road beyond the border post is still in Omani territory – you don't actually reach the UAE border until Al Ain, 40km distant. If you're visiting Buraimi only and then returning directly to Sohar it should be possible to not have your visa cancelled, but make this very clear when you present your passport to avoid having your visa cancelled. **Entering the UAE** from Buraimi, foreigners (excepting citizens of the UAE, Saudi Arabia, Qatar, Kuwait and Bahrain) have to pass through the **Hili border post** just north of the town centre.

Approaching **from Ibri** along Highway 21 the border is at **Mazyad**, about 25km before Buraimi, after which the road enters UAE territory, meaning that you will have to exit Oman here and then re-enter it at the Hili border post between Al Ain and Buraimi (paying the UAE exit tax of 35 AED, roughly US$10, in order to do so, plus 20 OR for a fresh Omani visa, if you don't have a multiple-entry one).

Re-entering Oman at either Wadi Jizzi or Mazyad, single-entry Oman visas are issued on the spot for a fee of 20 OR. In practice it can take as little as ten minutes to clear border formalities, although half an hour is a more realistic rule of thumb.

itineraries – which is a shame, given the town's bustling mercantile atmosphere and pair of fine forts.

Accommodation

Buraimi Hotel On the road to Sohar, about 2km east of the centre ⓣ2564 2010, ⓕ2564 2011. Pleasant, slighty old-fashioned three-star – not as upmarket as you'd think from the rather flashy entrance, although rates are still on the high side. Rooms are large and very comfortably furnished, while facilities include a decent-sized, if rather murky, pool in the scruffy little walled garden at the back and a passable restaurant (licensed) serving a wide range of international food, with mains around 2.5–3.5 OR. ❺

Al Jawarhar Hotel Opposite the *Buraimi Hotel* ⓣ2565 3440, ⓕ2565 3441. A fine budget option, with clean and bright (if slightly poky) rooms, and conveniently close to a good selection of local restaurants, including the one in the *Buraimi Hotel*. Not much English spoken. ❷

Al Salam Hotel ⓣ2565 5789, ⓦwww.alsalamhoteloman.com. Well-run three-star – not quite as nice as the *Buraimi Hotel*, but a fair bit cheaper. Rooms are pleasantly furnished with slightly chintzy wooden furniture, and there's a coffee shop and (unlicensed) restaurant downstairs. ❸

The Town

Modern Buraimi is an engagingly lively place, with a large Indian and Pakistani population and a distinct mercantile buzz – the main road through town just east of Al Hillah Fort is particularly colourful, with an incredible quantity of ladies' tailoring shops stuffed full of extravagantly embroidered clothes and adorned with brilliant neon signs. In many ways the town feels closer to Dubai and Abu Dhabi than Muscat, which of course geographically it is – every second or third car seems to be from the UAE, while you're likely to see as many white Emirati headrobes as Omani caps.

Khandaq Fort

There are several interesting things to see in Buraimi town – as well as a further slew of attractions over the border in Al Ain (see p.135). The main sight in Buraimi

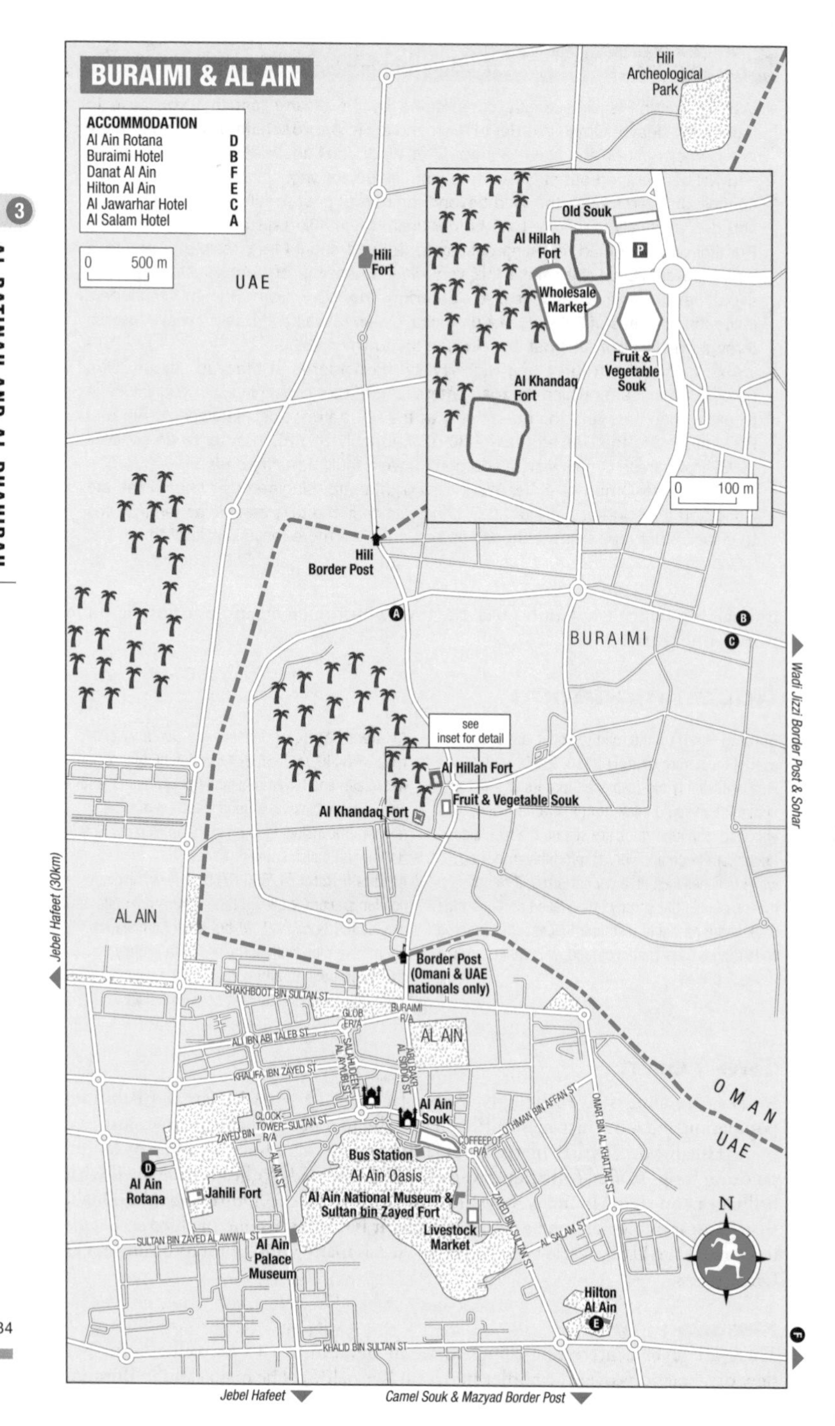

BURAIMI & AL AIN
ACCOMMODATION
Al Ain Rotana D
Buraimi Hotel B
Danat Al Ain F
Hilton Al Ain E
Al Jawarhar Hotel C
Al Salam Hotel A
0 500 m
UAE
Hili Archeological Park
Hili Fort
Old Souk
Al Hillah Fort
Wholesale Market
Fruit & Vegetable Souk
Al Khandaq Fort
0 100 m
Hili Border Post
BURAIMI
Wadi Jizzi Border Post & Sohar
see inset for detail
Al Hillah Fort
Fruit & Vegetable Souk
Al Khandaq Fort
AL AIN
Jebel Hafeet (30km)
Border Post (Omani & UAE nationals only)
SHAKHBOOT BIN SULTAN ST
GLOBE R/A
BURAIMI R/A
AL AIN
ALI IBN ABI TALEB ST
SALAHUDEEN AL AYYUBI ST
ABU BAKR AL SIDDIQ ST
KHALIFA IBN ZAYED ST
OMAN
UAE
OTHMAN BIN AFFAN ST
OMAR BIN AL KHATTAB ST
Al Ain Souk
CLOCK TOWER R/A
ZAYED BIN SULTAN ST
COFFEEPOT R/A
Bus Station
Al Ain Oasis
AL AIN ST
Al Ain Rotana
Jahili Fort
Al Ain National Museum & Sultan bin Zayed Fort
Livestock Market
ZAYED BIN SULTAN ST
AL SALAM ST
N
SULTAN BIN ZAYED AL AWWAL ST
Al Ain Palace Museum
Hilton Al Ain
KHALID BIN SULTAN ST
Jebel Hafeet
Camel Souk & Mazyad Border Post

Al Ain

Al Ain has a surprisingly rich collection of sights (for more on which, see the *Rough Guide to Dubai*). The **Al Ain National Museum** (Sat–Thurs 8.30am–7.30pm, Fri 3–7.30pm, closed Mon; 3 AED; Ⓦwww.aam.gov.ae) boasts interesting exhibits on the city's history, while the picturesque **Sultan Bin Zayed Fort** next door (same hours and ticket) is famous as the birthplace of Sheikh Zayed Bin Sultan Al Nahyan (ruled 1966–2004), the much-loved ruler of Abu Dhabi and first president of the UAE. The nearby **Livestock Market** and **Al Ain Souk** are also worth a look, as is the idyllic **Al Ain Oasis** (daily sunrise–sunset; free) immediately west of the museum, the largest of the seven oases scattered across the city.

Further sights lie spread out across the city. On the western side of Al Ain Oasis stands the sprawling but rather uninteresting **Al Ain Palace Museum** (Sat–Thurs 8.30am–7.30pm, Fri 3–7.30pm; free) and much more rewarding **Jahili Fort** (Tues–Thurs, Sat & Sun 9am–5pm, Fri 3–5pm; free), also home to an excellent little exhibition detailing the life and extraordinary exploits of legendary explorer **Wilfred Thesiger** (1910–2003), who stayed at the fort in the late 1940s. About 8km north of the city, the **Hili Gardens and Archeological Park** (daily 9am–10pm; 1 AED) is the site of one of the most important archeological finds in the UAE, and includes the Great Hili Tomb (though it may actually have been some kind of temple), dating from the third century BC.

Accommodation

If you want to **stay** in Al Ain, the city boasts three low-key five-stars. *Al Ain Rotana* (Ⓣ03-754 5111, Ⓦwww.rotana.com; 700–900 AED/❼) is the best of the bunch, conveniently close to the city centre, with pleasantly chintzy Arabian decor. The slightly cheaper but less attractive alternatives are the *Hilton Al Ain* (Ⓣ03-678 6666, Ⓦwww.hilton.com; 500–550 AED/❻) – rather dated, although with attractive grounds and pool – and the *Danat Al Ain Resort* (Ⓣ03-704 600, Ⓦwww.danathotels.com; 600–700AED/❻), in a very peaceful setting on the edge of town.

proper is the immaculately restored **Al Khandaq Fort** (Sun–Thurs 8am–2pm; free), thought to have been built during the rule of Sultan Said bin Sultan in around 1842 – as suggested by a brass cannon bearing this name and date which can be found inside. The fort occupies a slightly elevated position above a dried-up wadi, its somewhat vulnerable location compensated for by the deep moat which surrounds it. The exterior design of the fort is quite unlike any other in Oman (although somewhat reminiscent of nearby Jahili Fort just over the border in Al Ain): modest in size but prettily decorated, with diminutive, slope-sided round towers adorned with zigzagging triangles and chevrons. The interior of the fort is relatively bare, consisting of a large gravel courtyard from where ramps and steps lead up to a walkway around the battlements, with a couple of small buildings clustered below.

The souks

A couple of hundred metres north of the fort lies Buraimi's interesting huddle of souks. The large **Fruit and Vegetable Souk** occupies a rather grand edifice resembling a kind of postmodern fort. Inside, Indian and Pakistani traders preside over vast piles of colourful edibles; a couple of shops at the front sell quaint traditional wooden furniture, with ingenious lattice effects made out of mangrove poles and palm branches tied together with coconut string. The **wholesale souk** next door (in a similar building) is usually quieter, with merchandise including big piles of dried fish, sacks of dates and large bundles of wood.

Beyond the Fruit and Vegetable Souk, on the far side of the small car park, lies the **old souk**, the third and most interesting of the three souks, in a small white building with a fake watchtower at its centre. This is notably more traditional in flavour than its neighbours. The aisles to either side are full of little shops selling big stacks of spices, plus shoes, food, walking sticks and traditional toy rifles. There's also an unusual section at the back run by Bedu women selling spices alongside locally produced honey and rose-water, best appreciated while having a drink at the small café beneath the central tower.

Al Hillah Fort

Flanking the other side of the car park between the fruit and vegetable and old souks lies the second of Buraimi's two forts, **Al Hillah Fort** (Sun–Thurs 8am–2pm; free), a low-slung sandstone edifice, rather plain and box-like from the outside, although full of interest within. It's actually a walled residential complex rather than a proper fort – the walls come with the usual battlements and rifle slits, but there are no proper defensive towers or cannon on display. The entrance gateway leads into a large gravel courtyard, empty save for a small mosque with external *mihrab* and quaint little freestanding gateway with

The nasty affair at the Buraimi Oasis

A sleepy backwater for much of its history, Buraimi briefly captured the world's attention in the early 1950s as a result of the so-called **Buraimi Dispute** – one of the defining events in Oman's twentieth-century history, and one which neatly encapsulates the Wild West atmosphere of the early days of oil prospecting in the Gulf. The **origin** of the dispute was the result of Saudi Arabia's claim in 1949 to sovereignty over large parts of what was traditionally considered territory belonging to Abu Dhabi and Oman, including the Buraimi Oasis. The Saudis (supported by the US Aramco oil company) backed up their claim by referring to previous periods of Saudi occupation dating back to the early nineteenth century, although their real interest in Buraimi stemmed from the belief that large amounts of oil lay buried in the region

In 1952 a small group of Saudi Arabian soldiers occupied **Hamasa**, one of three Omani villages in the oasis, claiming it for Saudi Arabia and embarking on a campaign of bribery in an attempt to obtain professions of loyalty from local villagers. They also attempted to bribe **Sheikh Zayed al Nahyan**, governor of Al Ain, tempting him with the huge sum of US$42 million – an offer which Sheikh Zayed pointedly refused. The affair was debated in both the British Parliament and at the United Nations, although attempts at international arbitration finally broke down in 1955. Shortly afterwards the Saudis were driven out of Hamasa by the Trucial Oman Levies, a British-backed force based in Sharjah; for an eyewitness account of this action, read Edward Henderson's *Arabian Destiny* (p.239). The dispute wasn't finally resolved until 1974, when an agreement was reached between King Faisal of Saudi Arabia and Sheikh Zayed (who had subsequently become ruler of Abu Dhabi and first president of the newly independent UAE). Ironically, after all the fuss, the area proved singularly lacking in oil.

The dispute gave Buraimi its proverbial fifteen minutes of fame, even inspiring an episode of *The Goon Show* entitled "The Nasty Affair at the Buraimi Oasis". More importantly, it put a final end to centuries of Saudi incursions into Oman, as well as establishing the legendary reputation of Sheikh Zayed, one of the modern Gulf's most charismatic statesmen, who succeeded in repulsing the oil-rich Saudis and their American cronies long before Abu Dhabi had found its own huge oil reserves. As one foreign observer put it, "He [Zayed] was very proud that, when he had nothing, he told them to get stuffed."

wooden doors. Go right from here to reach the complex's **second courtyard**, where you'll find one of Oman's finest clusters of traditional residential buildings, with three impressive two-storey buildings, embellished with superb wooden doors and carved details including unusual windows formed out of interlocking triangles; climb to the roofs of any of the three for fine views over the complex.

Eating and drinking

There are the usual cafés scattered around town, including a particularly lively line of coffee shops and restaurants directly opposite the *Buraimi Hotel* (and alongside *Al Jawarhar Hotel*), serving up good shwarmas, grilled chicken, curries, samosas and juices. The only **licensed** venue in town is the restaurant at the *Buraimi Hotel*.

Ibri عبري

Strung out along Buraimi-Nizwa highway (Highway 21) more or less in the middle of nowhere, **IBRI** sees few foreign visitors, although it boasts a surprisingly absorbing cluster of traditional sights including a fine fort, interesting souk and one of the region's most memorable walled mudbrick villages at nearby As Suleif. The town was formerly a stronghold of Ibadhi conservatism, though modern Ibri derives its importance from its proximity to Fahud, where Oman's first oil was discovered in 1964.

The only **place to stay** in town is the *Ibri Oasis Hotel* (ⓣ2568 9955, ⓔiohotel@omantel.net.com; ④), situated 9km from the town-centre roundabout along the Buraimi highway, just past the Ibri College of Technology and the huge Ibri Sports Complex stadium. It's one of the nicest and best-value hotels in northern Oman – although unfortunately in a place very few tourists come to – with friendly service, spacious and very comfortably furnished rooms and a decent (licensed) restaurant plus bar with live Arabian music.

The Town

The main sight in town is the large and carefully restored **fort** (Sun–Thurs 8am–2pm; free). Inside, the spacious gravel courtyard is surrounded by an interesting jumble of buildings and towers. To the right of the entrance stands the main defensive tower, an impressive three-storey structure; to the left, the remains of a mudbrick mosque with a deep well built into the platform alongside; and, on the far side of the courtyard, a residential building. Head left across the courtyard, through a second gateway, to reach a subsidiary courtyard, where steps lead up to a sizeable **mosque**, one of the largest in any Omani fort and still in use today, although kitted out with eyesore modern glass windows and metal pillars. This is actually only half the fort; the rest, beyond the mosque, remains closed to the public.

The area **around the fort** is significantly less manicured, but ultimately much more memorable, with dozens of imposing mudbrick houses (and a particularly fine ruined mosque opposite the fort) in various states of ruin, dotted here and there with little patches of dead oasis with decapitated palm trees. It's a perfect picture of the physical passing of old Oman – intensely atmospheric, and rather sad. Pressed up hard against the west wall of the fort is the town's attractive old **souk**, including some neat little arcaded sections.

To **reach the fort and old town**, take the turning signed Ibri Souk and Town Centre from the middle of Ibri (on the right-hand side if approaching from Bahla), then take the unsigned left-hand turn about 100m beyond, heading up past the Makkah Hypermarket on your left then following the road for about 1km as it curves round to the right, bringing you to a small roundabout. Head straight across this and follow the narrow road through the souk to reach the fort (there's a large car park in front of it in which to leave your vehicle).

As Suleif

On the southern edge of town lies Ibri's most absorbing attraction, the remarkable walled village of **As Suleif**, a huge clump of collapsing mudbrick buildings which crown a small hill next to the main Nizwa highway. Like so many settlements in Oman, the old mudbrick village was abandoned a couple of decades ago in favour of the modern concrete villa development which now stands beside it, and the original settlement is now slowly crumbling into picturesque ruin – see it now before it collapses completely.

The entire village is impressively fortified, with high walls at the front and sides, and a string of watchtowers stuck like candles into the massive rock outcrop at the back. Inside is an incredibly labyrinthine, kasbah-like tangle of old roofless houses and other structures including a mosque, jail, various wells, *majlis*, food stores, a room for pressing dates and a "hanging tower" at the summit of the rock where unfortunates were taken to be executed. The remains of various inscriptions moulded onto arches or inscribed on rocks can also be seen. The resident guardian will meet you at the entrance and show you around. There's no admission price, although a couple of rials should suffice.

East of Ibri

East of Ibri, Highway 21 roars purposefully east towards Bahla, just under 100km distance. The area is home to two of Oman's most celebrated prehistoric sites: the beehive tombs at **Bat** and **Al Ayn**. The former is more likely to appeal to dedicated archeologists or students of ancient history than casual visitors, though the latter, with a string of beehive tombs lined up dramatically atop a rocky ridge, is well worth the detour from the main highway.

Bat

Around 30km east of Ibri, the small village of **BAT** is home to a remarkable array of **Bronze Age tombs**, towers and other remains, listed as a UNESCO World Heritage Site since 1988 (along with those at nearby Al Ayn; see opposite). The site dates back to between 2000 and 3000 BC, forming, according to UNESCO, "the most complete collection of settlements and necropolises from the 3rd millennium BC in the world". To the untrained eye, it's difficult to make much sense of the remains you see on the ground, although the sheer scale of the ruins is impressive and the whole place is particularly beautiful towards dusk, when the light turns the surrounding hills a rich russet, their ridges dotted with the enigmatic remains of one of Oman's most ancient civilizations. If you want to have a look at the tombs before visiting, there are a couple of nice 360-degree **panophotographs** of the site (and also of nearby Al Ayn) at ⓦwww.world-heritage-tour.org/middle-east/oman/bat/map.html.

The archeological site

Getting there is the first challenge. **From Ibri**, follow the road to Yanqul for about 15km then take the signed turn-off on the right to Bat and follow the road as it loops through a small village, past a mosque, straight on across a small roundabout and then turn right along the unsigned road in front of Al Dreez Modern Market. **From Yanqul**, take the signed turn-off on your left to Bat then the left turn signed to Al Wahrah, which brings you to the road in front of Al Dreez Modern Market. Follow the road past Al Dreez Modern Market for about 13km to reach a turning on the left signed to Al Banah and Al Hajar – this is the road on to Al Ayn (see below).

Ignore this turning for the moment and continue straight ahead for a further 2km to reach a blue sign on the left saying Wadi al Ain 23km and pointing down a dirt track. Follow this track for about 1km (you'll see the remains of a prominent white tower up on the hillside to your left) until you reach a ruined tower in a fenced enclosure next to the track on your right; park hereabouts. You're now pretty much at the centre of the archeological site, stretching for a couple of kilometres in every direction, although there are no signs or marked trails to guide you. There are some four hundred tombs scattered around the surrounding hills, although virtually all have collapsed and now look essentially like large mounds of rubble.

From here, it's a 5–10 minutes' walk up to the remains of the circular **white tower** you probably saw on the drive in, halfway up the hill overlooking the wadi. This is one of a number of such structures dotted around the site, now standing about 1m high after restoration (although they may originally have been up to 10m tall), with a distinctive triangular door, walls formed from beautifully carved and carefully fitted pieces of stone and an interior divided into two "rooms" by a single wall down the middle. The exact function of this and other similar towers around Bat – or, indeed, what they originally looked like – remains unknown.

Two further towers stand next to one another in the wadi below; one has been restored using white stones, and the other using ochre, which makes for a nice photo, although the underlying archeological reasoning behind two-tone restoration remains unclear. Continue walking up the wadi for another ten minutes to reach an enclosure protected by a green wire-mesh fence (padlocked at the time of writing). Inside are three neatly restored beehive **tombs** (very similar to the towers, though a little smaller), one constructed out of white stones, the other two out of ochre, along with half-a-dozen other tombs in various stages of collapse. The remains of further partially intact beehive tombs can be seen along the ridgetop beyond.

Al Ayn

Some 37km further east from Bat, the small village of **AL AYN** is home to another superb collection of Bronze Age necropolises. The appeal of the tombs here is their spectacular setting, strung out along a narrow ridgetop and dramatically backdropped by the craggy outline of **Jebel Misht** (literally "Comb Mountain", named on account of its distinctively serrated ridgetop), one of the largest of the various geological "exotics" which dot this part of Oman. There are 21 tombs in total, most of them well preserved, and late afternoon is a particularly magical time to see them.

To reach Al Ayn **from Bat**, follow the directions outlined above. Follow the road to Al Ayn until you reach a T-junction just before the village. Turn left here and you'll see the tombs up on your left on top of the ridge as you drive into the village, around 500m past the T-junction. It's a straightforward ten-minute walk from the road up to the tombs, although there's no obvious path. Cross the wadi bed and scramble up a track roughly opposite the big mosque at the entrance to the village.

Al Ayn is also accessible via two side-roads **from the Ibri–Nizwa highway**. Approaching from Ibri, take the turn-off at the village of Kubarah signed to Amla. Approaching from Nizwa, take the turning about 13km further down the road by the Al Maha petrol station, also signed to Amla.

Musandam

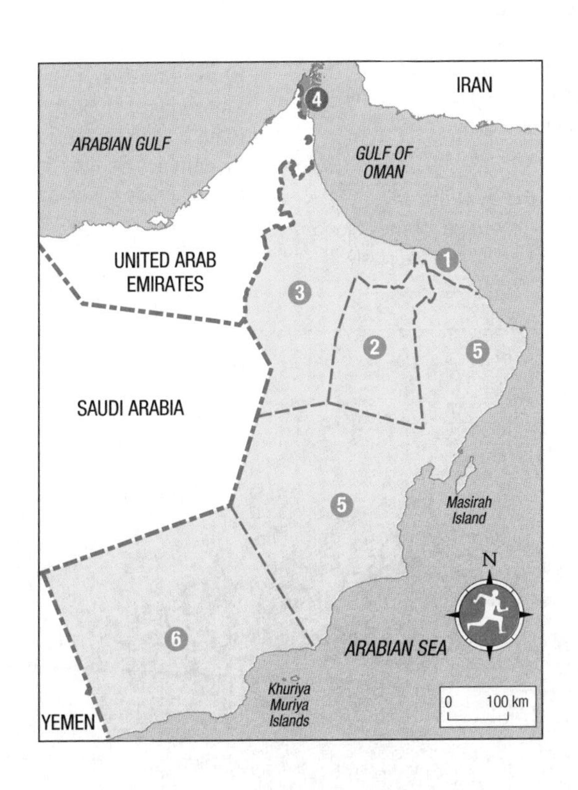
IRAN
4
ARABIAN GULF
GULF OF OMAN
1
UNITED ARAB EMIRATES
3
2
5
SAUDI ARABIA
5
Masirah Island
N
6
ARABIAN SEA
Khuriya Muriya Islands
0 100 km
YEMEN

CHAPTER 4 Highlights

* **Khasab Fort** Engaging Portuguese fort, with old wooden dhows lined up in the courtyard and absorbing displays on traditional life in Musandam. See p.146

* **Khor ash Sham** Musandam's largest and most beautiful *khor*, the perfect place to spend a day on the water, swimming, snorkelling and dolphin-spotting. See p.152

* **Sea trip to Kumzar** Marvellous sea journey along the coast to the famously isolated town of Kumzar, at the northernmost tip of Musandam. See p.153

* **Jebel Harim** Drive up Musandam's highest peak, rising amid dramatic mountain landscapes at the heart of the peninsula. See p.156

* **The coastal road from Khasab to Bukha** Explore Musandam's stunning coastal road, a spectacular feat of modern engineering, as it hugs the cliff-lined coast south from Khasab. See p.158

▲ Dhow journey in Musandam

4

Musandam

At the northeastern most tip of the Arabian peninsula (and separated from the rest of Oman by a wide swathe of UAE territory) the dramatic **Musandam peninsula** is perhaps the most scenically spectacular area in the entire Gulf. Often described as "The Norway of Arabia", the peninsula boasts a magical combination of mountain and maritime landscapes, as the towering red-rock Hajar mountains fall precipitously into the blue waters of the Arabian Gulf, creating a labyrinthine system of steep-sided fjords (*khors*), cliffs and islands, most of them inaccessible except by boat. Musandam remains one of Oman's great wildernesses, with a largely untouched natural environment ranging from the pristine waters of the coast, where you can see frolicking dolphins, basking sharks and the occasional whale, through to the wild uplands of the *jebel*, dotted with fossils and petroglyphs.

The main town in Musandam proper is lively little **Khasab**, at the top of the peninsula and connected to the outside world by the spectacular **coastal road** which runs down via Bukha to the UAE border at Tibat. Khasab offers the perfect base for boat (or diving) trips out on the marvellous **Khor ash Sham** or, further afield, to the remote town of **Kumzar**, as well as for mountain safaris up the mighty **Jebel Harim** and beyond.

Getting to Musandam

Musandam is separated from the rest of Oman by around 70km of the UAE, although getting to the peninsula has become increasingly easy in the past few years thanks to the introduction of daily **flights** and a weekly **ferry** service from Muscat. Even so, it's still much easier to reach Khasab from Dubai (a drive of around 3–4hr) than from the Omani capital; for information on driving to Musandam from the rest of Oman, see the box on p.145.

By plane

The easiest way of getting to Musandam is to fly. Oman Air operate **daily flights** from Muscat to Khasab (and back again) in small twin-prop planes. The flight takes 1hr 10min, with **fares** in the region of 50 OR. Convenience aside, the flight also offers spectacular views of the mountains: the last ten minutes before landing in Khasab must be one of the world's most spectacular plane journeys, and is worth the ticket price alone. Oman Air also offer a convenient "Cruise 'n' Fly" package (143 OR/person), giving you the chance to fly up to Khasab and then return by ferry (or vice versa) and including two nights at the *Golden Tulip* hotel.

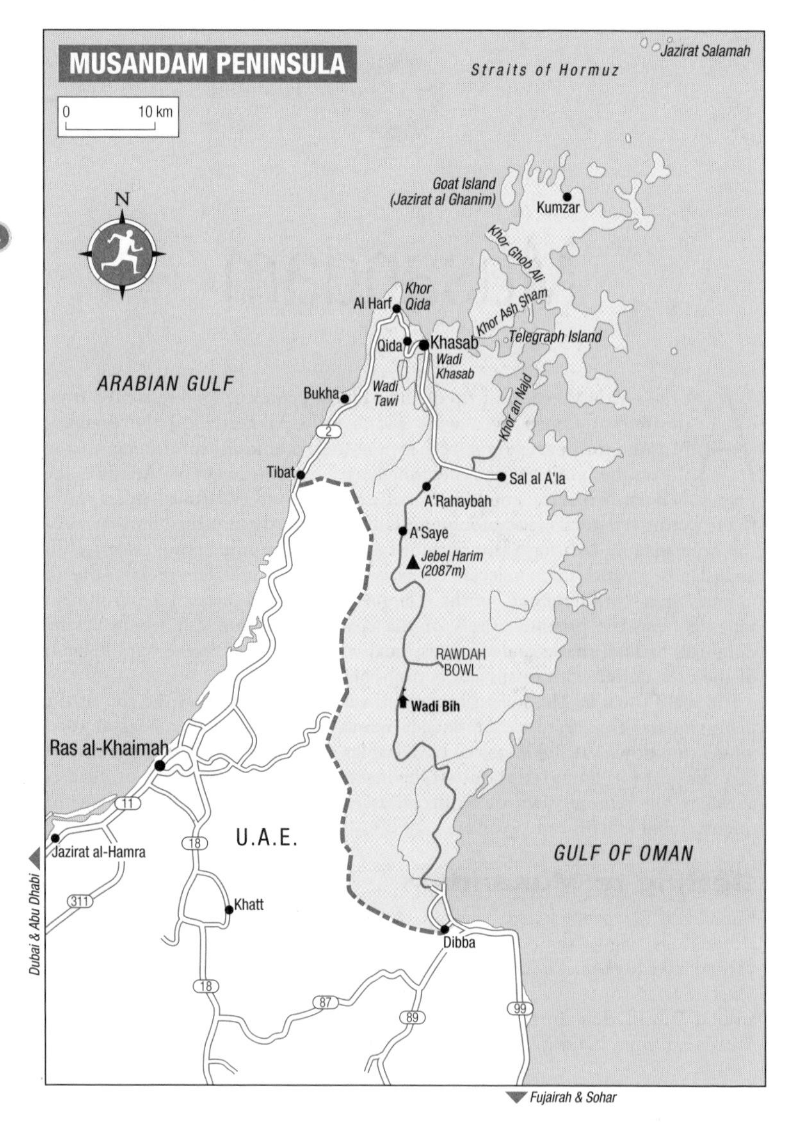

By ferry

Two state-of-the-art **high-speed ferries** operated by the National Ferries Company (Ⓦ www.nfc.om) sail regularly between Muscat and Khasab. From Muscat, there are departures every Wednesday and Friday at 3pm (plus an additional Monday departure in winter), arriving in Khasab at 8pm. From Khasab, ferries depart on Wednesdays and Fridays at noon (plus an additional Monday departure in winter), arriving in Muscat at 5pm. The **fare** is 23 OR in "tourist class" or 45 OR in "business class" (which offers better views from the front of the boat); children aged 4–12 travel roughly half price, under 4s go free. The ferry wasn't carrying cars at the time of writing, although they may have begun to do so by the time you read this.

There are two options for buying **tickets in Muscat**. The first, and easiest, is to book your ticket through a local travel agent (tour operators in all the city's upmarket hotels should be able to organize this for you). Alternatively, reserve by phone on ⓣ800 72 000 or by email via ⓔreservation@nfcoman.com and then collect your ticket from the booth at Sultan Qaboos Port prior to departure. You can buy **tickets in Khasab** at the National Ferries Company office (ⓣ2673 1802) down by the port, or, more conveniently, through Khasab Travel & Tours or Musandam Sea Adventures (see p.148).

Khasab خصب

Musandam's major town, **KHASAB** sits at the far northern end of the peninsula in a narrow plain squeezed in between the mountains – one of the few sizeable areas of flat coastal real estate in the entire peninsula. It's a small but lively place, and one which feels a long way from the rest of Oman, the slightly Wild West atmosphere stoked up by hordes of locals charging around in pick-up trucks, bands

Driving to Musandam

The road trip up to Musandam **from the rest of Oman** may look like an interesting adventure on paper, but is actually a bit of a slog, involving four sets of border formalities and many kilometres of largely featureless driving. This is especially the case if you take the tedious western route via Dubai, although the route up the east coast of the UAE is significantly more pleasant, and offers the chance to have a look at the relatively little-visited eastern and northern edges of the UAE en route.

Travelling from Oman, the trip can also work out to be surprisingly expensive. If you don't have a multiple-entry visa, you'll have to buy two new **Omani visas**, each at a cost of 20 OR – one for when entering Musandam and one for when re-entering the rest of Oman. You also pay 35 dirhams (around $10/£6) each time you exit the UAE. If driving yourself you'll need to get additional **car insurance** from your car-rental operator covering you to drive in the UAE – expect to pay around 20 OR, which will cover you for a week. By the time you've paid for visas and insurance, you might well be looking at a total cost of around $170/£100 – slightly more than the average plane fare.

There's only one surfaced road into Musandam: this enters the west side of the peninsula at **Tibat** from Ras al Khaimah emirate, then runs up the coast to Khasab. The border post at Tibat is open 24hr. Count on around thirty minutes to clear Omani and UAE border formalities, although it can take significantly longer at weekends and on public holidays. There's a second entry point to Musandam on the eastern side of the peninsula at **Dibba**, but this is open only to citizens of Oman and the UAE.

There are **two main routes** from the rest of Oman up to the Musandam border post at Tibat, taking roughly 4–5 hours from Sohar or Buraimi, or around eight hours from Muscat. The first starts at **Buraimi** and then follows Route E66 from Al Ain down to the edge of Dubai, and then the Emirates Road (Route 311) up to Ras al Khaimah, a boring and often stressful drive along two of the UAE's busiest highways (maps show some quieter cross-country roads, but these are surprisingly difficult to find without local knowledge). A slower but more pleasant option is the drive exiting Oman **north of Sohar** at Khatmat Milalah then heading up the attractive east coast of the UAE along Highway 99 through Fujairah and Khawr Fakkan to Dibba, before looping back round to Ras al Khaimah via highways 87 and 18.

Unfortunately, whichever route you take there's no way of avoiding **Ras al Khaimah**, a major bottleneck, exacerbated by the hopeless lack of signage – if in doubt, try to keep driving in the general direction of the mountains.

of Iranian traders loading up goods in the Old Souk and the occasional roar of an Omani airforce jet or the daily flight from Muscat coming in to land.

Khasab is the obvious place to base yourself while exploring the peninsula. The town is also home to virtually all Musandam's accommodation (excepting the two places listed on p.160), while its location and the number of tour agents in town makes it a good base for dhow rides out into the *khors*, diving trips and 4WD excursions into the mountains. Many visitors to Khasab are here on day-trips from Dubai and the people who do stay tend to stick to the *Golden Tulip* hotel. You'll see surprisingly few visitors in town after around 4pm in the afternoon – which is perhaps all the more reason to stay the night.

Arrival, orientation and information

Khasab is very spread out, and there are **no taxis**. If you're arriving by ferry or plane, you'll need to arrange for your hotel to pick you up or you'll be facing a long, hot and dusty walk with your luggage. The town divides into two parts: the modern **New Souk**, and the more ramshackle **Old Souk** down near the port, which is where you'll also find the interesting **fort**.

Car rental is available through any of the travel agents listed on p.148 (and many other agents around town as well), although it's a good idea to book in advance. Travel agents are also the best source of local **information**. There are a couple of reliable **internet** places in the New Souk charging 100bz per 15 minutes. Al Malik Computer Service in front of *Al Shamaliah* restaurant is usually quieter than Quick Age in the next square, which tends to get rammed after dark with local Indians making webcalls home.

Accommodation

Khasab has a passable range of **accommodation** given its modest size, although rates everywhere are comparatively high for what you get.

Esra Apartments Around 2km south of the New Souk ⓣ2673 0464, ⓦwww.khasabtours.com. These sixteen spacious and comfortably furnished apartments are run by Khasab Travel & Tours (whose office stands opposite). All come with a kitchen, and most with a sitting room as well, plus a pool in the attractive little garden around the back. A bit of a way out of town, however, if you don't have your own transport. ⑥

Golden Tulip About 3km from Khasab on the main road to Bukha ⓣ2673 0777, ⓦwww.goldentulipkhasab.com. A few kilometres out of town, this lacklustre establishment is the most upmarket option in Khasab, occupying a dramatic (if rather windy) hillside overlooking the coast, with an attractive pool and terrace overlooking the sea. Unfortunately, the whole place is beginning to look decidedly shabby and unloved, with peeling paint, dated decor and a moribund atmosphere. Rooms are bland but comfortable, with balconies and either sea or mountain views, while facilities include an overpriced restaurant and bar – the only licensed venues in town – and a small spa. ⑥

Khasab Hotel 750m south of the New Souk ⓣ2673 0267, ⓦwww.khasabhotel.net. Simple, pleasantly old-fashioned three-star, with spacious rooms set in a low-lying orange building overlooking surrounding gardens. There's also a nice little terrace, decent-sized pool and a passable restaurant. Weekdays ④, weekends ⑤

Lake Hotel Old Souk ⓣ2673 1664. Simple budget hotel on the edge of the Old Souk. Rooms are small but cosy and comfortably furnished in soothing marine blues, although televisions may not work, mattresses are hard and you may find yourself playing host to the occasional small but inquisitive cockroach. ③

Khasab Fort

Down near the Old Souk, the town's pretty stone **fort** (Sat–Thurs 9am–4pm, Fri 8–11am; 500bz) was built by the Portuguese in the seventeenth century as part of their efforts to control passing maritime trade. The fort was originally on the

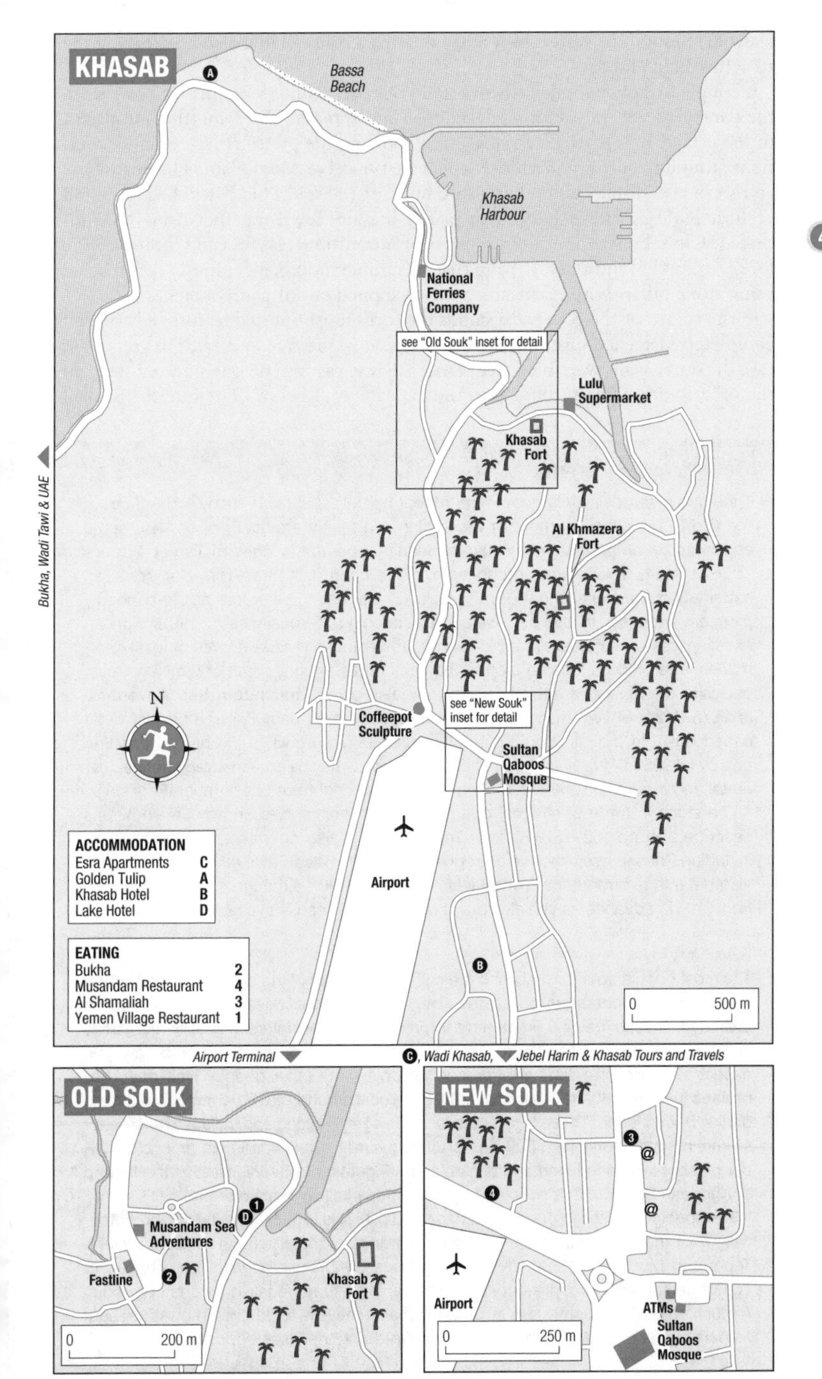
KHASAB
Bassa Beach
Khasab Harbour
National Ferries Company
see "Old Souk" inset for detail
Lulu Supermarket
Khasab Fort
Al Khmazera Fort
Coffeepot Sculpture
see "New Souk" inset for detail
Sultan Qaboos Mosque
Airport
N
ACCOMMODATION
Esra Apartments C
Golden Tulip A
Khasab Hotel B
Lake Hotel D
EATING
Bukha 2
Musandam Restaurant 4
Al Shamaliah 3
Yemen Village Restaurant 1
0 500 m
Bukha, Wadi Tawi & UAE
Airport Terminal
C, Wadi Khasab, Jebel Harim & Khasab Tours and Travels
OLD SOUK
Musandam Sea Adventures
Fastline
Khasab Fort
0 200 m
NEW SOUK
Airport
ATMs
Sultan Qaboos Mosque
0 250 m

seafront, though the waters have since receded a considerable distance, leaving the structure high and dry.

A couple of large wooden **dhows** stand outside, while three smaller boats sit in the courtyard within – a *battil*, *mashuwwah* and *zaruqah*. The *battil* (the one closest to the entrance) is particularly attractive, sporting the pretty cowrie-shell decorations around the prow and rudder which are typical of Musandam. The boat's bow and stern also display a rare extant example of the traditional "stitched" method of boat building (see p.172), with planks literally sewn together using coconut thread. Close by stand modern replicas of a traditional *bait al qufl* ("house of the lock"; see p.156) and a *barasti* (palm thatch) summer house, ingeniously constructed using stone pillars with permeable walls fashioned out of palm branches.

In the centre of the courtyard stands the fort's most unusual feature: a large and completely detached **circular tower**, intended to provide an additional refuge in case the outer walls were breached. Entrance is via a ramp on one side and steps on the other, with a hearth built into the exterior wall below. The interior is filled

Tours and activities from Khasab

There are a surprisingly large number of tour operators in town, many with offices in the Old Souk, although most of these places are only erratically open, and some appear to be on permanent siesta. The leading operator is **Khasab Travel & Tours** (Ⓣ2673 0464, Ⓦwww.khasabtours.com; office open daily 8am–1pm & 4–7pm), an extremely professional and well-run operation that has more or less single-handedly pioneered tourism in the peninsula since opening for business in 1992, with an excellent roster of guides, many of whom are veritable treasure-troves of local information. The office is located around the back of the airport, south of the New Souk, opposite the *Esra Apartments* (which they also own). **Musandam Sea Adventure** (Ⓣ2673 0424, Ⓦwww.msaoman.com; office open daily 8am–8pm), a smaller outfit based down in the Old Souk, is another reliable option, while the helpful **Fastline** nearby (Ⓣ9950 0425, Ⓦwww.khasabholidays.com) may be able to arrange cheap car rental and mountain safaris (although their guides might not speak much English).

The stock in trade of all local operators is the *khor* cruises and mountain safaris described on pp.152–157. Khasab Travel & Tours also operates handy **city tours** including Khasab itself and the petroglyphs at nearby Wadi Tawi. All operators should also be able to arrange **car rental** (either 2WD or 4WD), although it's a good idea to book this in advance as vehicles may not always be readily available.

Khor cruises

The most popular tour from Khasab is a half- or full-day boat trip down **Khor ash Sham** (see p.152). All operators offer essentially the same packages at the same prices (although Khasab Travel & Tours tend to provide the most interesting and informative guides). Trips are on traditional wooden dhows, sitting on deck under an awning; expect to share your boat with around ten to twenty other people. **Half-day khor cruises** (usually 9.30am–1.30pm or 1.30–5pm) cost around 15 OR per person including drinks, but no lunch. These trips go as far as Telegraph Island and include one stop for swimming and snorkelling. **Full-day cruises** (usually 10am–4pm) cost around 20 OR per person, including lunch and drinks, and will get you to Seebi Island at the far end of Khor ash Sham, with a couple of swimming/snorkelling stops en route.

The spectacular sea journey to **Kumzar** (see p.153) is slightly more tricky and potentially a lot more expensive. It's possible to arrange a dhow through Khasab Travel & Tours and Musandam Sea Adventures (around 35 OR/person with four people, or 70 OR/person with two; pre-booking advised); the return trip takes around five hours. A much cheaper (if slightly less atmospheric) alternative is to do the trip by speedboat as part of one of Extra Divers' snorkelling and diving trips (see opposite).

with wide-ranging and informative exhibits covering various aspects of Musandam's geology, culture and history.

From the entrance, steps lead up to the walls and a walkway on which you can make a circuit of the fort and its various towers – a couple of which still have their mangrove-pole ladders set into the interior walls. The second tower around houses various colourful but rather unedifying displays on **traditional Musandam culture** featuring colourful rugs, crockery and some droll mannequins. There's also an interesting re-creation of a traditional apothecary's shop and a display of fine traditional silver jewellery including enormously chunky elbow rings, necklaces featuring characteristic pouches ("Qur'an boxes") used to store texts from the holy book (worn as magic charms to ward off evil). A couple of these also incorporate the large silver Maria Theresa Thaler coins which were widely used throughout the Gulf and East Africa during the eighteenth and nineteenth centuries and which were often incorporated into traditional Omani jewellery (and are still widely available in souvenir shops around the country to this day).

Most operators can also set up **overnight dhow trips** (perhaps combining Khor ash Sham and Kumzar, for around 65 OR/person) either sleeping on board or camping on the beach. Khasab Travel & Tours and Musandam Sea Adventure both have **kayaks** for rent which can be carried on board dhows going into the fjords, although no guides are available, so you'll have to have a reasonable understanding of what you're doing before venturing onto the water.

Diving

The waters around the northern Musandam peninsula boast some of the finest diving in the Middle East, home to a superb range of marine life including magnificent manta and eagle rays, hammerhead, zebra, leopard and whale sharks, minke whales and turtles as well as myriad smaller tropical fish. Underwater habitats include beautiful coral gardens, sponge-covered rocks, dramatic submarine walls and a couple of wrecks. Despite what's often said, diving around Musandam isn't only for experienced divers with many hours in their log books – even unqualified divers can take the plunge.

Currently, the only dive centre in Khasab is the very well-run **Extra Divers** centre (ⓣ9987 7957, ⓦwww.musandam-diving.com), based at the *Golden Tulip* hotel; other agents around town advertising diving trips will be booking them through here. Trips (full-day only) currently cost 20/33 OR (for one/two dives) plus 17 OR equipment hire if needed. Alternatively, you can go along as a non-diver and **snorkel** for 15 OR plus 4 OR equipment hire. The centre also runs PADI courses and can provide reasonably inexpensive accommodation (divers only) in their comfortable six-room villa (34 OR/double) near the centre of town. They offer trips to around 25 sites. The best are around **Kumzar** (see p.153), a 45min–1hr journey by speedboat (although trips are often cancelled in bad weather), while there are a couple of further sites in the more sheltered waters of Khor ash Sham and elsewhere.

Mountain safaris

As with *khor* cruises, most operators offer a largely identikit range of **mountain safari tours** (see pp.154–157). These last either a **half-day** (around 25–30 OR with a minimum of two people), which will get you as far as Jebel Harim, or a **full-day** (around 50–55 OR, minimum 2 people), which will get you all the way to Rawdah Bowl (see p.157). You may be able to save a few rials off the price by shopping around, although discounted prices will probably mean you may get a dud guide as a result. As ever, the guides provided by Khasab Travel & Tours are particularly informative.

The tower diagonally opposite, on the breezy sea-facing side of the fort, houses the **Wali's Wing**, with the usual old rugs and coffeepots alongside more unusual *wali*-related bric-a-brac including antique sewing and writing boxes, expired tins of boot polish and bottles of ink, and an old Philips radio.

The Old Souk and Al Khmazera Fort

West of the fort lies Khasab's **Old Souk**, a huddle of shops, cafés and travel agents which was formerly the epicentre of the town's vibrant contraband industry (see box opposite). Many of the businesses here still advertise themselves as specializing in "Import & Export" – a polite way of saying smuggling – and even now the souk still sees regular boatloads of Iranian traders pitching up during the day to take delivery of assorted household goods which they load into boats and cart off for resale back home.

Sprawling away behind the fort lies Khasab's extensive **oasis**. Tucked away in the middle of this, halfway between the old and new souks, lies the recently restored **Al Khmazera Fort**, a rather plain structure with two round towers at opposite

The Shehi

Musandam is inhabited by three main tribes; the Dahoori, Kumzari (see p.154) and, by far the largest of the three, the **Shehi** (often anglicized to "Shihuh"). The Shehi formerly had a rather mysterious and fearsome reputation, said to speak a language unintelligible to anyone but themselves and living a reclusive life up in the mountains, ekeing a frugal and difficult existence out of one of Arabia's most inhospitable environments. Notably different from the Bedu and townspeople of the plains, many of the Shehi formerly lived in mountain **caves** or natural rock shelters, which were converted into simple little dwellings with the addition of a couple of stone walls and wooden doors. They also carried a small axe on a long handle (known as a *jirz*), rather than the *khanjar* found elsewhere in Oman, which could serve both as a weapon and a climbing stick. The Shehi remain the dominant clan in modern Khasab – you'll see the name Al Shehi on shop signs all around town, especially in the Old Souk – although many have now moved out to exploit the greater economic opportunities in neighbouring Ras al Khaimah (RAK), and RAK-registered cars are a common sight around town.

The **origins** of the Shehi remain unclear. One theory is that they were the original inhabitants of Oman who were gradually driven north into the mountains by waves of Yemeni and Nizari Arabs arriving from the south. Another, more colourful, tradition claims that they are descended from the survivors of shipwrecks marooned on Musandam's rocks over thousands of years – anecdotes record the occasional birth of Shehi children with fair hair and blue eyes. Their language, too, had a similarly cosmopolitan flavour, although, unlike Kumzari, it remains a dialect of Arabic, rather than an original language. As Ronald Codrai, writing of a visit to the peninsula in the 1950s in his entertaining *Travels to Oman: 1948–1955*, put it: "That they spoke a different dialect was soon obvious, but it was Arabic, although sometimes spoken more gutturally through closed teeth and, once or twice, I thought I detected a Somerset accent."

The Shehi (along with other Musandam tribes) formerly migrated on a **seasonal** basis, spending the winters farming in the mountains or fishing in the *khors* before heading down to Khasab to harvest dates during the summer. Not surprisingly, given Oman's rising prosperity, the Shehi and other tribes of Musandam, the younger generations particularly, are steadily abandoning the hard traditional life of their ancestors, meaning that many of Musandam's villages are being steadily **depopulated** as their inhabitants depart in search of a more comfortable existence in Khasab or elsewhere, leaving nothing behind but locked houses and wandering goats.

Marlboro Time: Smuggling in Khasab

Khasab was formerly infamous as the epicentre of the Oman–Iran contraband trade, thanks to its strategic location at the tip of the Arabian peninsula, just 45km from Iran across the Straits of Hormuz – a mere 45 minutes by speedboat. Up until 2001, taxes on US goods in Iran encouraged a flourishing trade in smuggling, with as many as five thousand Iranian boats visiting Khasab daily, arriving laden with boatloads of goats destined for the slaughterhouses of RAK and returning across the Straits of Hormuz weighed down with consignments of tea, electronics and, especially, cigarettes. Locals describe the golden age of smuggling as "Marlboro Time", and the sight of thousands of Iranian speedboats loading up with piles of duty-free fags was formerly a tourist attraction in its own right. The smuggling trade also provided a major source of income for locals in Khasab, who provided transport and other logistical services – accounting for the extraordinary number of pick-up trucks around town, formerly used to shift vast quantities of contraband tobacco and other goods down to the waiting boats.

Since 2001, successive changes in customs regulations in Iran and the UAE have led to the virtual demise of smuggling in Khasab. Cigarettes are now exported legally from Jebel Ali Free Port in Dubai, while the goats with which the Iranians formerly made themselves welcome are delivered directly to Ras al Khaimah in the UAE. The town still sees a fair number of Iranian traders even so – perhaps two or three hundred boats a day – although they now come to buy up electronics and surplus household appliances for resale in Iran, an entirely legal activity, making them shoppers rather than smugglers. They're granted a 12-hour pass, although they aren't allowed further into town than the Old Souk (where you'll often see them loading up trucks with old washing machines, fridges and suchlike) and must leave by sunset – a rather tame legacy of the town's former customs-busting bravado.

corners and a sequence of rooms inside arranged around a little courtyard. The fort is signed from the New Souk; follow the road through the oasis and you'll see it on your left in front of a prominent blue-domed mosque. Look out, en route, for the particularly eye-catching villa (on the left) with an enormous model dhow poised precariously above the gateway.

Bassa Beach

Heading out along the coastal road, about 1km past the harbour (and just before the *Golden Tulip* hotel) lies **Bassa Beach**. Despite its name, Bassa isn't so much a beach as an enormous car park, although there are majestic views of the coast and the tiny ribbon of muddy sand is piled high with a treasure-trove of washed-up seashells (along with less appealing domestic rubbish) – perfect for an hour's idle beachcombing.

Eating and drinking

You won't actually starve in Khasab, but don't expect any culinary surprises. The only **licensed** venues are at the *Golden Tulip* hotel, which has a bar and a rather expensive licensed multi-cuisine restaurant, although being 4km from the town centre it's not much use unless you're actually staying there.

In town itself, the best place is *Al Shamaliah* in the **New Souk**, which does above-average kebabs, shwarma and fruit juices, plus a less inspiring range of Chinese and Indian options (mains 1–2.5 OR); there's also nice outdoor seating on the square in front. The nearby *Musandam Restaurant* is similar, but not quite as nice, and has indoor seating only.

There's a further string of low-key cafés in the **Old Souk**, though nothing to get very excited about. *Bukha* is probably the best place for the usual kebabs and shwarma, while the *Yemen Village Restaurant* serves up a passable range of Yemeni-style fish, mutton and chicken biryanis, with seating either in the restaurant itself or, more attractively, on the pavement overlooking the water outside. A number of places in the Old Souk also double as **shisha cafés**, with huddles of pipe-smoking locals sitting out on the pavement after dark amid clouds of fragrant tobacco.

The khors and Kumzar

Looked at on the map (or from the window of a plane), the northernmost tip of Musandam resembles a strange Rorschach blob: a mad tangle of mountains and water, dotted with dozens of *khors*, bays, islands and headlands, and ringed about with sheer cliffs and craggy red-rock mountains. The peninsula's remarkable landscape is the result of unusual geological processes: the *khors* themselves are actually flooded valleys, formed as a result of Musandam's progressive subduction beneath the Eurasian continental plate, which is causing the entire peninsula to tilt down into the sea at the dramatic rate of 5mm a year.

The chance to get out on the water and see something of the magnificent *khors* and coastline around Khasab is the unquestioned highlight of any trip to Musandam. The easiest and most popular trip is out along the marvellous **Khor ash Sham** – the largest of all the *khors*. Further afield, the remote town of **Kumzar** is the endpoint of the perhaps even more spectacular sea trip out along the coast and into the Straits of Hormuz.

Khor ash Sham خور الشم

The longest and most dramatic of all the Musandam *khors*, **Khor ash Sham** stretches for some 16km in total, hemmed in between two high lines of mountains, the bareness of the craggy surrounding rocks offering a surreal contrast with the invitingly blue waters of the *khor* itself. A string of remote **hamlets** dots the shoreline, accessible only by boat; each is home to just ten or so families. All water has to be shipped in by boat, while children must commute to school in Khasab. Not surprisingly, the *khor*-side settlements are becoming steadily depopulated as the younger generation of villagers tires of the rather monotonous life of their ancestors and move off to Khasab or beyond. Those who remain live in the villages for just six months a year, earning a living through fishing, before decamping to harvest dates in Khasab during the summer months, when the water in the *khor* becomes too hot for fish.

The *khors* also boast a healthy population of **dolphins**, and you've got probably an eighty percent chance of seeing at least one pod during a full-day dhow cruise. Dolphins are attracted by the sound of boats' engines and the water churned up in their wake – they'll often swim alongside passing dhows, dipping playfully in and out of the water, reaching remarkable speeds and keeping up quite easily with even the fastest dhows.

About halfway down Khor ash Sham lies lonely **Telegraph Island** (or Jazirat Telegraph), an extremely modest bit of rock named after the British telegraph station which formerly stood here (see box opposite). The extensive foundations of the old British buildings survive, along with a flight of stone steps leading up from the water. The island is a popular stopping point on dhow cruises which often halt here for lunch. Boats can moor next to the island at high tide; at low tide you'll have to swim across.

Going round the bend in Musandam

Despite its rather unprepossessing appearance today, **Telegraph Island** was once a crucial hub in the nineteenth-century information superhighway, and a vital link in the chain of communication between Britain and her Indian empire. At a time when mail between London and Bombay took at least a month to arrive, messages could be sent between the two cities in as little as two hours via submarine telegraph cables – or the "Victorian internet", as it has been neatly described.

In 1864, the governments of India, Turkey and Persia agreed to join up their existing land telegraphs using a submarine cable through the Gulf and on to Karachi. Almost 2400km of cable was manufactured and laid out, passing through Musandam en route. In 1865, a small telegraph repeater station was constructed on the island formerly known as Jazirat al Maqlab, but ever since as **Telegraph Island**, a site chosen since it offered greater security than the mainland against potentially hostile local tribes. The station played a crucial role in the success of the cable. Telegraphic signals relayed over copper cable inevitably fade with distance, and the function of the station was to receive and relay, or "repeat", signals received from either London or Bombay.

Unfortunately, the location was one of the remotest in the empire. The mental and physical privations suffered by officials marooned on Telegraph Island quickly became the stuff of colonial legend, so much so that relief crews sailing eastwards around the tip of the Musandam peninsula coined the expression "**going round the bend**" to describe their mercy missions – an expression which has since become Oman's lasting contribution to the English vernacular and a fitting tribute to the sufferings of Telegraph Island's Victorian castaways.

The station lasted just three years and in 1868 the cable was diverted away from Musandam and rerouted via the Iranian island of Hengham.

Kumzar كمزار

One of the most inaccessible settlements in Oman, the famously remote town of **KUMZAR** sits perched in solitary splendour at the northernmost edge of Musandam, hemmed in by sheer mountains and accessible only by boat. Sadly, outsiders (meaning non-resident Omanis as well as foreign tourists) have been banned from landing in the town since 2010 as a result of locals complaining about the intrusive behaviour of tourists. A "visit" to the town therefore involves sitting in your boat in the harbour about 100m offshore and seeing what you can, although it's still well worth making the trip out here for the magnificent coastal scenery en route, as well as for the tantalizing glimpse of Oman's most reclusive town at the end of it. Many of Musandam's best **diving** spots are also located in the waters around Kumzar; see p.149 for more details. For details about **boat trips** to Kumzar, see the box on p.149.

Geographically, Kumzar is a paradox. By land, this is one of the most remote and inaccessible settlements in Oman. By sea, however, the town overlooks the Straits of Hormuz, one of the world's busiest shipping lanes, a fact reflected in the unique language spoken by its inhabitants, **Kumzari** (see box, p.154). The village is said to be around seven hundred years old, its inhabitants including a hotchpotch of ethnic groups ranging from Yemeni to Zanzibari – the colourful theory that sailors shipwrecked off the nearby coast were also integrated into the population is backed up by the remarkable number of European and Hindi loan words found in Kumzari. The town's population currently stands at around five thousand, with its own school, hospital, power station and desalination plant. The inhabitants live largely by fishing for nine months of the year, netting barracuda, tuna, kingfish and hammour (much of which ends up in the restaurants of Dubai), before retreating to Khasab for the hot summer months.

Kumzari

Kumzar is famous for the fact that it preserves its own language, **Kumzari** – a remarkable linguistic monument to the region's surprisingly cosmopolitan past. Kumzari is still very much a living language, despite the fact that it is spoken only in Kumzar town itself and on Larek Island in Iran, just across the Straits of Hormuz. Local children speak Kumzari as their first language, and don't necessarily learn Arabic until they get to school. Until quite recently older generations remained determinedly monoglot, speaking nothing but Kumzari – and according to local reports there's at least one old man in the village who remains resolutely unfamiliar with any other tongue.

The basis of Kumzari is **Farsi** (the language of Iran, which Kumzari most obviously resembles), mixed up with a significant dose of **Arabic** and **Hindi** (the result of long-standing trade with India), plus a significant number of loan words from assorted **European** languages including English, Portuguese, French, Italian and Spanish – a remarkable linguistic melting pot. The numbers for one to five – *yek, do, so, char, panch* – for example, are almost identical to their Hindi equivalents, while the Kumzari word for bread, *naan*, will also be strangely familiar to anyone who has ever eaten in an Indian restaurant. Many **European** loan words have also entered the language, including (to name just a few) *upset*, *door*, *light*, *starg* (stars), *cherie* (child), *toilette* (meaning, in Kumzari, a haircut) and *bandera* (from Spanish, meaning "flag"). Things have occasionally got slightly lost in translation, however: the word *kayak*, for instance, means a speedboat rather than a canoe, while the words *open doro* can serve as an instruction not only to open the door, but to close it too.

The trip out to Kumzar by speedboat takes around 45min–1hr from Khasab, or around 2hr 30min by dhow. The ride takes you out past the magnificent sea cliffs enclosing the entrance to Khasab harbour, past the entrance to the fine Khor Ghob Ali, and then **Goat Island** (Jazirat al Ghanim), ringed with fluted limestone cliffs. In the past, local Kumzaris would often bring their sheep and goats across to the island by boat to graze, given the lack of suitable pastureland around Kumzar itself – hence the name. Throughout the trip, there is remarkably little sign of human habitation, saving a few military buildings on Goat Island.

Beyond Goat Island you enter the **Straits of Hormuz**, with magnificent seascapes, craggy headlands and a considerable number of oil tankers; the three rocky islands way out to sea are collectively known as the **Jazirat Salamah**, the most northerly piece of Omani territory. Ten minutes or so later you round a final headland, getting your first sight of Kumzar, with its colourful huddle of buildings backed up against the sheer wall of the mountains behind. Although you can't actually land, you can approach close enough to get a reasonably good view of the town. Space is very much at a premium here; it's said that the village cemetery was filled hundreds of years ago, and that locals are now obliged to bury their relatives in the grounds of their own houses.

The mountains

Although the *khors* are the principal attraction of Musandam, the peninsula's mountainous interior runs them a close second. Here you'll find some of the wildest and most spectacular landscapes in Oman, comprising a string of great limestone peaks and massifs known by locals as the Ru'us al Jebel, or "Peaks of the Mountains". These are usually explored from Khasab on either a half-day or full-day **mountain safari** with a local driver aboard a 4WD (for details on operators see p.148). Half-day safaris usually take in Wadi Khasab, Khor an Najd,

Khalidiya, A'Saye and Jebel Harim. Full-day trips continue beyond Jebel Harim as far as the Rawdah Bowl. It's worth doing the full-day safari if possible – the Rawdah Bowl itself isn't especially memorable, but the mountain scenery beyond Jebel Harim and the ridgetop drive above Wadi Rawdah are simply magnificent.

There's nowhere to stay up in the mountains, although **camping** is possible in a number of places, including the beach at Khor an Najd, among the acacia trees at Khalidiya or in the remote Rawdah Bowl.

Wadi Khasab and Khor an Najd

Safaris begin by following the new tarmac road which runs from the southern end of Khasab, behind the airport and down through the broad **Wadi Khasab**. The wadi has provided mixed blessings. Rich alluvial soil, washed down the valley from the mountains, has long underpinned Khasab's agricultural prosperity (the name Khasab, in Arabic, means "fertility"), although the wadi has also been the source of devastating flash floods; a large dam, built in 1986 across the wadi just south of Khasab, now protects the town.

After about 7km you'll see the unsurfaced road up into the mountains and Jebel Harim (signposted to Dibba) heading off on the right. Beyond here you enter the area known as **Sal al Asfal** ("Lower Plain"), a dead-flat plain which was formerly sea bed. Some 5km past the turn-off for Dibba you'll reach an unsigned dirt road off on the left leading to **Khor an Najd**. It's a stiff climb – 4WD is essential – up past a military firing range to the crest of the ridge, from where there are bird's-eye views of the *khor* far below, and of the road hairpinning precipitously to a small scrap of rather unattractive beach. It's also possible to **camp** here, and it's a popular spot at weekends with Dubaians. Drinking water is available, but there are no other facilities.

From here tours return to the main road, where your driver may show you a **bait al qufl** (see box, p.156), which can be found here and in most other parts of Musandam. The next stop is usually the end of the tarmac at **Sal al A'la** ("Higher Plain"), about 20km from Khasab, also known as **Khalidiya** after the local Birkat al Khalidiya, meaning "Spring of Eternity" – somewhat ironic, since it has now dried up. The area is one of the most fertile in the peninsula, thanks to its location in a bowl at the foot of the mountains in which rainwater naturally collects, both at the surface and underground. The plain is dotted with pretty stands of acacia trees and, following periods of rainfall, lush green grass, looking a bit like an unlikely patch of African savannah in the middle of the Gulf. Dozens of goats wander the area, feasting on acacia leaves, which explains why the lower branches on all the trees have been stripped bare up to a certain height – in summer hungry goats may even climb up into the branches of the more accessible trees in search of fodder.

A'Rahaybah to A'Saye

Tours now return along the main road back towards Khasab then take the left turn onto the dirt road to Dibba which you passed earlier. The track is well maintained and graded, but steep in places; 4WD is essential.

From Wadi Khasab the track climbs doggedly upwards, offering increasingly wide-ranging views over the surrounding mountains. Most of these are an enormous mass of stratified, greyish limestone, interrupted in places by pockmarked extrusions of igneous rock created by volcanic explosions under the sea bed – a distinctively gloopy-looking substance, like a kind of geological cheese fondue. The porous rock is riddled with caves, many of which were formerly occupied by the reclusive Shehi.

The first village en route is **A'RAHAYBAH** (pronounced "A'Raheebah"), where you'll see patches of dried-up agricultural terracing – a result of the

Bait al qufl: the house of the lock

Almost every village in the mountains of Musandam is home to at least one **bait al qufl** ("house of the lock"), a distinctive type of local building – looking more like an antique bomb-shelter than a traditional house – which is unique to the peninsula. The *bait al qufl* developed in response to the migratory lifestyle of the local Shehi, who would leave their mountain homes during the summer months to go and work on the coast. Valuable possessions which they could not carry with them were left behind in the village, locked up in these miniature vaults. Although designed primarily for storage, *bait al qufl* were also used as living quarters, particularly in the depths of winter.

The *bait al qufl* was designed with the emphasis firmly on strength and security. Walls often reach thicknesses of 1m or more, fashioned out of enormous slabs of stone; the thickness of the walls had the additional benefit of keeping the interior cool in summer and warm in winter, as well as protecting its contents (and anyone inside) from the ever-present threat of rockfalls. *Bait al qufl* are usually around 6–7m high, although they look smaller from the outside since the floor is dug out 1m or so below ground level for additional strength and security; the buildings are also often surrounded with a raised platform to help drain rainwater and provide something to sit on. Huge earthenware jars were placed inside to store provisions such as water, dates and grains – the jars were often bigger than the actual door to prevent them being carried off, and had to be put in place before the walls were built up around them. Access is usually via a single tiny door, formerly secured with one or two chunky wooden padlocks, although most are now left open.

mountains' increasing aridity due to the falling water table. There's also a fine collection of *bait al qufls* on the mountainside above.

Above A'Rahaybah, your guide may point out a series of distinctive **rock formations**. One (popularly referred to as the "Titanic") on the top of the ridge above bears an uncanny similarity to a steamship with a pair of funnels; nearby stands a distinctive rock pinnacle claimed to resemble the outline of a praying man. Halfway up the cliff-face between the two formations lies **Sultan's House** (occupied until as recently as six or seven years ago), a tiny cluster of primitive stone buildings perched on the narrowest of rock ledges. It's apparently accessible on foot or by donkey, although to the uninitiated it looks like only an accomplished rock climber could reach it. Assorted abandoned cave houses can be spotted slightly further up the track, tucked away beneath rock overhangs in similarly rocky and inaccessible locations.

About 45 minutes from the turn-off you'll arrive at the village of **A'SAYE** (also spelled "Sayh"; pronounced "See"), clustered around a neat little plateau set in a bowl in the mountains at 1105m. As at Sal al A'la, the bowl serves as a natural collection point for rainwater and fertile silt washed down off the mountains, offering an unlikely little patch of agricultural prosperity amid the arid surrounding mountains. The plateau is dotted with a patchwork of square fields in which the five hundred-odd villagers grow wheat, dates, figs and vegetables, with donkeys and goats rambling here and there.

Jebel Harim جبل حارم

From here, it's another 20 minutes or so to the highest point of the road, below the summit of **Jebel Harim**, literally "Mountain of Women" and at 2087m the highest peak in Musandam. The mountain takes its name from the days when local women would retreat to caves up here in order to avoid being carried off by pirates or rival tribes while their menfolk were away on extended fishing or trading expeditions. The actual summit is home to a radar station monitoring shipping way below in the Straits of Hormuz and is out of bounds, although there are superb all-round views from the road, with breathtaking views back to Khasab and onwards towards Dibba. Many of the rocks up here are also studded with superbly preserved **fossils**, offering the remarkable sight of ancient submarine creatures – molluscs, fish, clams and numerous trilobites – now incongruously stranded near the summit of one of Arabia's highest mountains.

The highest point of road (at around 1600m) sweeps through a large rock cutting next to an air-traffic control radar installation. Just below here, a track leads off to a fine collection of **petroglyphs** carved into mountaintop boulders: rudimentary but evocative weathered images chipped out of the stone, including matchstick human figures alongside animals such as gazelle, oryx, Arabian leopards and even what is thought to be a man on an elephant. Further fossils can be seen in the surrounding rocks.

Past the summit, there are sensational views of the road ahead, as it runs along a narrow ridge before descending towards the Rawdah Bowl, plus stomach-churning views into the deep gorge below. En route you'll pass a remarkable **fossil wall**, formed out of what was originally a chunk of sea bed rock and covered in a dense layer of fossilized impressions among which the outlines of crabs, starfish and shells can clearly be made out.

The Rawdah Bowl

The road runs along the ridgetop then descends sharply into the wide bed of **Wadi Rawdah**, flanked by huge limestone cliffs. From here, a turning on the left runs down a side wadi into the expansive **Rawdah Bowl** (signed as "A'Rowdhah"), a neat little plateau a few kilometres across, enclosed by mountains – it all feels a long way from anywhere, and pleasantly sheltered compared to the exposed landscapes en route. Despite its name (Rawdah means "garden", or a nursery of flowers), the plateau is rather bare, with large expanses of sand and gravel, dotted with acacia trees, telephone poles and a scatter of modern houses, with the occasional wild camel wandering around – a strange sight this high up in the mountains.

The plateau is also home to a handful of more venerable remains including abandoned old stone buildings, several *bait al qufl* and a couple of **cemeteries**, both Islamic and pre-Islamic, with neat lines of headstones formed out of roughly hewn pieces of stone; the bowl was formerly used as a local tribal battleground, which presumably accounts for the large number of people buried here.

Petroglyphs

Musandam boasts an unusually rich collection of **petroglyphs** (from the Greek *petros*, meaning stone, and *glyphe*, meaning carving): simple rock art images which have been chipped out of boulders, cave walls or other convenient pieces of stone using sharp bronze, iron or stone tools and highlighted using a white pigment made from coral. Ancient petrogylphs can be found throughout the peninsula, often in the remotest places, and depict a wide range of subjects including people, animals (particularly horses and camels), as well as abstract symbols and geometrical patterns whose meaning has been lost. Dating the images is difficult, although the fact that most of them depict human or animal figures suggests that they may well pre-date the arrival of Islam (which prohibits the making of images of living creatures). Of Musandam's many petroglyphs, the most easily accessible are those at the top of **Jebel Harim** (see above) and those in **Wadi Tiwi** (see p.158).

The coastal road: Khasab to Bukha

The **coastal road** (Highway 2) between the UAE border at Tibat and Khasab is still the only reliable land connection between Musandam and the outside world (at least if you discount the very rough road over the mountains from Khasab to Dibba described above). The 35km highway (around a 45min drive) is one of the most dramatic in the country, a fine feat of modern engineering with jaw-dropping sea views. If you fancy stopping for a picnic there are numerous little patches of beach with palm thatch sunshades dotted along the road – the best is just before the village of Al Jadi, about 3km north of Bukha.

Wadi Tiwi rock carvings

The first 10km of the highway immediately south of Khasab's *Golden Tulip* hotel are perhaps the most dramatic of them all, as the road twists around **Khor Qida**, perched on the narrowest of ledges blasted out between the towering cliffs on one side and the sea on the other.

On the far side of the bay, some 4km south of Khasab, **Wadi Tiwi** sports some fine prehistoric petroglyphs, showing boats, houses and soldiers on horseback. To reach the carvings, take the signed left turn to the village of **QIDA**, 4km from Khasab. Follow the road through the village for around 750m until the tarmac runs out, keeping a wary eye out for goats – of which there are many – en route (running one over could prove surprisingly expensive). It's another 750m from the end of the tarmac along a dirt track, driveable, with care, in a 2WD, although it's a lot more pleasant to walk.

After about 500m you'll reach a cluster of ramshackle houses. Shortly afterwards, the track curves to the right in front of a brownish-white house, just past a well surrounded by three small trees. On your left you'll see a terrific mass of fallen boulders, a couple of which have been walled in to create tiny cave houses beneath the rocks (although they're no longer inhabited – or only by goats). These boulders are where you'll find the **rock carvings**. Easiest to spot is the boulder with five separate carvings, including a trio of camels. A boulder to the right has a stylized figure on horseback, while you'll find another virtually identical horseman on the rock next to the door of one of the miniature boulder houses. It's fun to hunt around for other pictures, although in many places it's nigh on impossible to tell whether the white dots are the remains of carvings or simply a natural mineral effect. Even if you don't find the carvings, it's a lovely valley walk between high limestone cliffs, pockmarked with caves, and with goats everywhere, often in the most unlikely places.

Al Harf

Past Khor Qida, the road climbs sharply upwards from the water to the ridgetop above, cresting the summit through a deep rock cutting before reaching the village of **AL HARF**, roughly halfway between Khasab and Bukha. This is the highest

On to Dibba and the border

It's around another 50km (45min–1hr) from Rawdah to **Dibba** (see opposite) and the UAE border. The actual border post is at **Wadi Bih**, just a few kilometres south of the turn-off to Rawdah Bowl, but this is closed to all foreigners apart from citizens of the UAE. If you want to explore Dibba and the southern part of the peninsula you'll have to exit Musandam at Tibat and make your way cross-country via the UAE to reach Dibba itself.

point of the road, with fabulous views – it's said that on a clear day you can see the coast of Iran. Unfortunately it's difficult to find anywhere to stop to enjoy the views along the narrow highway itself. The best option is to take the unsigned side-turning off the main road on the right about 500m past the summit rock cutting, then turn right again. This brings you to a peaceful vantage point with bird's-eye views out to sea, over Khor Qida and to the mountains inland.

Bukha بخة

Around 25km twisting kilometres south of Khasab lies the modest little town of **BUKHA**. The principal attraction here is the fine old **fort** (Sun–Thurs 8.30am–2.30pm, closed Fri & Sat; free), which sits right next to the coastal highway backdropped by huge mountain cliffs (ignore the blue signs pointing inland to Bukha village). Built in the early sixteenth century, the fort originally stood right on the shore (which has since receded somewhat) and is surrounded on three sides by a now-dry moat in which, legend has it, unfortunate prisoners were formerly chained up and left to drown by the rising tide. Boxy rectangular towers sit on opposite corners of the fort, separated by the circular southeastern tower with its distinctively curving upper storeys, designed to reduce the impact of cannonballs. There's not much to see inside, apart from a couple of unfurnished rooms set around a small courtyard with the *wali*'s apartment in the centre and a large pit covered by an iron grille – possibly some kind of prison.

Just behind the fort stands the town's old and extremely unusual **mosque** – it actually looks much more like a house than a place of worship, and lacks both dome and minaret. At the time of writing the mosque was disused and locked up, although it was possible to get inside through a large broken stone window for a look at the atmospheric interior with its solid, strangely shaped arches decorated with delicately carved plaster, plus *mihrab* and *minbar*.

Dibba دبا

At the southern end of Musandam, sprawling across the border with the UAE, lies the small city of **DIBBA** – a pleasant enough place, although not really worth a visit unless you can afford to stay at the idyllic *Six Senses Zighy Bay* resort (see p.160) further down the coast or have a particular yen to explore the southern portion of the Musandam peninsula. Foreigners are only allowed to travel as far as the border post at Wadi Bih (see opposite), however, which somewhat limits the area available for exploration.

Sleepy though it may now be, Dibba was the site of one of the most important **battles** of early Islamic history. In 632 AD, shortly after the Prophet Mohammed's death, the forces of his successor, the caliph Abu Bakr, defeated those of a local ruler who had renounced Islam. A large cemetery on the plains behind the town (on the UAE side of the border) is traditionally believed to house the remains of the ten thousand rebels killed in the battle.

The Town

Modern Dibba has something of a split personality, being divided into three parts: Dibba Bayah on the Omani side, Dibba Muhallab, part of the UAE's Emirate of Fujairah, and Dibba al Hisn, part of the UAE's Emirate of Sharjah. There's a police checkpoint at the **UAE–Oman border** where you'll have to show your passport when entering Oman, but no visa formalities. It's possible to travel north from here along the rough, graded track into the mountains as far as the official border

Madha

South of Musandam, about halfway between Dibba and the Omani border at Khatmat Milalah, lies the curious Omani exclave of **Madha** – a tiny dot of Omani territory (comprising just 75 square kilometres) completely surrounded by the UAE. The area is reached via a single surfaced road off the main coastal highway between Khawr Fakkan and Fujairah city near the district of Qurayya.

The enclave is notable mainly for one geopolitical oddity: the village of **Nahwa** (a few kilometres further along the road past Madha town, at the end of the tarmac). Bizarrely, this village actually belongs to the UAE emirate of Sharjah, creating a Russian-doll effect whereby the UAE territory of Nahwa is enclosed within the Omani district of Madha, which is enclosed by the UAE emirates of Fujairah and Sharjah – which are themselves bookended by Omani territory on either side.

post at **Wadi Bih** some 35km further on, though the border is closed to all but Omani and UAE nationals, so you can't go any further than this.

Fujairah's **Dibba Muhallab** is easily the largest and most developed of the three areas, and one of the UAE's more pleasant towns, built on a pleasingly human scale, with neat apartment blocks, tree-lined streets and a sweeping seafront corniche giving the whole place a pleasantly Mediterranean air. Sharjah's **Dibba al Hisn** is smaller, with a rather toy-town main street lined with identikit faux-Arabian villas and office blocks.

Things are even quieter and significantly less built-up over on the Omani side of the border in **Dibba Bayah**. The pleasant seafront is fringed with a fine arc of golden sand, plus the occasional fishing boat, while just inland stands the obligatory fort, which isn't open to the public. To get to the fort, follow the brown signs inland to Daba Castle, left of the main road through town about 750m north of the border checkpoint.

Accommodation

Dibba has the only **accommodation** in Musandam outside Khasab, and makes an interesting alternative base from which to explore the southern end of the peninsula; you can reach both places listed below from the UAE without having to buy an Omani visa, and both establishments can organize dhow cruises and mountain safaris (although you can only get as far as the border post at Wadi Bih). It's also possible to set up **diving** trips via the *Golden Tulip* or through local operator Ocean Divers (ⓣ2683 6602), although unless you've a special interest in diving this particular area, it's preferable to head to the much better organized Extra Divers in Khasab (see p.149).

Golden Tulip 2km north of the border on the coast ⓣ2683 6653, ⓦwww.goldentulipdibba.com. The location of this old-fashioned four-star is pleasantly crashed-out, although the hotel itself is decidedly run-of-the-mill, with rooms arranged around attractive but rather cramped gardens and a smallish pool. Lacklustre food, erratic service and noisy kids come as standard, although the nice swathe of beach at least partly compensates. ❻

Six Senses Zighy Bay ⓣ2673 5555, ⓦwww.sixsenses.com/SixSensesZighyBay. This very exclusive resort is hidden away on the coast, a 15min speedboat ride or 23km drive north of Dibba (4WD required); guests approaching by road also have the option of making the last part of the journey by tandem paraglide – either the maddest publicity stunt in Arabia or a wonderfully exhilarating way of arriving at reception. Gimmicks apart, the setting is blissful, tucked away beneath the mountains, with a fine swathe of beach and accommodation in attractively rustic villas sporting rough-hewn stone walls and lots of palm thatch. All come with their own small pools and every imaginable convenience, and there's also a top-notch spa, although with rates from around US$1500 per night it's a very expensive pleasure. ❾

5

Sharqiya

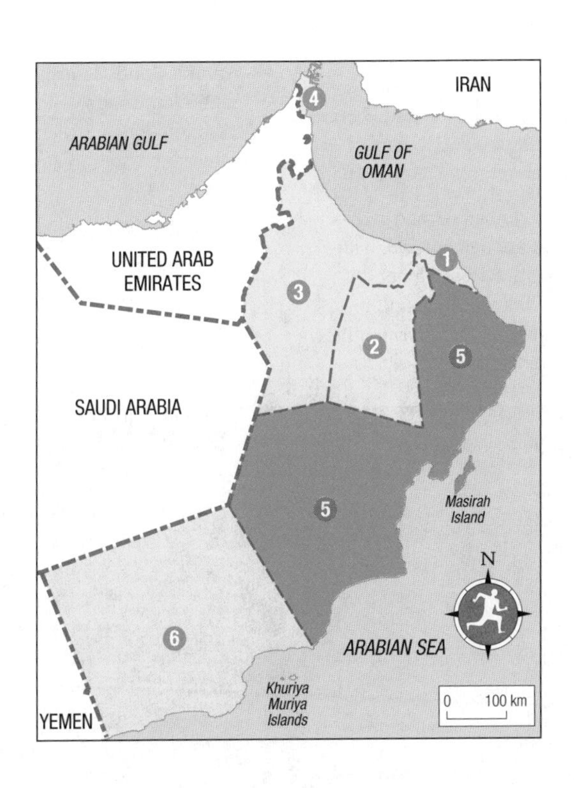
IRAN
ARABIAN GULF
GULF OF OMAN
UNITED ARAB EMIRATES
SAUDI ARABIA
Masirah Island
N
ARABIAN SEA
Khuriya Muriya Islands
0 100 km
YEMEN
1
2
3
4
5
5
6

CHAPTER 5

Highlights

* **Wadi Shab and Wadi Tiwi** Two of Oman's most picture-perfect wadis, with palm-fringed ravines running between sheer sandstone cliffs down to the sea. See pp.167–168

* **Jaylah and the Salma Plateau** Superb off-road drive across the top of the Eastern Hajar mountains, passing the spectacularly located Bronze Age tombs and towers of Jaylah en route. See p.168

* **Sur** Southern Oman's most appealing town, with a pretty harbour fringed with watchtowers and the country's only surviving dhow-building yard. See p.170

* **Ras al Jinz** Arabia's premier turtle-watching destination. See p.174

* **Ibra** One of the region's liveliest and most personable towns, with a colourful souk and a pair of fine old traditional mudbrick villages. See p.176

* **Wahiba Sands** Iconic desert landscape, with towering dunes, roving camels and superb sunsets. See p.179

* **Jalan Bani Bu Ali** Staunchly traditional Sharqiya town, centred on the country's most magnificently dilapidated mudbrick fort. See p.183

▲ Beehive Bronze Age tomb, Jaylah

5

Sharqiya

South of Muscat stretches **Sharqiya** ("The East"), a generous swathe of sea, sand and mountain spread across the southeasternmost tip of the Arabian peninsula. Scenically, Sharqiya is the most diverse region in the country, offering a beguiling snapshot of Oman in miniature, from the sand-fringed coastline, through the rugged Eastern Hajar mountains to the rolling dunes of the Wahiba Sands. Culturally, too, the region retains a distinct appeal. This is the most traditional part of the country, with a long and proud history of tribal independence – and occasional insurrection against the authority of the sultan in Muscat. The interior of Sharqiya is also one of the few places in Oman where you'll still see evidence of the country's traditional Bedu lifestyle, with temporary encampments dotted amid the rolling sands – albeit the camels of yesteryear have now been largely replaced with Toyota pick-up trucks and 4WDs.

Sharqiya divides into three main parts. The first is **the coast**, with a string of attractions including the historic town of Quriyat, Qalhat and Sur, and the turtle beach at Ras al Jinz. Running parallel to the coast, the craggy heights of the **Eastern Hajar** mountains (Al Hajar Ash Sharqi) provide numerous spectacular hiking and off-road-driving possibilities, including the celebrated ravines of Wadi Shab and Wadi Tiwi. On the far side of the Eastern Hajar, the Sharqiya **interior** boasts a further swathe of rewarding destinations, including the magnificent dunes of the Wahiba Sands and a string of interesting towns, notably the personable market centre of Ibra and the staunchly traditional Jalan Bani Bu Ali.

It's possible to make a satisfying **loop** through Sharqiya by heading down the coastal highway to Sur and Ras al Jinz described on p.165, and then returning along the inland route via Ibra described on p.175 (or vice versa), passing virtually all the region's major attractions en route.

Some history

Something of a backwater nowadays, Sharqiya's rather sleepy present-day atmosphere belies its illustrious past, when its boat-builders, merchants and mariners made the region one of the most commercially vibrant and cosmopolitan in the country. Sharqiya's prosperity was founded on the sea, with a string of bustling ports and entrepots, most notably **Qalhat**, whose fame attracted visits by both Ibn Battuta and Marco Polo, as well as **Quriyat** up the coast. The pivotal moment in Sharqiya's history was the arrival in 1508 of the **Portuguese**, who sacked both Qalhat and Quriyat – an event from which neither town ever completely recovered. The demise of Qalhat, however, spurred the growth of nearby **Sur**, which subsequently became the major town in the region, growing wealthy

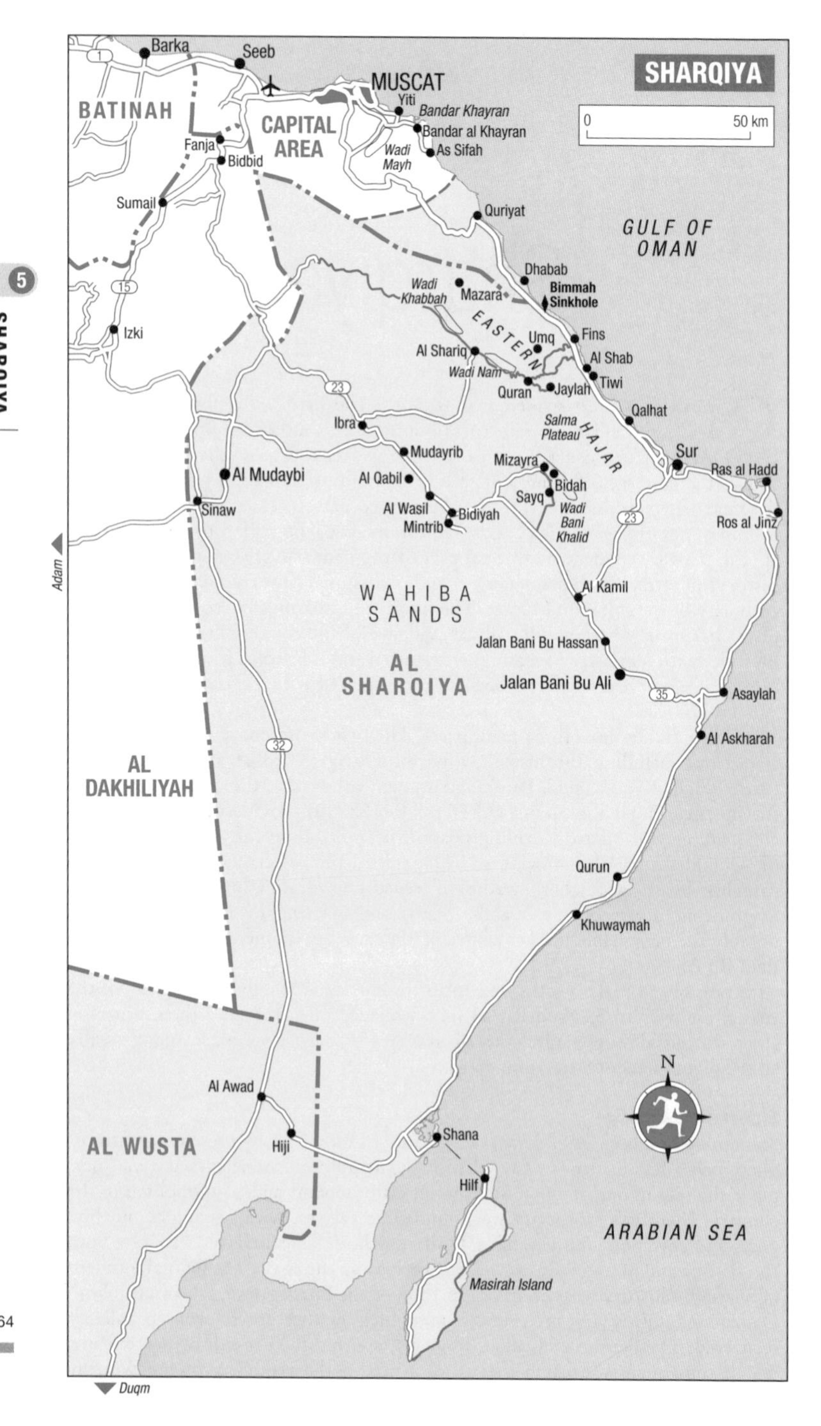
SHARQIYA
0
50 km
Barka
Seeb
MUSCAT
BATINAH
CAPITAL AREA
Yiti
Bandar Khayran
Bandar al Khayran
As Sifah
Wadi Mayh
Fanja
Bidbid
Sumail
Quriyat
GULF OF OMAN
Dhabab
Bimmah Sinkhole
Wadi Khabbah
Mazara
EASTERN
HAJAR
Izki
Umq
Fins
Al Shariq
Al Shab
Wadi Nam
Tiwi
Quran
Jaylah
Qalhat
Salma Plateau
Ibra
Mudayrib
Sur
Ras al Hadd
Mizayra
Al Mudaybi
Al Qabil
Bidah
Sayq
Al Wasil
Bidiyah
Sinaw
Mintrib
Wadi Bani Khalid
Ros al Jinz
Adam
Al Kamil
WAHIBA SANDS
Jalan Bani Bu Hassan
AL SHARQIYA
Jalan Bani Bu Ali
Asaylah
Al Askharah
AL DAKHILIYAH
Qurun
Khuwaymah
N
Al Awad
Hiji
Shana
AL WUSTA
Hilf
ARABIAN SEA
Masirah Island
Duqm
1
15
23
32
35

thanks to its dhow-building yards and lucrative trade in arms and slaves, while inland, **Ibra** also became rich for a time thanks to passing trade. Increasing **British** restrictions on slaving and arms smuggling during the nineteenth century led to a gradual eclipse in the region's fortunes, however, and during the early twentieth century Sharqiya became a major crucible of rebellion against the sultan in Muscat (see p.226), usually spearheaded by leaders of the powerful **Al Harthy** tribe, based in Ibra.

As with many of the country's other leading ports, Sur's fortunes have been revived since the accession of Sultan Qaboos by the construction of a massive new industrial complex, while the opening of the new dual-carriageway **coastal highway** in 2008 has further reinvigorated the region's economy – albeit at the cost of some of the area's former sleepy, slow-motion charm.

The Muscat–Sur coastal road

The principal route into Sharqiya follows the new coastal highway from Ruwi in Muscat south to Quriyat and Sur, with the Arabian Gulf on one side and the rugged summits of the Eastern Hajar on the other. Attractions here feature an interesting blend of the historical and the natural, including the old fort of **Quriyat** and the ruined city of **Qalhat**, along with **Wadi Shab** and **Wadi Tiwi**, two of Oman's most scenic wadis, while the off-road drive up across the top of the Eastern Hajar to Ibra via the Bronze Age tombs of **Jaylah** is another highlight. Past here lies **Sur**, the historic centre of Oman's famous ship-building industry, and still one of the prettiest towns in the south, and the turtle beach at **Ras al Jinz**.

Access to the eastern coast of Sharqiya is via the **Sharqiya coastal highway** (opened in 2008), which sweeps travellers south from Quriyat to Sur in little more than an hour. Plans to subsidize construction costs by a system of road tolls have been mooted but have not yet been put into effect, although a line of toll booths stands ranged across the highway 18km south of Quriyat ready to spring into action. The highway has provided a boon to development in the area, although it has also taken a toll on the various natural attractions it passes en route, while the increase in high-speed traffic and fly-by tourists has destroyed some of the area's original, slow-motion charm – an inevitable, if slighty depressing, consequence of Oman's ineluctable modernization.

Quriyat

The first town of any significance south of Muscat, **QURIYAT** lies some 80km from the capital, a 45-minute drive from Ruwi along a fast and relatively empty new stretch of dual carriageway which weaves between the craggy foothills of the Eastern Hajar. Quriyat had the dubious honour of being one of the first towns in Oman to experience the destructive attentions of the **Portuguese** fleet under Afonso de Albuquerque (see p.221). Albuquerque's soldiers attacked the town in August 1508, setting it ablaze and massacring its inhabitants – captives, it is said, had their noses and ears cut off, a popular Portuguese way of discouraging further resistance to their rapacious rule.

The town centre – a modest huddle of buildings and a low-key souk – lies around 7km off the coastal highway. The principal attraction is Quriyat's **fort**, which sits right in the middle of town, on your left as you drive in. Unfortunately, like so many other forts in Oman, it was closed at the time of writing for renovation – long overdue, judging by the crumbling exterior plasterwork and general

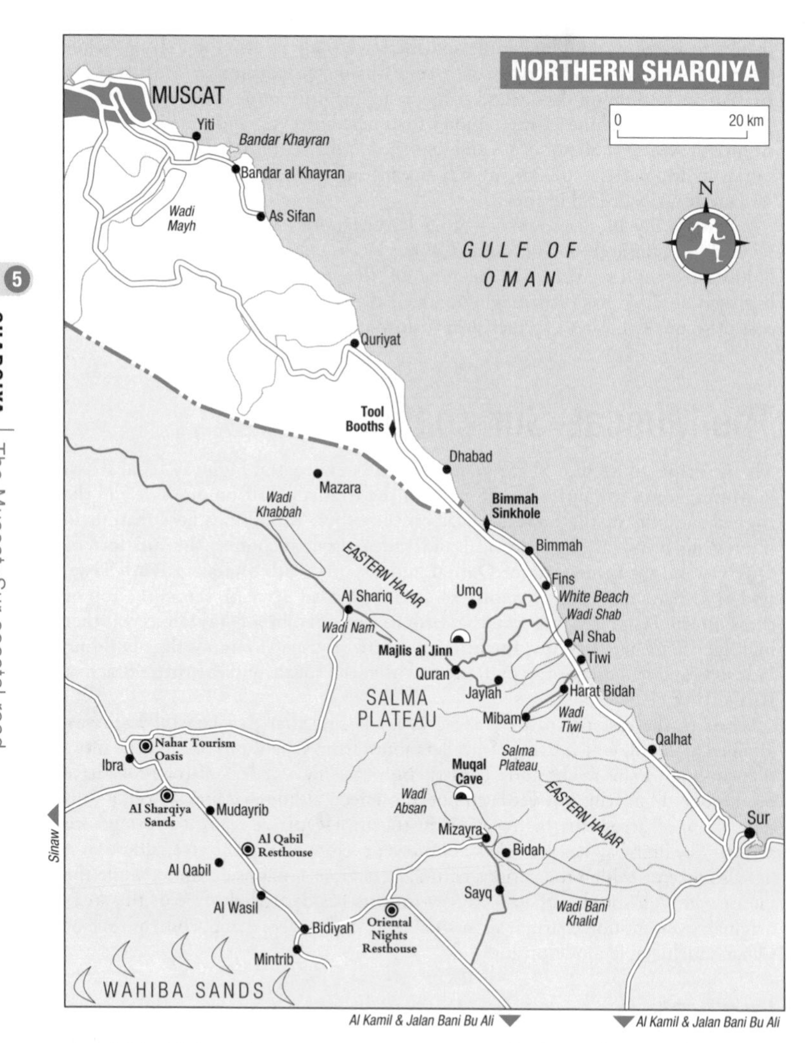

air of dilapidation. In the meantime, you can still admire the fine old wooden entrance door flanked by two rusty cannon and the shuttered ground-floor windows which ring the building on three sides, suggesting that domesticity, rather than defence, was formerly the principal concern.

Continue along the road past the fort and a large mangrove swamp to reach the town's pretty **seafront** corniche, at the end of which is the harbour, with boats drawn up on surrounding sands overlooked by a round watchtower sitting proudly on the headland above.

Bimmah Sinkhole and Fins

The next major sight heading south along the coast is the **Bimmah Sinkhole**, now enclosed within (and signed as) the Hawiyat Najm Park. The exit to the park is signed off the coastal highway 38km south of the Quriyat turn-off. Follow the road under the highway and down to the sea, then turn left at the (unsigned) T-junction towards Dhabab for 1.5km, then left again at the brown sign to the park.

Sadly, the sinkhole itself – formerly one of the coast's most magical beauty spots – has now been utterly defaced in the name of tourism, with an ugly stone wall erected around its rim and hideous concrete steps with bright blue handrails running down inside, which has succeeded in reducing the whole place to the level of suburban naff. If you can ignore all this, the interior of the sinkhole is still rather lovely, with a miniature lake at the bottom, its marvellously clear blue waters populated with shoals of tiny tadpole-like fish, and reflections from the water playing on the layered limestone above.

Continuing south from here, it's possible to drive along the **old coastal road** (tarmacked hereabouts) which runs close to the sea through Bimmah village and on to the village of **FINS**, 18km further on, where the tarmac ends – a pleasant change of pace and scenery from the coastal highway. There's a turn-off back to the highway past Bimmah 10km along the road, and another one at Fins. Fins itself is flanked by an attractive string of white-sand **beaches** including the popular "White Beach", 5km south of the village, although the whole place attracts a steady stream of visitors, particularly at weekends.

Wadi Shab

South of the Bimmah Sinkhole lie the dramatic Wadi Shab and Wadi Tiwi, a pair of spectacularly narrow mountain ravines, hemmed in by vertiginous sandstone walls with a verdant ribbon of date plantations and banana palms threading the base of the cliffs. Driving south, **Wadi Shab** is the first of the two you'll encounter, and perhaps the most rewarding. There's no road into the wadi (unlike Wadi Tiwi) – which is a significant part of its charm – even if the entrance has now been disfigured by the concrete flyover carrying the coastal highway. In a 4WD you can negotiate the first kilometre or so over deep, loose gravel, but after this progress is on foot only, as the gorge narrows, with a small footpath running along a small rock ledge just above the wadi floor, choked with huge boulders. It's possible to walk for another 45min–1hr up the wadi before the track becomes difficult, passing the ruins of old villages, further plantations, and deep rock pools en route – those around the end of the trail are a refreshing place for a swim, although the wadi's popularity with local and foreign tourists means that you're unlikely to have the place to yourself.

Getting to Wadi Shab

The coastal highway runs directly above the entrance to Wadi Shab on a high bridge, affording brief but wonderful views; there's a layby just past the bridge if you want to park up for a photograph or longer look. Actually **reaching the wadi** is surprisingly tricky, however, due to the fact that the access road (to which brown signs still direct you) has collapsed into the sea. Approaching from the north, ignore the brown signs, drive over the bridge past the mouth of the wadi and continue for 3km south to the signed Tiwi exit. Turn around here and head back up the coastal highway to reach a second, signed Tiwi exit slightly further north. Exit here, following the road as it ducks under the highway and heads down to the coast to reach a T-junction. Turn left here, following the narrow road as it twists through Al Shab village, eventually running down to the sea and then looping back under the highway to reach the entrance to the wadi, where there's a large parking area.

Wadi Tiwi

A couple of kilometres south of Wadi Shab lies the almost identical **Wadi Tiwi**, another spectacularly deep and narrow gorge carved out of the mountains, running between towering cliffs right down to the sea. It's less unspoiled than Wadi Shab, thanks to the presence of a road through the ravine (although, as at Wadi Shab, the dramatic scenery at the entrance has been ruined by the construction of a large flyover), although it compensates with its old traditional villages, surrounded by lush plantations of date and banana, and criss-crossed with a network of gurgling *aflaj*.

The road into the wadi was being widened and modernized at the time of writing (and should be complete by the time you read this), running along the valley floor, between plantations and past the rock pools which collect between the huge boulders below. After around 5km you'll reach the picturesque village of **Harat Bidah**, where the road narrows dramatically, squeezing its way between old houses and high stone walls. Past here the tarmac ends and a rough track climbs steeply for a further 5km up to the village of **Mibam** – a spectacular, if nerve-jangling, drive.

Getting to Wadi Tiwi

As with Wadi Shab, the coastal highway runs right past the entrance to the wadi via a high bridge, offering spectacular glimpses of the ravine, although actually **reaching the wadi** is somewhat more difficult. Exit the coastal highway at the signed Tiwi exit then follow the road as it loops back under the highway and towards the village. The tarmac runs out almost immediately, however, and the track becomes rough, narrow and, in a couple of places, difficult to follow. It should be okay in a 2WD, assuming it hasn't been raining, in which case things might be tricky.

Jaylah and around

Some 4km south of the turn-off for Fins, brown signs point inland to the ancient tombs of **Jaylah** (or Gaylah) and the village of Quran. This is one of the most memorable drives in Sharqiya, a spectacular off-road traverse of the barren uplands at the top of the Eastern Hajar with a cluster of wonderfully atmospheric Bronze Age beehive tombs en route. The track also offers a convenient short cut from the coast to Ibra (see p.176), although it's probably no quicker than taking the main road through Sur. The route comprises about 50km of generally good graded track, but there are some pretty rough, and sometimes extremely steep, sections here and there – 4WD is essential, as are strong nerves if you're driving yourself.

The route begins by switchbacking vertiginously up the flanks of the Eastern Hajar, a breathless thirty-minute drive with increasingly spectacular views down to the coast below. At the top, you reach the sere **Salma Plateau** at the summit of the Eastern Hajar: a rolling expanse of gravel plain, dotted with only the sparsest of vegetation. There's virtually no sign of human habitation until you reach tiny **Quran**, one of the loneliest villages in Oman – little more than a haphazard cluster of houses tucked away in the lee of cliff, and feeling an awfully long way from anywhere.

The tombs and towers

Past Quran, keep left, navigating a boulder-strewn section of wadi bed for a few hundred metres, after which the track resumes, becoming increasingly rough. About 7km west of Quran you reach an unsigned T-junction. Turn right here

Majlis al Jinn

Hidden away in the depths of the Eastern Hajar around 8km north of Quran village lies the celebrated **Majlis al Jinn** ("Meeting place of the Jinn"), one of Oman's most spectacular and challenging destinations for adventurous speleologists. The Majlis is one of the world's largest cave-chambers, some 120m high – larger than the great pyramid of Cheops. Entrance to the cave is via three vertical sinkholes, involving a free descent of between 118m and 158m and including the sinkhole now popularly known as "Cheryl's Drop", after the daring lady who first tackled the descent. Unfortunately, the cave has been closed since 2008, when the government, inspired by the success of Al Hoota Cave (see p.99), announced plans to develop the cave as a major tourist attraction, though no further news is currently forthcoming on the state of the project, or any likely future reopening date.

for Ibra, or left to reach the first of a marvellous collection of Bronze Age **tombs and towers** which dot the surrounding uplands. The most notable structure here is a single large tower, restored to a height of around 10m (you'll already have seen it up above on your left as you approach the T-junction), while the remains of six beehive tombs, which have survived in varying stages of completion, sit in a line along the very edge of the precipitous ridge beyond. The tombs are perfect examples of their type, crafted from finely cut stones, each with a small opening at the base, although it's the marvellously wild and remote location which really captures the imagination – a perfect example of the ancient Omani predilection for constructing funerary monuments in the highest, wildest and most remote places.

Turning right at the T-junction and continuing towards Ibra you'll see more tombs scattered about the mountainside to the right of the road. After another 3km you reach a **second cluster** of monuments spread out on either side of the road, including ten or so beehive tombs and a trio of well-preserved towers – perhaps even finer than the first group, although the location is less spectacular.

Beyond here, a series of isolated and ramshackle villages dot the bewildering network of tracks which crisscross the plateau, tucked away in hollows among the mountains. A few kilometres beyond the second group of tombs you reach another unsigned T-junction. Turn right here for Ibra, descending steeply down a poorly maintained track to **Wadi Nam**, a dramatic little valley hemmed in by sheer black-earth walls. From here, it's a straighforward, if bumpy, ride down the wadi to the village of **Al Shariq**, where the tarmac resumes and leads to Ibra, some 50km further on.

Qalhat

The ancient city of **QALHAT** was, up until the sixteenth century, one of the most important on the Omani coast – "A sort of medieval Dubai" as travel writer Tim Mackintosh-Smith described it in his *Travels with a Tangerine* (see p.239). Qalhat's importance derived from its status as the second city of the Kingdom of Hormuz (see p.221), serving as a major commercial hub in the Indian Ocean trade routes. The fame of the city attracted visitors including both Marco Polo and Ibn Battuta. Despite its prosperity, the city suffered from certain strategic weaknesses. A *falaj* system provided a reliable source of water, but there was almost no agricultural land available and all food had to be imported by land or sea. Qalhat's already tenuous foothold on the Omani coast was futher undermined by a serious earthquake at the end of the fourteenth century, while just over a hundred years later, in 1508, the newly arrived **Portuguese** delivered the *coup de grace*, sacking the city, massacring its inhabitants and setting its buildings and large fleet of boats on fire, an event from which Qalhat never recovered.

The ruins

The **ruins** of the city, originally triangular in plan, cover an area of over sixty acres, although it's difficult to make much sense of the confusing wreckage of assorted walls and towers scattered over a rocky headland and along the adjacent wadi (look out for shards of antique Persian pottery and Chinese procelain which litter the site). The only notable surviving structure is the **Mausoleum of Bibi Maryam**, a quaint little cuboid building enshrining the remains of the saintly Bibi Maryam who, according to Ibn Battuta, had ruled the city until a few years before his visit in 1330. The colourful tiles which covered the walls right up until the nineteenth century have now vanished, and the dome has also collapsed, though the remains of the delicately moulded arches and doorways have somehow survived the years.

The site was officially closed at the time of writing, although there's nothing to stop you walking up for a look anyway.

Getting to Qalhat

Finding Qalhat presents the usual navigational challenges. Exit the coastal highway at the brown sign for Ancient City of Qalhat, turn back under the highway and then veer right, down to the coastal road (this area had been turned into a fenced-off building site at the time of writing, but will hopefully have cleared by the time you read this). Reaching the coastal road turn right (south) and drive for around 1.5km until the tarmac ends and you see a brown sign saying Madinat Qalhat. Continue along the track (passable in a 2WD) as it veers to the right around a small palm grove, past which you'll see ruins up on a hillock to your left. Park along here and walk up.

Sur

Far and away the most appealing town in Sharqiya, **SUR** enjoys one of the eastern coast's prettiest locations, with the old part of town sitting on what is almost a miniature island, surrounded by a tranquil lagoon and offering views of mingled water and land in every direction. Sur is also one of the most historic settlements in the south, formerly a bustling port and trading centre whose maritime traditions live on in the intriguing **dhow-building yard**, the only surviving one of its kind in Oman. Further reminders of Sur's illustrious past are provided by the trio of forts and string of watchtowers which encircle the town and harbour.

Sur's attractions are quite spread out. The small but lively town centre and **souk** – a colourful tangle of brightly illuminated shops and cafés – lies at the western end of the island, from where the breezy seafront corniche runs down the coast for 1km or so to reach the old **harbour**, home to Sur's dhow-building yard and a trio of watchtowers, beyond which lies the pretty village of **Ayjah**.

Some history

The easternmost major settlement in Oman, Sur has always looked to the sea. Following the demise of Qalhat in 1508, the town developed as the region's most important port, shipping goods to and from India and East Africa, and also established itself as the country's most important ship-building centre (vestiges of which remain – see p.172). A succession of reverses during the nineteenth century eroded the town's fortunes, including the arrival of European steam-ships in the

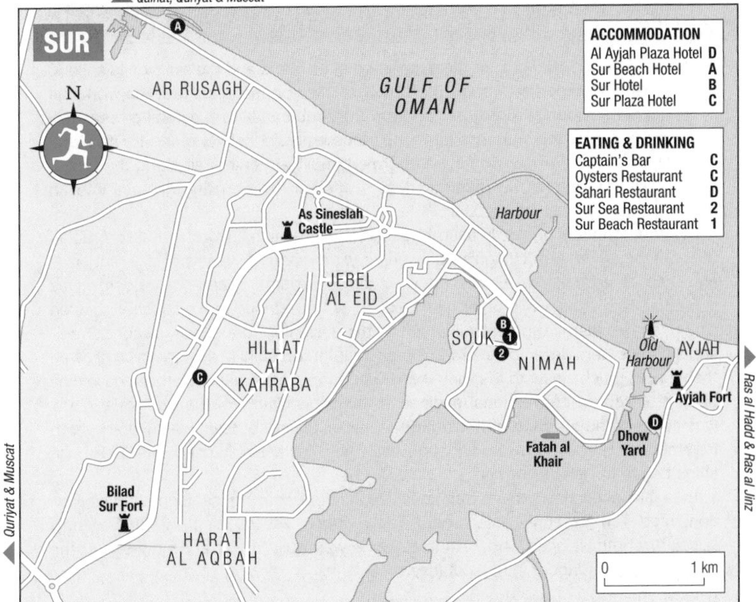

Indian Ocean, the British prohibition of slavery, the split with Zanzibar and the rise of the port of Muscat. Recent years have seen a modest revival in the town's fortunes thanks to the opening of the massive OLNG natural gas plant just up the coast.

Accommodation

Sur musters a reasonable spread of accommodation to suit most budgets, although only the *Sur Hotel* is actually in the centre of town.

Al Ayjah Plaza Hotel Just outside Ayjah village (see p.172) ⓣ2554 4433, ⓦwww.alayjahplazahotel.com. Smart, newly opened hotel with a fancy atrium painted in clashing colours and attractive rooms kitted out with stylish furnishings; some rooms also have fine views over the neighbouring lagoon. There's good food in the adjacent *Sahari Restaurant* (see p.173), while there are plans to open a live-music bar, and a swimming pool may eventually follow. ❺

Sur Beach Hotel 3km from town on the road to Qalhat ⓣ2554 2031, ⓔsurbhtl@omantel.om. This old-fashioned three-star resort looks like it's stuck in the 1970s, but compensates with a reasonable spread of facilities and a helpful and welcoming atmosphere. Accommodation is in a mix of cosy, old-fashioned rooms (all with sea view and balcony) or in two-storey villas (sleeping two), with living room and small kitchen, plus more modern and stylish furnishings. There's a stretch of slightly stony beach and a rather drab little pool, while facilities include an in-house international restaurant, sports pub, Indian, Arabian and Russian live-music bars, tennis court and internet café. ❹, villas ❻

Sur Hotel ⓣ2554 0090, ⓦwww.surhotel.net. In a convenient location right in the middle of the souk – although inevitably not the quietest place in town. Rooms are simple but perfectly clean and comfortable, and reasonable value at the price. ❶–❷

Sur Plaza Hotel Around 4km inland from the centre ⓣ2554 3777, ⓦwww.omanhotels.com/surplaza. The town's most upmarket option, with pleasant public areas arranged around a central atrium, although rooms themselves are looking a little drab and tired. Facilities include the cosy *Captain's Bar* (see p.173) and dull *Oysters Restaurant* (see p.173), and there's also a medium-sized pool with basic sun terrace and loungers, plus gym, business centre and a Budget rent-a-car office. ❻

The Omani dhow

Oman was formerly famous for the excellence of its boats and the skills of its sailors, whose maritime expertise – backed up by a detailed understanding of the workings of the local monsoon (a word derived from the Arabic *mawsim*, meaning "season") – laid the basis for the country's far-reaching commercial network, and for its string of colonies in East Africa. Boats were formerly built at centres all along the coast, though only the one at Sur now survives – offering a fascinating glimpse into an almost vanished artisanal tradition.

The word **dhow** is generally used to describe all traditional wooden-hulled Arabian boats, although locals distinguish between a wide range of vessels of different sizes and styles. The traditional Arabian dhow – such as the large, ocean-going *boom* – was curved at both ends, while other types – such as the *sambuq* and *ghanjah* – boasted a high, square stern, apparently inspired by the design of Portuguese galleons. Traditional dhows were driven by enormous triangular **lateen sails** (a design which allowed them to sail much closer to the wind than European vessels), although these have now been replaced by conventional engines. Another peculiarity of the traditional dhow was its so-called **stitched construction** – planks, usually of teak, were literally sewn together using coconut rope, although nails were increasingly used after European ships began to visit the region.

For a fascinating insight into traditional Omani boat-building, seafaring and navigation, read Tim Severin's entertaining *The Sindbad Voyage* (see p.240); Severin's specially commissioned dhow – the *Sohar* – was built in Sur and now sits in the middle of a roundabout in Muscat (see p.68).

The harbour and dhow-building yard

The prettiest part of town – and the obvious place to start a visit – is around the harbour at the southern end of the seafront corniche opposite the contiguous village of **Ayjah** (see below). Three watchtowers on successively higher rock outcrops sit above the harbour, overlooking the suspension bridge connecting Sur and Ayjah and the restored lighthouse nearby, backed by an attractive sprawl of low white houses – one of southern Oman's prettiest views.

Just past the suspension bridge is Sur's **dhow-building yard**, all that remains of the town's once flourishing boat-building trade and the only surviving dhow yard in Oman. There are usually a couple of boats under construction here while the carcasses of further old dhows can be seen further along the beach, awaiting restoration or recycling. Visitors are welcome to look around and watch the (now exclusively Indian) workforce chiselling, hammering, sawing and planing.

Continuing south past the dhow yard, the road runs along the edge of the lagoon to where the old **Fatah al Khair**, an elegant ocean-going dhow built in Sur some seventy years ago, stands propped up next to the road on the waterfront. Plans to open a maritime museum in the adjacent building have yet to bear fruit.

Ayjah

From the *Fatah al Khair*, you can either continue all the way around the lagoon-side road to reach the main souk or return past the dhow yard and across the suspension bridge into the neat little village of **AYJAH** (also spelled Aygah), spread out along the headland bounding the western side of the harbour. The village is one of the prettiest in Sharqiya: a low-lying huddle of simple old whitewashed waterside houses interspersed with more chintzy modern villas – many sport porticoes supported by the village's unique style of pillars topped with goblet-shaped capitals. It's worth going all the way through the village to the seafront road and modern **lighthouse**, with fine sea views, plus a surprising number of goats.

Driving into the village you'll pass a brown sign on your left pointing to the neat little **Al Ayjah Fort** (also known as Al Hamooda Fort). This is allegedly open to the public (Sun–Thurs 8am–2pm; free), but was closed at the time of writing.

As Sineslah Castle and Bilad Sur Fort

A couple of other forts lie dotted around town. A few kilometres west of the town centre, **As Sineslah Castle** (also spelled Sunaysilah) sits in a commanding position on a hill above town. There's not much inside apart from a neat little mosque, a Qur'an school and a surprisingly civilized prison – unusually for an Omani dungeon, it even has windows. Steps climb up to the eastern and western towers, from where a walkway stretches around the parapet offering fine views over the white sprawl of Sur below, spiked with dozens of minarets and the occasional watchtower. Entrance to the castle is from the main road between the town centre and the *Sur Plaza Hotel* (you can drive through the gates and right up to the fort rather than parking on the road).

Further down the same road, the large **Bilad Sur Fort** is currently closed for renovations, though it's still possible to have a look at the outside, notable mainly for the pair of unusual two-tier towers on its southern side. It's signed down a narrow lane off the main road past the *Sur Plaza Hotel*.

Eating and drinking

There's not much in the way of culinary diversion in Sur. The most upmarket **restaurant** in town is the *Oysters Restaurant* at the *Sur Plaza Hotel*, which dishes up thoroughly pedestrian Indian, Chinese and international fare at inflated prices (mains 2.5–4.5 OR). Another possibility is the *Sahari Restaurant* next to the *Al Ayjah Hotel*. The restaurant (and outdoor terrace) boasts a fine location overlooking the lagoon, with an upmarket selection of Italian dishes, plus other cuisines including Indian, Arabian and Mexican (mains 4–6 OR).

There are plenty of **cafés** scattered around the souk. The virtually identical *Sur Sea Restaurant* and *Sur Beach Restaurant*, opposite one another in the middle of town by the *Sur Hotel*, are two of the best, with reasonable, well-priced food and lively streetside seating – a great place to people-watch. Both menus feature the usual mix of quasi-Indian dishes and shwarmas, plus some Chinese and seafood options, with most choices under 2 OR, or considerably less.

For an alcoholic **drink**, the nicest place in town is the *Captain's Bar* at the *Sur Plaza Hotel*, a pleasant nautically themed pub, which is usually fairly quiet.

Ras al Hadd

The eastern coast of Sharqiya ends with a watery flourish at the little village of **RAS AL HADD**, sitting at the far southeastern corner of the country, overlooking the point where the waters of the Arabian Gulf merge with the Indian Ocean. The village's main attraction is as a convenient base from which to explore the turtle beach at Ras al Jinz (see p.174), although it's well worth a visit in its own right thanks to its pleasantly sleepy, somewhat end-of-world feeling, and impressive old fort, backed by a pair of extensive lagoons.

The main sight hereabouts is the sprawling **fort** (Sun–Thurs 8.30am–2.30pm; free), close to the sandy shore, looking (along with the rather grand mosque next door) incongruously oversized compared to the tiny buildings of the rustic village which surrounds it. Most of the interior consists of a huge empty courtyard, with a walkway stretching the length of the parapet and a large round tower at either end, each with a neat little toilet projecting from its topmost level.

Accommodation

There are a couple of **places to stay** in Ras al Hadd, although neither is particularly inspiring.

Ras al Hadd Beach Hotel On the main road through the village, about 2km past the fort ⓣ2556 9111, ⓔsurbhtl@omantel.om. Large, functional eyesore occupying a prime piece of real estate on a strip of sand between the sea and lagoon. Accommodation is in bright, spacious tiled rooms with nice views over either the lagoon or sea (with a wide but rather scrubby patch of beach, on which you may spot turtles in July and August). Cheaper, if somewhat bizarre, lodgings are available in a string of converted Portakabins set around the hotel forecourt – comfier than you might expect, albeit a bit stuffy, and expensive at the price. Facilities include a multi-cuisine licensed restaurant and bar, while the helpful staff can arrange motorboat trips on the lagoon or dolphin-spotting cruises out to sea (30 OR for a boat taking up to 6–7 people; one day's notice required for sea trips). ❺, Portakabins ❸

Turtle Beach Resort ⓣ2554 3400, ⓦwww.tbroman.com. This small fenced compound of densely packed barasti huts looks something like a desert concentration camp at first sight, an impression reinforced by the caged Alsatian kept at the entrance barrier. The location is nice, squeezed between sea and lagoon, and has an attractive sliver of beach, while the restaurant (in a recycled dhow) is fun. Unfortunately, the accommodation provided in the barasti huts (cheaper ones with shared bathroom and no a/c) is desperately small and basic – a total rip-off for the price. The miserable staff might be able to arrange a boat trip, if you ask very nicely, but there are no turtles here, despite the resort's name. To reach the resort, turn left at the roundabout at the entrance to the village shortly before the Al Maha petrol station. Follow this road for 6km around the back of the lagoon then go down the good graded track (signed) off on the right for a further kilometre to reach the resort. Half-board only ❹

Ras al Jinz

Some 35km from Sur at the easternmost point of the Arabian peninsula, **RAS AL JINZ** is home to Oman's most important **turtle-nesting beach**, visited by thousands of magnificent green turtles every year, who haul themselves up out of the sea to lay their eggs in the sand. This is perhaps the finest natural spectacle anywhere in Oman (even if, ironically, you can't actually see very much after dark) – a magical glimpse into a natural cycle which has been in existence for the best part of two hundred million years.

Visits begin with a walk across the sands in the darkness to the edge of the waves, from where you'll see the ghostly silhouettes of perhaps a dozen or more green turtles emerging slowly from the surf and then heaving themselves laboriously up the beach – a Herculean trial of strength for these enormously heavy creatures. Half an hour later, having found a suitably sheltered location, the turtles begin digging themselves carefully into the beach, scooping out clouds of sand with their flippers to create a sizeable hole in which they then proceed to lay their eggs.

The whole scene is particularly magical at daybreak, as the sun rises, revealing the beautiful, cliff-fringed beach dotted with the great humped outlines of departing turtles, leaving great plough-tracks in their wake as they make their way slowly back down the beach before disappearing, exhausted, into the waves.

Practicalities

Turtle-watching **tours** depart from the very smart modern **visitor centre** (ⓣ9655 0606, ⓦwww.rasaljinz-turtlereserve.com) at 9pm and 4am, last around 60–90min and cost 3 OR. It's a ten-minute walk from the centre to the beach (visitors with impaired mobility are offered transport). **Access** to the 3km-long beach (part of a larger 45km protected zone) is now strictly controlled, with a maximum of 100 visitors per evening and another 100 visitors per morning session. Unfortunately, demand for outstrips supply, and bookings either by phone or email are essential; three weeks or more in advance is recommended since places usually get booked up early, even for early-morning tours and in the height of summer.

The **best time** to see turtles laying their eggs is from June to August, when anything up to a hundred may arrive on the beach each night (although you're pretty much guaranteed to see at least one or two come to lay their eggs on any night of the year). Nesting turtles prefer dark nights rather than those when the moon is full. No torches or photography (even without flash) are allowed on night tours, while photography is allowed on morning tours only after sunrise.

It's also possible **to stay** at the centre, which has fourteen comfortable modern rooms (7), including two family rooms sleeping four or five (8). Rates include dinner, breakfast, and evening and morning tours. A cheaper although much less pleasant alternative is the *Al Naseem Camp* (bookings through Desert Discovery Tours in Muscat T 2449 3232, W www.desert-discovery.com, half-board only, 4), 4km inland from the visitor centre next to the road. Accommodation is in a compound of extremely basic, very small palm-thatch huts (with fan only), and with no furniture apart from beds; all share rudimentary shower and toilet facilities.

South to Al Ashkharah

South of Ras al Jinz it's a pleasant drive along the coast through a string of small, ramshackle villages. The landscape beyond **Asaylah** is particularly beautiful, with an unusual combination of mountain and desert, as the craggy limestone outcrops at the far southern end of the Eastern Hajar merge with the outlying dunes (some of them surprisingly large) of the Wahiba Sands (see p.179).

A short drive beyond Asaylah and some 90km from Ras al Jinz, **AL ASHKHARAH** is the largest settlement along this stretch of coast, although not really much more than a tumbledown little fishing town with low ochre-coloured houses straggling along a wide stretch of beach. The only **accommodation** option is the *Al Ashkhara Hotel* (1), a run-down one-star which has seen better days (probably in around 1950) but is tolerably clean and will do for a night if you get stuck. The *Golden Beach Restaurant and Coffee House* next door does good chicken or fish set dinners. The hotel is on the right-hand side of the main road through town about 100m past the Shell station.

Al Ashkharah to Shana

There's a choice of routes from Al Ashkharah: either northwest along **Highway 35** to Jalan Bani Bu Ali and on to Ibra, or south along the scenic new coastal road to **Shana**, the departure point for ferries to Masirah (see p.184), a journey of some 180km. The drive to Shana takes 90min–2hr along the fast single-carriageway road; note that the last petrol is at Qurun, 60km from Ashkharah. It's a fine drive, with pleasant coastal scenery including a stretch of large rolling dunes beyond **Khuwaymah** (and with brief, distant glimpses of the high dunes of the Wahiba Sands rising further inland). The region is totally uninhabited apart from the ramshackle Bedu camps you'll see pitched alongside the road, from which children may occasionally emerge to chuck stones at passing traffic.

South from Muscat: the inland route

An alternative route into Sharqiya and out is via the inland **Highway 23**, which heads down from Muscat to Ibra and on to Al Kamil, before turning northeast towards Sur or continuing south towards Jalan Bani Bu Ali and the southern coast. The major attraction en route is the magnificent **Wahiba Sands**, while the lively commercial centre of **Ibra** and the time-warped **Jalan Bu Bani Ali** are also worth a visit.

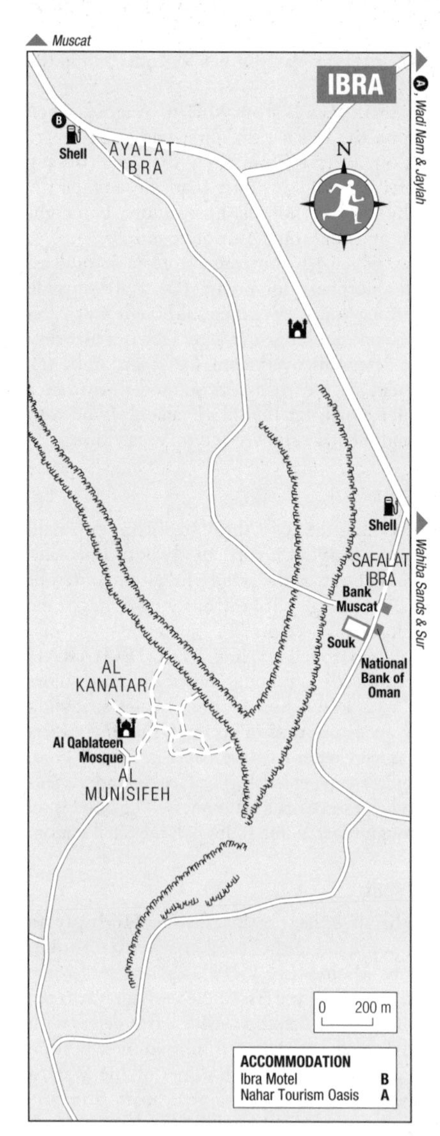

Ibra

The principal town of inland Sharqiya, **IBRA** grew rich thanks to its location on the major trade route between Muscat, Sur and Zanzibar – evidence of the wealth accumulated by the town's former notables can be seen in the magnificent old mudbrick mansions of Al Munisifeh (see p.177). The town is also the home of the redoubtable **Al Harthy tribe**, whose repeated rebellions against the sultans of Muscat were such a feature of early twentieth-century Omani history (see p.226).

Modern Ibra may have lost some of its strategic importance (especially since the opening of the new coastal highway, which has further isolated the town) but it still has a lively mercantile buzz, centred on the colourful **souk**, as well as some of Sharqiya's finest traditional mudbrick architecture in the nearby villages of **Al Munisifeh** and **Al Kanatar**. It also makes a good base for explorations of the nearby Wahiba Sands (see p.179), as well as a possible starting point for the magnificent off-road drive to the coast via the tombs of **Jaylah** described on p.168.

Accommodation

If you don't fancy either of the places below, there's a trio of places south of town along the main road to Sur, covered on pp.181–182.

Ibra Motel Just north of the Wadi Nam roundabout next to the Shell station ⓣ2557 1666, ⓔibramtl@omantel.net.om. One of the nicest budget hotels in southern Oman, with smart, spacious and very attractively furnished rooms at bargain prices. The adjacent *Fahad bin Saleh Coffee Shop* does a reasonable range of basic curries and shwarma. ❶

Nahar Tourism Oasis 3km east of Ibra down Wadi Nam road ⓣ9938 7654, ⓦwww.emptyquartertours.com. Peaceful rural retreat in a pleasant spot a few kilometres outside Ibra. Accommodation is in quaint, if slightly battered-looking, pseudo-mudbrick chalets (more expensive ones with attractive traditional Arabian decoration), and there's an attractive garden restaurant. ❸–❹

Desert Oman

Beyond the mountain chains which line the coast stretch Oman's deserts – a forbidding, fascinating patchwork of dunes, gravel plains and coastal flats, dotted with arid wadis, surreal wind-sculpted rock formations and patches of near-indestructible vegetation. Home to a few hardy Bedu, who continue to eke out a living amid the wilderness, as well as to rare and elusive wildlife such as the Arabian oryx, the desert represents Oman at its most unforgettably challenging and inhospitable.

Rub al Khali, also known as "The Empty Quarter" ▲

Salt flats near Mahut, Al Wusta province ▼

Ghaf tree, Rub al Khali ▼

The deserts

Much of Oman is desert – just not quite in the way that most visitors might imagine. The **sandy deserts** which are synonymous with the Arabian peninsula in the imagination of most foreigners can be found here, although they cover only a relatively small portion of the country. The magnificent dunes of the **Wahiba Sands** are the most notable and accessible example, although there are even grander dune formations in the remote **Rub al Khali** (Empty Quarter), sprawling across the Omani border in northern Dhofar and on into Saudi Arabia.

The majority of Oman's desert, however, is not sandy but **stony**, covering much of Dhofar, Al Wusta and Al Dhahirah provinces. The deserts here consist of windswept plains covered in a mix of gravel and rock, dusted with a fine layer of hardy vegetation; these expanses are less immediately picturesque than the dunes of Wahiba, but still compelling in their own austere way. **Coastal deserts** are also a feature of southern Oman. A mixture of sand, gravel and salt flats (*sabkha*), these areas are punctuated with secluded creeks and backed by cliffs sculpted into outlandish shapes by the combined effects of wind, sand and sea.

Flora and fauna

Oman's deserts are home to some of the hardiest **flora** on the planet, which have evolved over the millennia to survive in the interior's arid environments. These include the wispy *ghaf* trees, which somehow suck a living out of the inhospitable sands of the Wahiba, and the gnarled **frankincense trees** of Dhofar, as well as many smaller shrubs and plants which subsist on a daily diet of desert dew.

The desert also supports a remarkable diversity of incredibly resilient **fauna** (see p.236), ranging from scuttling camel spiders, scorpions and beetles through to larger mammals, such as the ubiquitous camel and the more rare desert fox, ibex and **oryx**.

▲ A Bedu man and his camel in the Wahiba Sands

The Bedu

Life in the desert is synonymous with the **Bedu** (see p.180), the hardy nomads whose austere lifestyle was immortalized in Wilfred Thesiger's *Arabian Sands*. Despite Oman's comprehensive modernization over recent decades, small Bedu populations continue to scrape a living from the desert regions, particularly around the Wahiba Sands, and colourfully dressed Bedu women still frequent the souks at Ibra and Sinaw. Traditional pursuits do persist, such as raising livestock during the winter (camels especially) and cultivating dates in the hot summer months, although many Bedu have reinvented themselves as tourist guides, working out of the desert camps in Wahiba and the Rub al Khali.

▼ Bedu woman wearing traditional mask

Exploring the desert

The most popular way to explore the desert is to go **dune-bashing** (see p.23), careering and skidding over the dunes in a 4WD amid huge plumes of sand. **Camel- and horse-riding** offer a more peaceful and environmentally friendly way of experiencing the desert, as does **hiking**. These activities can be arranged through camps in the Wahiba Sands, or through specialist tour operators (see pp.21–22). Whatever you do, you'll need a competent local **guide** before venturing into the sands on foot; travelling with local Bedu offers unparalleled insights into desert ecology, culture and traditions.

▼ Dune-bashing in Wahiba Sands

Bedu children, Wahiba Sands ▲

Arabian oryx ▼

The ten best desert experiences

▸▸ **Wahiba Sands** The classic Omani desert destination, with magnificent dunes and largely unspoiled scenery within a couple of hours' drive of Muscat, best appreciated by spending a night in one of the local desert camps. See p.179.

▸▸ **Ibra and Sinaw Souks** Two of Oman's most absorbing traditional markets, attracting a steady stream of colourfully attired local Bedu who come to shop for provisions or sell elaborately embroidered fabrics. See p.177 & p.178.

▸▸ **The Al Ashkharah to Shana coastal road** Newly opened coastal highway, running along the southern fringes of the Wahiba Sands, with glimpses of nomadic Bedu encampments en route. See p.175.

▸▸ **Masirah Island** Oman's ultimate desert island, ringed with secluded beaches and turtle-nesting sites. See p.184.

▸▸ **Arabian Oryx Sanctuary** Remote haven for the threatened animal, hidden away amid the rocky desert of the Jiddat al Harasis. See p.186.

▸▸ **The Duqm to Dhofar coastal road** Little-travelled route (by foreigners, at least) through the deserts lining the coasts of Al Wusta and eastern Dhofar. See p.187.

▸▸ **Shisr (Ubar)** The fragmentary remains of the legendary city of Ubar, once a pivotal location on southern Arabia's fabled incense route. See p.213.

▸▸ **The Rub al Khali** Oman's final frontier, the vast sands of the Rub al Khali (Empty Quarter) offer a taste of the Arabian desert at its most memorable and untouched. See p.213.

▸▸ **The Muscat to Salalah highway** Challenging desert drive across the interminable gravel plains of Oman's windswept interior. See p.193.

▸▸ **Dune-bashing** Buckle up that seat belt and hold on tight as you bump and slide across the desert in a high-powered 4WD. See p.23.

Sign language, Oman style

One charmingly old-fashioned aspect of every souk in Oman is the lack of advertising. Visit any market in the country and you'll see lines of similar little shops all boasting exactly the same, resolutely factual, signs in Arabic, with their English translations below. "Coffee Shop" is probably the most common, closely followed by "Gents Tailoring" (with "Ladies Tailoring" not far behind), while other signs are similarly matter of fact – "Sale & Repairing of Dish & Television" for a TV shop, for instance, or "Sale of Fresh Mutton & Frozen". The accuracy of English translations is consistently high, and mistakes rare, although when things do go wrong they can do so spectacularly, such as the shop in Ibra souk advertising "Asle of Freah Ghigken" (they mean "Sale of Fresh Chicken"). Occasionally bursts of unintentional linguistic whimsy also catch the eye, notably the local outlet advertising "Sale of Tobacco, Smoke & Derivatives" – a pleasantly fanciful way of saying they sell cigarettes.

The Town

Ibra is one of the few settlements of its size in Oman that doesn't have a fort, although the jagged surrounding hills are topped with a dozen or so watchtowers standing guard over the approaches to town.

Modern Ibra – or **Ayalat Ibra** (Upper Ibra) – is strung out along the main highway, a functional ribbon of banks, petrol stations and cafés. It's around 3km from here to the older part of town, **Safalat Ibra** (Lower Ibra), which is where you'll find the lively **souk**, one of the largest in Sharqiya. The heart of the souk is occupied by a large open-air pavilion mainly given over to the sale of fruit and vegetables, although look out for the small shop in the corner devoted to the (as the sign says) "Sale of Traditional Rifle Maintenance and Fire Arms", usually busy with a few old-timers bent over antiquated-looking weapons of slight destruction. There are also a few shops selling jewellery and *khanjars*, while the block immediately beyond the central pavilion is occupied by a string of carpentry shops turning out old-fashioned wooden doors and other traditional wooden items, although the workforce is now exclusively Indian. To reach the souk from the main highway, take the turning signed Safalat Ibra directly beyond the Shell station (not to be confused with a second Safalat Ibra turning signed about 2km further south).

Ibra is also home to a celebrated **Women's Souk** (Souk al Hareem, or Souk al Arba'aa, meaning "Wednesday souk"), held close to the main souk on Wednesday mornings from around 7am to 11am. The souk is restricted to female traders and shoppers (in theory at least – although the rule is not strictly enforced), with a wide selection of goods ranging from piles of cheap clothes and factory cloth through to traditional cosmetics and textiles; look for examples of the colourful and distinctive local Bedu embroidery which is sewn onto black abbayat or around the ankles of trousers.

Al Munisifeh

A couple of kilometres beyond the souk lie the atmospheric old walled villages of Al Munisifeh and Al Kanatar, two of the finest in the region. To **reach the villages**, continue past the souk until the road veers to the left, then turn right, following the brown signs to Al Munisifeh Village, Al Kanatar Village & Al Qablateen Mosque.

Approaching by road, you come first to **AL MUNISIFEH**, surrounded by the remains of its original walls, with gateways at either side linked by a central street. The village comprises an assortment of modern houses interspersed with rather grand old buildings in a mix of mudbrick and stone – their size testifying to the wealth amassed by the village's merchants during Ibra's heyday athwart the trade route between Muscat and Zanzibar. The quality of the decorative work on many of the old houses is unusually high – look out for the remains of elaborate plasterwork, and finely carved wooden doorways and window frames. All the old buildings are now uninhabited and partially derelict, although many have been discreetly restored, which has managed to preserve much of their original character while giving the comforting sense (unlike so many other abandoned Omani houses) that they aren't in danger of collapsing in the next heavy shower.

Exiting the village through the gateway at the far end you'll pass a very old mudbrick **mosque**, raised on a platform above street level. As with similar very early mosques elsewhere in the country, such as the nearby Al Qablateen (see below) or the Masjid Mazari in Nizwa (see p.90), there's no minaret, just a tiny pepperpot dome on one corner.

Al Kanatar

Continue past the mosque, through the second gateway and along the path (keeping right at the first fork) as it winds for a few hundred metres through rather battered-looking palm groves, dotted with the crumbled outlines of more mudbrick structures. Over on your right, close to the wadi, you'll notice a cluster of rather cubist-looking two-storey fortified houses.

Just before you reach Al Kanatar village you'll notice the venerable old **Al Qablateen Mosque** to your left, another ancient structure, standing on a raised platform and lacking the customary minaret. Fifteen stumpy columns stand massed inside, strikingly similar to those at the Al Hamooda Mosque in Jalan Bani Bu Ali (see p.183), though the roof they originally supported has long since collapsed. Turn right out of the mosque to reach another cluster of venerable old buildings, one sporting an exceptionally fine carved wooden door.

Continue along the main pathway to reach **AL KANATAR** village. Like Al Munisifeh, this is encircled with the remains of its old walls, with gateways at either end connected by a single, narrow street lined with mudbrick houses – an absolutely picture-perfect sight, although the houses are now completely abandoned, with little more than rubble inside.

West to Sinaw

West from Ibra, a little-travelled (by foreigners, at least) road heads cross-country to join up with Highway 15 at Izki (see p.82), some 125km distant – a useful short cut through to the Western Hajar. There's not much to see on the road itself, although if you're travelling this way there's a worthwhile diversion to the town of **SINAW**, 25km south of the Ibra–Izki road. The town is best known for its colourful **souk** – a rectangle of shops arranged around a large courtyard with an open-sided pavilion in the middle. The souk is in the centre of town; turn left at the big roundabout if approaching from Ibra via Al Mudaybi or from Izki. The souk attracts large numbers of Bedu from the nearby Wahiba Sands, including local women dressed in vibrantly coloured shawls, patchwork tunics and embroidered anklets, and others, less flamboyant, swathed in black abbayat and face masks.

Tucked away in the extensive date plantations behind the souk lie the atmospheric remains of **old Sinaw**, comprising a pair of neat little villages nestled among the palms. The first is close behind the souk; the second lies further into the plantations; both are crammed with fine two- and three-storey mudbrick buildings, some still surprisingly well preserved.

Mudayrib and Mintrib

Back on Highway 23, some 18km south of Ibra, a sign points left to **MUDAYRIB**, 1km off the main highway. One of the prettiest villages in Sharqiya, Mudayrib is surrounded by an unusually fine cluster of six watchtowers on the encircling hills which form a tight protective necklace around the small village below, all beautifully backdropped by the craggy peaks of the Eastern Hajar. The village boasts a number of imposing old **fortified houses** built, as at Ibra, by merchants who had grown wealthy on the back of trade with Africa. Some of them look almost like miniature forts, with battlemented rooftops, miniature towers and musket slits in the walls.

A further 25km south of Mudayrib and 3km west of the highway, the little town of **MINTRIB** (also spelled Mintarib and Minitraib) is an important access point for the Wahiba Sands, which rise immediately to the rear of the town. Mintrib is also home to a small **fort** (Sun–Thurs 8.30am–2.30pm; free), with unusual, slightly inward-sloping walls and a single, undernourished tower rising just a metre or so above the battlements. Access to *Al Raha* and the *1000 Nights* camps (see p.181) is along the road running past the fort. There's a handy garage in the middle of town where you can have your tyre pressure reduced before venturing onto the sands.

The Wahiba Sands

South of Ibra stretch the magnificent **Wahiba Sands** (Ramlat al Wahiba; also known as the Sharqiya Sands) – "a perfect specimen of sand sea", as they have been described. This is the desert as you've always imagined it: a huge, virtually uninhabited swathe of sand, with towering dunes, reaching almost 100m in places, sculpted by the wind into delicately moulded crests and hollows. Tourist resorts apart, there are no permanent settlements in the sands, although some local **Bedu** still live here in somewhat ramshackle temporary encampments, particularly on the southern fringes of the sands around Al Ashkharah (see p.175). Otherwise, Wahiba remains hauntingly empty, although the endless tracks churned up by cavorting dune-bashers tearing around the sands in their souped-up 4WDs (and, along the main routes, obscene quantities of litter) mean that it's not quite as unspoiled as you'd expect. As a general rule of thumb, the further into the sands you penetrate, the more dramatic and untouched the landscape becomes.

The **dunes** themselves follow a surprisingly regular pattern, as a glance at Google Earth makes strikingly clear, running in long lines from north to south – an orderly sequence of so-called "linear" dunes formed by the conflicting winds blowing in from the eastern and southern coasts (and meaning that travelling across the sands from north to south is significantly easier than tackling them from east to west). They are also constantly on the move, shifting inland at an estimated rate of 10m per year.

Exploring the sands

The sands cover a considerable area: some 180km from north to south, and almost 80km from east to west. There are no **roads** here. A network of tracks (for which

Desert ecology in the Wahiba Sands

Empty though they may look, the sands support a fascinating **desert ecology**. A celebrated expedition by the Royal Geographical Society in 1986 discovered 150 species of plant, including the hardy ghaf (*Proposis cinera*), which plays a major role in stabilizing the dunes, as well as providing firewood and shade. In addition, 200 mammal, bird and reptile species were discovered, ranging from side-winding vipers to desert hares and sand foxes. Most of these creatures are nocturnal, however, so you're unlikely to see much during the day apart from their tracks. For more on desert wildlife, see p.236.

The Bedu

Arabia's most iconic inhabitants, the **Bedu** (often Anglicized to "Bedouin") have long been seen – by Westerners at least – as the human face of the desert peninsula. For outsiders, the Bedu have come to personify a rather romanticized ideal of nomadic life amid the sands, with their distinctive lifestyle of ferocious independence, ceaseless tribal feuds and outbursts of legendary hospitality. Some of which is at least partly true.

Scattered across the interior of Oman and other countries around the peninsula, the nomadic Bedu tribes formerly eked out a marginal existence amid one of the world's most hostile natural environments, surviving in the depths of the desert by a combination of camel-raising, goat-herding and inter-tribal raiding – a lifestyle founded on a complex network of tribal allegiances, intimate knowledge of the local environment and extraordinary levels of physical resilience. Wilfred Thesiger's *Arabian Sands* remains essential reading for anyone with even a cursory interest in the region, offering a fascinating glimpse into the Bedu tribes' unique customs and traditions and a salutary corrective to some of the more flowery received notions of nomadic life.

Not surprisingly, virtually nothing survives of the harsh traditional Bedu existence described by Thesiger. Many Bedu in Oman have now adopted settled, sedentary lifestyles, emigrating to the cities and merging with the population at large, while others have reinvented themselves as tour guides, offering modern visitors rewarding insights into the flora, fauna and traditional culture of the Wahiba Sands. Traditional Bedu culture and customs do, however, linger on in many parts of southern Oman, particularly around the Sands themselves. Local Bedu here still follow a modified form of their traditional pursuits, raising livestock for part of the year before decamping to their plantations around Mintrib to harvest dates during the hot summer months. Bedu families can also often be seen frequenting the souks of Ibra and Sinaw, with the distinctive sight of local Bedu women in traditional face masks and elaborately embroidered shawls, trousers and tunics offering a colourful reminder of the interior's traditional, if now increasingly threatened, past.

you'll need 4WD) crisscrosses the sands, although these are sometimes difficult to follow without local knowledge, being notional routes rather than physical tracks – meaning it's possible to get badly lost if you don't know what you're doing. Getting **stuck** in the desert is also a real possibility, and no laughing matter during the hot summer months; it's best to travel with at least one other vehicle if you're venturing away from established routes.

The principal attraction of a visit here is simply the chance to be out among the dunes, and to spend a night in the desert. All the camps listed below also lay on various **desert activities**. Dune-bashing (see p.23) is a popular, if not particularly restful or environmentally friendly, way of exploring the sands; camel or horse rides (sometimes guided by local Bedu) offer a more peaceful alternative, while other activities include sandboarding, trekking and quad-biking.

Accommodation

For many visitors, overnighting amid the Wahiba Sands at a **desert camp** is one of Oman's most memorable experiences – surrounded by the majestic outline of moonlit dunes, and with a twinkling tapestry of stars overhead. Unfortunately, you don't get much for your money at any of the extensive string of establishments dotting the dunes. Even the most basic camps come with a sizeable mark-up, while the nicer spots can cost as much as a plush Muscat five-star hotel. On the plus side, rates include breakfast and dinner, plus free coffee, tea and fruit.

Most camps feature accommodation in some kind of pseudo-traditional tent or palm-thatch hut (which may be concrete inside). Many places can also get noisy at weekends, when locals and expats descend on the region; if possible, visit during the week. None of this should deter you if you've got your heart set on a night in the desert, however – but it's worth knowing you can explore the sands without actually staying in them, either by opting for one of the two places on the main highway listed below, or by staying in Ibra (see p.176). All desert camps, with the exception of *Al Areesh*, require 4WD to reach, although all places can arrange to collect you from the main road, albeit often at a considerable price.

Desert Nights Camp, *Nomadic Desert Camp* and *Sama Al Wasil Tourism Village* are reached from **Al Wasil** village, 30km south of Ibra; *1000 Nights*, *Safari Desert Camp* and *Al Raha* are reached from **Mintrib**, 40km south of Ibra.

In the sands

1000 Nights 20km further into the sands beyond *Al Raha* camp ⓣ9944 8158, ⓦwww.1000nightscamp.com. Nice-looking camp with accommodation mainly in Bedu-style tents – simple, but pleasantly authentic. The standard "Arabic" tents (with shared bathroom) are pretty bare, have just two beds and not much else; the pricier "Sheikh" tents are bigger, with attractive woven decorations, a couple of pieces of furniture and nice attached open-air bathrooms (cold water only); or there's more conventional and comfortable accommodation in the two a/c "Sand Houses", built in traditional mudbrick style. Facilities include a small but pretty pool and mudbrick-style sun terrace, a quirky sit-out area in an old dhow, a lovely (unlicensed) restaurant scattered with colourful cushions, and free wi-fi. Pick up from Mintrib is 40 OR return. Arabic tent ❹, Sheikh tent ❻, Sand House ❽

Al Areesh Turn-off from Highway 23 around 27km south of Ibra (7km past Mudayrib turn-off), then 8km into the sands ⓣ9945 0063, ⓦwww.desert-discovery.com. Built in the lee of the dunes in a rather tame section of desert, this is one of the oldest and drabbest of the main camps, and beginning to look its age. The only real selling point is that it's accessible by sealed road (apart from the last 750m or so, which should be fine in a 2WD), although this means the scenery is less majestic than at other places further into the dunes. Accommodation, in simple rooms (with or without en suite) covered in withered palm fronds, is decidedly basic, and there's no electricity – alternatively, you can move your bed and sleep outside. It's very expensive for what you get. Shared bathroom ❹, en suite ❺

Desert Nights Camp Turn-off from Al Wasil, then 11km into the sands ⓣ9281 8388, ⓦwww.desertnightscamp.com. The most luxurious camp in Wahiba, offering a real dash of Arabian style in the desert, although at a hefty price. Accommodation is in a string of individual "units" modelled after traditional Arabian tents. The "double units" (240 OR) are attractively furnished with traditional bric-a-brac and fabrics under a tent-style canvas roof; "attached units" are cheaper (195 OR) but not nearly as nice. There's also an attractive licensed restaurant (with a live oud player nightly) and a nice bar, plus complimentary pick-up from the main road. ❾

Nomadic Desert Camp Turn-off at Al Wasil, then 20km into the sands ⓣ9933 6273, ⓦwww.nomadicdesertcamp.com. A long-established camp deep in the sands, owned and operated by a local Bedu family and therefore offering a touch of authenticity other places lack. Accommodation is in simple but nicely furnished barasti huts, with shared bathroom only and no electricity, and there's an attractive *majlis*-cum-dining area. ❻

Al Raha 20km along the road past Mintrib Fort ⓣ9934 3851, ⓦwww.alrahaoman.com. This is the best value of the various camps, set a considerable distance into the sands in a neat and shady little garden surrounded by towering dunes. Accommodation is in rather unappealing concrete rooms (all en suite) that come either with fan or a/c. There's a licensed restaurant, and free tea and coffee are served in the *majlis*. Fan ❹, a/c ❺

Safari Desert Camp 25km from Mintrib ⓣ9200 0592, ⓦwww.safaridesert.com. Recently opened camp with accommodation in nicely furnished Bedu-style tents (with en-suite bathrooms) scattered across a rather flat and unexciting stretch of sand, plus a pleasant *majlis*-style restaurant with cushion seating on the floor. ❻

Sama Al Wasil Tourism Village Turn-off from Al Wasil, then 20km into the sands ⓣ2449 9309, ⓦwww.samavillages.com. Newish and well-equipped camp with accommodation in a neat circle of attractive sandstone chalets (all en suite) in traditional Omani style, with pretty little rug-covered verandas. It lacks some of the atmosphere of more traditional tented camps, but compensates with above-average creature comforts, including proper beds, modern bathrooms, electricity and good food. ❻

On the main highway

Al Sharqiya Sands 8km south of Ibra on the west side of Highway 23 (just south of the turn-off to

Sinaw and Al Mudaybi) ⓣ2558 7099, ⓦwww.sharqiyasands.com. Comfortable three-star with unexciting rooms but attractive gardens around a decent-size pool. Facilities include a licensed restaurant, the pleasant *Lausanne Pub*, and the *Ahlan Lounge*, with a live Arabic band nightly. ❹

Al Qabil Rest House 23km south of Ibra next to Highway 23 ⓣ2558 1234, ⓦwww.desert-discovery.com. A homely little place, set around an attractive garden courtyard and with comfortable rooms – if you don't mind the naff bedclothes and carpets with which some are equipped. There's also a licensed restaurant, and trips to the sands can be arranged (1–4 people 35 OR for 2.5hr). ❸

Oriental Nights Rest House 14km south of Bidiyah. Next to Highway 23 (on the right-hand side of the road approaching from Ibra) just east of Al Maha petrol station ⓣ9900 6215. Simple, comfortable lodgings in a modern hotel with in-house restaurant. ❷–❸

Wadi Bani Khalid

Some 15km beyond Mintrib along Highway 23, a side road heads northeast into the dramatic **Wadi Bani Khalid**, perhaps the most attractive of the various wadis which dissect the western flanks of the Eastern Hajar. The wadi is one of the greenest in Oman, dotted with a string of villages and plantations – the red-skinned banana is a local speciality, particularly in Bidah village.

It's 22km off the main highway to the little village of **Mizayra**. The road splits here: turn right for Bidah (see below) or head left into Wadi Absan (a subsidiary branch of the main Wadi Bani Khalid) and follow the tarmac through the plantations before reaching the end of the road and a small car park at tiny Muqal village. Several large **pools** dot the wadi hereabouts, a popular swimming and picknicking spot, especially at weekends. Taking the path to the right of the pools and following the very rough, boulder-strewn track up the wadi for around 15 minutes brings you to **Muqal Cave**. It's possible to enter the cave, although, depending on how tall you are, you'll have to crawl – or at least stoop painfully – through the narrow entrance in order to reach the main chamber. A torch is essential.

Returning to Mizayra and taking the right-hand turn (see above) brings you after about 3km to the village of **Bidah**, framed by a beautiful series of waterfalls, the Shalalaat al Hawer, which run down above the village after rain. Bidah is also the starting point for a challenging hike through the canyon-like upper reaches of Wadi Bani Khalid, taking around 4–5hr to reach the village of Sayq on the far side.

Al Kamil

South of the Wadi Bani Khalid turn-off, the main road continues for a further 40km to the small town of **AL KAMIL**, where the road splits, with Highway 23 heading east to Sur (50km distant) and Highway 35 heading south to Jalan Bani Bu Hassan and beyond. Al Kamil itself is home to a cluster of imposing fortified houses lined up in a row just off the main road: large and severely simple mudbrick boxes, almost completely unadorned save for their rooftop crenellations and turrets. The houses are on your left as you reach the roundabout on the far side of town, identifiable by the large Muscat Pharmacy sign. A short walk beyond, on the far side of the open-air souk, stands the crumbling remains of a three-towered fort.

Jalan Bani Bu Hassan

Sixteen kilometres south of Al Kamil, the modest town of **JALAN BANI BU HASSAN** is home to a sprucely restored **fort** (Sun–Wed 7am–6pm; free). Most of the interior consists of a large, empty courtyard. The residential quarters sit at the far end, with a disorienting complex of rooms arranged around a sloping terrace surrounded by an Escher-like tangle of steps, doors and battlements. Continuing along the road past the fort brings you to the oldest part of town, home to a fine cluster of traditional **fortified houses**, including one particularly impressive tower-house, five storeys high, with distinctive layers of crumbling off-white *sarooj* (plaster) still clinging to its upper floors.

To **reach the fort**, turn left off the main road at the sign to Jalan Bani Bu Hassan and follow the brown signs to the fort; the first sign, on your right, is rather easy to miss, given how small the English words are compared to the Arabic.

Jalan Bani Bu Ali

A further 10km south of Jalan Bani Bu Hassan, the town of **JALAN BANI BU ALI** is the most interesting in this part of Sharqiya: staunchly traditional, and with a certain reputation for religious conservatism and political independence. During the early nineteenth century, following repeated Saudi incursions into Oman, the local Bani Bu Ali tribe converted to the Wahhabi form of Islam practised in Saudi Arabia. It was the only tribe in the country ever to do so, and subsequently repudiated the rule of the sultan – who responded by dispatching a large armed force to crush the fledgling rebellion. Even now, the town retains a decidedly old-fashioned atmosphere, and visitors remain a source of (usually friendly) curiosity.

The Town

The modern part of town along the main highway is indistinguishable from any other in Oman. The **old town**, however, remains relatively untouched by the twenty-first century, with a sprawl of low, sand-coloured buildings and stands of dusty-looking palm trees sprawling around one of Oman's most marvellously atmospheric **forts**. This is probably the single largest unrestored mudbrick structure in the entire country: a huge, crumbling colossus which rises high and proud above the surrounding streets. Large parts of the structure have collapsed, though several soaring towers and the magnificent central keep survive – for the time being, at any rate.

Access to the **interior** is either via the various gaps in the partially collapsed walls, or a single small door around the far side. Inside there's a fascinating tangle of ruined buildings boasting the remains of fine arches and arcading. Look out for the quaint little mosque, topped by a pair of domes – remarkably similar to the famous old fifteenth-century mosque at Bidiyah in the eastern UAE (the oldest in that country), suggesting a similar vintage for the building here.

Nearby stands the rustic **Al Hamooda Mosque**, a low, squat structure topped by 52 tiny domes and with a *falaj* running across its main facade. Unlike the fort, this has been carefully restored. Non-Muslims aren't allowed inside, though the main door is usually left open, allowing you a view of the unusual interior, filled with a dense cluster of stumpy columns – a very old style of mosque design which can also be seen at the Al Qablateen Mosque in Ibra (see p.178).

To **reach the mosque**, follow the road past the front of the fort until you reach a brown sign (partially collapsed) announcing the beginning of the Wahiba Sands. Turn left here and follow the road for about 500m as it swings round to the left; the mosque is clearly visible next to this road on the right-hand side.

Practicalities

Approaching from the north, turn right at the main roundabout in the centre of town to reach the souk, and follow this road through the souk to reach the fort and old town on the far side.

If you want **to stay**, your only option is the *Al Dhabi Tourist Motel* (Ⓣ2555 3322; ❷), a simple but homely little one-star, jazzed up with fancy wooden doors and masses of plastic flowers; it's 1km south of the main roundabout, next to the Shell station. There are a few low-key **cafés** scattered along the main road in the vicinity of the hotel.

Masirah Island

Oman's largest island, remote **MASIRAH** remains largely off the tourist radar. Development here is muted, infrastructure basic and the whole place still sees far more turtles than tourists, offering plenty of unspoiled coastline and beaches to explore for adventurous and well-equipped travellers with time (and a 4WD) on their hands. The major attraction of a visit here is the chance to go **turtle-watching** (see opposite), while the island's somewhat end-of-the-world ambience may also appeal to idle beachcombers and birdwatchers. If you've got camping gear and a 4WD, the island's pristine beaches offer numerous opportunities to sleep out under the stars.

Not that Masirah is entirely untouched. The northern tip of the island has already been swallowed up by industrial and military installations, while ambitious plans for the construction of a 40km **bridge** linking Masirah with the town of Mahut on the mainland (scheduled to open in 2014 at a cost of US$1.5 billion) are likely to massively accelerate the pace of change, assuming it actually ever gets built. For the time being, however, Masirah remains a pleasantly sleepy sort of place, bordering on comatose.

The ferry from the mainland deposits you at the small town of **HILF**, the only major settlement on the island and home to a trio of petrol stations, a couple of ATMs and a pharmacy, plus a modest selection of shops in the town's small centre. There are no facilities elsewhere around the island.

Getting to Masirah

Driving directly down to Masirah from Muscat is a bit of a slog – a good four or five hours along the single-carriageway Highway 33 (later becoming Highway 32) which branches off the Nizwa highway at Izki. It's a lot nicer to approach from Sharqiya along the recently opened coastal road from Al Ashkharah. Either way you'll have to make it to the harbour at **Shana** – a very modest scatter of official buildings and a small café – from where car-ferries depart for **Hilf**.

The **ferry** costs 8 OR per car and the crossing takes around 90 minutes. Ferries leave when full – roughly every 1–2hr – and should run until around 5pm, although it's best to be at the jetty by 3pm, just in case. The service occasionally stops running in rough weather.

If you get stuck on the mainland, there's basic **accommodation** at the *Mahut Guesthouse* in Hijj, 60km from Shana back along the road to Muscat. The

The Baron Innerdale

Tucked away in the military area at the northern end of the island (and therefore out of bounds, although pictures can be found online) stands a touching memorial to the unfortunate crew and passengers of the **Baron Innerdale** (or "Inverdale", as it's often incorrectly called, including on the monument itself). The *Innerdale* was travelling from Karachi to Liverpool in 1904 when she ran aground amid the Khuriya Muria islands. After three days, crew and passengers abandoned the ship in two lifeboats. One disappeared; the other (with 17 people aboard) made it to Masirah.

What happened next remains unclear. Probably a misunderstanding led to a fight, during which the stranded passengers were massacred – although there's no basis for the outlandish rumours that they were subsequently eaten by the islanders. Sultan Faisal responded by visiting the island, banishing the local ruling sheikh and having nine of the murderers executed. He also razed the village of Hilf and forbade the islanders to build permanent houses for 100 years – a ban which wasn't lifted until 1970.

open-deck ferries are decidedly lacking in frills: there's limited seating on wooden benches around the bridge, but otherwise no facilities on board; it's more comfortable to do what the locals do and just sit in your car.

Around the island

Masirah is small enough to explore in a day but, at around 60km long, big enough to get lost in, if that's what you want, with plenty of off-road tracks and coastal nooks and crannies in which to picnic or set up a tent. Much of the coastline is fringed with wide, sandy, windswept beaches, while inland rises a ribbon of low, rough-edged hills. A tarmac road stretches down the west side of the island and along parts of the east coast, though to reach the island's most scenic beaches you'll need 4WD. Assuming you have your own tent and 4WD, there are superb, and still largely unexplored, **beach camping** possibilities all along the coast, particularly around the southern tip of the island.

Wild camping apart, Masirah's major attraction is its wildlife. In addition to the island's turtles (see below), 328 species of **bird** have been recorded here, more than anywhere else in Oman, ranging from flamingos to plovers and parakeets. The island is also known for its remarkable **seashells** and other marine relics, including molluscs, gastropods, bivalves, cowries and sponges, a result of the cold currents which flow along the coast during the *khareef* (see p.191).

It's for **turtles**, however, that Masirah is best known. Four of the five main species of marine turtle nest here (while the fifth species, the leatherback, can occasionally be seen feeding in the waters offshore). Masirah is believed to host the world's largest population of **loggerhead** turtles, while hundreds of green, hawksbill and olive ridley can also be found. Satellite tracking studies have shown that Masirah's loggerheads "commute" around the edge of the Arabian peninsula between the Red Sea and the Arabian Gulf, only rarely going further afield, nesting an average of four to five times a year, adding up to a staggering total of 15,000–30,000 egg-layings annually. Note that turtles nest only on the **east and far southwestern coasts** of the island; loggerheads favour the northeastern coast, while other species can be seen further south.

There are currently no official guided **turtle watches**, however, which means that you'll have to make your arrangements and ask locally about the best places to turtle-spot. Your best bet might be to head to the nesting sight on the beach by the *Swiss Belhotel*, 10km from Hilf.

Accommodation

Masirah has a passable selection of **places to stay**, including three relatively cheap options in Hilf itself, and the more expensive *Swiss Belhotel* some 10km distant on the far side of the island. Arriving at the island, turn left (north) out of the harbour for the *Masirah Hotel*, or right (south) for everywhere else.

Danat al Khaleej ("Khalig" on sign) ⓣ2550 4533, ⓦwww.danat-hotel.com. A pleasant place on the seafront road about 1km south of the harbour, although not as nice (or as conveniently located) as the similarly priced *Masirah Hotel*. Accommodation is in bright, medium-sized tiled rooms, and there's also an in-house restaurant – useful, since it's too far to walk into town. ❷

Masirah Hotel About 1km north of the harbour at the end of the main road through town, just past the Shell station ⓣ2550 4401, ⓔbooking@omantel.net.om. The nicest of the cheaper options in town, with big, comfortably furnished rooms, and also the closest to the souk, which is less than ten minutes' walk down the road. ❷

Serabis Hotel On the seafront road about 1km south of the harbour and souk ⓣ2550 4698. There are just nine rooms here at present, including one double, one triple, and seven suites-cum-apartments with sitting room (but no kitchen), sleeping two to four people. All are modern and spacious, albeit rather lacking in furniture. A new extension with forty doubles is planned. ❷–❹

Swiss Belhotel On the east side of the island about 10km from Hilf (follow the brown signs) ⓣ2550 4274, ⓦwww.swiss-belhotel.com. Opened in 2010, this upmarket establishment has added a welcome splash of luxury to Masirah's accommodation options. The building sits on the beach, which is wide but rather stony – considerable numbers of turtles nest right in front of the hotel from May to Sept (although there are no guided turtle watches). There are just fourteen standard rooms, all sea-facing with balcony, plus three attractive chalets with kitchen, sitting room and bedroom (sleeping two, though more beds can be put in). Facilities include a big pool, gym and jacuzzi, plus licensed restaurant and bar, and staff can arrange diving, snorkelling, jet-skiing and fishing trips. Interesting displays in the lobby cover the history and wildlife of the island. ❼

Eating and drinking

The only upmarket (and licensed) **restaurant** in Masirah is at the *Swiss Belhotel*. There are a few simple cafés scattered around Hilf, the best of which is the *Restaurant and Coffee Shop Masera for Turkish Meales* [sic], a popular little spot with outdoor seating and a well-prepared selection of grills, kebabs, shwarma and some meze (mains around 2 OR). It's on the way to the *Masirah Hotel* and Shell station. The *Swiss Belhotel* is also home to the only licensed **bar** on the island.

Al Wusta

Beyond Sharqiya lies the province of **Al Wusta** (literally, "The Central Region"), a great expanse of gravel desert known as the **Jiddat al Harasis** which stretches southwest all the way to Dhofar. Economically, the area is one of Oman's main oil-producing regions, but few tourists make it here, unless passing through while tackling the long drive to Salalah, and even fewer stop. The only mainstream attraction is the **Arabian Oryx Sanctuary**, although the long off-road journey down **the coast** south of Duqm offers a classic slice of wild Omani at its most unspoiled.

The Arabian Oryx Sanctuary

An hour's drive south of the Muscat–Salalah Highway 31 lies the **Arabian Oryx Sanctuary**, one of the most important wildlife conservation sites in Oman – albeit now in rather reduced circumstances (for more on the oryx, see p.237). The sanctuary was founded in 1982, becoming the first place in the Arabian peninsula to reintroduce free-ranging oryx herds into the wild following their virtual extinction during the 1970s. The reserve's early years were an unquestioned success: by 1994 the resident oryx population had risen to 450 and the sanctuary was added to the UNESCO World Heritage Site list. Unfortunately, the increasing oryx population also attracted less welcome human attention. Over the following decade, the vast and vulnerable sanctuary was systematically decimated by local poachers and the resident oryx population fell to 65 – including just four breeding pairs. Faced with this disaster in 2007, the government announced its plans to reduce the size of the sanctuary by ninety percent in order to be able to guard it effectively. Shortly afterwards, it also acquired the dubious distinction of becoming the first place ever to be struck off the UNESCO World Heritage Site list.

The sanctuary as it now exists is an altogether more modest affair: a fenced enclosure covering an area of just four square kilometres in which breeding pairs are protected. The surrounding area is also home to the world's largest population of wild Arabian gazelle, as well as the only breeding sites in Arabia of the endangered houbara bustard. Other rare species such as the Nubian ibex, Arabian wolf, honey badger and caracal also live here, although they are very rarely seen.

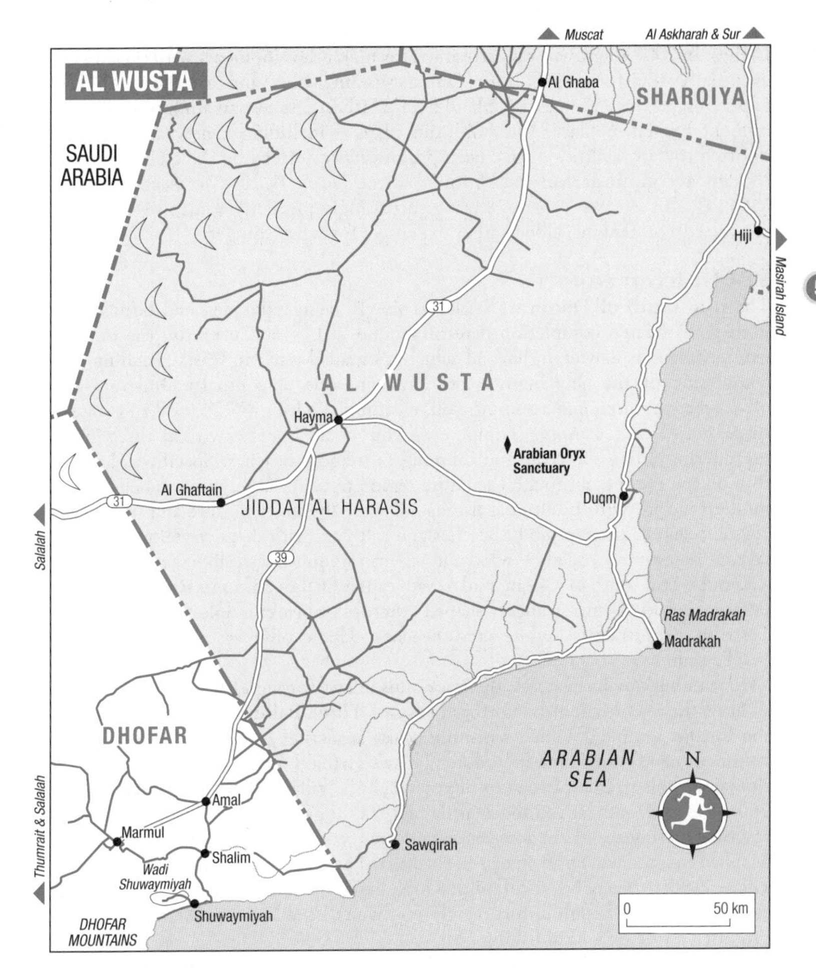

Practicalities

To visit the reserve you'll need to arrange a **permit** in advance from the Office of the Advisor for Conservation of the Environment in Muscat (T 2469 3536, E acedrc @omantel.net.om). Entrance **costs** 20 OR per group, which includes the services of a guide from the local Harasis tribe, who have guarded the reserve since its foundation – although be aware that they probably won't be able to speak English.

The turn-off to the sanctuary is at the modest town of **HAYMA**, on the main Muscat–Salalah highway; it's about an hour's drive from here to the site. There are a couple of simple places **to stay** in Hayma: the *Haima Motel* (T 2329 7103; 1) and *Al Wusta Resthouse* (T 2343 6016; 1); the *Duqm Tourist Guesthouse* in Duqm (see p.188) is another possible base. There's also a **campsite** at the sanctuary.

Duqm and beyond

A further hour down the road past the Arabian Oryx Sanctuary lies the port of **DUQM** (also reachable via the road from Al Ashkharah which serves Masirah

Island). In 2007 the town was earmarked for major development, with the aim of eventually transforming it into Oman's leading port and a major hub for exporting oil from the nearby inland fields. Although a certain amount of development has taken place, the ambitious plans – including a new airport plus assorted tourist facilities – have been progressively delayed by the credit crunch. Modest **accommodation** can be found at the *Duqm Tourist Guesthouse* (Ⓣ2542 7191; ❸) in the town centre, offering surprisingly pleasant rooms in a string of converted Portakabins, albeit rather expensive for what you get.

South from Duqm

The road **south of Duqm** to Salalah is slowly being upgraded and tarmacked, with an estimated completion date of around 2014–15. Currently, the tarmac extends as far as Sawqirah, beyond which it's graded track to Hasik. Pending the completion of the new highway, this remains one of southern Oman's great off-road adventures, and assuming you're equipped with a 4WD, food and water, spare petrol and camping equipment, you could spend two or three days meandering down the coast and camping on remote beaches. Specific sights are thin on the ground, although the entire region remains largely untouched by the modern world, with traditional fishing villages, abundant birdlife and unspoiled coastal scenery, mixing sandy beaches and salt flats with distinctive low cliffs of layered limestone, eroded by wind and sea into sinuous, wave-like shapes.

About 60km south of Duqm a side-road leads a further 25km to **Ras Madrakah** peninsula, dotted with strangely shaped outcrops of blackish dolomite rock above a string of attractive white-sand beaches which offer good camping and beachcombing.

Continuing down the coast, the track runs inland through barren desert, out of sight of the sea, skirting the northern edge of **Three Palm Tree Lagoon**, one of the various sea inlets which score the coast, attracting colourful flocks of pink flamingoes and other aquatic birdlife. There's virtually no sign of human habitation along this stretch of road until you reach the village of **SAWQIRAH**, some 250km from Duqm. It's a modest little place, although its small cluster of houses, toytown harbour and shallow lagoon, dotted with fishing boats, will feel like Manhattan after what you've driven through. The coast immediately south of the village is particularly beautiful, with a high line of sea cliffs dropping sheer to the water below – although unfortunately you won't be able to see them unless you can hitch a ride on a local fishing boat.

Beyond Sawqirah the tarmac comes to an end. The main track to Salalah veers inland to the small town of **Marmul** at the centre of the Al Wusta oilfields and then continues cross-country, eventually rejoining the Muscat–Salalah highway at Thumrait (see p.213). A second track turns south across the Jebel Hadiah, descending to the coast at the village of **SHUWAYMIYAH**. This is the starting point for the rough drive inland along the spectacular **Wadi Shuwaymiyah**, a dramatic canyon lined with towering white limestone cliffs and dotted with rock pools and palm groves – one of the region's remotest and most memorable sights.

Beyond Shuwaymiyah you reach the wild, cliff-fringed escarpment at the eastern edge of the **Dhofar Mountains**. The new coastal highway to Hasik is currently being blasted out of the inhospitable terrain here, and promises to be one of the most spectacular roads in the whole of Oman upon completion. For the time being, however, you'll have to retrace your steps back to Shuwaymiyah, and continue onwards via Marmul.

Dhofar

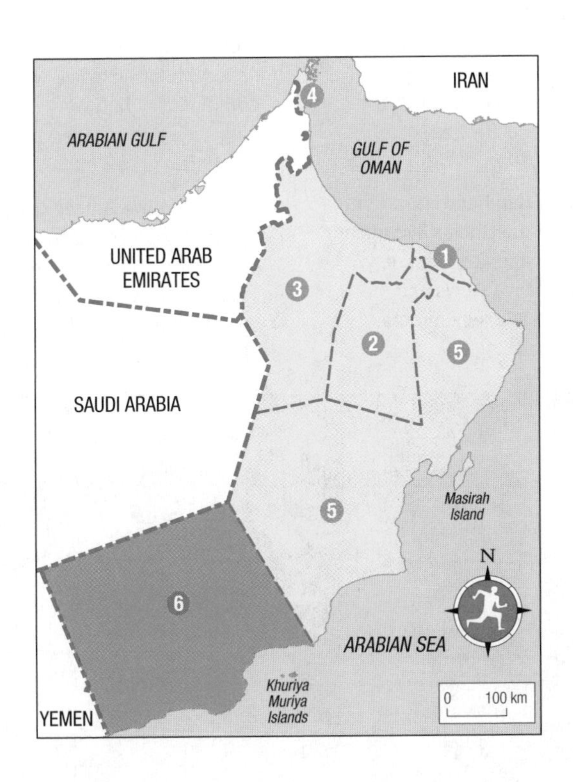
IRAN
ARABIAN GULF
GULF OF OMAN
UNITED ARAB EMIRATES
SAUDI ARABIA
Masirah Island
N
ARABIAN SEA
Khuriya Muriya Islands
YEMEN
0 100 km
1
2
3
4
5
5
6

CHAPTER 6

Highlights

* **The khareef** Arabia like you've never seen it, as the countryside around Salalah turns a lush, misty green during the annual *khareef* rains. See p.191

* **Al Husn Souk** A magical traditional souk in old Salalah, piled high with frankincense and *bukhoor*. See p.198

* **Wadi Darbat** Scenic wadi, full of rock pools, roving camels and – during the *khareef* – Oman's most spectacular waterfall. See p.204

* **Jebel Samhan** Ride to the top of the Dhofar Mountains, with magnificent scenery, superlative views and a pair of vast sinkholes en route. See pp.204–206

* **Sumhuram and Khor Rori** Explore the ruins of ancient Sumhuram, perched above the idyllic waters of Khor Rori. See pp.206–207

* **Mirbat** Dhofar's most personable town, with a neat fort and fascinating collection of old-style Dhofari houses. See p.207

* **The Mughsail to Fizayah road** Oman's most spectacular highway, weaving dramatically between frankincense-studded mountains. See p.210

* **Ubar and the Empty Quarter** Explore the ruins of the legendary "Atlantis of the Sands", then head out for a night amid the mighty dunes of the Empty Quarter. See p.213

▲ Omani men at Salalah's Al Husn Souk

Dhofar

Hugging the southern coast of the Arabian peninsula, the province of **Dhofar** (in Arabic, Zafar) can seem like a world away from the rest of Oman. Separated from pretty much everywhere else in the country by a thousand kilometres of stony desert, the region's history and identity have always been largely separate from that of the rest of the Sultanate. Fabled in antiquity as the source of the legendary **frankincense** trade, Dhofar boasted one of Arabia's oldest and most cosmopolitan cultures – whose remains continue to exercise historians and archeologists to this day. The region was only finally brought under the control of the sultans of Muscat in the mid-nineteenth century, while the Dhofaris continued to assert their independence until as recently as the 1970s (see p.229) before finally being brought into the Omani fold.

Centrepiece of the region is the laidback city of **Salalah**, capital of Dhofar and by far the biggest settlement for hundreds of kilometres in any direction. This is Oman with a distinct, tropical twist: endless white-sand beaches line the coast, while coconut and banana palms replace the ubiquitous date trees of the north and neat little pastel-painted houses stand in for the fortified mudbrick mansions found elsewhere in the country. The differences are especially striking during the annual **khareef** (June to August/early September), when the rains of the southeast monsoon brush along the coast around Salalah, turning the area to a fecund riot of misty green which has no equivalent anywhere else in the Arabian peninsula. During this period Salalah is thronged with visiting Omanis and other Gulf Arabs, who flock here to experience the unusual pleasures of rain – an attraction that might well be considered overrated by most visitors from outside the region – although the magical explosion of green, accompanied by the bursting into life of seasonal waterfalls and streams, more than compensates.

Numerous attractions dot the hinterland of Salalah, enclosed by the arc of the scenic **Dhofar Mountains**, including the rugged Jebel Samhan and Jebel al Qamar dotted with wadis, gorges, sinkholes, blowholes and other geological curiosities. Down at sea level, the **coast** is lined by huge, and largely deserted, strips of pristine white-sand beach, picture-perfect *khors* (creeks) and a string of further attractions including the quaint old town of Mirbat and the ruins of ancient Sumhuram. Beyond the mountains you enter the vast stony **desert** which stretches from here to Muscat, where you'll find the slight remains of the legendary Ubar and, further on, the enormous dunes of the majestic Empty Quarter.

Some history

The history of Dhofar is quite separate from that of the rest of the country, looking west towards neighbouring Yemen rather than north towards the Omani heartlands. The region as a whole rose to prominence, and economic prosperity,

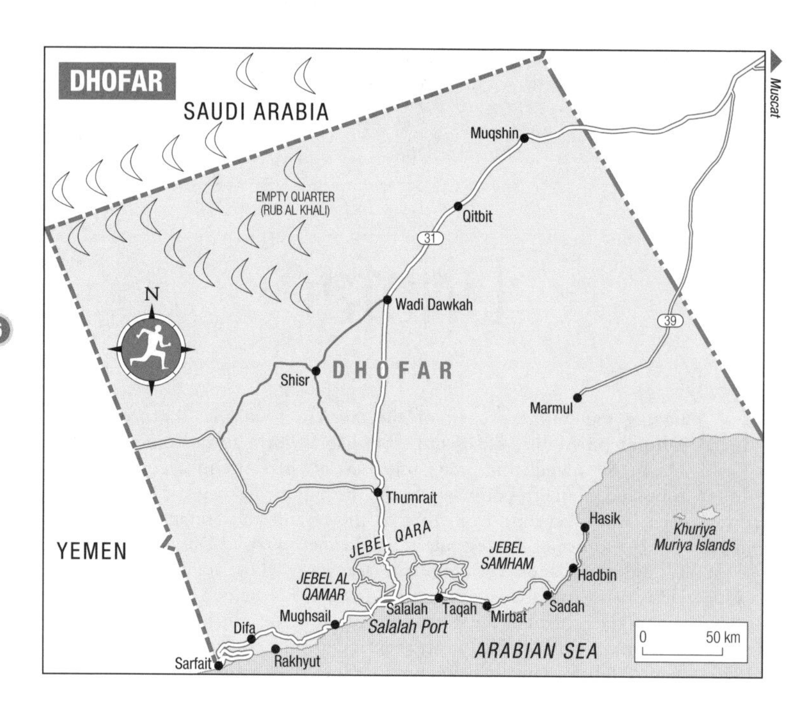

much earlier than most other parts of Oman, thanks to the lucrative local **frankincense** trade. Frankincense was traded through the region from Neolithic times onwards, gradually developing into the so-called **Incense Route**, one of the ancient world's most extensive and important commercial networks. Frankincense was transported by sea from the coast of Dhofar westwards up the Red Sea to Egypt, Africa and Europe, and east into the Arabian Gulf and on to India. By land, caravans headed up via Shisr across the Empty Quarter to Bahrain and, westwards, into Yemen and then north to Medina, Petra and, ultimately, Egypt.

A string of **ports** developed along the coast of Dhofar to service the frankincense trade, including Sumhuram (see p.206), followed by Mirbat, Sadh, Hasik and Zafar (the forerunner of modern Salalah, and the origin of the name "Dhofar"). The internal politics of the area remain obscure. The kingdom of Hadhramaut, in what is now southern Yemen, appears to have enjoyed some control over the region, while the influence of the Persian Parthians may also have been strong at various times. From around 300 AD onwards, the international frankincense trade went into a gradual decline, although Mirbat and Zafar, at least, continued as major commercial centres, exporting horses and spices in addition to frankincense and attracting many foreign visitors, including Marco Polo and Ibn Battuta.

The region was only finally brought into the Omani fold in 1877, during the reign of **Sultan Turki bin Said** (ironically, just as his own capital in Muscat was coming under increasing threat from the marauding Sharqiya tribes). Outside control was minimal to begin with, however, and in 1896 the local tribes rebelled, overran the sultan's fort in Salalah and murdered the garrison. Muscat eventually reasserted control, though its authority rarely ran much further than the immediate environs of Salalah itself, with the mountains remaining more or less autonomous under the patchwork of competing tribes.

Salalah played an increasingly important role in national affairs during the reign of **Sultan Said bin Taimur** (reigned 1932–70; see p.228), who effectively moved the court from Muscat to Salalah, rarely leaving the city (or, indeed, his palace) during the final years of his rule. The province was wracked during the 1960s and early 1970s by the protracted **Dhofar Rebellion** (see pp.229–231). In 1970, Sultan Said was overthrown in a bloodless coup in his Salalah palace and replaced by his son, Sultan Qaboos.

Despite having largely grown up in the region, Qaboos returned the court to Muscat. Notwithstanding the loss of its resident sultan, Salalah shared the benefits of the Omani Renaissance (see p.230), while the comprehensive aid and infrastructure programmes which followed the end of the Dhofar Rebellion in 1976 also hastened economic development and helped quieten political unrest. Swift growth followed, centred on the huge Raysut Industrial Area and Salalah Port, assisted by the opening of the local airport to international flights in 1975.

Getting to Salalah

The easiest and most comfortable way of getting to Dhofar is **to fly** from Muscat to Salalah. There are also regular **bus services**, or the challenge of **driving yourself** (see box below) along one of Arabia's longest desert highways.

Driving to Salalah

It's slightly over a thousand kilometres **from Muscat to Salalah** along Highway 31, one of Arabia's epic road-trips, although notable more for its sheer length (and the stamina involved in driving it) than for any scenic appeal. This is Oman as its emptiest and bleakest, although the views are not of romantic dunes but of an endless expanse of largely flat and stony desert.

Driving nonstop at the 120km/h speed limit you could theoretically do the trip in under nine hours, though a minimum of twelve is more realistic, and unless you're going to be sharing the driving you'd be well advised to break the journey overnight somewhere en route. The challenges of the drive shouldn't be underestimated. The sheer monotony of the road provides a certain kind of mental water torture, and the endless unchanging kilometres can easily lull one into a sense of hypnotic boredom and inattention in which accidents can occur, compounded by the sense of ant-like slowness you'll feel when traversing the desert, even when travelling at velocities well in excess of 100km/h.

There are a number of **places to stay** en route, spaced at strategic intervals along the highway. Advance bookings aren't usually needed. The following are listed in the order you reach them travelling towards Salalah. All provide simple lodgings for around 15 OR per double per night, with unlicensed in-house restaurants but not a great deal else.

Al Ghaba Resthouse Al Ghabah, 320km south of Muscat, 755km north of Salalah ⓣ9935 8639.

Haima Motel Hayma, 520km south of Muscat, 555km north of Salalah ⓣ2329 7103.

Al Wusta Resthouse Hayma, 520km south of Muscat, 555km north of Salalah ⓣ2343 6016.

Al Ghaftain Resthouse Al Ghaftain, 600km south of Muscat, 475km north of Salalah ⓣ9948 5881.

Qitbit Resthouse Qitbit, 775km south of Muscat, 300km north of Salalah ⓣ9908 5686.

Thumrait Hotel, Thumrait, 1000km south of Muscat, 75km north of Salalah ⓣ2327 9371 (also see p.213).

By plane

Oman Air operates **four flights daily** from Muscat to Salalah with a flying time of around 90 minutes; at the time of writing the return fare was 63 OR, inclusive of taxes. Book well in advance for flights during the *khareef*.

By bus

The bus journey **from Muscat to Salalah** takes around twelve hours, with tickets costing 6–7.5 OR one-way. Buses are adequate but not exactly luxurious, and it's a fair old slog, although significantly cheaper than the plane. The Oman National Transport Company (ONTC; two buses daily at 6am and 7pm, plus an additional departure at noon during the *khareef*; ⓣ2470 8522, or 2449 0046) operates out of the bus terminal in Ruwi, while the Gulf Transport Company (6 daily; ⓣ2329 3303 or 3307, in Muscat ⓣ2479 0823, ⓦwww.gulftransportco.com) also has an office nearby, just behind Sultan Qaboos Mosque. You may be able to pick up a bus from the Salalah roundabout just outside **Nizwa**, but you'll need to ring the relevant operator to reserve a seat and guarantee pick-up in advance.

Salalah صلالة

Roughly midway along the Dhofar coast lies **SALALAH** ("The Shining One" in the local Jebali language), hemmed in between the spectacular crescent of the Dhofar Mountains on one side and the blue waters of the Arabian Sea on the other. Much of modern Salalah, Oman's second-largest city (although barely a quarter of the size of Muscat), is not much different from anywhere else in the country. Away from the functional city centre, however, it's still possible to sense something of the old-time Salalah's alluringly languid, subtropical magic, with its lush banana plantations, lopsided coconut palms and superb white-sand beaches, more reminiscent of Zanzibar than Muscat – a feeling emphasized by the considerable quantities of African blood swilling around the local gene pool.

Salalah's exotic appeal is strongest around the old parts of town: in the aromatic alleyways of **Al Husn Souk** and in the marvellous stretch of palm-fringed beach which spreads along the coast east from here to the remains of the ancient city of Zafar – now protected as the **Al Baleed Archeological Park**. Inland, the modern city is less striking, but still boasts plenty of contemporary mercantile character, particularly along bustling **As Salaam Street** and in the engaging **New Souk**. The city also makes an excellent base for explorations of the region as a whole, putting you within a day-trip of pretty much everywhere worth visiting.

Arrival

Salalah's **airport** is very central, just 1km north of the city centre along a sweeping avenue lined with coconut palms – a dramatically stage-managed entrance for one's first sight of Dhofar. There are a number of **car-rental** agencies (see p.201), plus money exchange and ATMs. There's also a **pre-paid taxi** kiosk (turn left as you exit the building). Arriving by bus you'll come in at the main **bus station**, right in the middle of the city.

Accommodation

Salalah boasts a good selection of **budget** hotels, most of them handily located right in the city centre and close to all the action. **Mid-range** options are thinner on the ground, while at the **top end** of the scale it's a choice between the *Crowne Plaza* and *Hilton* resorts, set on the beach at opposite ends of town; there's also a

Moving on from Salalah

For general details of tackling the journey between Salalah and Muscat, see the "Getting to Salalah" section on p.193.

Buses to Muscat take around 12 hours. Services are operated by the ONTC (Ⓣ2329 2773; 3 daily to Muscat at 7am, 10am & 7pm, plus one to Dubai at 3pm), whose small office is tucked away on the northeastern corner of the square from which buses depart. Buses are also operated by a number of private companies, with offices clustered around the bus station. The most reputable is probably Gulf Transport Company (Ⓣ2329 3303; 6 daily to Muscat at 7am, 10am, 1.30pm, 5pm, 6pm & 7pm; one to Dubai at 3pm, 16hr); other options include Al Turky Transport (Ⓣ9258 9089; 2 daily at 5.30am & 9am) and Capital Transport (Ⓣ2329 1314; 2 daily at 9.30am & 6.30pm). Tickets cost 6–7.5 OR one-way to Muscat. Note that if you're heading to **Nizwa**, you should be able to arrange to be set down at Firq Roundabout, 10km east of Nizwa, where you'll find plenty of taxis and micros to take you into town – although you'll probably still have to pay the full fare to Muscat. Another option is to catch one of the various **Dubai** buses, which continue on through Nizwa to Ibri and Buraimi, and then on to the UAE border at Al Ain.

smart new *Marriott* (see p.208) down the coast at Mirbat. Note that prices at most places more or less double (or more) during the **khareef** (June–Aug), when the town gets overrun with visitors – advance booking is strongly recommended.

City centre

Dhofar Hotel Al Matar St Ⓣ2329 2300, Ⓕ2329 4358. Old-fashioned Arabian-style two-star, with chintzy foyer and plenty of rather solemn-looking grey marble. Rooms are spacious and comfortable – albeit a tad dated – and those on the higher floors have nice views over town. ❷

Haffa House Hotel Al Matar St Ⓣ2329 5444, Ⓕ2329 4873, Ⓦwww.shanfarihotels.com. Chintzy four-star with fancy marbled corridors and pretty Moroccan-style tilework. Rooms have nice Arabian touches and good views from higher floors, and there's a passable in-house restaurant (see p.201) and coffee shop. ❹

Al Hanaa Hotel 23 July St Ⓣ2329 0274, Ⓕ2329 1894. One of the nicest of Salalah's cheapies, with cosy, good-value rooms in a central location. It's also superb value during the *khareef*, when the already cut-price room rates rise by just 5 OR – not surprisingly, advance booking during this period is more or less essential. ❶

Al Naser Hotel Al Matar St Ⓣ2329 4815, Ⓕ2329 4816. Simple one-star with absolutely no frills, but some of the cheapest beds in town. Rooms are spacious, but look a bit battered and are somewhat lacking in furniture. It's not such good value during the *khareef*, when prices triple. ❶

Redan Hotel As Salam St Ⓣ2329 2266, Ⓕ2329 0491. Along with *Al Naser*, this is the cheapest address in town, right in the thick of the As Salam Street action, although virtually all rooms – which are a bit nicer than the rather grubby public areas would suggest – are around the back away from the street, so it's quieter than you might think. There's street parking only, which can get chock-a-block after dark. ❶

Salalah Hotel As Suq St Ⓣ2329 5626, Ⓕ2329 2145. In a brilliantly central location, close to the New Souk, bus station and many of the town's best restaurants. It doesn't have much character, but rooms are spacious, modern and well furnished. Excellent value at the price, and only a few rials more than *Al Naser* and *Redan*. ❶

City outskirts

Crowne Plaza Eastern edge of Salalah, around 5km from the centre Ⓣ2323 5333, Ⓦwww.crowneplaza.com/salalah. This rather old-fashioned five-star resort looks a tad frumpy and uninspiring but compensates with its beautiful setting and very civilized price tag. Rooms (sea view or land view) have been nicely refurbished, and there are spacious gardens to crash out in, plenty of pool space and a wide swathe of idyllic white-sand beach. Facilities include the run-of-the-mill *Darbat* and the more attractive seafront *Dolphin Beach* restaurants, a bar, a pool-bar, the *Al Luban* nightclub and an on-site nine-hole golf course. Tours and watersports (parascending, sailing and kitesurfing) can be arranged through the in-house Sumahram Falcon (Ⓦwww.sumahramfalcon.com), while there's also a booking office for the Mirbat-based Extra Divers (see p.202). Reasonable value during the *khareef*. ❼

Hilton Salalah Resort On the coast 5km west of the city centre ⓣ2321 1234, ⓦwww.salalah.hilton.com. Salalah's most upmarket hotel, slightly smarter and more expensive than the *Crowne Plaza*, although with a similar resort-like ambience (and some equally uninspiring architecture). The grounds, pool and beach are pleasant enough, although not quite as nice as those at the *Crowne Plaza* – and the view of the massed cranes over the bay at Salalah Port doesn't inspire. Rooms are attractive and extremely spacious and the hotel also boasts Salalah's best collection of restaurants (see p.201) plus sports bar and nightclub with live music. In-house amenities include the Sub Aqua dive centre (see p.202), while tours can be arranged through Sumahram Falcon (see box below).

Salalah Beach Villas (also known as *Beach Spa Tourism*) Off Al Dhahariz St, just east of the *Crowne Plaza* ⓣ2323 5999, ⓕ2323 5599. Long-running seafront establishment some 5km east of the centre, although the name is a misnomer – there are no villas here, just ordinary rooms in two large houses. The big attraction is the location: there's absolutely nothing between you and the sand (although rooms with a sea view cost a bit extra). On the downside, the rooms themselves are nothing special, and if you can do without the beach there are nicer lodgings in the city centre at less than half the price. There's a small pool out front, although you're rather exposed to the public gaze. The owner can also arrange tours around the city (60–80 OR for up to four people), trips to Shisr (100 OR for up to 4) and overnight stays at a camp beyond Shisr on the edge of the Empty Quarter (120 OR for two). ❹–❺

Samaharam Tourist Village 5km west of town, just before the *Hilton Salalah* ⓣ2321 1420, ⓦwww.shanfarihotels.com. Self-contained complex of chalets and villas catering to a mainly Arab clientele. Accommodation is either in large, modern (if rather bare) rooms with kitchenette, or in a string of much more appealing three-bedroom villas, with enough space for up to six adults and three kids. There's a simple in-house restaurant, plus big pool, while all the eating and drinking facilities of the *Hilton Salalah* are just a couple of minutes' drive down the road. Unfortunately the adjacent beach is fenced off, and covered in scrub, camels and 4WDs. Rooms ❹, villas ❼

The City

Like most of Oman's larger towns, Salalah is very spread out (plentiful taxis roam the streets, hooting for custom, should you become footsore). The modern city centre revolves around lively **As Salam Street** and the more sedate **23 July Street**, a block to the north. Old Salalah lies on the coast a couple of kilometres south of here. This is where you'll find the imposing **Sultan's Palace** and the marvellous **Al Husn Souk**, as well as a superb stretch of palm-fringed **beach**, lined with old-fashioned, pastel-coloured Dhofari houses. East of here lie the ruins of the city's original incarnation as the port of Zafar, whose sprawling remains have now been incorporated into the **Al Baleed Archeological Site** and the attached **Museum of the Frankincense Land**.

Tours in and around Salalah

Most tour operators offer a fairly standard range of half-day **city tours**, plus half- or full-day tours either **west** or **east of the city**, along with **desert tours** to Shisr (see p.213), with perhaps an overnight stay in the Empty Quarter beyond. Tours cost around 40 OR for a half day and 75–100 OR for a full day.

The largest tour operator in town is **Sumahram Falcon** (ⓣ9288 8591, ⓦwww.sumahramfalcon.com), with offices in the *Crowne Plaza* and *Hilton* hotels, which runs the usual range of city tours, plus watersports and fishing trips. Unless you're staying at one of these hotels, however, it's probably best to head for the extremely clued-up and helpful **Al Fawaz Tours** (ⓣ9700 3425, ⓦwww.alfawaztours.com) on 23 July Street in the city centre (it's upstairs in the block which also contains the *Udipi* restaurant). Al Fawaz also operates its own camp at Hashman in the Empty Quarter beyond Shisr (240 OR for up to 4 people) and offers off-road 4WD trips around Jebel Samhan (100 OR/day) as well as trips to the spectacular beach at Fizayah (see p.210).

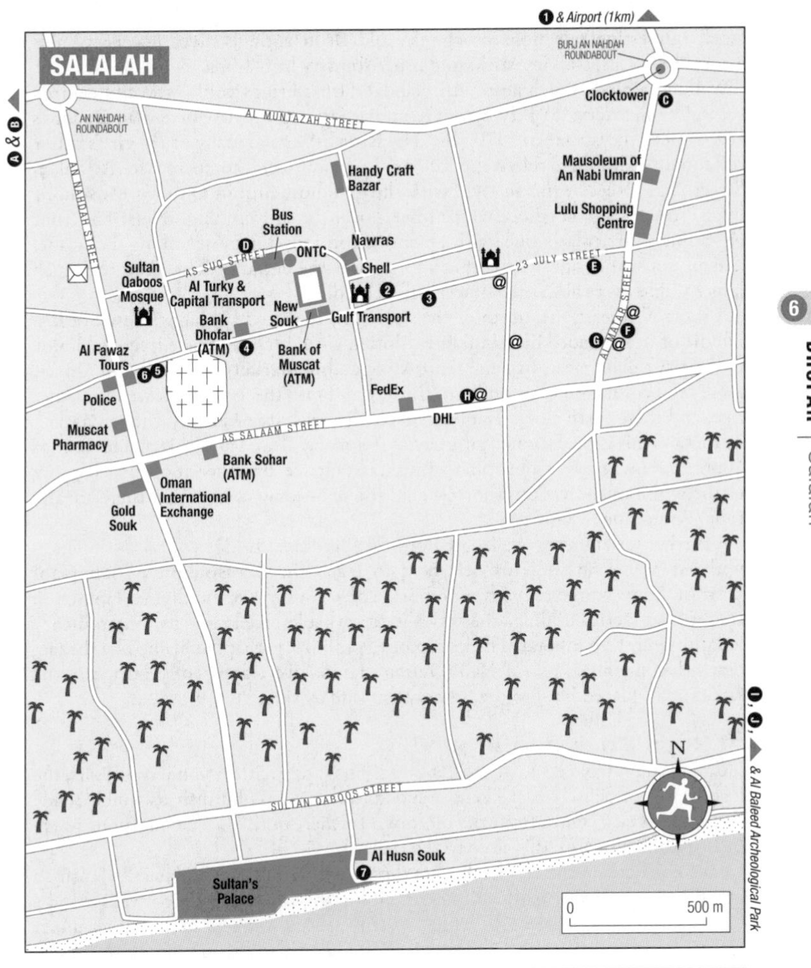

ACCOMMODATION				EATING			
Crowne Plaza	I	Al Naser Hotel	F	Baalbeck Restaurant	2	Al Kutaini	4
Dhofar Hotel	G	Redan Hotel	H	Bin Ateeq	3	Lialy Hadrmout Restaurant	7
Haffa House Hotel	C	Salalah Hotel	D	Chinese Cascade	5	Udupi	6
Al Hanaa Hotel	E	Salalah Beach Villas	J	Al Haffa Restaurant	C	Woodlands	1
Hilton Salalah	A	Samaharam Tourist Village	B	Hilton Salalah	A		

The city centre

Bisecting the heart of modern Salalah, **As Salam Street** is the city's main shopping drag, and usually the liveliest place in town, especially after dark, with a long string of closely packed shops selling anything and everything from gold and bespoke perfumes through to chintzy furniture and cheap shoes, dotted with dozens of low-rent cafés and a remarkable number of hairdressers (Salalah appears to boast more barbers per head of population than possibly any other city in the world). Just west of the junction with An Nahdah Street you'll find Salalah's modest **Gold Souk** (Souk al Dhahab), a single street of shops behind a small archway. There's actually probably more silver than gold on sale here – some shops stock interesting selections of chunky old Bedu antique silver jewellery, plus assorted *khanjars*, walking sticks and other touristy bric-a-brac.

Walking a block north along An Nahdah Street brings you to the city centre's second main artery, **23 July Street** (commemorating the date of Sultan Qaboos's accession to the throne in 1970), lined by large banks and many of the city's better restaurants, although relatively lacking in atmosphere compared to As Salam Street. The street begins in style with the grandiose **Sultan Qaboos Mosque**, a huge, brownish-pink edifice which towers over the surrounding streets. The front elevation is particularly fine, with a pair of enormous minarets flanking the facade, and an unusual design with a small dome over the entrance framed by the much larger dome over the central prayer hall behind.

A short walk east, just north of the street, lies the city's appealing **New Souk**, a huddle of neat arcaded little buildings, dotted with cafés and shade trees and home to the city's main meat, **fish** and **fruit & vegetable markets** (unusually for Oman, these tend to stay open throughout the day and into the evening as well). Further east, and then north along Tamiyah Street, lies the city's "Handy Crafts Bazaar". In theory, this is operational Saturday to Thursday from 9am to 1pm and 4pm to 10pm, and on Fridays from 4pm to 10pm; in practice, however, it opens according to the whim of the various shop owners and depending on whether there are any tour groups due to visit.

A further ten minutes' walk east along 23 July Street brings you to the junction with Al Matar Street. Turn left here to reach the **Mausoleum of An Nabi Umran**, home to the remains of a fourteenth-century Yemeni divine. Housed in a simple modern building, the tomb is remarkable chiefly for its extraordinary length, some 12m in total. The length of the tomb is perhaps explained by the fact that other members of An Nabi Umran's family were apparently buried in the same tomb, placed head to toe, rather than side by side.

Al Husn Souk and around

Heading south from As Salam Street down An Nahdah Street you'll soon reach the lush swathe of densely packed coconut and banana palm **plantations** which divide the modern city centre from the old town further south – an incongruous touch of tropical abundance this close to the centre.

South of here on the beachfront lies the sprawling **Sultan's Palace** (Al Husn): a grandiose complex of marbled modern buildings protected by high walls – and a far cry from the old palace, in which Sultan Qaboos was kept by his father under virtual house arrest until the coup of 1970. The palace is now home to various government offices, and serves as the sultan's residence during his intermittent visits to the city.

Right next to the palace is the marvellous **Al Husn Souk** (also known as Al Haffa Souk, after the district in which it's situated), a pretty little area of small shops arranged around a neat grid of pedestrianized alleyways. This is one of the most interesting souks in Oman, particularly famous for its frankincense, *bukhoor* and *attar* (perfumes). Various rare types of local frankincense can be found here: *shazri*, *sha'abi*, *najdi* and, perhaps finest of all, *hawjari* (or *hasiki*) from the wadis around Hasik. Many of the stalls selling aromatics are run by veiled female traders – you may find bargaining with someone when you can only see their eyes a little disconcerting.

Al Haffa beach and around

West of Al Husn Souk stretches the suburb of **Al Haffa**, home to one of Salalah's prettiest stretches of **seafront**, boasting a wide swathe of picture-perfect white-sand beach extending in either direction as far as the eye can see (although the strip flanking the Sultan's Palace is off limits). It's particularly lovely at dusk, as the sun dips into the ocean and locals come out to loll about or play football on the sand. A ten- to fifteen-minute stroll down the seafront promenade will bring you to a stand of windblown coconut palms sheltering some of the city's few remaining old-style Dhofari houses. Some are no more than minimalist cubist white boxes; others are more elaborate two-storey affairs with long arcaded balconies running the length of the upper storey. A few further examples can be found a block inland near here along Sultan Qaboos Street.

Al Baleed Archeological Site

A short distance further west lie the remains of the city of **Zafar**, the forerunner of the modern city of Salalah (and also the place which subsequently gave its name to the province of Dhofar). Zafar was originally founded some three thousand

Frankincense

Frankincense has been one of Oman's most famous and highly prized natural products since antiquity, and its heady aroma is never far away, wafting out of everything from homes, mosques and souks through to modern office blocks and hotel lobbies, providing the country with an instantly recognizable olfactory signature. The majority of the world's supply is now harvested in Somalia, while Yemen is also a major producer, although Omani frankincense – particularly that from Dhofar – is generally considered the finest.

Frankincense (in Arabic, *luban*) is a type of resin obtained from one of four trees of the Boswellia genus, particularly the **Boswellia sacra**, which thrives in the semi-arid mountainous regions around Salalah, often surviving in the most inhospitable conditions and sometimes appearing to grow straight out of solid rock. These distinctive trees are short and rugged, rarely exceeding 5m in height (and frequently shorter), often with a shrub-like cluster of branches rising straight from the ground, rather than a single trunk, and with a peeling, papery bark.

Frankincense is **collected** by making – or "tapping" – small incisions into the bark, causing the tree to secrete a resin, which is allowed to dry and harden into so-called "tears". Tapping and collection is a skilled but often arduous profession, now mostly done by expat Somalis. Trees start producing resin when they are around ten years old, after which they are tapped two or three times a year. Virtually all frankincense is taken from trees growing in the wild – the difficulty of cultivating the trees means that they're not generally farmed on a commercial scale, in the manner of, say, dates, adding to the resin's mystique.

There are many varieties of frankincense, sorted by hand and **graded** according to colour, purity and aroma. "Silver" (also known as Hojari) frankincense is generally considered the highest grade. The whiter and purer the colour, the better the grade. More yellowish varieties are less highly valued, while at the bottom of the scale come the rather blackish Somali varieties. The resin is then mixed with coals and burnt in a **frankincense burner**, ranging from simple clay pots to the colourfully painted examples favoured in Dhofar.

Frankincense is a key element in traditional Omani life; a frankincense burner is traditionally passed from hand to hand after a meal in order to perfume clothes, hair and beards; it is also used as an ingredient in numerous perfumes, as well as in Omani *bukhoor*. Besides its aromatic properties, frankincense has many **practical uses**. Its smoke repels mosquitoes, while certain types of frankincense resin are also edible, and are widely used in traditional Arabian and Asian medicines to promote healthy digestion and skin. Even more cutting-edge medical uses for the resin are currently being investigated, including its use as a treatment for Crohn's disease, osteoarthritis and even cancer.

years ago, but reached the height of its wealth and pomp from the twelfth to sixteenth centuries, when it served as a vital location in the trade routes linking Oman with the Gulf, East Africa, India and China, and whose fame attracted many visitors, including both Ibn Battuta and Marco Polo.

The remains of Zafar are now protected as the **Al Baleed Archeological Site** (Sat–Wed 8am–2pm & 4–8pm, Thurs & Fri 4–8pm; combined ticket for this and Museum of the Frankincense Land 2 OR). The ruins cover an impressively large area – a good kilometre from top to bottom – although most are extremely fragmentary, usually little more than the bases of walls and the occasional stump of pillar, and the greater part of the city still lies buried under the dunes, awaiting the trowels of future archeological expeditions. Helpful signboards dotted around the site offer interesting historical and archeological background. The most rewarding area is at the **western end** of the site, where you'll find the considerable remains of the citadel, a great tumbling heap of masonry which was formerly the ruling sultan's palace, and the similarly impressive ruins of the Grand Mosque opposite, which once covered an area of over 1700 square metres, centred on a huge prayer hall supported by 144 columns – the largest of the fifty-odd places of worship which originally stood dotted around the city.

Museum of the Frankincense Land

Right next to the entrance to the Al Baleed archeological site lies the somewhat mishmash **Museum of the Frankincense Land** (same opening hours and ticket), dedicated to the history of Salalah and Dhofar – although, despite the name, it offers only patchy coverage of the ancient frankincense trade itself. The museum occupies two large rooms. The first, the **Maritime Hall**, hosts interesting exhibits relating to Omani seafaring traditions and boat-building, with navigational instruments, displays on maritime history and beautifully crafted wooden models of various types of Omani boat – *boom*, *battil*, *ghanjah*, *sambuq* and so on.

The adjacent **History Hall** is altogether less interesting, with a muddle of utterly random exhibits and even more random explanations. Most of the exhibits are of prehistorical artefacts. The various pottery and metalwork finds from the local sites of Al Baleed next door and Sumhuram down the road are the most interesting, although you'll need to know a fair bit about Oman and its history to make any sense of the displays. Other exhibits, such as the spread on "Modern Oman" (complete with scale model of a motorway flyover and assorted suburban housing developments), are little better than low-grade nationalistic propaganda.

Eating and drinking

Salalah musters a reasonable spread of **places to eat**, with most of the best places clustered along 23 July Street, although if you want to wine and dine in style you'll have to head out to one of the two five-star resorts on the edge of the city. These are also the only **licensed venues** in the city, with the exception of the *Woodlands* restaurant in the airport (see opposite) and the *Oasis Bar*, a very well-kept local secret tucked away inside Salalah Port (about 15km west of the city centre), which attracts a lively crowd of sailors and local expats thanks to its affordable beer, good food and ten-pin bowling. For an alfresco coffee, tea or juice local style, the place to head is the New Souk, dotted with dozens of tiny cafés and busy at most times of the day or night with locals shooting the breeze.

For a drink with a difference, head out to one of the eye-catching lines of palm-thatched roadside **fruit stalls** which flank Sultan Qaboos Street just east of the *Crowne Plaza* turn-off. Mounds of fresh coconuts from the city's palm plantations sit piled up along the roadside here (along with plenty of bananas and papaya too), offering an authentically tropical thirst-quencher for under a rial.

Baalbeck Restaurant 23 July St. Friendly staff, a convivial atmosphere and a well-prepared selection of meze, grills and shwarmas pull in a regular crowd of locals and tourists to this deservedly popular Lebanese-style restaurant. Arrive early if you want to grab one of the handful of coveted outside tables – although the pleasantly rustic interior is just as nice. Mains 1.6–2.6 OR.

Bin Ateeq 23 July St. Identikit branch of nation-wide chain (see p.71), with the usual Omani-style food served up in stuffy and windowless little private dining rooms, with seating on the floor. Mildly interesting if you haven't tried it before, although the food is nothing to get excited about. Most mains 1–2 OR.

Chinese Cascade 23 July St. The best Chinese restaurant in town, turning out a reliable range of moderately priced Cantonese favourites. Mains 2–3 OR.

Al Haffa Restaurant 2F *Haffa House Hotel*, Al Matar St. Zero atmosphere, but one of the better places in the city centre for a curry, with a well-prepared range of North Indian meat and veg standards, including assorted tandoor dishes, along with a less appealing range of Chinese and international options. Most mains around 2.5 OR.

Hilton Salalah For the best food in Salalah, the *Hilton* is the place to head for. Choose between the attractive *Palm Grove*, a rustic open-air beachside restaurant offering a range of international, Indian, Italian and Mexican dishes (4–8 OR), *Hilton Sushi*, serving fine Japanese cuisine, or the more formal *Sheba's* steakhouse (prime US and Australian cuts from 11 OR). All venues are licensed.

Al Kutaini 23 July St. Busy, no-frills Pakistani restaurant featuring a short menu of mainly chicken and mutton curries and biryanis, plus assorted Indianized Chinese offerings. It's good, simple, nourishing fare at rock-bottom prices and perfectly acceptable if you don't mind the slightly manic service – the waiters seem to want to get rid of you once you've finished eating even quicker than they wanted to get you inside in the first place.

Lialy Hadrmout Restaurant Al Husn Souk. Entertaining Yemeni-style outdoor restaurant in a lovely location bang in the heart of the souk. It's a positive feast for the senses, with clouds of fragrant smoke, the noise of bread being endlessly pummelled and slapped into shape and a colourful local crowd sporting some of the city's most rakish turbans. There's no menu: take your pick from chicken rice or beef rice (1.5 OR) or beef or chicken kebabs (200bz/skewer), featuring pieces of chewy meat interspersed with lumps of charcoaled fat (much tastier than it might sound) served with hummus and huge round doughy breads.

Udupi 23 July St, opposite Sultan Qaboos Mosque. Cheerful Indian vegetarian restaurant drawing a steady subcontinental clientele. Food includes the usual mixture of South and North Indian veg favourites, with plenty of *dosa* and paneer dishes in every conceivable style. Most dishes are under 1 OR.

Woodlands Salalah Airport. Offshoot of the excellent Muscat original (see p.71), serving up the best Indian vegetarian food in town, as well as offering the unexpected bonus of the only alcohol licence anywhere near the city centre. Unfortunately it was closed for renovations at the time of writing, so you might want to check at your hotel that it's reopened before heading out there for a meal.

Listings

Banks and exchange There are ATMs all over town, particularly along 23 July St. For foreign currency exchange, try Oman International Exchange at the junction of An Nahdah and As Salam streets, or UAE Xchange on 23 July St near Bin Ateeq restaurant.

Car rental Most easily arranged at the airport, where you'll find branches of Europcar, Avis, Budget, Thrifty, Sixt and Mark; there's also a Budget office at the *Crowne Plaza* hotel and a Dollar office at the *Hilton*. A number of local firms have offices along 23 July St and around the bus station, usually undercutting rates offered by the international agencies, although vehicles may correspondingly be older and less reliable. It's a good idea to book ahead during the *khareef*.

Internet There are a quite a few internet cafés scattered around town; for locations see the map on p.197. Usual charges are around 1 OR/hr.

Pharmacies There's a cluster of pharmacies on An Nahdah St between 23 July and As Salam streets, including the Muscat Pharmacy (24hr) and branches of the Mazoon Pharmacy and Al Hashar Pharmacy. There's another Muscat Pharmacy (not 24hr) in the same block as the *Al Hanaa Hotel*.

Post and couriers The main post office is on the side road west of An Nahdah St (Sat–Wed 8am–2pm, Thurs 8am–noon), although service can be painfully slow. There are DHL and FedEx offices on As Salam St.

East of Salalah

Of the numerous attractions clustered in the countryside around Salalah, the majority are located to the **east of the city**. The construction of extensive new roads (plus generally helpful signs) has made many places – which formerly required 4WD and a large slice of local knowledge – independently accessible to anyone with a saloon rental car. Leading attractions include the remains of the ancient port of **Sumhuram**, once one of the key staging posts in the frankincense trade, overlooking the idyllic creek of **Khor Rori**. Close by lies **Wadi Darbat**, home to a spectacular waterfall during the *khareef*, and the even more dramatic uplands of the **Jebel Samhan**, whose sheer limestone walls tower above the coastal plain; the drive up to the top is easily combined with stops to see the cavernous sinkholes of **Tawi Attair** and **Taiq**. Further along the coast lies the magical town of **Mirbat**, while those with a sense of adventure and time to spare can follow the recently tarmacked coastal road all the way to **Hasik**, some 200km east of Salalah.

All the main sights are fairly close to one another and can be visited in various permutations. A particularly rewarding **day-trip** can be made by combining the highlights of the area: Sumhuram and Khor Rori with the road up Jebel Samhan via Wadi Darbat; or, alternatively, Sumhuram and Khor Rori with Mirbat. With an early start you could just about squeeze all three into a longish day.

Ain Razat and Ain Hamran

Heading east out of Salalah, the coastal highway is fast dual carriageway as far as Taqah (see p.204), running through scrubby coastal deserts just out of sight of the sea. En route to Taqah you'll pass two of the dozens of freshwater **springs** (*ain* or *ayn*) strung out along the base of the Dhofar Mountains where they meet the coastal plains. Many have now been turned into local picnic spots which tend to get crowded at weekends.

The first you reach is **Ain Razat**, 23km from the city centre. To get here, turn left off the coastal highway at the Al Mamurah roundabout and head north for 8km, then 1km down a signed side road on the right to reach a T-junction. Turn left here and follow the road as it loops (one-way) around a small fenced-in ornamental garden (Thurs & Fri, or daily during the *khareef*). From the parking lot at the far end of the garden you can see a large cave in the hillside nearby, beneath which the waters of the spring collect in a small concrete pool. Turn right below the cave, from where there's a pleasant five- to ten-minute walk along a cobbled

Diving in Dhofar

There's some rewarding – and still relatively little-known – **diving in Dhofar**. The main attraction here is the splendid sea life, including huge rays, moray eels, parrotfish and turtles, all attracted by the nutrient-rich waters close to the shore. There's also some good coral – Dhofar is one of the few places in the world where you find corals and kelp growing together due to the cold waters produced during the *khareef*.

The **dive season** runs from late September or early October through to the end of May, interrupted by the arrival of the *khareef*, during which the water becomes too rough for diving. It's possible to dive straight off the beach here – the best **dive sites** are around Mirbat – while there are also offshore sites around Mughsail. The two best local **operators** are Sub Aqua (Ⓣ9989 4032, Ⓦwww.subaqua-divecenter.com), based at the *Hilton Salalah Resort* (see p.196), and Extra Divers, based at the *Marriott* hotel (see p.208) in Mirbat. Both places can also arrange **snorkelling** trips, while Sub Aqua also run **fishing** and **dolphing-watching** expeditions.

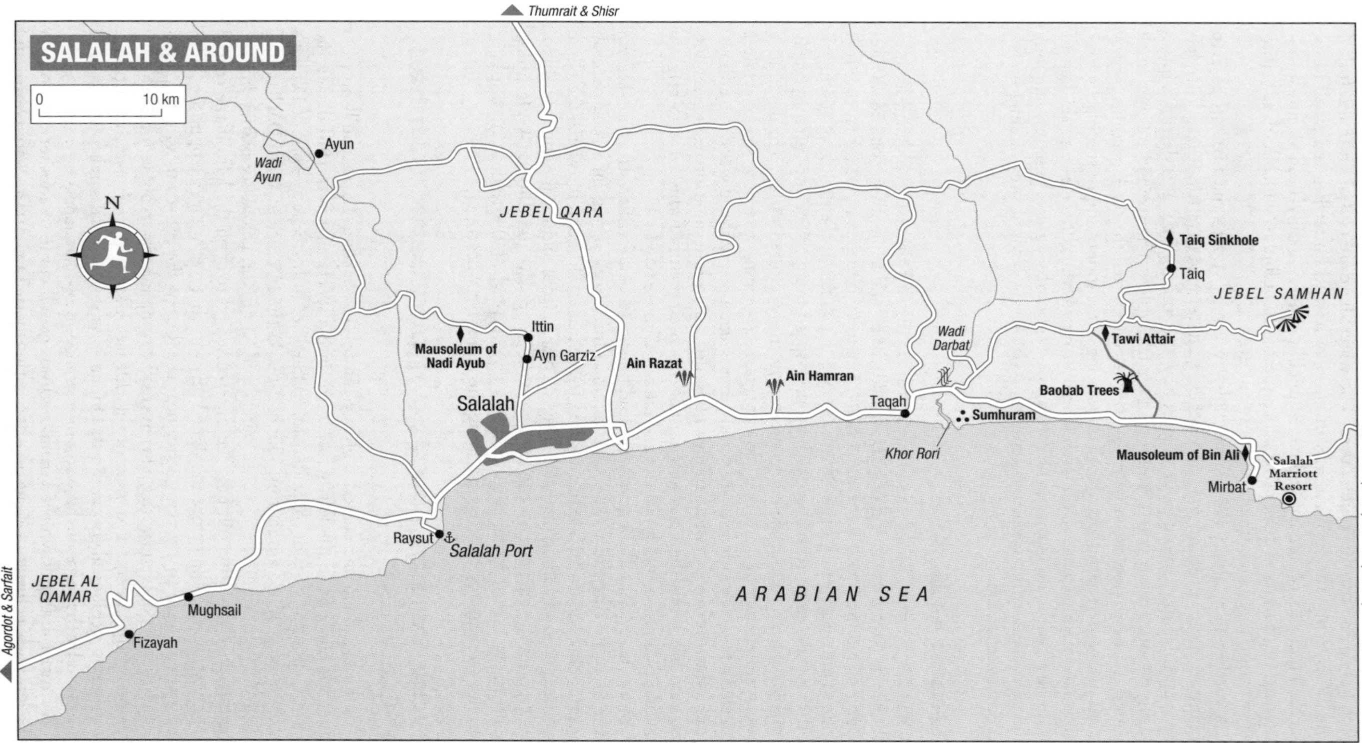
SALALAH & AROUND
0
10 km
N
Thumrait & Shisr
Ayun
Wadi Ayun
JEBEL QARA
Taiq Sinkhole
Taiq
JEBEL SAMHAN
Ittin
Mausoleum of Nadi Ayub
Ayn Garziz
Ain Razat
Ain Hamran
Wadi Darbat
Tawi Attair
Baobab Trees
Salalah
Taqah
Sumhuram
Khor Rori
Mausoleum of Bin Ali
Salalah Marriott Resort
Mirbat
Sadah (60km) & Hasik (120km)
Raysut
Salalah Port
JEBEL AL QAMAR
Mughsail
Fizayah
Agordot & Sarfait
ARABIAN SEA

path beside the narrow watercourse. The waters here are crystal-clear and full of small fish, while the surrounding bushes play host to butterflies and small birds, including flocks of canary-yellow Rüppell's weavers, stripy-headed cinnamon-breasted buntings and distinctive white-spectacled bulbuls – which look as if they are wearing tiny black hoods with cut-out eyes.

A further 6km along the coastal highway brings you to the turn-off to **Ain Hamran**, a very peaceful spot, and rather less developed than Ain Razat. Turn left here at Al Hamran roundabout, then follow the road for 5km as it descends into a lushly wooded area, where you'll find a parking lot. The springs are in a small round walled-in pool from which a *falaj* emerges to feed the small coconut plantations below. The spring occupies a fine setting at the foot of impressive black-stone cliffs, and it's a pleasant stroll from here up towards the cliffs, through thickets of trees alive with the incessant twittering of tiny birds – green pigeons, laughing doves, bee-eaters, kingfishers and pipits – with larger birds of prey circling on the thermals overhead.

Taqah طاقة

Some 37km east of Salalah, a signed right-hand turn off the coastal highway leads to the sleepy coastal town of **TAQAH**, spread out behind a fine stretch of wide white-sand beach dotted with boats and 4WDs. The town is worth a visit for its cute **fort** (Sun–Thurs 9am–4pm, Fri 8–11am; 500bz), which lies in the middle of town, just off the main street (turn left at the fourth speed bump). The fort isn't especially impressive from the outside but has been attractively restored within. The diminutive courtyard is centred on a fine old date palm, providing welcome shade, while a higgledy-piggledy jumble of stairs and terraces, equipped with old wooden handrails, leads off to the castle's various rooms. Those downstairs host some interesting exhibits on local life, while the *wali*'s suite upstairs has been prettily furnished with brightly coloured cushions, kitsch pictures and piles of Chinese bowls.

Immediately behind the fort, steps lead up to a second fortified structure, known simply as the **Burj**, or tower (same hours as fort; free), sitting on a rock outcrop overlooking the town. There's nothing to see inside, although it's worth the climb for the fine views along the palm-fringed coast in front and the mountains behind.

Opposite the entrance to the fort, note the impressive old **dhofari-style house** with finely carved wooden shutters – a style typical of the region. A couple of similar old houses can be found along the main street nearby.

Wadi Darbat (وادي دربات) and Jebel Samhan (جبل سمحان)

Continuing along the coastal highway, some 7km beyond Taqah you'll notice a dramatic cliff just to the left, which turns into a spectacular **waterfall** during the *khareef*, spouting cascades of water amid a tangle of lush greenery – one of Dhofar's most photographed attractions. This cliff marks the entrance to **Wadi Darbat** (also spelled Dhabat or Derbet), whose waters feed Khor Rori below (see p.207). For the best view of the waterfall, take the small unsigned road on the left off the coastal highway about 100m before the signed turn-off to Tawi Attair (see opposite). This leads after 1.5km to a parking space near the foot of the cliff-cum-waterfall, amid seasonal rock pools and with fine views of the tumbling waters above (or, in the dry season, of the pockmarked rocks of the cliff face – known as a "travertine curtain", a common geological formation in Dhofar – whose original sandstone has been dissolved by the force of the water into strange, wax-like shapes).

A further 100m down the coastal highway you'll come to another turn-off on the left with a cluster of signs pointing variously to Tawi Attair, Wadi Darbat and

Taiq Cave; this is one of several roads which climb into the lofty uplands of the **Jebel Samhan**, as the section of the Dhofar Mountains east of Salalah is known.

The road begins by climbing steeply up into the hills, with sweeping views down to the coast and Khor Rori below. After 2.5km a turn-off on the left leads (after a further 2.5km) to a car park in the middle of Wadi Darbat. It's an enjoyable ten-minute walk from here to the top of the waterfall, through wonderful trees, alive with small birdlife, with probably a few wandering camels for company. Seasonal rock pools form up here during the *khareef*, although a sign warns of the dangers of bilharzia, should you be tempted to take a dip.

Attair and Taiq sinkholes

Retrace your route to the Jebel Samhan road, turn left and continue another 15km to reach the junction just past the abandoned Al Maha petrol station. Continuing straight ahead here takes you down the graded track back to the coastal highway via the baobab trees (see p.207). Alternatively, turn left, down the road signed to Jebel Samhan. Follow this for 1km, and you'll see a sign on the right pointing down a side road to **Tawi Attair**, which ends after 250m in a parking space. Probably formed by the prehistoric collapse of the roof of an enormous subterranean cave, Tawi Attair is one of the world's deepest sinkholes, measuring some 210m from top to bottom – big enough to swallow a fifty-storey building. The name translates as "Well of Birds" on account of the many avian species which can usually be seen fluttering about in the sinkhole below, their calls magically echoed by the enclosing cliffs. Steps lead down from the parking area to the litter-strewn viewing platform, although the view of the sinkhole is disappointingly limited. You'll get a much better (and cleaner) view if you head from the car park across the hillside to the right, aiming for the improvised tripod-cum-pylon structure which sits above the sinkhole, although even from here you still can't see the bottom of the chasm.

Continue along the Jebel Samhan road for a further 3.5km to where a blue sign points left down a side road to Taiq Cave (also spelled Teyq or Teiq). Follow this road, passing through the village of **Taiq** en route, a thoroughly rustic little settlement, looking like one big farm, with large quantities of wandering livestock – cows and camels – to match.

Some 8km down the side road, a blue-signed turn-off on the right leads 500m to reach the car park above the so-called "cave", which isn't actually a cave at all, but a vast **sinkhole** (most likely formed, as was nearby Tawi Attair, by the collapse of an enormous underground cave). According to estimates, this is the world's third-largest sinkhole, at around 1km long, 750m across and some 200m deep, with a total volume of ninety million cubic metres – a magnificent chasm in the mountains surrounded by sheer cliffs, riddled in places with holes like gruyère cheese, and also much easier to see than Tawi Attair due to the lack of surrounding vegetation.

Up to Jebel Samhan

Returning yet again to the Jebel Samhan road it's another 15km to the **top of the escarpment**, whose high, sheer cliffs tower over the coastal plains and the town of Mirbat far below. The scenery becomes increasingly barren near the top, as the last stands of stunted trees give way to bare uplands covered in rocks and hardy, ground-hugging vegetation until you reach the summit of the escarpment, with magnificent views of the line of rugged cliffs ahead and (weather permitting) down to the coastal plain below. There are a couple of parking places up here right next to the cliff-edge from which to enjoy the vertiginous views: the first (after 13.5km) is near the large telecommunications station; the second is off on the left after a further 1.5km.

The uplands hereabouts are one of the final strongholds of the Arabian **leopard** (*nimr*, a smaller subspecies of the African and Asian *pantherus pardus*). A few leopards are believed to survive up here, based on the evidence of pugmarks, scat and the remains of kills, although the creatures themselves haven't been seen for many years, despite the best efforts of international scientific teams to track them down. A number of other rare mammals also inhabit the area, including wolves, foxes, hyenas, gazelle and hyrax (a type of small rodent, like a fat, furry rat, which is – improbably enough – distantly related to the elephant), although these are similarly elusive without the services of an expert local guide.

Sumhuram سمهرم

Back on the main coastal highway past the Wadi Darbat turning lie the absorbing remains of the old city of **SUMHURAM**, now protected as the **Sumhuram Archeological Park** (daily 8am–6pm; 1 OR). Along with the nearby city of Zafar, this was formerly one of the major ports of Southern Arabia and an important conduit for the international frankincense trade network. There are two wildly conflicting theories about the origins of the city based on the inscription found at the gateway (see below). According to the official handbook to the site, the city was founded in the third century BC by a local ruler named Sumhuram (or Samaram); according to Nicholas Clapp in *The Road to Ubar* (see p.240), the inscription states that the city was founded by King Il'ad Yalut I of the Hadhramaut (in what is now Yemen) "not earlier than 20 AD". The city survived for 500 (or possibly 800) years before being gradually abandoned in the fifth century AD, perhaps due to the formation of the sand bar across the mouth of Khor Rori, which closed the creek to shipping.

To **reach Sumhuram**, take the signed turning on the right off the main coastal highway 750m past the turning to Tawi Attair (and 8km beyond Taqah); follow this tarmac road for about 2km to reach the entrance to the site. There are a couple of misleadingly placed brown signs in the vicinity of Taqah which appear to be pointing you onto dirt tracks – ignore them. There's a useful printed **guide** to Sumhuram available at the ticket office for 2 OR, while informative signs dotted around the site provide interesting historical and archeological background snippets.

The site

The **ruins of Sumhuram** are far less extensive than those at Al Baleed (see p.199), but have been much more thoroughly excavated and restored, while the lovely natural setting between coast and hills adds to the appeal. The ruins sit atop a small hill above the tranquil waters of Khor Rori: a neat rectangle of off-white buildings enclosed by impregnable **walls** made out of huge, roughly hewn slabs of limestone; the walls are more than 3m thick in places, and perhaps originally stood up to 10m high. Entrance to the city is via the remains of a small **gateway**, inside of which you'll find two beautifully preserved **inscriptions** commemorating the foundation of the city, carved in the ancient South Arabic (or "Old Yemeni") *musnad* alphabet.

Inside, the town is divided into residential, commercial and religious areas, with the slight remains of a maze of small buildings packed densely together. These were originally at least two storeys tall (as the remains of stone stairways attest), although not much now survives of most beyond the bases of their ground-floor walls. The city's most impressive surviving structure is the **Temple of Sin** (the Mesopotamian moon god), built up against the northwest city wall – look out for the finely carved limestone basin in the ritual ablution room within. Nearby, the so-called **Monumental Building** is thought to have housed the city's main freshwater reservoir and well. At the rear of the complex stands the small **Sea Gate**, from which goods were transported down to boats on the water below.

Khor Rori خور روري

A couple of minutes' walk below the ruins of Sumhuram lies the tranquil **Khor Rori**, the most attractive of the various *khors* (creeks) which line the coastline around Salalah. A neat pair of symmetrical headlands flanks the mouth of the *khor*, which is separated from the sea by a low sand bank. As a result, the waters inside the creek (fed by Wadi Darbat) are freshwater, and full of fish, which in turn attract a fine selection of aquatic birds, while camels can usually be seen browsing the surrounding greenery. It's a wonderfully peaceful spot – so quiet that you can actually hear the splashes of fish in the water.

If you want to **reach Khor Rori** by vehicle, you need to continue past the Sumhuram turn-off for a further 2.5km, then take the good graded track signposted off on the right.

East to Mirbat

Beyond Sumhuram the road gradually runs down towards the sea, the approach to Mirbat heralded by a magnificent stretch of beach backed by dunes on one side and the craggy escarpment of Jebel Samhan towering over the other. Some 20km past the Wadi Darbat turn-off, a graded track (4WD only) heads off steeply up into the mountains above, eventually emerging at Tawi Attair after 13km. About 3km along you'll discover a fine cluster of **baobab trees** dotted close to the road – an impressive botanical reminder of Dhofar's links with Africa.

Back on the coast, between the main highway and the beach, lies one of Oman's weirdest curiosities, the baffling **Magnetic Point** (also known as Anti-Gravity Point). At one point along the track sloping down to the beach cars left in neutral will begin magically reversing themselves back up the hill. Local guides claim that this is the result of some mysterious magnetic phenomenon, although the more prosaic explanation is that it's probably just some kind of weird optical illusion – a local example of a so-called "Gravity Hill" (or "Magnetic Hill"), dozens of examples of which have been recorded worldwide.

Mausoleum of Bin Ali

Continuing east along the highway, just before you reach Mirbat itself, a brown sign points towards the **Mausoleum of Bin Ali** (turn right off the main road at the brown sign, follow the road for 1km and you'll see the distinctive mausoleum on your left). The mausoleum itself is a pretty little structure, topped by a pair of rustic onion domes. Inside, the saint's tomb lies in a darkened room heavy with incense; remove your shoes before entering.

An extensive **cemetery** stretches away on the landward side of the mausoleum, dotted with thousands of headstones; male graves are marked with three headstones, female graves with two. Some of the gravestones are elaborately carved, with ornate Arabic inscriptions and other decorative flourishes; others are little more than simple, roughly hewn pieces of undecorated stone wedged upright in the ground. The oldest and finest headstones are clustered around the shrine itself, becoming progressively more modern the further down the road you go.

Mirbat مرباط

A couple of kilometres beyond Bin Ali's Mausoleum lies personable **MIRBAT**, one of the Dhofar's most interesting smaller towns, and another in the chain of erstwhile frankincense ports which line the coast. Two miniature statues of prancing horses atop columns flank the entrance to the town – a whimsical memorial to its history as an important breeding centre for Arabian steeds. A short

The Battle of Mirbat

Mirbat Fort was the scene of perhaps the most important single conflict of the entire Dhofar Rebellion (see p.229), and what is also frequently claimed to be the finest moment in the history of the British SAS. The **Battle of Mirbat** began early in the morning of July 19, 1972, when around 300 heavily armed fighters of the Popular Front for the Liberation of Oman (PFLOAG) attacked the town's small garrison, based in the fort and surrounding buildings, guarded by just nine SAS soldiers and thirty-odd Omani troops, all under the command of Captain Mike Kealy, aged just 23.

The aim of the rebels was simple: to disrupt Sultan Qaboos's new policy of rapprochement; to demonstrate the weakness of the government's control even over towns close to Salalah itself; and to execute as many local government supporters as they could find in Mirbat itself once they had overwhelmed the garrison. The fact that this major political setback, and the potential murder of innocent civilians, was averted is mainly down to the skill and courage of the soldiers defending the garrison. The bravery of Fijian sergeant **Talaiasi Labalaba** in particular – who somehow succeeded in holding large numbers of PFLOAG fighters at bay by single-handedly operating an old World War II 25-pound artillery piece (a job normally requiring three men) despite severe injuries – has become the stuff of military legend. After hours of bitter fighting, but with the loss of just two men (including Labalaba), air support and SAS reinforcements arrived from Salalah, after which the rebel forces were driven back into the hills. The battle was a major setback for the rebels, who lost perhaps as many as 200 fighters. Their failure to seize Mirbat, even with vastly superior forces, also boosted the morale and standing of government forces, and the peace effort in general. Sadly, the UK government's anxiety to keep the fact that British fighters were involved in Dhofar secret meant that the battle received little attention overseas, and those involved largely failed to receive the recognition many people feel they deserve. Campaigns to have Sergeant Labalaba awarded a posthumous Victoria Cross have so far come to nothing.

distance further you'll see the town's small **fort** just off the road on your right, standing proudly above the waves, with fine views of the coast, beach and mountains beyond. The building is currently fenced off for renovations, though you can make out the unusual hexagonal tower at one corner and neat shuttered windows in square stone frames.

Immediately below the fort lies the **old harbour**, a picture-perfect little sandy cove, dotted with boats and enclosed by a low rocky headland at the far end. Walking across the sand brings you to Mirbat's **old town**, a wonderful area of old Dhofari-style houses. Most are simple one- or two-storey cubist boxes, painted in faded oranges, blues and whites, their minimalist outlines enlivened with distinctive wooden-shuttered windows. There's a particularly grand trio of large three-storey structures (one ruined) next to the main road, with diminutive towers and battlemented roofs, like miniature forts, strikingly similar to the domestic architecture of nearby Yemen. The one right next to the main road is particularly fine, with a couple of intricately carved wooden shutters, spiky battlements and a picture of a dhow etched into the plasterwork at the top of the small corner turret at the rear. Beyond here lies Mirbat's prettier-than-average **main street**, with shops painted in cheery pastel pinks and oranges and decorated with big green shutters.

Accommodation

The only accommodation option hereabouts is Mirbat's fancy new **Salalah Marriott Resort** (ⓣ2326 8245, ⓦwww.marriottsalalahresort.com; rooms ❻, chalets ❼). Set in solitary splendour on the coast around 10km east of Mirbat off the coastal highway en route to Sadah, this sprawling five-star resort looks like it's just crash-landed from another planet. Rooms are either in the main hotel building or in a costlier detached area of two-storey chalets. There's a large pool and pleasant gardens (looking a bit bare at the time of writing while the landscaping kicked in) with a rather rocky stretch of beach at the end. Facilities include a couple of restaurants and bars, a Budget car rental office and the Frankincense Spa by Chavana (Ⓦwww.chavanaspa.com). The hotel is also home to the well-run Extra Divers (see p.202).

Sadah (سدح) and Hasik (حاسك)

East of Mirbat, the coastal highway continues for a further 120km east to Hasik (and will eventually be extended all the way to Sawqirah – see p.188 – by around 2014–15). It's 60km from Mirbat on to the next major settlement along the coast, the small fishing town of **SADAH** (also spelled Sadh), the road twisting and turning through rocky coastal hinterland, out of sight of the sea, with the towering escarpment of Jebel Samhan rising proudly on the left. Sadah itself is a small but surprisingly pretty little town with slightly chintzy balconied houses and a small harbour enclosed by rocky headlands. Formerly one of the leading frankincense ports along the Dhofar coast, it has now reinvented itself as a major centre for the collection of abalone, a type of sea snail, gathered by local divers, and highly prized in Chinese and Japanese cuisine, which is where most of the Omani produce ends up. There's also a small **fort** here (Sun–Thurs 8.30am–2.30pm; free).

It's another 60km on through the village of **HADBIN** to the town of **HASIK** at the end of the road, through a largely barren landscape dotted with occasional frankincense trees – some of the region's finest frankincense, known as *hawjari* or *hasiki*, is cultivated in the wadis hereabouts. It's a long and rather lonely drive, although the section of road between Hadbin and Hasik provides some of Dhofar's finest **coastal scenery**, as the mountains of the Jebel Samhan run into the sea, with soaring sea-cliffs, rock pools and outlandish geological formations aplenty.

The Khuriya Muriya Islands

About 40km off the coast of Dhofar, due east of Hasik, lie the **Khuriya Muriya**: a miniature archipelago consisting of four small islands clustered around the main **Hallaniyah Island** (hence their alternative name, the Hallaniyah – or Hallaniyat – Islands), which is also the location of the islands' only permanent settlement.

The Khuriya Muriya have a rather curious **history**. In 1854, Sultan Said (see p.225) ceded the islands to the British after they had proposed a scheme for harvesting guano from them (the foreign secretary, Lord Clarendon, it is said, reciprocated the sultan's largesse by sending him a snuffbox in return). Guano was extracted for only a few years, however, and the islands were subsequently attached to the Aden Settlement, in what is now Yemen. They remained a British possession until 1967, when they were returned to Oman – despite Yemeni claims that, as part of the former Aden adminstration, they properly belonged to them.

The Khuriya Muriya's considerable tourist potential has yet to be tapped, although work began in 2010 on a US$100 million scheme to develop Hallaniyah Island's harbour, while plans to start a regular ferry service with the mainland have also been mooted. The islands boast a string of unspoilt beaches, plentiful birdlife and turtle-nesting grounds, as well as some fine **dive sites**, including the wreck of the British ship, *The City of Winchester*, sunk by German forces in World War I. There are currently no organized dive trips, and the only way to reach the islands – for now – is to arrange a ride with a fishing vessel in Hasik, Sadah or Mirbat.

West of Salalah

West of Salalah lies the **Jebel al Qamar**, one of the most dramatic sections of the Dhofar Mountains, which rear up out of the sea at the village of **Mughsail** (home to an impressive trio of blowholes) and march along the coast in a sequence of dramatically sculpted crags and sea cliffs, best appreciated from the tiny coastal village of **Fizayah**. Beyond here the road rides the top of the mountain plateau to the Yemeni border at Sarfait, although the border itself remains closed.

West to Mughsail مغسيل

Heading west out of Salalah, the main road is dual carriageway to the edge of the city and the vast **Raysut Industrial Area** and **Salalah Port**, one of the largest in the country, whose mass of towering gantries rises away to your left. Thereafter the road reverts to single carriageway, running across the rocky coastal plain beneath the mountains. The sea itself remains out of sight until a few kilometres before Mughsail when road and water finally come together, offering superlative views down the coast, with a long white-sand beach backed by the dramatic limestone mass of the Jebel al Qamar plunging sheer into the sea – reminiscent of the fjords of Musandam, at the opposite end of the country.

The tiny village of **MUGHSAIL** (also spelled Mughsayl) itself is little more than a clump of houses on the hillside above the road. Turn left opposite the Al Maha petrol station down the road signed Al Marneef Cave and continue 1km to get to Mughsail's **blowholes**, reached by a path beyond the parking lot and the *Mocca Cafe* (a good place for a drink). The blowholes comprise three small holes in the rock through which jets of seawater shoot into the air. They're particularly impressive during the *khareef*, when they spout plumes of water up to 30m high, regularly drenching unwary hordes of screeching tourists. Outside the monsoon they are less memorable, and during the driest parts of the year they cease to blow altogether, although the subterranean groaning of wind and water, eerily amplified by the blowholes themselves, is still strangely impressive. **Al Marneef Cave** itself is not actually a cave, but a kind of open-sided rock shelter at the base of the weathered limestone outcrop which towers up to the rear of the blowholes. The overhanging rocks here provide a convenient source of shade and shelter, and the "cave" is usually thronged with picnicking local day-trippers.

Jebel al Qamar

Past Mughsail the road begins to hairpin steeply up into the **Jebel al Qamar**, the "Mountains of the Moon" – as singularly wild and lunar as their name suggests, and utterly devoid of human settlement. Some 6km beyond Mughsail the road traverses the cavernous **Wadi Aful** via a spectacular set of hairpin bends which slalom downhill and then up for eight solid kilometres, the most dramatic feat of highway engineering in Oman (outdoing even the more celebrated road from Khasab to Tibat in Musandam), twisting and turning through deep rock cuttings chiselled laboriously out of the huge surrounding limestone cliffs. The mountainsides flanking this section of road are also one of the best places in the Salalah area to see **frankincense trees**, one of the few types of vegetation able to survive in this arid habitat.

Some 14km beyond Mughsail you reach the crest of the ridge with breathless views along the coast and down to the sea far below. On your left, a graded track (4WD recommended, though you might just get down it with care in a 2WD in the dry season) winds down to the coastal village of **FIZAYAH**, where you'll find one of Dhofar's most memorable beaches: an idyllic cove of sand hemmed in by spectacular sea-cliffs and wind-sculpted limestone formations.

Past the Fizayah turning the road continues along the top of the ridge for another 8km to a police checkpoint, where you'll need to show some kind of ID and vehicle documentation if driving yourself. It's another 10km from here to the village of **AGDOROT**, the first sign of human settlement along the road since Mughsail, with brief glimpses into some of the wild wadis which score the mountains inland.

Curiosity apart, this is probably as far as it's worth going (indeed you won't miss much if you turn back at Fizayah). Beyond Agdorot the road runs on across the plateau, dotted with a string of unremarkable villages (and an unlikely number of large government buildings) and the scenery becomes relatively humdrum. If you do persevere, you'll eventually be turned back at a second checkpoint some 40km short of the border.

There's no petrol along this road (and hardly any shops, either), so if in doubt, fill up at the Al Maha station in Mughsail.

North of Salalah

The section of the Dhofar Mountains north of Salalah, known as the **Jebel Qara**, is less spectacular than the ranges to the east and west, although it boasts a couple of worthwhile attractions, including the peaceful mausoleum of **Nadi Ayoub** (popularly known as Job's Tomb) and the **Pools of Ayoun**. The main attractions north of Salalah, however, lie in the interior beyond the mountains, in the fragmentary remains of the legendary city of **Ubar** at the village of Shisr and, further inland still, in the great sand dunes at the edge of the **Empty Quarter**, one of the world's greatest and most inhospitable deserts.

Ayn Garziz

Heading northwest out of Salalah towards the Jebel Qara, the first attraction you reach is the local beauty spot of **Ayn Garziz** (also spelled Jarziz), one of the various springs dotting the base of the mountains which ring Salalah. The springs (which may dry up late in the season) nestle in a quaint natural cul-de-sac hemmed in by low limestone cliffs, dissolved into strange, wax-like shapes by the *khareef* rains and draped with fronds of hanging greenery. It's an attractive spot, kitted out with little gazebos for picnicking, although the considerable quantities of litter (and even greater quantity of goat droppings) slightly detract from the ambience.

To **reach Ayn Garziz**, head down the Ittin road, a signposted right turn 3.5km west of the An Nadhah roundabout. The springs lie 7.5km north along this road, then 3km down a signed turning on your right.

Mausoleum of An Nabi Ayub

Beyond Ayn Garziz, it's a fine climb up into hills to reach the **Mausoleum of An Nabi Ayub**, also known as **Job's Tomb**, after the long-suffering biblical patriarch. Job/Ayub is an important figure in Islamic, Jewish and Christian theology, appearing in the Qur'an as a prophet who suffered a series of divine tribulations similar to those described in the Bible. Quite how or why his supposed mortal remains ended up in the hills above Salalah remains unclear, although it's worth bearing in mind that there's also a rival Druze tomb of Job in the Al Chouf region of Lebanon, and that the towns of Magdala in present-day Israel and Urfa in southern Turkey both claim to have been the site of Job's various trials and misfortunes.

Whatever the tomb's historical credentials, it's an attractive site, and well worth the visit. The **mausoleum** itself is a small, gold-domed building, sitting inside the gardens of a modern mosque: an enjoyably cool and peaceful spot, full of flowering shrubs and small birds, and with fine views over the *jebel* and down to Salalah way below. Inside the mausoleum lies the prophet's long tomb, covered in green cloth (don't forget to remove your shoes when entering); the size of the tomb is explained either by the theory that more than one person is buried in it, or by the more entertaining belief that human beings in the days of Job were of far greater size than ourselves, and that people are, contrary to all scientific thinking, not increasing in size, but shrinking. A chart on the wall of the tomb shows the genealogies (in Arabic) of various prophets including Abraham, Moses, Job, Jesus and Mohammed; outside lie the remains of a much older building, presumably a previous version of the mausoleum, along with a very roughly formed rock imprint in a concrete box in front of the tomb which is popularly claimed to be Job's own footprint, although it's difficult to be convinced.

To **reach the tomb**, follow the road past the Ayn Garziz turn-off for a further 14km, then head left for 1.5km down a steep, twisting side-road (signposted). The rather grand-looking *Prophet Ayoub Region Restaurant* immediately below the mausoleum is a good place for a drink, with wonderful views from the rear terrace, although it doesn't have much in the way of food.

Jebel Qara and Wadi Ayun

Back on the main road past the turn-off to Nadi Ayub's mausoleum the road continues to climb up towards the escarpment of the **Jebel Qara**. After 9.5km you

Tribes and languages of Dhofar

Ethnically and linguistically, the original inhabitants of Dhofar – an intricate patchwork of mountain and desert **tribes** of which the Qara, Mahra and Bait Kathir are perhaps the most notable – have far more in common with the people of neighbouring Yemen to the west than with their fellow Omanis to the north. Jan Morris, writing during the mid-1950s in *Sultan in Oman* (see p.239), described "tribes of strange non-Arab peoples, often living in caves, almost naked, speaking languages of their own and maintaining their own obscure manners and customs." Other distinctive cultural traditions persisted until recent decades. The Qara, for instance, refused to eat chickens or any kind of egg, while their women were forbidden from touching the udders of the tribe's cows (the cow being considered generally superior to a mere female, whose touch might offend it). Their religious beliefs also appeared somewhat unusual. As Morris described it, "They were nominally Moslems ... but their theological principles seemed to be a trifle hazy: whenever I saw any of them praying during my stay in Dhufar, they were turned not towards Mecca, but towards the sun."

Modernization and rising prosperity mean that physical reminders of traditional Dhofari life are now increasingly rare (and virtually extinct in Salalah itself), although up in the hills you may spot occasional examples of the region's traditional round stone huts with straw roofs, or come across elderly Dhofaris wearing the distinctive indigo-dyed robes which have been replaced everywhere else by the white Omani dishdasha.

The original Dhofari tribes are also interesting from a linguistic point of view, speaking a range of South Arabian Semitic **languages** closer to Amharic (one of the languages of modern Ethiopia and Eritrea) than Arabic, and offering a living link with the region's pre-Islamic history. The most important of these are Shehri (also known as Jebali – literally, "mountain"), spoken by the Qara, with around 25,000 native speakers, and Mehri (or Mahri), spoken by the Mahra, with an estimated 50,000 native speakers. All Shehri and Mehri speakers are also fluent in Arabic.

reach a T-junction. Turn right here and follow the road for an exhilarating drive up to and then across the top of the plateau, becoming increasingly rocky and barren as you gain height, with views down into steep-sided gorges and wandering camels strolling unconcernedly across the road – one of Oman's more exotic road hazards.

After 17km you reach a turn-off on the left signed to Ayoon. Go down this road for about 400m then bear left along the rough track (4WD only) for a further 4km to reach the secluded **Wadi Ayun**, a small, rocky declivity dotted with a picturesque series of reed-fringed rock pools. According to tradition, the pools are the source of the freshwater spring at distant Shisr (a comb dropped into the pools at Ayun is said to have reappeared at Shisr). According to another old tradition, related by Wilfred Thesiger in *Arabian Sands* (see p.240), "a monster serpent lived in the pool and sometimes seized a goat when the flocks came down to drink".

Thumrait ثمريت

The small town of **THUMRAIT** lies some 75km north of Salalah, an hour's drive at present, although ongoing road improvements to the highway (which is slowly being converted to dual carriageway) will speed things up. The town is basically a glorified service station, with dozens of no-frills coffee shops catering to passing truck drivers, who pull up here in droves. Heading north, Thumrait is the last source of petrol before Shisr. Accommodation is provided by the simple one-star *Thumrait Hotel* (☎2327 9371; ❶) at the end of the side road past the Shell station. There's no real incentive to stay, given how close you are to Salalah – unless you've been travelling south and really can't face spending any more time on the road.

Shisr الشصر

Way out in the desert north of Thumrait lie the celebrated remains of the town of **SHISR**, popularly believed to be the site of the mythical ancient city of **Ubar**. The ruins inspired one of the most famous archeological treasure-hunts of recent times (see p.214), although unless you have a particular interest in Arabian archeology, the site scarcely justifies the long journey, unless combined with an overnight stay in the dunes of the Empty Quarter further to the north.

The **remains** themselves are decidedly modest: the bases of a few walls and towers and the outlines of some buildings next to the rocky sinkhole into which the town suddenly disappeared some time between 300 and 500 AD. It will make a lot more sense if you've read Clapp's *The Road to Ubar*, although the book rather goes to prove that the hunt for Ubar was rather more exciting than Ubar (if that's actually what it is) itself.

To **reach Shisr**, head along the main highway for 41km north of Thumrait roundabout, where a turn-off points to Shisr (signed "Shasar") some 50km further on into the desert. The road is surfaced for the first 25km, and a good graded track thereafter, passable in a 2WD if you don't mind being rattled to bits. The journey from Salalah currently takes around 2 hours to 2 hours 30 minutes, although it should become considerably quicker once road improvements are completed.

The Empty Quarter

The legendary **Empty Quarter** (Rub al Khali) is one of the world's largest and most famous deserts, stretching northwards from Oman into Saudi Arabia, Yemen and up into the western UAE. The scale of the desert is jaw-dropping: a thousand kilometres long and five hundred wide – bigger than France, Belgium and the Netherlands combined. Most of the desert consists of huge swathes of dunes reaching heights of up to 300m, interspersed with gravel plains and occasional salt flats, such as the

Ubar: the search for the Atlantis of the Sands

The legend of **Ubar** (or Wubar) is one of the most persistent in the Arabian peninsula. The name seems originally to have referred to a region or a tribe in or near the Empty Quarter but later became associated with a legendary city – also known as **Iram** (or Irem) – which grew immensely wealthy as a result of trade between the coast and population centres inland to the north. According to the story as related in the Qur'an, the city's rich but godless inhabitants were repeatedly warned to mend their ways by the prophet Hud, but ignored him – after which God destroyed the city, which collapsed back into the sands, never to be seen again.

The first sign that the legend of Ubar/Iram might have a basis in historical fact was hinted at by English explorer **Bertram Thomas**, the first European to traverse the Empty Quarter in 1930–31 (a journey desribed in his *Arabia Felix*). Travelling north of Shisr, Thomas saw a series of "well-worn tracks", described by his Bedu companions as the "Road to Ubar", which they said lay buried under the sands, although no one could say where. A number of other explorers subsequently searched for the city during the 1930s and 1940s, but without success.

The trail then went cold until the 1980s, when American film-maker and amateur historian **Nicholas Clapp** had the bright idea of using high-definition radar imaging, carried on board the US Space Shuttle, to search for Ubar. A detailed satellite picture of the area in which Bertram Thomas had seen the "Road to Ubar" was slowly put together, and in 1990 a team including Clapp, British explorer **Ranulph Fiennes** and archeologist **Juris Zarins** set out to follow these leads on the ground. Some eighteen months later, they finally discovered the remains of an ancient trading town next to **Shisr**. The discovery made headline news around the world in 1992, while both Clapp and Fiennes subsequently wrote books about their part in the discovery (see p.240). Whether the ruins at Shisr are in fact those of the legendary Ubar remains something of a moot point, however – and one that will probably never be fully resolved.

notorious "quicksands" of **Umm al Samim** – first described by Thesiger – which even local Bedu ventured into only rarely and with extreme caution.

Most of the Empty Quarter lies within Saudi Arabia, although there are significant portions in Oman, stretching across the northern sections of Dhofar and Al Wusta and into Al Dhahirah, which is where you'll find the Umm al Samim. The scale of the dunes and the largely pristine natural environment (particularly when compared to the Wahiba Sands) is as memorable a taste of the desert as you're likely to get anywhere – although expeditions into the sands should only be attempted with a proper guide and full equipment. The cheapest way to explore the desert is by signing up for an overnight trip with Al Fawaz Tours (see p.196) or via Salalah Beach Villas (see p.196). The Empty Quarter also features on the itineraries offered by some of the companies listed on p.22, while upmarket tours with a Bedu guide can be arranged through Safari Drive (Ⓦ www.safaridrive.com).

Wadi Dawkah

North of the Shisr turn-off, the western side of the main highway is bounded by the shallow, sandy **Wadi Dawkah**. This is one of the cluster of places related to the ancient frankincense trade which were given World Heritage Site status by UNESCO in 2000 under the moniker "The Land of Frankincense" (also including the ruins of Sumhuram, Shisr and Al Baleed). Frankincense trees still dot the arid bed of the wadi, although many, especially those close to the road, have been damaged by amateurish incisions made by passing visitors. Part of the wadi has now been fenced in and planted with new trees – the nearest thing to a frankincense plantation you'll find in Oman – although the general effect is decidedly mundane.

Contexts

Contexts

History

Oman's history is a paradox. Much of the country's past remains blanketed in the sort of mystery that one would expect given its inhospitable terrain and remote location at the nethermost ends of the Arabian peninsula. And yet the country also boasts a recorded history stretching back well over five thousand years, and a wealth of archeological remains which are only now beginning to be slowly deciphered. Copper and other commodities were shipped from here to ancient Sumer, while the ancient frankincense trade in Dhofar has left tantalizing glimpses of ancient life in South Arabia. The armies of Persia's Cyrus the Great colonized parts of the region, while the early Islamic dynasties of Damascus and Baghdad also left their mark, as did later colonial powers including Portugal and Britain.

Put simply, the history of Oman is the story of two quite separate regions, each with its own distinct identity. The first is the inward-looking and staunchly conservative tribal **interior**, or "Oman proper" as it's sometimes described, an inhospitable and sparsely populated region, little visited by outsiders, and even less written about. The interior's barren geography, harsh climate and historically low population levels have all tended to work against the establishment of centralized authority, encouraging the patchwork development of independent regions under the control of competing tribes which endured right up until the second half of the twentieth century. The history of the interior is thus not so much that of a coherent nation as a vague confederation of clans, loosely joined by their shared Ibadhi beliefs (see p.219) and suspicion of outsiders – although as often as not at war with one another, when not confronting outside threats.

The second is the far more cosmospolitan history of **the coast**, shaped by its location on the Arabian Gulf and long-standing trading and cultural links with surrounding regions, from ancient Mesopotamia and Persia through to its wide-ranging connections with colonial European powers including Portugal, France and Britain. Omani settlements overseas in East Africa and Baluchistan (in what is now Pakistan) have also played a major role both in the country's economic past and present-day cultural make-up.

Magan (2300–1300 BC)

Evidence of human settlement in Oman goes back to at least 6000 BC, roughly around the time when rising sea levels stabilized at their current levels, establishing the outlines of the Arabian Gulf and Gulf of Oman. Early settlements were generally coastal – huge piles of shells have been excavated at various places along the seaboard, representing the remains of innumerable prehistoric shellfish suppers.

The first recorded references to Oman date back to the Bronze Age. From around 2300 BC the region, under the name of **Magan** (or Majan), begins to crop up in cuneiform texts written in nearby Sumeria, in what is now southern Iraq. According to these, Magan (which probably also covered parts of what is now the UAE) was an important source of copper and other materials, some of which doubtless came from the rich mines in Wadi Jizzi, inland from Sohar, along with other sites such as Wadi Samad near Nizwa. This period (roughly 2500–2000 BC) is often described as the **Umm an Nar** period, named after a small island near Abu Dhabi where remains from this era were first excavated. The Umm an Nar culture is best known for its distinctive style of circular and "beehive" tombs, of which fine examples survive at Bat and Al Ayn, as well as in the UAE at Hili, just over the border from Buraimi.

The Umm an Nar period was followed by the so-called **Wadi Suq period** (c.2000–1300 BC), after the wadi near Sohar in which remains from this period were first discovered – again characterized by large tombs, both round and rectangular. Oman's **Iron Age** (c.1300–500 BC) has left fewer notable archeological remains, though there is evidence of a network of mudbrick villages and fortified hilltop settlements. Copper production also reached a peak during this period.

Persians and Arabs (530 BC–630 AD)

The first of the various large-scale invasions and migrations which would shape the history of Oman occurred sometime around 530 BC, when the Achaemenids of **Persia**, under Cyrus the Great, conquered "Mazun", as they called Oman – the beginning of an Iranian presence in Oman that was to last until the coming of Islam, well over a thousand years later. The Persians are believed to have introduced advanced irrigation techniques which subsequently developed into the Omani *falaj* (see p.83), leading to the development of widespread cultivation and a prosperous agricultural civilization.

How long – and how much of – Oman remained under Persian control is unknown, although it seems likely that their power ebbed and flowed over the next few centuries. Of more importance in the subsequent history of Oman are the large-scale **migrations of Arabs** which took place in the centuries following the arrival of the Persians. Most of Oman's current population can trace its ancestry to one of two different Arab migrations into Oman during the centuries before and after the birth of Christ. The first was of large numbers of southern Arabs, or Qahtani, from Yemen (and including the powerful Ya'aruba and Azd tribes, both of whom were to play a leading role in the subsequent history of Oman). Many of these appear to have come from the **Ma'rib** area, home to the legendary Queen of Sheba and of the huge Ma'rib dam, one of the engineering wonders of the ancient world. Successive failures of the dam, however, resulted in the gradual collapse in the region's prosperity, leading to the migration of large numbers of people into Oman between roughly the second century BC and the second century AD; even today those who claim Yemeni origins are known as **Yamani**. The second major migration into Oman was of northern Arabs, or Adnani, also known as **Nizari**, from what is now the Nejd in central Saudi Arabia. Yamani–Nizari rivalries and quarrels would prove a lasting feature of Omani history, right through until recent decades.

The Yamani and Nizari gradually moved into Oman, slowly assimilating with the existing, Persianized population through a mixture of conquest and trade. The Arab immigrants tended to settle themselves in the Sharqiya and the Jebel Akdhar, while the Persians continued to dominate the northwest Batinah coast around Sohar – an early instance of the split between coast and interior which was to become a running theme in Omani history for the next two thousand years.

Islam, imams and Ibadhis (630–751 AD)

Oman was one of the first countries to embrace Islam, which was introduced to the country in **630 AD** by an envoy of the Prophet Mohammed, 'Amr ibn al 'As (who would subsequently earn a leading place in Islamic legend as the general in charge of the Muslim conquest of Egypt). 'Amr ibn al 'As decided to begin

The history of **Dhofar** – largely separate from that of the rest of Oman – is covered on p.191.

proselytizing in the town of Sohar, then the largest and most prosperous in the country, and home to a sizeable Persian population. In the event, however, it was the local Julandas, the rulers of the Arab tribes, who were converted to the new faith, rather than the city's Persian governor (the Persians were already followers of Zoroastrianism, one of the world's oldest monotheisms). The first act of the newly converted Julandas was to drive the Persians out of Oman.

The **death of the Prophet Mohammad** in 632 AD ushered in a period of instability, as various parts of the newly converted Islamic world revolted against the new caliph in Medina, Abu Bakr, leading to the so-called Wars of Apostasy (or Ridda Wars) – although despite the name these rebellions probably had more to do with politics than religion. One such uprising broke out at **Dibba**, led by the powerful Azd tribe under Laqit bin Malik. According to one version of events, Laqit was killed by an envoy of Abu Bakr in what was a relatively small struggle; other sources say that at least 10,000 rebels were killed in one of the biggest battles of the Wars of Apostasy.

Islam would henceforth remain unchallenged in Oman, although the exact form the religion would take in the country was still evolving. The turmoil which followed the Prophet Mohammed's death and subsequent fighting between his successors led to a dissident movement known as the **Khawarij** (meaning "Outsiders"; sometimes anglicized to "Kharijites"). Disillusioned with the conduct of their leaders, the Khawarij took an essentially democratic view of Islam, arguing that any suitable Muslim could be chosen as leader, and that any leader could be replaced if he failed to act in accordance with the teachings of Allah. Khawarij attitudes travelled to Southern Arabia, where they became known as **Ibadhism** (see box below).

Conflicts with the Islamic centre continued during the reign of the second **Ummayad caliph**, Abd al Malik bin Marwan. Wishing to crush the "heretical" Omanis, in around 694 Abd al Malik dispatched a large punitive expedition which eventually succeeded in subduing the Omani rebels with terrible slaughter. The

Ibadhism and the imamate

The school of Islam known as **Ibadhism** once flourished across Yemen, Oman and southern Saudi Arabia, but now survives almost exclusively in Oman, where it remains the most widely practised form of the religion, followed by around three-quarters of the population. Ibadhism began as a popular reaction against the perceived failings of the Caliphate, and its democratic character appealed to the independent-minded tribes of Oman and subsequently became an important marker of national identity.

Up until 1959, the nation's Ibadhi community was led by the **imam** – a kind of Omani pope. The imam – meaning "one who sets an example" – could come from any part of the community, so long as he (despite the sect's democratic credentials, the imam was always a man) possessed the necessary spiritual and personal qualities. The imam was traditionally elected by the *ulama*, a small council of elders; their choice then had to be ratified by the community at large. On occasion, an imam nominated by the *ulama* was rejected by the people, and a new one found. An imam could also be removed from power if he lost the support of the people, and if no suitable candidate was available the post could (and sometimes was) left vacant, often for considerable periods of time. At various times the offices of imam and sultan were held by the same person; at others, by two different figures – tensions between rival imams and sultans became a particular feature of Oman's troubled early to mid-twentieth-century history until the last imam fled the country in the wake of the Jebel War (see p.228), since when the office has lapsed, and shows no sign of being revived.

Ummayad dynasty collapsed, however, just over fifty years later in 750, offering Oman a new measure of independence, during which its leaders took the opportunity to elect the country's first **imam** (see box, p.219), Julanda bin Mas'ud, in 751.

The era of invasions (751–1507)

The independence was short-lived, however. Just four years later Julanda bin Mas'ud was murdered by the invading forces of the new **Abbasid caliph**, Abu al Abbas (reigned 750–754), popularly known as "The Shedder of Blood". As Abbasid power waxed and waned, so Oman enjoyed greater or lesser degrees of autonomy, though they had to wait until the reign of the legendary caliph Harun al Rashid (786–809) to elect a **second imam**, Sheikh Mohammed bin Abu Affan. Sheikh Mohammed proved an unhappy choice, however, and was replaced just two years later by imam Warith bin Kaab – an early example of Ibadhi democracy in action. Eventually, Harun al Rashid decided to send a punitive army, although his forces were destroyed in battle at Sohar.

This time Oman's independence lasted for around a century until 892 and the arrival of a new, 25,000-strong army, sent by the caliph and commanded by **Mohammed bin Nur**, governor of Bahrain, who led a murderous assault on the country, killing the imam and sending his head back to Baghdad. Next to arrive were the **Qaramita** (Carmathians), a radical Ismaili Shia sect from Bahrain, who had already caused widespread havoc across Syria and Iraq, and also sacked Mecca, killing 30,000 people and carrying off the Black Stone, one of Islam's most important relics, in the process. Not surprisingly, these constant attacks took a heavy toll on the region. Many of the country's *aflaj* were destroyed and large areas of agricultural land lost to the desert.

The gradual collapse of the Abbasid dynasty meant that the caliphs in Baghdad no longer interfered with Oman. New enemies rapidly appeared, however. In 971 and again in 1041 the **Persians** returned, sacking Sohar, followed, in 1064 by the **Turks**.

Omanis in East Africa

Despite the often chaotic situation at home, from early in its history Oman succeeded in extending its reach overseas, thanks to its expertise in shipbuilding and navigation. The Omanis are thought to have sent slaving expeditions to **East Africa** as far back as the seventh century, while the Julanda rulers defeated by the Ummayad caliph Abd al Malik bin Marwan in 694 (see p.219) are said to have fled to the "Land of Zanj", meaning East Africa. This Julanda arrival marked the beginning of a thousand years of continuous Omani presence, and often considerable power, on the East African coast, broken only briefly by a brutal Portuguese interregnum in the fifteenth and sixteenth centuries.

One of the oldest and largest of these settlements was the city-state of **Kilwa Kisiwani**, an island now belonging to Tanzania, founded as a trading centre in 957, becoming in its heydey the most important single entrepot along the East African coast; Ibn Battuta, visiting in 1332, described it as "amongst the most beautiful of cities, and elegantly built". Kilwa was just one of many such centres, and by the 1200s the Omanis had established a lasting presence at various locations along the African coast ranging from Mogadishu through to Mombasa and Zanzibar and down into Mozambique, trading in gold, iron, ivory, textiles, spices and, increasingly over time, slaves.

Despite the number of such settlements, and the riches passing through them, there was never such a thing as a formal Omani "empire" in Africa. These Omani settlements were largely independent from one another, and also from whoever happened to be ruling Oman, except during the rule of Said the Great, who actually transferred the entire Omani court to Zanzibar (see p.225).

In the midst of this constant upheaval, a new dynasty entered Omani history in 1154, following the death of Imam Jaber Moussa bin Ali. This was the **Bani Nabhan** (Nabhani) dynasty, whose rulers constructed the vast fortress at Bahla and styled themselves as *malik* (king) rather than imam. Their dynasty continued until 1500, when the last Nabhani ruler, Sulayman bin Sulayman bin Mudhaffar, was removed and the imamate belatedly restored. Little is known of the period, though it appears that Nabhani power fluctuated over time, with their influence sometimes restricted to parts of the interior and sometimes reaching down to the coast; they also had to face various Persian invasions and tribal rivalries.

Further attackers arrived from Persia during the thirteenth century – although these were most likely **Mongol** soldiers (the Mongols then being in control of Persia) – while the whole Omani coastline appears to have subsequently fallen under the control of the island **kingdom of Hormuz**, just over the eponymous straits, in Persia.

The Portuguese (1507–1624)

Oman would soon come into contact with a new imperial power in the Indian Ocean: the **Portuguese**. Vasco da Gama himself is sometimes claimed (though with no apparent evidence) to have stopped off in Oman during his historic first voyage to India in 1497–98, though the first sighting of the Portuguese in Oman had to wait another ten years until 1507, when a small fleet commanded by Admiral Afonso de Albuquerque appeared off Muscat. The Portuguese were offered safe passage by Muscat's governor and were in the process of taking on water on the beach when they were suddenly fired upon by soldiers sent by the king of Hormuz. The Portuguese responded by bombarding the city, overrunning and pillaging it and then reducing it to ruins – an unhappy start to a bleak 150 years of Portuguese rule over the coast of Oman.

The Portuguese gradually expanded their power along the coast east and west of Muscat, reaching as far as Sohar and Sur. Their conquests were accompanied with unprecedented levels of brutality and random cruelty: thousands of innocents were murdered, prisoners had their ears and noses chopped off and some coastal settlements, such as Qalhat, were so thoroughly destroyed that they never recovered.

The Portuguese thereafter remained in control of Muscat and the coast, largely unchallenged (bar an unsuccessful uprising in 1526) until 1550, when an **Ottoman fleet** set sail from Egypt to relieve Muscat, with thirty boats carrying 16,000 men. A month-long siege ensued in 1551, after which the victorious Ottomans sacked Muscat – proving no better than the Portuguese they had replaced. Ottoman control of the city lasted just two years, however, before the Portuguese retook it, subsequently fighting off another Ottoman attack in 1554, after which the Turks withdrew from the scene.

The Ya'aruba dynasty (1624–1742)

The next major turning point came in 1624, when **Nasir bin Murshid bin Sultan al Ya'aruba** was elected imam at Rustaq, initiating the **Ya'aruba dynasty**, one of the most important in Oman's history. The Ya'aruba (also spelled Ya'arubi or Yaruba) were possibly the oldest of all the Yamani tribes in Oman. They now provided the country with the charismatic leader it had craved for so long.

At the time of Nasir's election, the interior had splintered into at least five statelets, including Nizwa, Rustaq, Nakhal, Sumail and Ibra, with other forts and regions in the hands of independent tribal leaders and the Portuguese still ensconced in Muscat down on the coast. A strong leader for troubled times, Nasir set about reasserting the imamate's authority over the interior. The process took the remainder of his life, although he didn't live quite long enough to see its completion. By the time of his death in 1649, the last Portuguese were being driven from their strongholds in Muscat and it was left to his cousin and successor, Sultan bin Saif, to complete the work of recapturing the city, which was finally accomplished in 1650 (see box, p.61). In 1646 Nasir also signed a trade treaty with the British, the first of many such arrangements and the beginning of a relationship which was to last, on and off, for over three hundred years.

Like his cousin, **Sultan bin Saif** proved a strong and determined leader. Having seen off the Portuguese, he then launched a series of retaliatory missions, chasing them down to India and across to the east coast of Africa, gradually building up a stock of captured Portuguese ships until Oman had acquired the basis of a large and powerful navy. African-based Omani traders increasingly flourished, while considerable wealth began to pour into Oman for the first time in its history. The monies accumulated were used to fund a major overhaul of the country's *aflaj*, so crucial to its agricultural prosperity, and also to underwrite a countrywide building boom. Sultan bin Saif himself constructed the enormous round tower at Nizwa fort, while his successors added further major new castles at Nakhal, Al Hazm and Barka.

The later Ya'aruba rulers

Sultan bin Saif died in 1679 and was succeeded by his son, **Bil'arab bin Sultan**, thus confirming the principal of hereditary succession – despite the fact that this was completely at odds with the democratic principles of the imamate and Ibadhi faith (during the 900-year history of the imamate, there had previously been only one instance of hereditary succession; now, suddenly, there had been three in a row). Excepting the construction of the beautiful fort at Jabrin (in which Bil'arab is buried), much of the rest of Bil'arab's unhappy reign was spent fighting with his brother, **Saif bin Sultan**, who acceded to the throne after Bil'arab's death at Jabrin in 1692.

Saif bin Sultan once again focused on trade and agriculture, investing further money in *aflaj* throughout the interior and planting thousands of date palms along the Batinah in an effort to encourage Arabs from the interior to settle along the Persianized coast. Saif bin Sultan also continued to harrass the Portuguese along the African coast, and increase his own wealth in the process; his forces captured Mombasa in 1698 (after a siege lasting almost three years), and soon afterwards drove the Portuguese out of Pemba, Kilwa and, most importantly, **Zanzibar**, leaving the Portuguese with no remaining East African possessions north of Mozambique. Zanzibar would subsequently play a crucial role in the later history of Oman, although development of the island didn't really take off until the reign of Said the Great, over a hundred years later. By the time of Saif bin Sultan's death in 1711 he is said to have owned seven hundred male slaves, twenty-eight ships and a third of all the date trees in Oman.

Ya'aruba turbulence and decline

Saif was succeeded by his son, **Sultan bin Saif II**, whose death in 1718 signalled a new era of turbulence. He was nominally succeeded by his twelve-year-old son, **Saif bin Sultan II**, the popular choice of the people at large, although realizing that Saif's youth made him unsuitable for such an important office, the *ulama* secretly elected his elder brother **Muhanna** to serve as imam. This was not a popular decision, however, and Muhanna was rapidly supplanted by his cousin, Yaarub bin Bil'arab, who was himself then forced to resign in favour of the young Saif bin Sultan II, who was assisted by his uncle, and leader of the Bani Hina tribe, Bil'arab bin Nasir. Unfortunately, Bil'arab bin Nasir succeeded in immediately upsetting Muhammed bin Nasir al Ghafiri, a prominent Nizari leader, who quickly organized his tribes in rebellion against the new Bani Hina ruler.

Civil war promptly erupted, with the rival factions divided broadly along Yamani–Nizari lines. The Yamani tribes were led initially by Khalf bin Mubarak of the Bani Hina tribe, and thus became known as **Hinawi** (from Hina), while the Nizari tribes under the command of Muhammed bin Nasir al Ghafiri became known as **Ghafiri**. (The names Hinawi and Ghafiri survive even today as a description of tribal allegiance, being roughly synonymous with Yamani and Nizari respectively, although there has been much switching of allegiance since, including the Bani Ghafir themselves, who, ironically, are now counted among the Hinawi tribes.)

Mohammed bin Nasir al Ghafiri was initially victorious, taking both the young Saif bin Sultan II and his uncle Bil'arab prisoner. He was then elected imam (the third in as many years) and ruled the country for five years from Jabrin before being killed during a battle at Sohar in 1727, after which Saif bin Sultan II subsequently found himself elected imam for a second time.

Saif's position was far from safe, however. Confronted with further uprisings and popular disgust at his opulent and profligate lifestyle in Rustaq (including a particular weakness for Shiraz wine which would subsequently prove his undoing), he called upon the Persians for support. The Persians duly arrived in 1737 under the leadership of **Nadir Shah**, one of the most brilliant – and bloodthirsty – military commanders of his age, although it quickly became apparent that the Persians, having been unwisely invited in, were in no hurry to leave. Nadir's forces captured Muscat (excepting the forts of Jalali and Mirani, which remained in Omani hands) and then marched upon Sohar, where their initial attack against the city was repulsed by a certain Ahmad bin Said Al Bu Said, who was about to assume a pivotal position in Omani history.

By 1742 the Persians had seized control of large parts of the country and showed no signs of going home. The nadir occurred when Saif bin Sultan II was invited to a banquet by the Persian commander **Taqi Khan**. Saif and the rest of his entourage were rendered insensible with large quantities of wine, after which Taqi Khan stole his signet ring and forged an order commanding the forts of Jalali and Mirani to admit the Persian forces, which they did. The unfortunate sultan awoke to one of the worst hangovers in history and the discovery that two of his key forts had fallen to the enemy, and soon afterwards sickened and died. His cousin and would-have-been successor, Murshid al Ya'aruba, had already died fighting the Persians in Sohar, meaning Saif's death heralded the end of the Ya'aruba dynasty, leaving the country leaderless.

The Al Bu Said dynasty begins (1742–1806)

A man for the moment was already at hand, however, in the shape of the redoubtable Hinawi leader, **Ahmad bin Said Al Bu Said**, the *wali* of Sohar – a man of brilliant abilities but humble origins who, it is said, started off by selling wood from the back of a camel. Ahmad had already fought off one Persian attack on Sohar and was busy resisting a second at the moment of Saif's death. After a stubborn nine-month siege Ahmad finally capitulated on honourable terms, and was subsequently confirmed by Taqi Khan as governor of Sohar and Barka – on condition he pay tribute to the Persian authorities in Muscat. He was then elected imam in 1744, ushering in the **Al Bu Said dynasty**, which endures to the present day.

Ahmad bin Said Al Bu Said immediately set about undermining the Persian garrison in Muscat by finding a plausible excuse to fail to make the required payments, meaning many of the garrison's troops received no wages, and deserted. In 1747, still professing his loyalty to the Persian governor, Ahmad invited the entire garrison to his fort in Barka for a **banquet**, where, having assembled his enemy, he did away with the lot of them (see box, p.115), thus freeing Oman once again from the Persian yoke.

Peace and prosperity returned during the 39-year reign of the new imam. Ahmad bin Said encouraged trade by sea and a programme of agricultural development at home. Muscat flourished and, from his seat at Rustaq, Ahmad attempted to strike a balance between coast and interior. He also raised a standing army and navy for the first time in Omani history. Tribal intriguing still threatened his position, however, initially by the remaining members of the Ya'aruba tribe (despite the fact that Ahmad had diplomatically married the daughter of one of the last Ya'aruba rulers), then by the Ghafiri, and finally, towards the end of his reign, by two of his own sons, Saif and Sultan (the latter was eventually forced to flee to Baluchistan, where he fortuitiously inherited the province of Gwadur; see below).

Internal division and Wahhabi threats

Ahmad died in 1783, whereupon his second son, **Said bin Ahmad**, was elected imam (the last Omani leader to hold the post of both sultan and imam), in preference to the rebellious Saif and Sultan. Said appears to have been a reluctant ruler, however, and shortly afterwards his son **Hamad bin Said** wrested political control from his father and set up court in Muscat in 1784, where he took the title "Sayyid" (lord). His father remained as imam in Rustaq, a powerless religious figurehead, until his death in 1803. The union between coast and interior – and between religious and secular leadership – that Ahmad bin Said had carefully nurtured was once again split wide open.

Meanwhile, Muscat continued to flourish and the power of the city grew, even while the division between it and the interior widened. Sayyid Hamad died in 1792 of smallpox and was succeeded by his uncle, **Sultan bin Ahmad** (one of the two rebellious sons of Ahmad bin Said, who had subsequently found his way to Muscat from Baluchistan). Fearing challenges from his own family, Sultan came to an agreement at Barka in 1793 whereby he confirmed the position of his brother Said (who was still imam up in Rustaq) and handed over Sohar to another brother, Qais, effectively confirming the increasing importance of Oman's coastal areas, and the corresponding irrelevance of the office of imam.

In 1798, a new treaty was signed with the British East India Company, part of a system of military and diplomatic maneouvres by which the British hoped to ward off French designs on India, and by which Sultan hoped to benefit from the protection of the increasingly powerful British navy.

Not that all was peaceful at home. In 1800 Oman suffered the first of a string of invasions by the **Wahhabis**, from what is now Saudi Arabia, which were to plague it for the next century and a half. The Wahhabis besieged Qais bin Ahmad in Sohar and also occupied the Buraimi oasis, kicking off a long-running **territorial dispute** that would not finally be settled until 1974 (see box, p.136).

Gwadur and Omani Baluchistan

Sultan bin Ahmad's flight from Oman following his unsuccessful attempts to unseat his father Ahmad bin Said (see above) had one unexpected but important consequence. Sultan initially sought refuge abroad in **Gwadur** on the Makran coast of Baluchistan (in present-day Pakistan). The obliging local Baluchi ruler of Kalat granted Sultan possession of what was then an insignificant fishing village and the surrounding area, which Sultan retained following his return to Muscat and eventual accession to the throne, and which remained Omani territory until being finally sold back to Pakistan in 1958. Oman's long-standing links with Gwadur can still be seen in the large number of Omanis of Baluchi descent who migrated to the country over the years and who can now be found in towns and cities nationwide, in Muscat particularly.

Sultan's death in 1804 was followed by the predictable bout of intriguing and infighting. Sultan's cousin, **Badr bin Saif** (deeply unpopular thanks to his Wahhabi sympathies) was notionally in charge for the next two years until being assassinated by Sultan's son, Said. At the same time, the Wahhabis returned and took advantage of the confusion to gain control of large parts of the interior.

Said the Great (1806–56)

The new ruler, **Said bin Sultan** (reigned 1806–56), sometimes referred to as "Said the Great", was just seventeen when he assumed power following the assassination of Badr bin Saif – the beginning of a half-century reign which, despite its murderous start, would see Oman reach the high point of its power and prosperity. He was also the first Omani ruler to take the title of "Sultan", which is still used by the country's supreme ruler today – thus becoming (rather confusingly) Sultan Said bin Sultan.

Not that all went smoothly to begin with, however; Wahhabi incursions continued until 1820, when Said was able to repulse them with help from the British and Persians. Said forged increasingly close links with Britain, whose government offered him protection in return for his assistance in quashing local Qawasim pirates (based in their stronghold at Ras al Khaimah in the present-day UAE) and in putting a stop – eventually – to the slave trade between Africa and Oman.

Said and Zanzibar

The latter part of Said's reign is inextricably linked with **Zanzibar**. The island had been in Omani hands since 1698, but remained something of a backwater until the sultan's first visit in 1828, when he passed laws obliging all landowners to establish **clove plantations**. Despite being met with initial resistance, the clove trade subsequently proved massively successful, underpinning the island's rapid development and increasing prosperity.

Said himself was increasingly drawn to East Africa, and in 1832 moved his official residence from Muscat to Zanzibar, attracted by the island's congenial surroundings and far more promising economic prospects – which was very much to Africa's gain, and Oman's loss. Established in Zanzibar, Said ruled over a string of Omani settlements stretching for almost 1600km along the East African coast, and for considerable distances inland – as well as continuing to exercise nominal sovereignty over Muscat and Oman, although his prolonged absences led to inevitable intriguing and skirmishes among rival pretenders to the throne.

From his new base in Zanzibar, Said also provided invaluable assistance to Victorian explorers including Richard Burton, David Livingstone, Henry Stanley and, ironically, early Christian missionaries intent on penetrating the interior of the continent; Burton returned the favour by stating that Said was "as shrewd, liberal, enlightened a prince as Arabia ever produced." **Relations with Britain** remained warm: in 1834 Said gifted King William IV his largest ship, the seventy-four gun *Liverpool*, while in 1854 he presented an even grander offering in the shape of the Khuriya Muriya (Hallaniyat) islands (see p.209), off the coast of Dhofar.

Said, the British and the slave trade

Said's apparent willingness to assist British efforts in suppressing the huge **slave trade** between East Africa and Arabia was particularly notable – although whether such efforts were the result of political expediency or genuine humanitarian scruples is not entirely clear. An initial treaty was signed with the British in 1822, though this simply bound Said to forgo trading in slaves himself rather than take active steps to stamp out the Afro-Arabian slave trade between Omani settlements in East Africa and Oman – and the slave market in Muscat itself continued to flourish. The 1822 treaty was reinforced with a new agreement in 1839 before Said signed a third treaty in 1845 that finally outlawed the export of slaves from areas of Africa under Omani control. Nevertheless, the keeping of slaves remained legal in Zanzibar until 1897.

Whatever the reasons, Said's anti-slavery policy struck at the economic root of both Oman and its East African colonies. In Zanzibar, for example, no less than three-quarters of the estimated population of 200,000 were slaves, while a wealthy Zanzibari might have owned anything up to a thousand slaves – indeed Said himself is thought to have lost a quarter of his annual income as a result of the new prohibitions following the 1822 agreement.

Economic decline and tribal unrest (1856–1912)

Said's death in 1856 left the predictable power vacuum, with unhappy results for the country. Omani territories were divided between his two sons, **Thuwaini** and **Majid**, with the former taking Oman and the latter Zanzibar – a rather uneven arrangement, given that Zanzibar was then far richer than Oman. Thuwaini attempted to reclaim Zanzibar by force, but was beaten back, at which point the British Government of India intervened. Oman and Zanzibar would henceforth remain two separate states – with considerable economic costs to the former. Recognizing the financial implications of the loss of its former colony, Lord Canning, the Governor-General of India, ruled in 1861 that Zanzibar should henceforth pay the government of Oman an annual sum of 40,000 Maria Theresa Thalers, a settlement known as the **Canning Award**. Perhaps not surprisingly, Zanzibar almost immediately defaulted on its payments and the British authorities (having brokered the arrangement) were forced to make good the difference from 1871 until 1956. Zanzibar, meanwhile, remained under Al Bu Said rule until 1964, when it became part of Tanzania.

Thuwaini enjoyed his half of the inheritance for only ten years before being killed in 1866 by his son **Salim**, who then declared himself sultan. The unpopular Salim lasted just two years before being driven into exile by his cousin, the energetic but fanatical **Azzan bin Qais**. Azzan did slightly better than Salim, holding onto the throne for three years before being killed by **Turki bin Said** (another son of Said bin Sultan). Meanwhile, in 1869 the troublesome Wahhabis returned yet again, taking advantage of the confusion to occupy the Buraimi oasis for the fifth time before being once again repulsed.

Following his defeat of Azzan, Turki bin Said was proclaimed sultan in 1871 with the support of the British government in London – with whom he immediately signed a further treaty aimed at repressing the slave trade and curbing the trade in arms. The increasingly impoverished tribesmen of the interior, however, regarded their new sultan as little more than a British puppet and soon rose up in arms. A series of attacks against Muscat ensued, spearheaded by the powerful **Al Harthy** tribe from Sharqiya under **Salih bin Ali al Harthy**. Salih bin Ali led successive raids against Muscat in 1874 and 1877, capturing Muttrah and threatening Muscat itself until being bought off by the sultan. A third attack followed in 1883, this time repulsed, again with British naval assistance.

Meanwhile, in the far southwest of the country, the independent province of **Dhofar**, previously a somewhat anarchic patchwork of competing tribal areas, was slowly being brought into the Omani fold. Said the Great had already dispatched a force to the region in 1829, although it wasn't fully integrated into Oman until 1877, when Sultan Turki bin Said sent soldiers to take control of Salalah and garrison the town. Even then, the sultan's authority rarely ran much further than the immediate environs of Salalah itself – a situation that persisted right up until the final suppression of the Dhofar rebellion (see p.229) almost exactly a century later.

Turki died in 1883 and was succeeded by his son **Faisal**, though events continued largely as before. Despite constant Hinawi–Ghafiri conflicts in the interior, the two rival groups joined forces in 1895 for yet another march on Muscat, now led by **Abdullah bin Salih** (son of Salih bin Ali). This time the rebels succeeded in finally capturing Muscat itself, watched by the British, who studiously kept their distance, refusing to assist either side.

The rebels were, once again, eventually bought off by the increasingly indebted Sultan Faisal, who now found that his writ ran only from Muscat to Muttrah, along the Batinah coast and in Sur and a few places in the interior, including Izki, Nizwa and the strategic Sumail Gap. Inland, the tribes lapsed into poverty, and were driven to inter-tribal raids or even mass emigration.

The arrival of the French

One by-product of the British failure to intervene on his behalf during the 1895 insurrection was that (despite two sizeable loans from the British Government of India) the infuriated Sultan Faisal turned increasingly to the **French** – who also had the advantage of being altogether more pliable when it came to matters relating to the slave trade and arms smuggling. When Faisal granted the French coaling facilities at Bandar Jissah the British sent a warship to Muscat harbour to put the sultan in his place, after which he was forced to give up his flirtation with the French. Relations subsequently improved, and in 1903 the Viceroy of India, Lord Curzon, visited Muscat and wrote off the sultan's debts to the British Government of India.

Insurrection in the interior (1912–32)

The inhabitants of the interior, however, were not greatly impressed by such instances of imperial largesse. The last straw, so far as the Omani tribes were concerned, came in 1912, when the sultan, under British pressure, established an arms warehouse in Muscat, effectively strangling the lucrative trade in trans-Arabian arms smuggling which provided one source of income in the increasingly poverty-stricken country. Unfortunately for the Omanis, many of these weapons were subsequently used against British soldiers in northwest India – hence the British desire to wipe out the trade.

In 1913, a meeting of Ghafiri tribal sheikhs arranged for the election, at Tanuf, of a **new imam**, the first since the death of Said bin Ahmad 110 years earlier. The revival of the office of imam was intended as a direct challenge to the authority of the sultan in Muscat (although the chosen candidate, one Salim bin Rashid al Kharusi, would remain a largely ceremonial figurehead in the conflicts to come). Civil war once again ensued. Shortly afterwards the rebels captured Nizwa and then Izki, after which the Hinawi tribes joined the uprising.

Then, in October 1913, Sultan Faisal died, and was succeeded by his son **Sultan Taimur**. Taimur thus inherited his father's parlous finances and a full-blown rebellion in the interior. Attempts at negotiation proved fruitless, and in 1915 the British Government of India was forced to send a battalion of Indian troops to Muscat to beat off a rebel attack led by Isa bin Salih (another son of the rebellious Salih bin Ali), culminating in a fierce battle at Muscat's Bait al Falaj (see p.64). The attack was repulsed, although the rebellion dragged on for five more years. Finally, in 1920, the **Treaty of Seeb** was signed between the two warring factions, whereby the sultan effectively handed over control of the interior to its tribal leaders, confirming the final division of the Sultanate of Muscat and Oman into two more or less autonomous states. The luckless new imam, Salim bin Rashid, meanwhile was assassinated in 1920 and suceeded as imam by Mohammad bin Abdullah al Khalili, a nominee of Isa bin Salih.

Sultan Said bin Taimur and the search for oil (1932–55)

The new sultan, Taimur, proved a reluctant ruler. In 1920, finding himself the virtually powerless ruler of a bankrupt state, hamstrung (as he saw it) by British interference, he sailed to Bombay and attempted to abdicate. The Government of Britain refused to accept his abdication, however, and the sultan himself refused to return to Muscat. He spent the next eleven years in India, during which power effectively passed to a council of ministers led by his young son, Said.

Taimur returned to Oman in 1931. In 1932, he was finally able to relinquish the throne and hand over power to his son, who became **Sultan Said bin Taimur**. Sultan Said enjoys a rather ambiguous position in the history of Oman. His early rule was marked by a commendable level of fiscal and diplomatic prudence, as he succeeded in liquidating his inherited debts and maintaining peaceful relations with the imam in the interior for two decades – although Oman as a whole lapsed into a state of almost medieval torpor, with most of the country's population leading lives of unremitting hardship and poverty.

The possibility of Oman finally achieving the means to break out of its endless cycle of isolation and poverty came thanks to **oil**, which was by the 1930s already transforming the economies of many other countries in the Middle East. By the 1940s, oil exploration was proceeding apace in Oman, although efforts at prospecting were significantly hindered by the fact that the interior (where the oil was presumed to be) was effectively an independent state, not to mention the difficulties presented by the country's inhospitable and largely unmapped terrain.

The situation was also complicated by further military and political skirmishes, as the Saudis returned, re-occupying the **Buraimi oasis** yet again, largely in the hope that oil would eventually be found there (see box, p.136). Despite this setback, in October 1954 the sultan's forces captured Ibri, close to the site of the most important oil exploration in Fahud (see box, p.230), finally securing a base for oil exploration in the interior; for a first-hand account of this, read *Arabian Destiny* by Edward Henderson, who played a leading role in the affair (see p.239).

Following the loss of Ibri, and with the encouragement of the Saudis, the newly elected imam, **Sheikh Ghalib bin Ali al Hina'i**, launched attempts to have the Imamate accepted as a member of the Arab League – an effort to have the interior, or "Oman proper", recognized as an independent, sovereign state.

The Jebel War (1955–59)

Faced with the occupying Saudis in Buraimi and Imam Ghalib's attempts at secession, Sultan Said and the British finally took action. In 1955, the Saudi forces were expelled from Buraimi with the help of the Trucial Oman Scouts (a small, Sharjah-based force consisting of a batallion of Arab troops under British command), after which the sultan's forces, with continued British support, went on to occupy the whole country, taking Rustaq and Nizwa en route. Shortly afterwards, Sultan Said travelled from Salalah to Muscat through his newly reconquered dominions, a journey memorably described in Jan Morris's *Sultan in Oman* (see p.230).

Resistance to the rule of Muscat was far from over, however – although it had more to do with the self-interested ambitions of local tribal leaders (and their Saudi backers) rather than the tribal population at large. The three leaders most responsible were **Suleyman bin Himyar al Nabhani**, the self-styled "King of the Jebel Akhdar", Imam Ghalib and his brother Talib. Insurrection flared up again in 1957, the beginning of an eighteen-month rebellion subsequently known as the **Jebel War**. At the beginning of the conflict, the nervous *wali* of Nizwa abandoned the city and its fort to the rebels, while the towns of Bahla and Izki capitulated immediately afterwards.

Sultan Said turned for help to the British, who provided both air and land forces, retaking Nizwa after one and a half days' fighting (with just one casualty) and routing the rebels. Suleyman, Talib and Ghalib fled into the heights of the Jebel Akhdar, where they clung on until January 1959, until being ousted in a final assault by combined Omani and British forces, after which they fled abroad.

Insurgency and oil (1959–69)

The end of the Jebel War might have appeared to mark the final reunification of the country, but just as most of Oman was beginning to enjoy a new-found sense of peace and security (if not yet prosperity) the tribesmen of the Dhofar interior launched a new rebellion. The movement's figurehead was a dissatisfied tribal leader, Mussalim bin Nafl. In 1962, bin Nafl formed the **Dhofar Liberation Front** (DLF), obtaining arms and equipment from ever antagonistic Saudi Arabia, as well as support from the exiled imam Ghalib Bin Ali. From late 1962 onwards, bin Nafl and his troops began a series of sabotage attacks against oil vehicles, government posts and the British air base at Salalah.

Sultan Said's response to the insurrection was to assemble the so-called **Dhofar Force** (DF), a locally recruited irregular unit of just sixty men. The move backfired spectacularly when, in April 1966, members of the DF turned on their employer and attempted to assassinate the sultan. Sultan Said was so shaken by this that he subsequently rarely left the safety of his palace in Salalah – fuelling rumours that the British were running Oman through a phantom ruler. In fact, the sultan was still very much involved, launching a full-scale military offensive against the DLF despite the advice of his British advisors, including heavy-handed punitive missions against villages thought to be harbouring rebels.

The rebellion assumed even more serious proportions in **1967**, thanks to two events. The first was the Six Day War and the crushing Israeli victory over the combined forces of Egypt, Syria and Jordan – a military disaster which radicalized opinion throughout the Arab world. Even more important was the British withdrawal from Aden and the establishment of the neo-Marxist People's Democratic Republic of Yemen (**PDRY**), also known as South Yemen. The new Yemeni government became a reliable source of arms, supplies and training facilities just over the border from Dhofar, and fresh recruits from among Yemeni groups, meaning that the rebels were increasingly well armed and organized.

Yemeni and other outside influences led to the rebellion becoming increasingly radicalized. In 1968 the movement renamed itself the Popular Front for the Liberation of the Occupied Arabian Gulf (**PFLOAG**), adopting an increasingly Marxist–Leninist stance that resulted in increased backing from South Yemen, China and Russia. The situation had all the makings of an Arabian Vietnam, with an absolutist monarch backed by the old imperial power of Britain on one hand, and a highly trained and motivated proto-Communist force on the other.

The insurgents were by now excellently equipped with automatic rifles, heavy machine guns, mortars and rockets. The Sultan's Armed Forces, by contrast, were chronically under-resourced and badly trained, with no more than a thousand fighters, many of them equipped with World War II-era bolt-action rifles. In addition, no Omani held a rank above that of lieutenant (a result of the Sultan's fears of opposition to his rule among the armed forces). The Sultan's Armed Forces were generally restricted to Salalah and its immediate environs, while the British RAF and Royal Artillery had to be deployed to protect the airfield at Salalah. By **1969** PFLOAG fighters had overrun much of the Jebel Dhofar, and cut the only road across it, from Salalah to Thumrait, effectively paralyzing the region, and

Oil in Oman

The **search for oil** in Oman began in 1925 – although the very first geological survey of the country found no evidence of oil reserves. Despite this initial failure, hopes of oil remained, and in 1932 Sultan Said bin Taimur granted a 75-year concession to the Iraq Petroleum Company (IPC) to prospect for reserves.

Further prospecting was interrupted by World War II and serious exploration didn't begin until 1954, although oil company geologists were hindered by assorted tribal conflicts which blocked access to what was considered the most promising site, at **Fahud**, in the desert outside Ibri. Despite this, surveys of the Fahud region began later that year, although no oil was initially found. Further drillings followed, also without success. Continued logistical problems, allied to a surfeit of oil on the world market, led to most of the original stakeholders in the IPC withdrawing from the venture in 1960.

The perseverance of the two remaining companies, Shell and Partex, however, soon paid off. In 1962 oil was discovered at **Yibal**, in the Dhahirah desert south of Fahud, while in 1963 further reserves were discovered at nearby **Natih** and, finally, at **Fahud** (within a few hundred metres of the original IPC drillings). A 276km pipeline was laid, followed by the construction of a refinery at Mina al Fahal in Muscat, with the **first exports** being shipped in July 1967.

The effect of oil on Oman has been profound. Although the country has never enjoyed the fabulous oil revenues enjoyed by places such as Saudi Arabia, Abu Dhabi and Qatar, oil monies provided the funds with which to drag Oman out of poverty and give it a modern infrastructure. As of 2009, Oman was ranked the world's 25th largest oil producer, with its 23rd largest proven reserves (0.41 percent of the global total). Even so, steadily dwindling reserves and unstable oil prices have forced the country's leaders to take active steps to diversify the national economy (see p.232), with the aim of reducing oil's contribution to GDP to under ten percent by 2020.

persuading many observers, including the sultan's British advisors, that only a new ruler could save Oman from its gradual slide into anarchy.

The discovery of oil

Ironically, just as the Dhofar rebellion was threatening to tip the entire country into chaos, the key to its future prosperity was being uncovered, with the **discovery of oil** in 1962 at Yabil, and later at Natih and Fahud (see box above). Exports began in 1967, and although the reserves were modest compared to those in nearby Saudi Arabia, Abu Dhabi and elsewhere around the Gulf, they were at least sufficient to finally release the Omani population from the grinding poverty in which they had been previously trapped.

Unfortunately, Sultan Said's response to his new-found largesse was disappointingly half-hearted. Despite the new oil money pouring into the country, the sultan appeared struck immobile by a lifetime's habit of financial caution. These frugal habits had served him well in the past when the country was virtually bankrupt, but were no longer suited to massively changed circumstances. Instead of investing the money in much-needed development, Said simply consigned the new revenues of state to a chest under his bed – where they stayed.

The Omani Renaissance (1970–2000)

The end of Sultan Said's old-fashioned and autocratic rule finally came on July 23, 1970, when he was deposed in an almost entirely peaceful **coup** (organized with tacit British assistance and approval). His 30-year-old son, **Qaboos**, who had been kept under virtual house arrest by his father in the palace in Salalah, was installed in his place, while the deposed sultan was packed off into exile in England, where he spent the last two years of his life living in state at London's *Dorchester Hotel*.

The young sultan was faced with widespread dissatisfaction among his new subjects, endemic poverty and a nation which had totally lost touch with the modern world. His most pressing problem, however, was the continuing insurrection in **Dhofar**. To this he responded with characteristic decisiveness. His first act was to offer a general amnesty to all rebels, even offering cash incentives to surrendering insurgents. Allied to this was a comprehensive "hearts and minds" campaign, under the moniker "The Hand of God Destroys Communism" – an attempt to appeal to traditional Islamic values in opposition to the rebels' secular ethos. Rebels who surrendered were subsequently reformed into irregular units who were sent back out into the *jebel* as part of the propaganda war – and where, as locals, they had far more success than fighters from other parts of Oman. In addition, twenty British Royal Engineers were sent out to construct schools, health centres and to drill wells, an RAF medical team began operating out of Salalah hospital and money was provided for a Dhofar Development Programme. These peaceable efforts were also backed by strong military measures. The Sultan's Armed Forces were enlarged and re-equipped, while the Omani Air Force was also expanded.

As a result of these combined measures, the rebels were soon deprived both of local support and supplies from the PDRY. The decisive confrontation came at the **Battle of Mirbat** (see p.208), when 300 rebels attacked the Sultan's Armed Forces, which were under the command of nine SAS soldiers, only to be driven back with heavy losses. From this point on, the rebels were forced steadily backwards, their demise hastened by diminishing levels of support from the Soviet Union and China. The final defeat of the rebellion was announced in January 1976, although isolated incidents took place as late as 1979.

Modernization and reform

Meanwhile, Sultan Qaboos launched a far-ranging programme of modernization and reform – or the **Omani Renaissance**, as it is now popularly known. One of his first acts was to change the name of the country from the "Sultanate of Muscat and Oman" to "The Sultanate of Oman", thereby symbolically erasing the historical divide between coast and interior which had plagued the country for so long. Qaboos also made a concerted effort to have Oman recognized as a fully sovereign independent state, and by the end of 1971 the country had joined the United Nations, the Arab League and the International Monetary Fund.

At home, rapid development began. Qaboos had inherited a country with no newspapers, radio or television, no civil service and just one hospital, two graded roads and three schools. The average life expectancy was 47 (it has since risen to 74). Large numbers of new schools and hospitals were swiftly constructed and a civil service established. Efforts were also made to lure back home disaffected Omanis who had emigrated, while many Zanzibaris and Kenyans of Omani origin were welcomed to the country.

Political progress also followed. In 1981 a State Consultative Council, the **Majlis ad Dawla** (its members all appointed directly by the sultan), was established. Ten years later, the larger and more representative **Majlis ash Shura** (with 83 elected members) was created, although the Majlis has no legislative powers, and all final decisions are made by Sultan Qaboos and his advisors.

Oman in the 21st century

Twenty-first-century Oman is an increasingly modern and prosperous place – and virtually unrecognizable from the country of just four decades ago. A study in late 2010 by the United Nations Development Programme rated Oman as the "most improved" country over the past forty years out of the 135 it surveyed.

One measure of the country's stability was provided by events during the so-called Arab Spring of early 2011. What began as a political earthquake in Tunisia, Egypt, Bahrain and neighbouring Yemen, however, produced only a fairly modest ripple in Oman itself. Small-scale protests occurred in various parts of the country, centred on the Majlis ash Shura in Muscat and the Globe roundabout in Sohar, although notably these were aimed more at perceived government corruption and cronyism, along with practical concerns such as unemployment and the cost of living, rather than with making any attempt to upset the basic political status quo; without exception even the most vehement demonstrators were adamant in professing their loyalty to Sultan Qaboos. Only in **Sohar** did events turn serious when a handful of protesters were killed while attacking a police station, although even there the situation was rapidly returned to normal.

Future challenges

Significant challenges remain, however. The oil reserves which have underpinned the country's transformation are steadily dwindling. The country's leaders are taking major steps to **diversify the economy** with the aim of reducing oil's contribution to GDP from the current forty percent to less than ten percent by 2020. Tourism is one major growth area, while there have also been concerted attempts to strengthen the country's industrial and commercial base.

The country's burgeoning birth rate and youthful population (with a median age of just 24 years) has created a potential **demographic time bomb**, given the shortage of jobs for the large numbers of educated young Omanis entering the workplace. There is also an increasing resentment against the country's reliance on **expatriate labour**, and the perception that foreigners are taking what should, by rights, be Omani jobs (even if, in fact, at least some of these jobs are ones which Omanis themselves are unwilling or unqualified to perform).

The **role of women** in Omani society is also evolving. The first women members of the Majlis ad Dawla were appointed in 2000, with women finally being given the vote in 2003. There are now more women than men in higher education, while they also make up around a third of the country's civil service. Women can also stand for election to the Majlis ash Shura, although there are so far only two elected female councillers out of a total of 83. This under-representation doesn't seem likely to change in the near future: in the last Majlis ash Shura elections in 2007 not a single one of the twenty new female candidates was elected – although the Majlis ad Dawla, whose members are directly appointed by the sultan, now boasts nine women among its 59 members.

The succession question

The question of who will eventually **succeed Sultan Qaboos** (aged 71 at the time of writing) is another concern, given that the sultan remains childless (his only marriage, in 1976, having ended soon afterwards in divorce). Qaboos has failed to name his choice of successor, although it is said that he has written the names of his two favoured candidates in an unopened letter, copies of which are now kept in Muscat and Salalah, to provide guidance in the event that the royal family cannot agree the choice of new sultan following his death. The three sons (all now in their fifties) of Qaboos's uncle and former prime minister Tarik bin Taimur al Said are considered likely successors, although none has especially distinguished himself, and speculation is rife. For the time being, however, Sultan Qaboos remains in good health, and the nation whose spectacular transformation he has overseen can face the future with genuine, if cautious, optimism.

Fortified Oman

Oman is one of the world's most extensively fortified nations, a reflection of the unsettled nature of life in the peninsula in times past. There are more than five hundred **forts** in the country – indeed there's hardly a town in Oman which doesn't boast at least one, and often several – while numerous other examples of fortified architecture can be found, ranging from **surs** (fortified houses) and **walled villages** through to the innumerable **watch-towers** which dot the summits of ridges and hilltops across the land.

Omani forts

Forts played a vital role in the life of traditional Oman. Their principal function was, of course, military, providing a home to local militia and also serving as a refuge for the entire population of the village or town in case of attack. Forts also usually housed the residence of the local *wali* (governor) and his *majlis*, used to receive visitors and as a forum in which the *wali* and other local leaders would meet to discuss matters of importance. Not surprisingly, therefore, possession of the local fort offered whoever held it de facto control over the entire surrounding region.

Fort design

No two forts in Oman are exactly alike. Those built on flat ground along the coast tend to be square, typically – but not always – with a tower at each corner. Those in the mountains are usually built above the surrounding countryside on easily defensible rock outcrops, being moulded to the contours of the stone on which they sit, and thus more irregularly shaped. A few forts, notably those at Buraimi and Bukha, also have moats, although these are relatively rare. All forts have at least one tower (although most usually have several), which offered a good vantage point over the surrounding countryside and a raised position from which to fire in the event of hostilities.

Designs also changed over time. The introduction of the **cannon** into the Arabian military arsenal, in particular, had far-reaching effects on the design of Omani forts. Walls were thickened massively, while rounded towers also became the norm – both features which helped absorb and reduce the impact of cannon-fire. Inside the fort, reinforced towers and terraces were constructed to provide a stable platform from which to fire cannon on approaching attackers; the great round tower at Nizwa, providing support for twenty-plus cannon offering a 360-degree line of fire, is perhaps the most famous example.

The interior of most forts is typically divided into military and domestic areas; the word "fort" can be translated in Arabic as either *qala* or *hisn* (or *husn*), although the former more properly refers to the military portions of a fort, while *hisn* describes the residential sections. Most forts include a large **courtyard**, with the *wali*'s **residential quarters** usually grouped together in one corner. These lodgings typically consist of the *wali*'s own bedroom/apartment, along with other bedrooms, a *majlis* (and perhaps a women's *majlis* as well), a kitchen, stores for dates and arms, barracks for the resident soldiers and at least one jail.

Defensive features

Whatever the design, defensive considerations were always paramount. All Omani forts are surrounded by high **walls** topped by battlements, ranging from spiky, saw-tooth crenellations to more rounded designs. Inside the walls, loopholes provided safe cover from which to fire on enemies below, along with openings down which boiling date juice could be poured (or heavy objects dropped) onto the heads of attackers. Windows, where they existed, were reinforced with heavy iron grilles and thick wooden shutters which could be secured from inside.

Potential attackers, assuming they managed to survive the barrage of musket and cannon fire (not to mention the cascade of boiling date juice) from above, would then have to breach the **gateway**. All Omani forts, even the largest, were provided with just a single entrance to limit access and provide security. Gateways themselves were typically protected by massive hardwood doors (often elaborately carved), reinforced with iron spikes. Inset within each large door was a second, much smaller, door with an unusually high sill, limiting access to one person at a time and forcing anyone entering into an awkwardly bent posture.

Inside, many forts feature a disorienting labyrinth of narrow stairways, designed to confuse intruders and restrict access to one person at a time. Some stairways (at Nizwa fort, for example) also boast further defensive features such as "murder holes" – overhead openings down which boiling date juice and heavy objects could be poured or dropped onto the enemy, or down which water could be poured to extinguish fires – and "pitfalls", deep dark holes into which unsuspecting attackers could easily tumble.

Given the general impregnability of Omani forts, many attackers chose to **besiege** them rather than storm them, although this too brought no particular guarantee of success; Nizwa Fort, for example, is said to have successfully resisted one siege lasting several years. All Omani forts boast their own well, while many also have dedicated *aflaj*, which guaranteed a reliable source of water; these were often designed to issue from the ground within the walls of a castle, avoiding the possibility of the water supply being poisoned by attackers outside. Some forts were also equipped with secret escape tunnels in the event that the trapped *wali* or other bigwigs decided to beat a hasty retreat.

Surs, watchtowers and walls

Slightly different from the traditional fort is the **sur**, or fortified house. Exactly where a fort ends and a *sur* begins is difficult to say, although *surs* tend generally to be smaller, taller and most domestic in character. Examples include the magnificent Bait Na'aman near Barka; the more modest but still solid and largely windowless mudbrick cubes which are such a feature of Sharqiya towns such as Ibra, Jalaan Bani Bu Hassan, Al Kamil and Mintrib; and the distinctive Yemeni-inspired examples found in Dhofar, Mirbat in particular.

Even more numerous than the country's forts are its **watchtowers** (*burj*). In parts of the country (particularly driving up the Sumail gap, or around Ibra and other towns in Sharqiya) it seems that virtually every ridgetop and rock outcrop is dotted with at least one of these characteristic structures. Watchtowers were generally arranged in defensive chains surrounding an important town, mountain pass or oasis. The towers – usually circular, occasionally square – were designed to be impregnable, with earth or stone-filled bases, a single, difficult-to-reach doorway on an upper level (entrance would have been via a ladder, which was pulled up afterwards) and crenellated rooftops commanding 360-degree views of the surrounding area and offering elevated lines of fire over attackers below.

Walled towns and villages are also common throughout the country. The old walled quarter of Al Aqr in Nizwa, with its elaborate, crumbling gateways, is a particularly fine example, as is the nearby old town of Bahla, whose magnificent walls extend for some 12km. Walled villages include well-preserved Al Munisifeh and Al Kanatar in Ibra, and the remarkable fortified village of As Suleif in Ibri.

Building materials

The basic building material of all traditional Omani architecture is **mudbrick** (or adobe, from the Arabic *al tob*, meaning "mud"). Bricks were made from alluvial clay, containing a mixture of grit and silt – that from date plantations was generally considered to be the best for building. Chopped straw was added to the clay to reduce shrinkage and warping during the drying process and to improve resistance to erosion. The resulting mixture was then left to "cure" for four or five days before being moulded into bricks. **Stone**, readily available throughout the mountains, was relatively little used, perhaps because of the difficulty in transporting and cutting it, although it can often be seen in parts of larger structures, particularly in the foundations.

All structures, whether mudbrick or stone, were traditionally bound together with and then covered in **sarooj**, a type of mortar-cum-plaster. This was made from mudcakes which were fired together with limestone at extreme temperatures (in excess of 850°C) for as long as a week. The ashy residue was then pulverized and mixed with water and the resultant substance used to bind bricks and stone, and to provide a smooth lustrous finish.

Restoration

At the time of Sultan Qaboos's accession in 1970, most forts in Oman were in advanced states of dilapidation. Since then, the Omani government has made huge strides in the massive project of restoring the nation's traditional landmarks and making them safe for posterity – a massive undertaking covering hundreds of buildings. Many major forts have now been beautifully renovated, although work on others continues; travelling around the country you're still likely to find that every third or fourth fort you visit is closed for maintenance (notable examples at the time of writing included the Batinah forts of Rustaq, Al Hazm and Sohar, while work continues on the mighty Bahla fort, closed since 1987). Others, such as the mudbrick monster fort at Jalan Bani Bu Ali, remain entirely untouched despite their perilous condition, and with no sign of restoration in sight.

The fate of Oman's traditional **domestic architecture** remains even more parlous. Many of the country's old mudbrick fortified villages are steadily crumbling away, with large numbers now little more than roofless shells – undeniably picturesque at present, although in danger of vanishing completely in the next decade or so if urgent work is not begun to stabilize them.

Wildlife

Despite its largely arid and inhospitable environment, Oman supports a surprisingly wide range of animal life – although many creatures are rarely seen by casual visitors. The **mountains** are home to many of the country's most distinctive species, ranging from the shaggy tahr through to the legendary but famously elusive Arabian leopard. Inland, the **desert plains** of the interior are home to the iconic Arabian oryx and occasional herds of gazelle, while the **coastal** lagoons and salt-flats support large numbers of migratory bird species, including colourful flocks of pink flamingoes. The **waters** around Oman are rich in sea life, including an exceptional range of dolphins and whales, plus thousands of turtles which nest on shores around the country.

Mammals

Oman is home to around 75 species of **mammal**, although almost all are rare, and very seldom sighted in the wild. Perhaps the most famous is the **Arabian leopard** (*Panthera pardus nimr*) – the world's smallest, at under 1m long and half the weight of its African cousin. Based on the evidence of pugmarks and scat, an estimated hundred or so leopards are believed to survive in the Dhofar mountains, particularly around Jebel Sumhurum; there are also perhaps a few more in the mountains of Musandam, although actual sightings in either location are virtually unknown. The best scientific estimates suggest that, overall, there are now perhaps fewer than two hundred Arabian leopards left in the wild, including some in Saudi Arabia and Yemen. Not surprisingly, the animal is currently listed as "critically endangered" – one step up from "extinct" – on the International Union for Conservation of Nature and Natural Resources' "Red List".

Hunting and conservation in Oman

Hunting has always played a crucial role in traditional Bedu life, as a combination of practical necessity (a large Arabian oryx could feed a family for a week) and sheer pleasure in the traditional thrill of the chase. In times past, this was a carefully matched contest between the hunter, on foot or camel-back, and his wary, fleet-flooted prey. The advent of modern motor vehicles and sophisticated rifles and other firearms in the mid-twentieth century destroyed this delicate balance, however, plunging many species into near extinction. In parts of Arabia the traditional Bedu hunt was replaced with posses of urban thrill-seekers in 4WD trucks literally machine-gunning their way across the desert, massacring as many as a hundred oryx and other creatures in a single afternoon. Not surprisingly, by 1972 the Arabian oryx had become extinct in the wild, with many other species, such as the region's gazelles and leopards, not far behind.

Oman's response to this ecological cataclysm was commendably swift, and under Sultan Qaboos the country has been in the vanguard of **conservation** efforts in the peninsula. The hunting of endangered species was made a criminal offence in 1979, and in 1982 the Arabian Oryx Sanctuary (see p.186) became the first of its kind in the Gulf. Important areas are now protected (in some form) across the country, including the Ras al Jinz turtle beach (see p.174), the Daymaniyat Islands (see p.122), and the Jebel Samhan Nature Reserve (see pp.205–206), as well as various *khors* along the Salalah coast.

Despite its modest size, the leopard is still the apex hunter in Arabia and has no natural predators (except humans), although leopard cubs are potentially at risk from foxes, hyenas and wolves. Male leopards have a territory of around 300 square kilometres and are opportunistic hunters, feeding on a range of smaller mammals and birds, plus human livestock – something which has brought them into conflict with humans in the past, most notably in Musandam in the 1980s, when a systematic cull of local leopards was undertaken by tribesmen protecting their herds. Fortunately, killing a leopard now entails a fine of 5000 OR and up to five years in jail.

Antelopes and other mammals

The deserts of southern Oman are home to populations of various small- and medium-sized antelopes. Of these, the best known is the **Arabian oryx** (or white oryx; *Oryx leucoryx*; in Arabic, *al maha*). This has become one of the iconic animals of Oman – and, indeed, of other countries around the Gulf (particularly Qatar, where it's the national animal) – thanks to its distinctively long, sweeping horns. One theory holds that the oryx is a possible source for the myth of the unicorn, given that the two horns can easily merge into one when seen in side profile. Living in herds of around ten to fifteen animals, the remarkably strong and hardy oryx is perfectly adapted to desert life, and capable of going without water for months, surviving entirely off moisture contained in foliage. Despite being a favoured prey of Bedu hunters, the oryx's speed and well-developed reflexes meant that only relatively few were ever killed – at least until the advent of motorized vehicles and modern rifles in the twentieth century (see box opposite).

Other resident antelopes are the **Arabian gazelle** (or mountain gazelle; *Gazella gazella*) and the less common **reem gazelle** (or sand gazelle; *Gazella subgutturosa marica*). The unusual **Arabian tahr** (*Arabitragus jayakari*) is a mix of antelope and goat, with thick curved horns and a dense woolly fleece. It's now extremely rare in the wild, clinging to a few remote spots in the mountains. The **Nubian ibex** (*Capra ibex nubiana*) is another rare goat-antelope – males sport particularly impressive curved horns, reaching up to 1m in length.

Other rare mammals include canine species such as the Arabian wolf, striped hyena and Blanford's fox, small felines including the caracal, Gordon's wildcat (or sand cat), and the prettily named but famously ferocious honey badger. Rodents include the colourful Indian-crested porcupine and the small hyrax.

Birds

Oman's location between Europe, Asia and Africa makes its something of an ornithological crossroads, attracting a wide range of migrants, some of which also breed here – only 85 of the nearly 500 species of bird recorded in Oman are actually permanent residents.

Eye-catching common indigenous species which can be seen at any time of the year – even in Muscat – include Indian rollers, green bee-eaters, yellow-vented bulbuls and purple sunbirds. Large numbers of migratory **aquatic birds** frequent the coastal lagoons and creeks, including herons, sandpipers and plovers, which migrate here from their breeding grounds in northern Europe and Siberia. Even more seemingly incongruous are the colourful flocks of greater flamingo which frequent the south coast. Common **birds of prey** include the striking Egyptian vulture, often seen floating on the thermals over the Western Hajar, and the Steppe eagle.

Mountains, coast and desert all have their characteristic avian residents. **Dhofar** and southern Oman are particularly rich in birdlife thanks to the lush habitats produced by the annual *khareef* (monsoon), and the abundance of coastal lagoons. Some thirty species which aren't encountered elsewhere in the country can be found here, including Rüppel's weaver, Didric cuckoo and the African Scops owl.

For further information about the birds of Oman, see the **books** listed on p.240, visit Ⓦwww.birdsoman.com, run by local experts Hanne and Jens Eriksen, or Ⓦen.wikipedia.org/wiki/List_of_birds_of_Oman.

Marine life

Oman's extensive coastline and relatively unspoilt marine environment plays host to an outstanding array of marine life. Larger marine creatures are particularly well represented – no less than twenty types of cetaceans can be found in the waters around Oman – although your only chance of seeing any of these is by going diving with one of the operators listed on p.49, p.123, p.149 and p.202.

Dolphins are a common sight in the *khors* of Musandam (especially the humpback variety) and along the coast near Muscat. The most common species around Muscat are spinner dolphins (named for their spinning leaps through the air), often in mixed groups with common dolphins, plus less frequently spotted bottlenose dolphins.

Oman's waters are also rich in **whales**, including blue, humpback, sperm and Bryde's, as well as false killer whales, killer whales and whale sharks. These are all much less frequently seen by casual tourists than dolphins, although they might occasionally be spotted on diving trips. The coast around Mirbat is probably the most likely area, thanks to the kilometre-deep submarine trenches, which run relatively close to shore. The southern coast is particularly interesting thanks to the effects of the annual *khareef*, which produces a stream of cold, nutrient-rich water in which sea kelp and other edibles flourish. A population of humpback whales inhabits the waters here – studies suggest it is one of the very few groups of humpback around the world which don't migrate, given that the seasonal variations in the local waters provide them with all they need.

Oman is also a superb **turtle-watching** destination. Four of the seven main species of marine turtle – the green, olive ridley, hawksbill and loggerhead – nest in Oman, while a fifth, the leatherback, can also occasionally be found in Omani waters. The major turtle-nesting sights are the green turtle beach at Ras al Jinz (see p.174), and the beaches of Masirah island (see p.185), which see visits from all four species. Turtles can also be seen nesting around Ras al Hadd (see p.173) and at Bandar al Jissah in Muscat (see p.69).

Books

There's a surprising amount written about Oman, largely by the various explorers, adventurers and soldiers who tramped through the country between the 1950s and 1990s in search of oil, insurgents and ancient ruins. Accounts of the modern nation are thinner on the ground, as are reliable accounts of the sultanate's earlier history. Books marked with the ★ symbol are particularly recommended.

History, exploration and travelogues

Ranulph Fiennes *Atlantis of the Sands*. Rambling account of Fiennes' twenty-year quest to discover the fabled city of Ubar (see p.214), starting during his service as an officer in the Sultan's Armed Forces in Salalah in the late 1960s through to the discovery of the ruins at Shisr in 1992. First-hand accounts of military action against Dhofari rebels and some interesting (if haphazard) forays into Arabian prehistory are the highlights, although the latter part of the book is marred by far too much autobiographical waffle, pointless name-dropping and random irrelevant accounts of assorted polar expeditions.

Ian Gardiner *In the Service of the Sultan: A First-Hand Account of the Dhofar Insurgency*. Written by a former Royal Marines officer, this crisply written account of the Dhofar rebellion offers a fascinating description of the conflict, while the early chapters of the book paint an absorbing picture of local life in Dhofar and elsewhere at the very beginning of the Omani Renaissance.

Hussein Ghubash *Oman: The Islamic Democratic Tradition*. This scholarly tome by a leading Gulf historian is the nearest thing currently available to a comprehensive history of the country. The book focuses on Oman's unique imamate and Ibadhi traditions, but also provides wide-ranging coverage of other events from the Bronze Age through to the 1960s, with particularly strong coverage of the colonial period.

Edward Henderson *Arabian Destiny*. An autobiographical account of Henderson's years in Oman and the UAE from 1948 to 1956 working for the Petroleum Development Trucial Coast, a position which gave him a privileged insight into the development of the modern Gulf. There are eyewitness accounts of the battle for Buraimi and of events preceding the outbreak of the Jebel War, and the book also features fascinating portraits of Muscat, Dubai, Abu Dhabi and Al Ain in the early 1950s. Unfortunately, it's difficult to get hold of outside the Gulf.

Tim Mackintosh-Smith *Travels with a Tangerine: A Journey in the Footnotes of Ibn Battutah*. Enjoyable account of the English Arabist and adventurer's journey in the footsteps of Ibn Battutah from Morocco to Istanbul, with visits to Sur, Salalah and the Khuriya Muriya islands en route. Beautifully written, with a heady blend of often hilarious contemporary travelogue and recondite snippets of historical information.

★ **Jan Morris** *Sultan in Oman*. One of the best books ever written about the country. It provides a memorable first-hand account of Sultan Said bin Taimur's triumphal overland journey from Salalah to Muscat following the reassertion of his authority over the interior in 1955 (see p.228), offering an unusually sympathetic portrait of one of Oman's most misunderstood rulers. The almost medieval nation portrayed in the book has long since vanished, but still comes off the page with marvellous vividness, described in Morris's inimitably laconic and chiselled prose.

Tim Severin *The Sindbad Voyage*. Entertaining account of Severin's attempts to build an Omani dhow according to traditional Arabian boat-building techniques, and then sail it from Oman to China. The first part of the book covers the incredibly complex and laborious process of constructing the boat, while the second records the voyage itself, during which Severin and his crew of eight Omani sailors and fifteen international passengers sailed for seven months and 10,000km from Muscat to Canton, braving monsoonal typhoons, international pirates and assorted maritime mishaps en route.

Wilfrid Thesiger *Arabian Sands*. Arguably the finest book ever written about the Arabian peninsula, Thesiger's classic tome recounts his two epic crossings of the Empty Quarter and other remote wanderings around Oman, Saudi Arabia, Yemen and the UAE accompanied by a handful of trusted Bedu companions. The sheer difficulties, dangers and immense physical privations of Thesiger's various journeys make for a compelling read, while the detailed portrait of Bedu life among the sands offers unparalleled insights into the region's harsh, but also surprisingly intricate, tribal cultures, customs and beliefs – an elegiac memorial to a remarkable culture which was beginning to disappear even as Thesiger wrote about it.

Nicholas Clapp *The Road to Ubar: Finding the Atlantis of the Sands*. Entertaining account of the protracted hunt for Arabia's most famous lost city – far superior to Ranulph Fiennes' haphazard work (see p.214) on the same subject, and with a nice blend of ancient history and contemporary archeological adventure.

Specialist guides

Michael Hughes Clarke *Oman's Geological Heritage*. Beautiful coffee-table book bursting with wonderful photographs of Oman's weird and wonderful landscapes, plus interesting accompanying text.

Dave E. Sargeant, Hanne Eriksen, Jens Eriksen *Birdwatching Guide to Oman*. Detailed practical guide to birdwatching in the sultanate, including coverage of over sixty top birdwatching sites and lists of birds likely to be encountered, plus lots of maps and photos. The companion *Common Birds in Oman*, by Hanne and Jens Eriksen, provides comprehensive background (with 400 photos) on 250 species found in the country and the neighbouring UAE.

Explorer Publishing *Oman Trekking*. In-depth coverage (with basic maps) of twelve of Oman's finest trekking routes, mainly in the Western Hajar.

Explorer Publishing/Mark Grist *Oman Off-Road*. Lavish volume covering 26 of the best off-road drives countrywide with routes plotted on large-scale satellite maps, plus detailed directions and GPS coordinates to help keep you on the right track.

Samir S. Hanna *Field Guide to the Geology of Oman*. Detailed coverage of Oman's unique geology, followed by seventeen field trips around the country (mostly in the Western Hajar). It's tricky to follow in places if you're not a trained geologist, but is full of absorbing insights into the formation of the country's remarkable landscapes.

Language

Language

Arabic

The national language of Oman is **Arabic**, spoken as a first language by almost all the country's native Omanis, and by many Asian expatriates as a second language; a few other indigenous languages still survive, including **Shehri** and **Mehri** (see box, p.212) in Dhofar and the remarkable **Kumzari** (see p.154) in Musandam. **English** is used widely in the business and tourism sectors – most people working in these areas will likely have at least a basic command of the language – and is also widely spoken and understood by the country's Indian and Pakistani community. Out in the sticks, however, knowledge of English can often be minimal, or even completely nonexistent. Various Asian languages are also widely spoken among the expat community, notably **Hindu**, **Urdu** and **Bengali**, while other languages like **Swahili** (spoken by Omanis of Zanzibari descent), **Baluchi** and **Iranian** may also occasionally be heard, particularly in Muscat.

Modern Gulf Arabic

Modern Arabic (*'arabiya*), the world's fourth most widely spoken language, is the mother tongue of around 300 million people across the Middle East and North Africa. Variations in the language between different areas are considerable, both in vocabulary and pronunciation – the form of the language spoken in Oman and neighbouring countries, known as **Gulf Arabic**, is particularly distinctive.

Arabic is not an easy language, for various reasons. It contains a range of **sounds** which are not generally encountered in European languages (such as the notorious *'ayn*, ع, whose production involves a kind of back-of-the-throat choking spasm which most westerners only experience immediately prior to being sick). These sounds are represented by a range of characters in Arabic which have no equivalent in the Roman alphabet, and although various ingenious systems have been developed to express the full range of Arabic sounds using Roman script, these require a certain amount of study. The transliterations given below are based on the simplest and most common-sense approach – although like all transliterations from Arabic they are, at best, somewhat approximate. The only way to properly write Arabic is to use the Arabic script, and the only way to learn correct pronunciations is to listen to locals.

Arabic **script** is another – albeit fascinating – challenge. There are no capital letters in Arabic, but many characters change (sometimes dramatically) depending on whether they appear at the beginning, middle or end of a word.

If you're interested in **studying Arabic**, this is a language where it really pays to get hold of a native speaker, if at all possible. Failing this, the rather expensive Rosetta Stone Arabic course is the next best thing. Of the standard book-plus-CD courses available, Palgrave Macmillan's *Mastering Arabic* by Jane Wightwick and Mahmoud Gaafar is probably the best all-round introduction, while Routledge's *Colloquial Arabic of the Gulf and Saudi Arabia* by Clive Holes is the only course specifically devoted to modern Gulf Arabic, although it has the major drawback of not covering Arabic script. For a more accessible and unusual introduction to the language, try the innovative *Earworms Arabic* (Ⓦ www.earwormslearning.com, also available from iTunes), which teaches the basics of the language by setting simple phrases to music.

Greetings

Perhaps the most notable feature of Gulf Arabic is its almost courtly array of **greetings** and other salutations (see below for the basics). Meetings between Omani friends are generally celebrated with a barrage of enquiries and responses concerning one's health, one's news, the health of one's wife, children, cousins, and so on which can go on for a considerable amount of time. Even total strangers can keep the pleasantries going for a surprisingly long time. Reference to a higher power is also a feature of the language, most commonly in two of Arabic's most characteristic phrases – *insh'allah* ("God willing") and *al hamdu'lillah* ("Thanks be to god"), both of which you'll hear incessantly.

Useful Arabic words and phrases

Greetings and common expressions

Hello	salaam aleikum (literally "Peace be upon you")
Hello (response)	wa aleikum a'salaam ("And peace upon you also")
Hello (informal)	marhaba
Hello/welcome	ahlan wa sahlan (response: ahlan beek/ya hala)
How are you?	Shlonak? (to a woman: shlonek?)/ kaif al haal? (response: bi khair/zayn, meaning "good/well", or al hamdu'lillah)
Goodbye	ma'assalaama/fi aman illah
Good morning	sabaah al khair
Good afternoon/ evening	masaa al khair
Good night	tisbah ala khair
How are you?	kaif al haal? (response: al hamdu'lillah)
Fine, thanks	be-khair/al hamdu'lillah/ tamaam
God willing	insh'allah
thanks be to god!	al hamdu'lillah

Basics words and expressions

Yes	aiwa/na'am
No	la
Please	min fadlak (to a woman: min fadlik)
Thank you	shukran
Thank you very much	shukran jazeelan
You're welcome	afwan
OK	tayib/n'zain/kwayyis
Not OK	mish kwayyis
Come in/after you	tafaddal (to a woman: tafaddali)
Excuse me	afwan/lau samaht
Sorry	afwan/muta'assif
Can I...?/ It is possible?	mumkin?
I don't know	ma ba'raf
No problem	ma fi mushkila
Perhaps	mumkin
Not possible	mish mumkin
What time is it?	Kam as saa?
How much?	Bikam?
How many?	Kam?
What?	Shu?
What is this?	Shu hadha?
There is	fi
There is not	ma fi
Let's go/hurry up	yalla
Slow down	shwaya-shwaya
old	kadeem
new	jadeed
big	kabeer
small	saghir
beautiful	zayn

hot	haar	**too expensive**	ktir ghali
cold	baarid	**very expensive**	ghali jidan
open	maftuh	**money**	fulus
shut	mughlag	**no money**	mish fulus
cheap	rakhees	**I'm ill**	ana mareed
expensive	ghali		

Meeting people

My name is ...	ismi ...
What's your name?	shu ismak? (to a female: shu ismik?)
Where are you from?	Min wayn inta?
I'm ...	ana ...
British	Britani
Irish	Irlandee
American	Amerikanee
Canadian	Canadee
Australian	Ostralee
New Zealand	Newzeelandee
I like	ana bhib
I like this	bhib hadha
I don't like	ana ma bhib
I don't like this	ma bhib hadha
I understand	ana fahim/fahma
I don't understand	ana ma fahim/fahma
Do you speak English?	Tehki ingleezi?
I'm (not) married	ana (mish) mitjawaz (fem: mitjawazah)
I don't speak Arabic	ma'atkallam arabi (or just *la arabiya*)
I have 1/2/3/ children	andi walad/waladain/ thalathat awlaad
How do you say ... in Arabic	kaif tegool ... bil'arabi?
May I take your photo?	Mumkin sura, minfadlak? (to a female: Mumkin sura, minfadlik?)
Leave me alone!	Imshi!

Getting around and directions

How far is it to ...?	Kam kiloometre ila ...?
Where is the ...?	Wayn al ...?
room	ghurfah
toilet	hammam/bait maoi
museum	mat-haf
hotel	funduq/otel
airport	mataar
post office	maktab al bareed
bank	bank/masraf
police	shurta/boulees
chemist	saydaliyeh
doctor	doktor
hospital	mustashfa
to	ila
from	min
in	fi
left	yasaar
right	yameen
north	shimaal
south	janub
east	sharq
west	gharb
straight	ala tool
here/there	hina/hunak
near/far	gareeb/ba'eed
town/city	madina/madinat
street	shari
bus	baas
car	sayaara
taxi	taksee
petrol	benzeen
diesel	maazout

Days

today	al yoom	Monday	yoom al ithnayn
tomorrow	bokra	Tuesday	yoom ath thalatha
yesterday	ams	Wednesday	yoom al araba'a
early	mobakkir/badri	Thursday	yoom al khamees
late	mit'akhir	Friday	yoom al jum'a
day	yoom	Saturday	yoom as sabt
daytime	nahaar	Sunday	yoom al had
night	layl		

Numbers

0	٠	sifr	50	٥٠	khamseen
1	١	wahid	60	٦٠	sitteen
2	٢	ithnayn	70	٧٠	sab'een
3	٣	thalatha	80	٨٠	thimaneen
4	٤	arba'a	90	٩٠	tis'een
5	٥	khamsa	100	١٠٠	maya
6	٦	sitta	150	١٥٠	may wa khamseen
7	٧	saba'a	200	٢٠٠	mayatayn
8	٨	tamaniya	300	٣٠٠	thalattmaya
9	٩	tis'a	400	٤٠٠	rab'amaya
10	١٠	ashra	500	٥٠٠	khamsamaya
20	٢٠	aishreen	600	٦٠٠	sittamaya
21	٢١	wahid wa aishreen	700	٧٠٠	sabamaya
22	٢٢	ithnayn wa aishreen	800	٨٠٠	tamnamaya
30	٣٠	thalatheen	900	٩٠٠	tissamaya
40	٤٠	arba'een	1000	١٠٠٠	alf

Arabic numbers

Numbers in Oman are usually written western style as 1, 2, 3 and so on, although you'll also often see the traditional Arabic numerals as shown in the box above. One curiosity of Arabic numerals is that they're written right-to-left, like western characters, rather than left-to-right, like Arabic characters.

Food and drink

Basics

mat'am	restaurant
futour	breakfast
ghadaa	lunch
ashaa	dinner
finjaal/gelaas	glass
zojaja/botel	bottle
ana ma bakul laham	I don't eat meat
ana nabaati (female: ana nabaatiya)	I'm vegetarian
ladhidh	delicious
Bas, shukran	Enough, thanks
fatturra, hisaab	bill

Accompaniments, drinks and deserts

salata	salad
jubn	cheese
zibda	butter
bayd	eggs
samak	fish
'asal	honey
llaban	yoghurt
Murabba	jam
balah	dates
zatoon	olives
sukkar	sugar
bi/bidun sukkar	with/without sugar
mai	water
mai ma'adaniya	mineral water
halib	milk
shay	tea
Western style coffee (not necessarily Nescafe)	Nescafe/Nescoffee
coffee (usually Arabian style)	gahwa
beera	beer

Menu reader

arus	rice
arus abyad	white rice
biryani	biryani
dijaj	chicken
ghanam	mutton
habsha	intestine
kabsa	Saudi-style biryani (see p.28)
kabuli (or qabooli)	Afghan-style biryani (see p.27)
laham	meat (usually beef, although also possibly lamb or goat)
makli	fried
mandi	Yemeni-style slow cooked meat with rice (see p.28)
maqboos (or machbus)	Saudi-style biryani (see p.28)
marakh	curry
shuwa	slow-roasted meat with rice
kenadh	king fish
samak	fish
samak al qersh	shark
sharkha	lobster
halwa	traditional desert (see p.28)
khubz	Arabian-style flatbread
thereedh	Omani bread

Common dishes and Arabian meze

baba ghanouj all-purpose dip made from grilled eggplant (aubergine) mixed with ingredients like tomato, onion, lemon juice and garlic

burghul cracked wheat, often used as an ingredient in Middle Eastern dishes such as tabouleh

fatayer miniature triangular pastries, usually filled with either cheese or spinach

fatteh dishes containing pieces of fried or roasted bread

fattoush salad made of tomatoes, cucumber, lettuce and mint mixed up with crispy little squares of deep-fried flatbread

foul madamas smooth dip made from fava beans (foul) blended with lemon juice, chillis and olive oil

jebne white cheese

kibbeh small ovals of deep-fried minced lamb mixed with cracked wheat and spices

labneh thick, creamy Arabian yoghurt, often flavoured with garlic or mint

loubia salad of green beans with tomatoes and onion

moutabal a slightly creamier version of baba ghanouj, thickened using yoghurt or tahini

saj Lebanese style of thin, round flatbread

saj manakish (or mana'eesh) pieces of saj spinkled with herbs and oil – a kind of Middle Eastern mini-pizza

sambousek miniature pastries, filled with meat or cheese and then fried

shwarma See p.27

shish taouk basic chicken kebab, with small pieces of meat grilled on a skewer and often served with garlic sauce

tabouleh finely chopped mixture of tomato, mint and cracked wheat

tahini paste made from sesame seeds

waraq 'enab vine leaves stuffed with a mixture of rice and meat

Glossary

Abbasid third of the major Islamic caliphates (750–1258)

Adnani people from northern Arabia (see p.218)

aflaj plural of falaj (see p.83)

attar perfume

ayalat upper

ayn/ain spring

Azd Major Yamani (see p.250) tribe

barasti traditional palm-thatch hut

bait house

bait al qufl "House of the Lock" (see p.156)

barzah see majlis

bilad village

bin "son of" (Sultan Qaboos bin Said, for example, means Sultan Qaboos, son of Said)

burj tower

bukhoor a kind of incense (see p.32)

caliph religious and political leader of the Islamic world

corniche seafront road, often with a pedestrian promenade as well

balah dates (see p.129)

dallah traditional Arabian coffeepot

dishdasha the long robes (in Oman usually but not always white) worn by men throughout the Gulf; also known as *thawb*

falaj water channel (see p.83)

fanar lighthouse

gahwah/kahwah traditional Arabian coffee (see p.28)

ghafiri See p.223; often used interchangeably with Nizari (see p.250)

halwa traditional Omani sweet (see p.28)

hegira The Prophet Mohammed's flight from Mecca to Medina, from which the beginning of the Muslim calendar begins, written "AH" (1 AH = 622 AD)

hinawi See p.223; often used interchangeably with "Yamani" (see p.250)

hisn/husn fort

Ibadhism The version of Islam professed by most Omanis (see p.219).

ibn son; variant of bin (see opposite)

imam religious rulers of the Omani interior

Imamate area of interior Oman ruled by the imams

jamal camel

janubiah northern

jawhara jewel

jazirat/juzor island/islands

jebel mountain or hill

khanjar traditional Omani curved dagger

khor creek, inlet or (in Musandam) fjord

kummah Omani cap

luban Frankincense

Magan old name for Oman during Sumerian era

majan coral

majlis meeting/reception room in traditional Omani house

manatiq region; Oman in divided into five regions (Ad Dakhiliyah, Al Batinah, Al Wusta, Ash Sharqiya and Ad Dhahirah) each of which is further subdivided in wilayats. There are also four Governorates, or *muhafazah* (Muscat, Musandam, Dhofar and Buraimi).

mandoos traditional Omani wooden chest with metalwork decoration

masjid Mosque

Mazoun Old Persian name for Oman

mihrab arch inside (or sometimes outside) a mosque indicating the direction of Mecca

minbar raised platform or steps inside a mosque on which the presiding cleric stands to deliver his address during Friday prayers; roughly equivalent to Western pulpit

misfat/misfah pool

mubrick traditional Omani building material, with bricks made out of mud mixed with pebbles and straw

mukkabbah, traditional round airtight containers with fluted lids, made from copper, used to store volatile items like frankincense and perfume

musalla prayer hall in mosque

musar turban

nakheel/nakhl palm

Nizari Omani of Saudi or north Arabian descent

ophiolite type of red rock typical of Oman (see box, p.100)

qadi Judge

qal'at/qala fort

qahtani People of southern Arabia (see p.218)

qurum mangrove

ras headland

rasul/nabi messenger/prophet (used as synonym for the Prophet Mohammed)

sarooj traditional plaster (see p.235)

sharqiya eastern

shatti beach

safalat lower

sur fortified house (see p.234)

tawi well

thawb alternative name for *dishdasha* (see p.249)

travertine type of rock formation caused by evaporation of mineral-rich waters

Ummayad second of the major Islamic caliphates (661–750)

Umm an Nar Period of Arabian pre-history, see p.217

wadi generic term for any kind of valley or riverbed, usually dry

wali local governor

wilayat administrative district (see manatiq, above)

Yamani "Yemeni", signifying an Omani of Yemen descent

Khasab Travel & Tours
Oman Office
P.O. Box: 464,
Tel.: (+968) 26730464
khastour@omantel.net.om
Dubai Office
P.O. Box: 34110
Tel.: (+971) 4 2669950
khaztour@emirates.net.ae
KTT
The Pioneer & Leading Tour Operaters with 19 years experience in region of Musandam
• Daily Dhow Cruises with Dolphins to Musandam - Khasab.
• 4WD Mountain Safari to Jebel Harim.
• Cultural Tours of Musandam
• Overnight Packages including Hotels, Furnished Apartments & Dhows.
• Fleet of Traditional Dhows & Speedboats.
• Fleet of Luxury Cars & Coaches.
Your Satisfaction is Our Success
www.khasabtours.com

swiss-belhotel RESORT
MASIRAH ISLAND · OMAN
Perfect Locations for Business or Leisure
SOHAR BEACH
by swiss-belhotel
OMAN
Sohar Beach by Swiss-Belhotel and Swiss-Belhotel Resort Masirah Island are two jewels in the Sultanate of Oman. Both situated on the edge of the Arabian Sea, perfect for business by the beach or the ideal resort escape.
www.swiss-belhotel.com
swiss-belhotel INTERNATIONAL

Small print and

Index

A Rough Guide to Rough Guides

Published in 1982, the first Rough Guide – to Greece – was a student scheme that became a publishing phenomenon. Mark Ellingham, a recent graduate in English from Bristol University, had been travelling in Greece the previous summer and couldn't find the right guidebook. With a small group of friends he wrote his own guide, combining a highly contemporary, journalistic style with a thoroughly practical approach to travellers' needs.

The immediate success of the book spawned a series that rapidly covered dozens of destinations. And, in addition to impecunious backpackers, Rough Guides soon acquired a much broader and older readership that relished the guides' wit and inquisitiveness as much as their enthusiastic, critical approach and value-for-money ethos.

These days, Rough Guides include recommendations from shoestring to luxury and cover more than 200 destinations around the globe, including almost every country in the Americas and Europe, more than half of Africa and most of Asia and Australasia. Our ever-growing team of authors and photographers is spread all over the world, particularly in Europe, the US and Australia.

In the early 1990s, Rough Guides branched out of travel, with the publication of Rough Guides to World Music, Classical Music and the Internet. All three have become benchmark titles in their fields, spearheading the publication of a wide range of books under the Rough Guide name.

Including the travel series, Rough Guides now number more than 350 titles, covering: phrasebooks, waterproof maps, music guides from Opera to Heavy Metal, reference works as diverse as Conspiracy Theories and Shakespeare, and popular culture books from iPods to Poker. Rough Guides also produce a series of more than 120 World Music CDs in partnership with World Music Network.

Visit www.roughguides.com to see our latest publications.

Rough Guide credits

Text editor: Harry Wilson
Layout: Jessica Subramanian
Cartography: Animesh Pathak
Picture editor: Rhiannon Furbear
Production: Rebecca Short
Proofreader: Jan McCann
Cover design: Nicole Newman, Dan May
Editorial: **London** Andy Turner, Keith Drew, Edward Aves, Alice Park, Lucy White, James Smart, Natasha Foges, James Rice, Emma Beatson, Emma Gibbs, Kathryn Lane, Monica Woods, Mani Ramaswamy, Alison Roberts, Lara Kavanagh, Eleanor Aldridge, Ian Blenkinsop, Charlotte Melville, Lorna North, Joe Staines, Matthew Milton, Tracy Hopkins; **Delhi** Madhavi Singh, Jalpreen Kaur Chhatwal, Dipika Dasgupta, Prema Dutta
Design & Pictures: **London** Dan May, Diana Jarvis, Mark Thomas, Nicole Newman; **Delhi** Umesh Aggarwal, Ajay Verma, Ankur Guha, Pradeep Thapliyal, Sachin Tanwar, Anita Singh, Nikhil Agarwal, Sachin Gupta
Production: Liz Cherry, Louise Minihane, Erika Pepe
Cartography: **London** Ed Wright, Katie Lloyd-Jones; **Delhi** Rajesh Chhibber, Ashutosh Bharti, Rajesh Mishra, Jasbir Sandhu, Swati Handoo, Deshpal Dabas, Lokamata Sahu
Marketing, Publicity & roughguides.com: Liz Statham
Design Director: Scott Stickland
Rough Guides Publisher: Jo Kirby
Digital Travel Publisher: Peter Buckley
Reference Director: Andrew Lockett
Operations Coordinator: Becky Doyle
Operations Assistant: Johanna Wurm
Publishing Director (Travel): Clare Currie
Commercial Manager: Gino Magnotta
Managing Director: John Duhigg

Publishing information

This first edition published November 2011 by
Rough Guides Ltd,
80 Strand, London WC2R 0RL
11, Community Centre, Panchsheel Park, New Delhi 110017, India

Distributed by the Penguin Group

Penguin Books Ltd,
80 Strand, London WC2R 0RL

Penguin Group (USA)
375 Hudson Street, NY 10014, USA

Penguin Group (Australia)
250 Camberwell Road, Camberwell, Victoria 3124, Australia

Penguin Group (NZ)
67 Apollo Drive, Mairangi Bay, Auckland 1310, New Zealand

Rough Guides is represented in Canada by Tourmaline Editions Inc. 662 King Street West, Suite 304, Toronto, Ontario M5V 1M7

Cover concept by Peter Dyer.

Typeset in Bembo and Helvetica to an original design by Henry Iles.

Printed in Singapore

264pp includes index
A catalogue record for this book is available from the British Library
ISBN: 978-1-84836-598-8

11 12 13 14 8 7 6 5 4 3 2 1

MIX
Paper from responsible sources
FSC™ C018179

Help us update

We've gone to a lot of effort to ensure that the first edition of **The Rough Guide to Oman** is accurate and up-to-date. However, things change – places get "discovered", opening hours are notoriously fickle, restaurants and rooms raise prices or lower standards. If you feel we've got it wrong or left something out, we'd like to know, and if you can remember the address, the price, the hours, the phone number, so much the better.

Please send your comments with the subject line "**Rough Guide Oman Update**" to Ⓔ mail@uk.roughguides.com. We'll credit all contributions and send a copy of the next edition (or any other Rough Guide if you prefer) for the very best emails.

Find more travel information, connect with fellow travellers and book your trip on Ⓦ www.roughguides.com

Acknowledgements

Gavin Thomas At Rough Guides, thanks firstly to Martin Dunford, who backed the project from the start and without whom this book would probably not exist. Thanks also to all the various people involved along the way – Jo Kirby, Keith Drew, Emma Gibbs, Kathryn Lane and Clare Currie, and to my editor Harry Wilson, for helping to thrash the beast into shape. In Oman, thanks to Alex Crasta and Dee Marusic in Muscat; Vish Ranasinghe, Abraham V.M. and Jon Rhind in Salalah; Sameh Ibrahim Taha and Muzaffer A. Bulgurcuoglu in Sohar; Walter Menezes at Barka; and Ali Al Rashidi in Nizwa. Particular thanks to Khasab Travel & Tours for making my second visit to the Musandam peninsula so enjoyable and informative, particularly to Barakat U'llah and Malalah al Kumzari for showing me the mountains and khors, and to Tomy and Sinesh for setting the whole thing up. Elsewhere, thanks to Ayla Haas at Swiss Belhotel and to Matt Grainger at Oman Air/Black Sheep PR for his invaluable assistance and enormous patience. And, finally, to my long-suffering wife Allison, with whom my long journey through Oman properly began, and who put up with ever-increasing levels of marital infelicity and grumpiness during the writing of this book – and who I hope will one day get to ride the wadis and see the mountains for herself.

Photo credits

Title page

Dome of Sultan Qaboos Grand Mosque © Gunter Fischer/Pictures Colour Library

Full page

Schoolboys at Jabrin Fort © Walter Bibikow/AWL Images

Introduction

Pottery © Cahir Davitt/AWL Images
Muscat © Jose Fuste Raga/age footstock/Robert Harding
Nakhl Fort © Patrick Dieudonne/Robert Harding World Imagery/Getty
Swimming at Wadi Bani Khalid © Eric Nathan/Robert Harding
Rub Al Khali © imagebroker.net/Superstock

Things not to miss

01 Green turtle © Hanne & Jens Eriksen/Nature Picture Library
02 Sultab Qaboos Grand Mosque © Gavin Thomas
03 Muttrah Souk © Eric Nathan/Robert Harding
04 Khor ash Sham © Gavin Thomas
05 Dawn mist near Zayk, Dhofar © Malcolm MacGregor/AWL Images
06 Stone tomb © age fotostock/Superstock
07 Sur dhow yard © John Warburton-Lee/AWL Images
08 Hikers © Fotograferen.net/Alamy
09 Frankincense © Eye Ubiquitous/Superstock
10 Jebel Harim © Edward North/Alamy
11 Bani Habib, Saiq Plateau © Niels van Gijn/AWL Images
12 Jabrin Fort © imagebroker.net /Superstock
13 Misfat al Abryeen © Pixtal /Superstock
14 Yellowtail clownfish © Charles Stirling/Alamy
15 Rustaq Fort © Walter Bibikow/Photolibrary
16 View of Nizwa from fort © altrendo travel/Getty
17 Desert campsite © Dominic Byrne/Alamy
18 Jebel Shams © Manfred Gottschalk/Getty
19 Wadi Bani Awf © Mark Hannaford/AWL Images

Mountain Oman colour section

Jebel Misht © Malcolm MacGregor/AWL Images
North face of Jebel Shams © Travel Library Limited /Superstock
Waterfall in Dhofar mountains, near Gogub © Hanne & Jens Eriksen /Nature Picture Library
Al Hoota Cave © Aurore Belkin/Photolibrary
Village in Wadi al Ayn © Gavin Thomas
Traditional *falaj* © imagebroker.net/Superstock
Snake Gorge © Eric Nathan/Pictures Colour Library
Wadi Shab © Tom Till/Alamy

Desert Oman colour section

Wahiba Sands, Bedu man sitting in sand © Photononstop/Superstock
Rub al Khali desert © DanitaDelimont/AWL Images
Salt flats, Mahut © Giovanni Mereghetti/Superstock
Ghaf tree © Lonely Planet Images/Getty
Bedu man and camel © John Warburton-Lee/AWL Images
Bedu woman with traditional mask © imagebroker.net/Superstock
Dune-bashing, Wahiba Sands © Andrew Whitehead/Alamy
Bedu children, Wahiba Sands © Travel Library Limited/Superstock
Arabian oryx © Hanne & Jens Eriksen/Nature Picture Library

Black and whites

p.46 Muscat waterfront and Muttrah Fort © Gavin Thomas
p.78 Earthenware pots, Nizwa © Photononstop/Superstock
p.108 Nakhal Fort © Egmont Strigl/Superstock
p.142 Dhow © Gavin Thomas
p.162 Beehive tombs, Jaylah © Gavin Thomas
p.190 Old Souk, Salalah © Mike Nelson/Corbis

Index

Map entries are in colour.

E

F

G

H

I

J

K

L

M

N

O

P

Q

R

S

T

U

V

W

Y

Z

INDEX

Map symbols

maps are listed in the full index using coloured text

- International boundary
- Province boundary
- Chapter divisions boundary
- Major road
- Minor road
- Unpaved road
- Track
- River
- Ferry route
- Wall
- Bridge
- One-way street
- Cliff
- Gorge
- Peak
- Dune
- Ruins
- Waterfall
- Spring
- Cave
- Palace
- Baobab
- Oasis
- Viewpoint
- Mosque
- Gate
- Boat
- Point of interest
- Fortress
- Border crossing
- Tower
- Castle
- Museum
- Accommodation
- Internet access
- Transport stop
- Airport
- Petrol station
- Hospital
- Post office
- Parking
- Lighthouse
- Stadium
- Market
- Building
- Cemetery
- Park/reserve
- Beach

ROUGH
GUIDES